# ICT for Education
*A Few Concepts and Researches*

# ICT for Education
## *A Few Concepts and Researches*

### Vinod Kumar Kanvaria

NEW DELHI PUBLISHERS

ICT for Education *A Few Concepts and Researches* by Vinod Kumar Kanvaria New Delhi Publishers, New Delhi.

© Vinod Kumar Kanvaria Editor

First Edition 2018

ISBN:9789386453433

*All rights reserved. No part of this book may be reproduced stored in a retrieval system or transmitted, by any means, electronic mechanical, photocopying, recording, or otherwise without written permission from the Editor*

**NEW DELHI PUBLISHERS**

90, Sainik Vihar, Mohan Garden, New Delhi – 110 059

**Branch Office Kolkata**

216, Flat-GC, Green Park, Green Park, Narendrapur, Kolkata – 700103 (W. B.)

**Tel:** 011-23256188, 9953694312, 9582248909

**E-mail:** ndpublishers@gmail.com

**Website:** www.ndpublisher.in

**Dedicated to Every Learner, learning through ICT,
Facilitator, teaching through ICT
and Parent, believing in strength of ICT**

*All the authors, teachers, learning-facilitators, developers, managers, and proprietors of the websites, published and unpublished material, whose works are cited or quoted, with or without any changes, with or without their names, in this entire document, including texts, images and pictures, are highly and heartily acknowledged.*

# Preface

The current book is an endeavor to look into practices, stories, experiences, ideas and researches pertaining to ICT for education. The specific focus is on ICT for learning, teaching, evaluation, management and policies and the current book looks at all these educational areas as intact for use and application of ICT. These practices are presented in the form of concept-based scenario and activities. Some of the practices are being used in the educational institutions which were found to be very useful and fruitful; some others are used by individual academic while some others are suggested under innovations for applying ICT in the field of education with learning through ICT as a major area. Facilitators and learners encounter with a lot of problems while dealing with concepts in learning through ICT. The difficulties are spread over throughout the content from humanities, sciences, social sciences and languages to all other aspects of education as a discipline. This book focusses on specific researches, areas and techniques for making teaching-learning through ICT interesting and easier for educators, learning-facilitators as well as learners. Specific topics are dealt for either past methods through newer ICT platform or software; or newer methods in an innovative manner to make the pedagogy, learning and evaluation innovative, interesting, easier and learner-friendly with inculcating several other values to these aspects. This book gives an insight to practitioners, facilitators and educators for dealing with the earlier concepts in a newer and innovative ICT-based manner so that the learners can learn, facilitators can facilitate, researchers can research, educational managers can manage, evaluators can evaluate and stakeholders can plan policies in a more enthusiastic, ready and welcoming environment for ICT and its application and dealing with subjects of all streams and their concepts through ICT.

ICT for learning, pedagogy, evaluation, educational management and policy implications should not be delimited by classrooms or institutional boundaries. If one thinks that education is possible only in classrooms, then he/she might be wrong. The current book presumes that learning, pedagogy, evaluation, educational management and policy implications should not be limited by the four walls of any classroom or institution. Learners, facilitators, practitioners and stakeholders should enjoy their plans and actions within and outside these boundaries. Even within the boundaries, the learning, pedagogy, evaluation, educational management and policy implications should be free from the boredom and be participatory for one and all. This can be endeavored to achieve by more and more ICT-based activities in the field of education. The current book suggests a lot of researched activities which can easily be executed inside and outside the institutional boundaries for the learning, pedagogy, evaluation, educational management and policy implications.

In fact it is at all levels, where ICT can be made interesting and popular among the learners, practitioners and stakeholders. If the base is strengthened at initial level, they all can enjoy ICT for education throughout the educational field. Not only in formal setting, but in informal setting also, they would love dealing with ICT and its implications for education. The current book is a sincere research-based endeavor in this direction.

The content in this book looks forward to cope up with phobia attached with ICT for education. The concepts pertaining to application of ICT in education which seem to be highly difficult and technical are dealt in a simplistic manner in order to present them in an easier research-based manner for all. The phobia towards ICT can be controlled by various activities in education. The well-researched activities provided in this book can be part of ICT for education club and associations also in order to remove phobia for ICT for education among all.

The research-based activities, within and outside the boundaries, can be one of the best strategies for continuous and comprehensive evaluation also. Evaluation should be an integrated part of the pedagogy, learning, management and policy implication. Within and outside the boundaries, learners, facilitators, educational practitioners and stakeholders can cooperate, collaborate, plan and execute various activities for education through ICT which can lead a path for the evaluation as well. The researched activities shared and suggested in this book, hence, can better be used for evaluation in an integrated and transparent mode.

The current book is a good, directional and research-based fruitful document for all the practitioners including learners, pre-service facilitators, in-service facilitators, facilitator educators, practitioners and stakeholders. Anyone can use this book to make his/her learning, pedagogy, educational practice, management and policy implication easier and interesting.

*Vinod Kumar Kanvaria*

# Acknowledgment

Admiration is our polite recognition of another's resemblance to ourselves.

*Ambrose Gwinnett Bierce*

First of all, all the authors, facilitators, developers, managers, and proprietors of the websites, published and unpublished material, whose works are cited or quoted with or without any changes in this entire document, including units, text and pictures, are highly and heartily acknowledged. Moreover, all of my learners, along with all the past and present colleagues, during this life are acknowledged for fruitful interaction to bring the entire book to the current shape.

A book is never the whole sole contribution of any author or editor, rather it is the result of many people's efforts and interests and paying thanks to their contribution is more a matter of realization and less that of expression. With the depth of my heart, I express my sincere thanks to all of them.

Acknowledgement is due towards experts of consultative and review meeting for their inputs for enrichment, improvement and moderation in the content of this book. I am thankful to all the contributors in addition to facilitating experts for their valuable inputs and contribution, without whom this book could not be even completed and that, too, well in time. I am indebted to my team of learners Ms. Bharti and others for their support in the entire phase.

I am extremely grateful to my family members, without whose continuous cooperation, guidance and motivation, this book would not have been a reality.

I am deeply grateful to all of those, whose suggestions helped me, directly or indirectly, and so generously, in various aspects of this book. Their discussion and worthy suggestions gave me inspiration and confidence. Without their interaction and prescriptions, it would have been very difficult to give the present shape to the book.

I pay my due regards to Prof. A. B. Saxena, Dr. R. P. Maurya, Prof. H. K. Senapaty and Prof. A. K. Behera for providing me insight before, during or after my formal academic life, which helped me a lot in developing the current book, as well.

Administrative as well as library staff of Faculty of Education, DU, Delhi, CPDHE-ILL (DU, Delhi), CRL (DU, Delhi), NCERT (New Delhi), NUEPA (New Delhi), IGNOU (Delhi), JNU (New Delhi), RIE (NCERT, Bhopal) and USOL, PU, Chandigarh and all those libraries which I have ever visited were of great help to me in the completion of this book. I express my sincere thanks to all of them.

I am extremely thankful to the publisher for the proper printing and binding, and giving the current shape to this book.

MHRD, Govt. of India and IASE of University of Delhi are acknowledged for their support for the activity which, in turn, has led to the publication of this book and to facilitate the consultation with the experts in the field.

Lastly, I, once again, express my sincere thanks to all of my learners and colleagues, since the beginning of my professional career; all of my friends, since the beginning of my understanding of friendship; all of my facilitators, since the beginning of my academic career, and all of my well-doers, since the beginning of lighting the life-lamp in this body.

*Vinod Kumar Kanvaria*

# Contents

*Preface* vi
*Acknowledgment* ix

## Expert Section

1. **New College Student and Programa Permanecer's ICT Platform** 1
   Matheus Batalha Moreira Nery

2. **Utilising ICT in Education: Focus on Distance Education** 13
   Simon-Peter Kafui Aheto

3. **ICT: New Paradigms for Old Problems** 21
   Renato Bulcao de Moraes

4. **ET for Higher Education: Innovative Practices at Global Level** 25
   Ramesh C. Sharma & Maria Antonia Lima Gomes

5. **ICT-based Evaluation of Professionals and Researchers** 33
   Vinod Kumar Kanvaria

## Specific Section

6. **Educational Technology: A Tool for Facilitating Learning** 43
   A. Subramanian

7. **Learning through Social Networking** 55
   Bharti Nagpal

| 8  | Web 2.0 Technologies in Learning-Facilitator Preparation through Educators<br>*Binulal K. R.* | 61 |
|---|---|---|
| 9  | Social Media for Learning: Perception of Pre-University Learners<br>*Devaki T. C.* | 69 |
| 10 | Awareness of OER at Higher Education<br>*Dinesh Maharana* | 75 |
| 11 | Psycho-Utopianism among Learning-facilitators and ICT<br>*Divya Rajkumar Panjwani* | 87 |
| 12 | ICT: Learning in Own Way<br>*Dolly Pachouri* | 95 |
| 13 | Perception of School Learners towards ICT in Science Learning<br>*Geetika Nidhi* | 101 |
| 14 | ICT Mediated Pre-Service Learning-Facilitator Training<br>*Kartikeswar Behera* | 109 |
| 15 | ICT for Learners and Educators<br>*Lovish Raheja* | 121 |
| 16 | ICT Integration in Teaching and Learning<br>*M. Satheeshkumar* | 131 |
| 17 | ICT in Administration of Higher Education Institutions<br>*Manju Gupta* | 141 |

| | | |
|---|---|---|
| 18 | **Computer Phobia towards Using ICT among B.Ed. Learning-facilitators**<br>*Mohit Dixit* | 155 |
| 19 | **ICT Integration in School for Technological Teaching and Learning**<br>*Pramod Kumar Gupta* | 167 |
| 20 | **Functioning of ICT@School Scheme at Secondary Level**<br>*Ranjan Kumar Sahoo* | 175 |
| 21 | **Digital Games for Mathematics: Spatial Learning**<br>*Robin Sharma* | 183 |
| 22 | **ICT Embedded Experiential Learning Progression: Learning Outcomes**<br>*Sanjay Kumar* | 191 |
| 23 | **ICT for Environmental Education and Sustainable Development**<br>*Santosh Kumar Parida* | 201 |
| 24 | **ICT as a Tool for Capacity Building of Learning-facilitators**<br>*Sapna Yadav* | 217 |
| 25 | **ICT Enabled Learning: Digitalizing Homework**<br>*Sourabh Garg* | 229 |
| 26 | **ICT in Learning Processes in Higher Education: Attitude of Learners**<br>*Susmita Mondal* | 239 |

| | | |
|---|---|---|
| 27 | **Potential of Radio Jamia for Functioning of Schools: An Exploration**<br>*Syedah Fawzia Nadeem* | 247 |
| 28 | **ICT and Administration in Education**<br>*Tanuj Sharma* | 257 |
| 29 | **Geogebra as an ICT Tool for Learning of Mathematics**<br>*Tarun Aggarwal* | 265 |
| 30 | **Self-Esteem and Attitude in Using ICT for Language Teaching**<br>*Vandana Chaudhary* | 275 |
| 31 | **ICT Intervention in Schools of Madhya Pradesh**<br>*Vandana Khare* | 284 |
| 32 | **ICT in Teaching Learning of Chemistry at School**<br>*Zeba Tabassum* | 291 |
| | ***Bibliography*** | 299 |

# Chapter 1

# New College Student and Programa Permanecer's ICT Platform

    **Matheus Batalha Moreira Nery**

*Uninassau, Aracaju, Brazil, South America*

## Preview at a Glance

This article aims to discuss the main transformations in Brazilian higher education, with the special focus on the changes that happened in the life of students after Brazil introduced affirmative action programs that expanded the access to higher education for lower-income families' students, providing them also with information and communication technologies (ICT in education) tools through online education platforms. The research concentrated in a Brazilian federal program for student aid called Programa Permanecer, which was designed to give support to students from lower-income families, providing them with the necessary condition so they can be able to be mentally and emotionally prepared to pursue university studies. The analyses focused on the main students' characteristics, and the data collection was conducted through the program's online platform. The conclusions points outs to necessary improvements in the Brazilian government strategy, especially regarding academic permanence and to student retention. Brazil needs a more comprehensive system regarding access and permanence in higher education, and also needs to improve its uses of information and communication technologies for education initiatives. The students from lower-income families are arriving in federal universities without being fully informed about the realities of their undergraduate programs, which can lead to false expectation. A more intensive use of ICT in education tools could improve students' academic skill and maximize student retention.

## Introduction

The access to higher education in Brazil, for a long time, was restricted to the youth's elite, who could afford to leave the country to carry out their university studies in Europe. Before the transfer of the Portuguese royal family to Brazil, in 1808, the Portuguese government considered important to maintain a policy designed to suppress any cultural sign of independence in their South America colonies. This policy generated a cultural and intellectual isolation in which no concrete project of higher education could be developed during 308 years.

The first Brazilian higher education institution was created in 1808 at Salvador, in the north-east of Brazil. The *Escola de Cirurgia da Bahia* was created as soon as the king of Portugal arrived in Brazil in the same year. This institution provided undergraduate medical training to Brazilian students, and 140 years later, became the Federal University of Bahia (UFBA), when it was integrated into the Brazilian higher education federal system (Favero, 2006).

Historically, UFBA academic project was a mix between two western university academic models: (a) The 1810 Humbolt report, which established the primacy of scientific research in university life. This document was fundamental for the establishment of the University of Berlin, and in its core developed a professor chair system and included elements of institutional governance, and the distribution and separation of fields of knowledge (Barreto and Figueiras, 2007); (b) the Flexner report, which summarized the North American university reform of 1905. This document had focused on training in health care, but also addressed important issues for the American universities reorganization. Its core element was the adoption of academic major and minor curriculum components, called the undergraduate college, which gave the possibility to the student to join a vocational training, called the master's degree programs, and a specialization in the subject area or field of research, called Ph.D. It was instituted also a separation between the academic management, delegated to Deans (appointed heads of schools and colleges), and the academic governance, conducted by the departments composed by full-time professors (Filho, 2007).

As a higher education project, the Brazilian federal university system took several years of political debate to take shape. The cultural isolation imposed by Portugal to Brazil, and the cologne's dependence administrative model, generated consequences in the subsequent organization of Brazilian universities, such as its institutional organization. In the Brazilian law, especially in Brazil's Federal Constitutions of 1934 and 1946, the public universities appear represented through an institutional composition organized by various segments connected to a central Ministry of Education, such as islands depended on a centralized administration. For more them a century, the student population of the Brazilian public universities was the country's elites, who no longer needed to travel to another continent to get, educated (Favero, 2006).

More recently, the Brazilian higher education scenario has passed for substantial changes. In the past two decades, the Brazilian government restructured public universities and opened new programs and institutions, which are operating under a new affirmative action policy. Called *Reestruturacao e Expansao das Universidades Federais* (REUNI), this government action helped to increase the number of enrolments in public institutions by 85% (Rossetto and Goncalves, 2015). At least

10% of the students enrolled in public universities were accepted through affirmative action programs (SESU, 2014). The Brazilian government also created programs with the objective of increasing the number of students from lower-income families in private institutions, such as *Fundo de Financiamento Estudantil* (FIES) and *Programa Universidade Para Todos* (PROUNI). Combined, those actions helped to create a new profile for Brazilian undergraduate students.

Case in point, Federal University of Bahia (UFBA) was a pioneer higher education institution in Brazil, being among the first that adopted new rules for students' admission, accepting students through affirmative action programs. UFBA also implemented one of the first financial aid programs in Brazil, called *Programa Permanecer*, and established online platforms so the students could engage in different learning experiences by using information and communication technologies.

ICT in education has become an important phenomenon, as has impacted profoundly in people's lives, as it provides different experiences for teaching and learning. Mainly there were two major online platforms at UFBA designed to serve the purpose of ICT for education: (a) UFBA's Moodle platform, which functions as a virtual learning environment in which the students can have access to different learning tools, in way to complement what students learn in the classroom; (b) UFBA's SISPER platform, which was designed specifically for students from lower-income families who needed financial aid and academic support to perform their universities studies.

Therefore, this journal aims to discuss the main transformations in Brazilian higher education, with the special focus on the changes that happened in the life of students after Brazil introduced a new affirmative action program that expanded the access to higher education for lower-income families' students, providing them also with information and communication technologies through online education platforms. First, it will be presented the principal elements that help to transform the Brazilian higher education system, taking UFBA as a case study. In sequence, the author will present an analysis of the *Programa Permanecer*, its online platform, and the data collected through the program's online platform with the students that were part of the first cohort of grantees. In the analysis, the author sought to balance his own experience managing government programs with the survey's data.

## Brazilian Higher Education Federal System: The Historical Path

The University of Bahia, known now as UFBA, was created in 1946. Its creation document, a decree-law, designates the unification of five public higher education colleges that already existed at the time in Salvador, Bahia: the Bahia Medicine College, the Bahia Law School, the College of Fine Arts, the Polytechnic College and the Philosophy College. The first of those colleges, the Bahia Medicine College, was founded in 1808 with Portugal's king arrival to Brazil. Called initially Bahia Surgery Medical Center, it was created to provide medical assistance to Salvador's population, and also to serve as a healthcare training center.

The academic management model proposed by Humbolt report inspired the model adopted early on by UFBA. In the early 1960s, as the Brazilian government decided to implement a new and more innovative academic model at the University of Brasilia (UNB), the country's new capital federal university. The government proposal was to build a modern university, with more academic freedom and autonomy. UNB academic model sought to set new standards for all Brazilian universities. For this proposal to have success, it was necessary that four key essential points were achieved: (a) The university should be able to form and maintain a high intellectual and diverse Faculty; (b) scientific research should be massively incorporated to academic life; (c) the academic isolation should be overcome and the university needed to create integration in academic life; (d) and finally, the general problems of Brazilian higher education should become a central concern for the university, and the higher education administrators would have to make the necessary efforts to understand their students' academic and economic problems and provide them with solutions (Ribeiro, 1978).

With the military coup of 1964, most of the universities reorganization projects, especially these that directed efforts to expand academic freedom, had to be redirected. The military government put in place a national project to modernize all federal universities, using only some parts of the academic models proposed by UNB, UFBA, and also the University of São Paulo (USP). The USP was not formally integrated into the federal system but had achieved a lot of prestige due to its academic project, especially regarding integrating international scholars into its academic life. The military government had isolated UFBA and UNB institutional leaders. They were not allowed to participate in designing of the new national plan. UNB was occupied by the military in 1964 and many professors were fired or forced to retire (Cunha, 2007; Filho, 2007).

The military government viewed the students as fundamental human capital, which needed to be integrated into a major economic development plan. This project proposed a substantial increase in the number of students enrolled in public universities. The Brazilian government estimated that they needed to create 180,000 new vacancies in public universities in the early 1970s. The idea was that the university had a student per hundred inhabitants. This modernization plan did not take into consideration the demands of economic sectors for professionals or the expectations of the population regarding higher education. They only considered that a specific segment of the population, who had the opportunity to have access to a good private secondary education, was able to enroll at federal universities. The concept of affirmative action policies or even the possibility of giving access to higher education for people that hadn't the selected background was not discussed (Cunha, 2007).

The project of modernization of the Brazilian universities culminated in 1968 into a University Reform Law. This new law organized and standardized procedures for Brazilian higher education federal universities. The law was built around four core ideas: (a) replacing the old chairs system by the department system; (b) unified enrollment exam for all undergraduate students; (c) basic cycles and a system of enrollment by majors; (d) a career plan for all faculties (Favero, 2006).

Despite criticism related to the reduction of academic freedoms, the academic model implemented by the military government provided a major growth for the

Brazilian federal universities. The government funds were used mainly for the development of national research activities, which was almost inexistent prior the military coup. On the other hand, the military higher education reform was unable to create instruments that would provide an active link between the university, society and the productive sector (Macedo, Trevisan, Trevisan and Macedo, 2005).

There were two factors that impacted substantially the life of Brazilian higher education institution after the military reform: (a) The project only encompassed the least interesting parts of the Flexner report, using some of his concepts without pursuing major social change results, as, for example, the mere replacement of the professors chair system for departments without decentralize management of academic life; (b) the implementation of graduate programs and scientific research incentives, which enabling the Brazilian federal universities to train, at a higher level, researchers to serve different purposes. The second factor was positive and relevant and opened up a gap for new changes in Brazilian universities (Filho, 2007).

## Federal University of Bahia: New Brazilian Academic Model and ICT in Education Challenges

It was through the 1968 higher education reform that the University of Bahia adopted its current name, Federal University of Bahia (UFBA), and became known as UFBA. The number of undergraduate majors and graduate programs are an example of UFBA's importance for the regional development of northeast of Brazil: By 2015, they offered 99 undergraduate majors, 10 online programs, and 129 graduate programs, providing higher education to almost 40,000 students (UFBA, 2016).

In 2004, the UFBA's board of trustees established a working group to design a new academic development plan. After deliberations, an academic reform plan was approved. UFBA's decision gained momentum when the Brazilian government opened the debate for a new law proposal, which would provide a new policy for higher education through the creation of a national affirmative action program. This program was set to facilitate the enrollment of students from secondary public schools in federal universities. Traditionally, placements in Brazilian federal universities are very competitive, and the majority of students come from private schools (Lima, Azevedo and Catani, 2008).

The academic debate about a national affirmative action policy in Brazil became more prominent in 2001 when Rio de Janeiro State University enrolled the first cohort of students under an affirmative action program (Maggie and Fry, 2004). Other Brazilian universities, such as UFBA, soon followed this decision, and also created procedures for their affirmative action program (Bevilaqua, 2005). There were critics about this new policy: (a) Some emphasized that Brazil, a country composed by a lot of cultural mixtures, with the new policy, was condemned to be the nation of those who have or do not have the right to affirmative action; (b) others emphasized that the new system of enrollment would represent a setback for the Brazilian non-racist tradition (Maggie and Fry, 2004). Despite many contrary opinions, the new enrollment system, which reserved vacancies in public universities to students from the public school, was implemented and today stands as a reality.

However, UFBA's proposal only included a few modifications in administrative and enrollment procedures, and a deeper change in the university's academic life and infrastructure would be necessary to accommodate the new cohort of students. Therefore, the Brazilian government implemented the *Reestruturacao e Expansão das Universidades Federais* (REUNI) action plan, which provided funds for all federal universities, so they could be able to increase enrollments substantially. The Brazilian government main objective was to use the federal universities campuses in its maximum capacity (Brazil, 2007).

As the REUNI was introduced in 2007, UFBA's board of trustees approved a strategic plan that would modify the institution's main social characteristics in the following decade (UFBA, 2007). Entitled *Universidade Nova* (New University), UFBA's academic reform project was subject to many debates, promoted by stakeholder interested in the university's future. Although it represented a step forward, the project suffered criticism, particularly from those that believed that the expansion of the enrollments would not be accompanied by improvements in the university's infrastructure. The critics pointed out that the new students would share the same problems faced by the students that were already enrolled.

UFBA's strategic project covered all the major criticisms pointed out by the protestors. As an example of a quick response to the critics was the establishment of a new student aid program, developed by a specific vice-provost that was created to work directly to improve the support of the university to students that were having social and financial difficulties in their universities studies. The vice-provost actions aimed to support the students so that they are able to study and work or devote themselves exclusively to their major. The appointment of a vice-provost for student aid at UFBA was a landmark for other Brazilian universities (UFBA, 2007).

The 2004 and 2007 academic reforms also made possible for UFBA to develop a more consistent ICT for education platform. The institution increases its investment on the Moodle platform, making possible to students from all majors to use the platform resources. UFBA also developed a specific platform for students from lower-income families that were enrolled in the *Programa Permanecer*. This online platform, called SISPER, allowed the scholarship holders to interact with their supervisor, whom, on the other hand, could request them to do specific academic tasks.

Since 2005, a year after UFBA started to enroll students through affirmative action programs, the number of students from public schools approved in the entrance examination increased significantly, showing a significant change in UFBA's student population. This new population of students from lower-income families needed support from the university to pursue their studies. The online platforms made available to the students are fundamental tools for their development.

## ProgramaPermanecer: From Student Aid to ICT in Education Platform

In 2006, the vice-provost for student aid created the Permanecer Program with the main objective of ensuring the permanence at UFBA of students in socio-economic vulnerability, considering that those students may interrupt their studies when they encounter economic and social difficulties, during their undergraduate major. For the purpose of the Permanecer Program, the faculty and administrators of UFBA are allowed to submit proposals for grants in three different academic areas: (a) UFBA's relations with the community, focusing on projects that establish relationship between the university and society; (b) institutional projects, which aims to support the projects from technical-administrative and artistic-cultural areas of the university; (c) and education, represented by academic grants for undergraduate students engaged in research projects (UFBA, 2007).

In 2007, the ProgramaPermanecer program provided 600 scholarships to UFBA students; this number grew to 1,029 in 2015 (UFBA, 2016). The students receive a financial aid to stimulate their permanence at the university and, in exchange, they must comply with all requirements stipulated by the program management, including the meet twenty hours per week in activities supervised by specific coordinators.

The requirement of compensation in social projects was the object of analyzes by Sposito and Corrochano (2005) that highlighted the importance of this mechanism as an agent that breaks with the aid's bias present in many proposals for social policy. These initiatives require more social engagement, and the participants are encouraged to seek independence of the financial aid. However, the compensation system can be presented in social policies rhetoric as a multifaceted concept, which ranges from a more limited scope, such as requiring school attendance, to a more complex, such as requiring that students perform tasks that could overwhelm them, preventing them to reach the individual goals planned for them by program.

The *ProgramaPermanecer* aims not only to provide financial aid to students. The program also secures that all activities undertaken by the scholarship holders should contribute to their education. As a requirement for the grant, the students, after approved in the affirmative action program entrance exam, must remain enrolled in their undergraduate major throughout the duration of his or her grant. The program's actions were controlled by the management team that works under the supervision of the vice-provost of student aid. They developed an ICT in education online platform called *Sistema Permanecer* (SISPER), which made it possible and easy for the management team to manage the activities of the program's grantees, and to interact continuously with them. Supervisors and grantees can also interact and have learning experiences through the online platform.

## Research Methodology: The Use of Program Permanecer Online Platform to Survey UFBA's Student Population

Since all the scholarship holders were spread in different departments of UFBA, the survey data collection was carried out by an online platform designed and used by the *ProgramaPermanecer*, and all the communications with the grantees were made through the e-mail that they register on the program's website. All 511 scholarship holders from the first cohort of the 2007 *ProgramaPermanecer*, who had registered at the website and had valid e-mails address, received a communication about the research, in which it was described research goals, and the students were invited to participate in it the study.

The mains goal of this research with the grantees from the *ProgramaPermanecer* was to identify their mains social characteristics. Thus, the research instrument was composed of forty-six items that questioned aspects related to academic life, to the use of internet to have access to knowledge, to the main characteristics of the student's education in elementary school and in high school, to their family educational and economic background, and to the use of the grant provided by the program.

On average, one of every two students who received the e-mail inviting them to participate in the study responded to the research instrument, totaling 252 questionnaires collected. Dillman, Smyth and Christiam (2007), when analyzing the Internet use for scientific research pointed out that this tool has shown an upward curve in the number of the response of the participants. They argue that this is because the virtual network has become part of daily life and the ease and convenience that it provides to the potential research participant. The collected data were submitted to statistic descriptive analysis.

## Key Learning Points of the Main Characteristics of the *ProgramaPermanecer*'s Student Population

The distribution of participants by academic areas had a higher concentration in the majors related to life sciences and health training professions (37.3%), followed by the humanities (30.2%), STEM sciences (23%), liberal arts (6.7%) and romance languages and literature (2.8%). When divided into projects areas of concentration submitted to the *ProgramaPermanecer*, 64.5% are proposals linked to the university relations with community projects, 19.4% are institutional projects and 16.1% are research projects. The effective participation of students in projects related to university relations with the community plays a key role in UFBA's academic life, by making a connection between knowledge produced by science with the needs of society.

The scholarship holders of the *ProgramaPermanecer* have a few characteristics in common: 92.4% of the participants reported being single, 96% said they did not have children, 92.1% use public transportation as the main transportation, 96.4% own a mobile phone, 69% have a personal or a family computer, 59.9% have personal access to the Internet, although 56.8% of students claimed only use computers that are available at UFBA. A substantial number of students participated in preparatory courses for entrance exams for at least one year in a way to improve what they learned in high school (65.5%) and almost half (45.6%) had taken the entrance exam only once.

More than half of scholarship holders (53.9%) were enrolled in courses in the fifth and seventh semester, 23.9% were between the eighth and tenth semester, and 20.6% were between the first and fourth semester during the time they received financial aid from the *ProgramaPermanecer*. These data indicate that the program helped, for the most part, students who are in their mid-university undergraduate major's courses. Despite being a positive factor, this represents also a contrast from what the scientific literature indicates about the permanence of students in universities. Coulon (2008) and Albuquerque (2008) pointed that the beginning of students' academic life in the university is the moment that involves the most complex social situations that affect the student's decision to stay and pursue their majors or to drop out of the university. Both authors, when analyzing this phenomenon, said that dropouts are more frequent in the first months after entering university or in the first year.

Scholarship holder's educational background was also part of the survey. It was identified that most students graduated from high school between 2002 and 2006 (71.6%). Local, state and federal public schools have graduated more than 80% of the *ProgramaPermanecer*' students, of which approximately 50% were living in the interior of Bahia State and the other 50% were divided by those who lived at Salvador, Bahia' state capital, and at other Brazilian states. Students' migration was intense and 83.1% of the scholarship holder's move to Salvador to pursue their universities studies, 4.4% were living in cities closer to the capital, such as Camaçari, Lauro de Freitas, and SimoesFilho, and 7.2% in more distant cities. Few scholarship holders said they use university dorms and residences (13.5%).

The power of public education to promote social change has been in debate in Brazil since the implementation of affirmative action programs. Critics say the government should resume investments in primary and secondary education (elementary and high schools), rather than invest in affirmative action policies, in order to carry out a "not racist" educational project. However, the critics forget that for years the federal, state and municipal governments scrapped these schools with poor academic proposals, ranging from automatic approval for all students in the first year of elementary school, regardless with those students achieved the necessary grades, to actions that tried to minimize distortions in an attempt to decrease the number of students with advanced age who remain in the same stage for failing year after year in their school assignments. Therefore, it is understandable that the public school has lost some of its quality, but that doesn't mean that the university should be silent and deny access to their students, and trying to develop them as human beings (Maggie and Fry, 2004).

The students' families are seen as the most responsible for the scholarship holders' support, as 78.7% of all the students indicated that his or her father or his or her mother as responsible for their financial support. The survey also requested that the participant indicated the educational background of his or her father and his or her mother. Parents who have never attended school adds up to 4.0%, those with incomplete and complete elementary education account for 33.7%, incomplete and complete junior high education accounts for 13.9%, and incomplete and complete high school account for 33.7%. The percentage of fathers with incomplete and complete higher education is 9.2% and mothers are 13.1%. Moreover, the survey also indicated that there were a significant number of mothers who have a superior education background if compared to the scholarship holder's fathers.

Regarding working during school time, the survey results indicated that 33.7% of students said they had worked during his or her elementary school time, and mostly (89.9%) worked during their high school time. Almost half of the students (46.6%)

said they receive financial assistance from family or from other persons beyond the scholarship from the *ProgramaPermanecer*, 29.9% declared that they are responsible for their own financial sustainability, 22.7% said they need to help monthly with their family expenses and 0.8% defined themselves as the leading provider of their family financial resources. Most of the scholarship holders (72.1%) reported that their families have a monthly income between one and three minimum wages, 15.5% have a minimum wage income, which in Brazil stands for R$ 937,00 (approximately US$ 289,00).

In the last two decades, sociology of education has been interested in the relationship between students from lower-income families and the university. For Zago (2006), this discussion passes through indicators such as students' exceptional trajectories in public schools. The social network of support formed by the relationship between the student and the family portrays this condition, in which parents contribute substantially to family support and help financially in the education of their children. Although the family assist with financial resources, the need to work during the university time was also described by participants and 13.5% of the scholarship holders said they supplement their income with some kind of paid work, such as tutoring classes for elementary and high school students, moonlight jobs, manual sewing work, selling cosmetics, trinkets, and snacks, babysitting work and working in artistic and cultural events.

The scholarship holders were asked also about the intention to search for a full time or part time job during their time in the university: 50.3% of the students said yes, but only for internship opportunities. This information shows that the relationship between work, need for financial resources and specialized training in higher education is geared to obtaining a future job that combines what the students have learned in the university with the possibility to earn some money. In addition to having the income from scholarship, 25.2% of students said they received other funds from the vice-provost of student aid. Among others, the most common are: funds for housing and food, for buying medicines, for making photocopying, for participating in English as Second Language courses and exemption from university tuitions and fees.

A peculiar and contradictory aspect of network strategy to support the students' higher education studies formed by the family was observed when the scholarship holders were asked about what was the main influence for their university major choice. More than a third of participants (34.4%) indicated that anyone or anything influenced them. Moreover, the number of students who were influenced by their parents, spouses, brothers, friends or relatives account for just over 10% of valid responses, a relatively low influence compared to the effort that those families made to conduct their children to university.

The scholarship holders pointed the training for future employment as the main expectations regarding their higher education (40.1%). In a research conducted at the University of Coimbra, Estanque and Nunes (2003) highlighted that the expectations about higher education have changed with the democratization of access to the universities. Such as Brazil, Portugal also held a university reform aimed to give more access to educational opportunities for students from lower-income families. The universities face today a new social stratification in the students' population, which are divided between students who have consistent financial support from their families and those who need financial aid, so their permanence in the university can be guaranteed.

Therefore, the Brazilian wealthier students come to believe that their undergraduate major lost prestige with the democratization process and they are now shifting the focus of their expectations to MBA programs and Ph.D. degrees, in a way to pursue an exclusive expertise that differentiates them in the labor market. Students from lower-income families have different expectations, which are revolving around the possibility to have access to a future professional position. The prestige for them is not in the undergraduate degree itself, but in corresponding to the investment made by their families, who used part of the household budget so they could study in the university and had the possibility of pursuing a good job.

The survey also questioned about how the scholarship holders often use the grant from the *ProgramaPermanecer*. They were asked to organize their responses in order of expenditure importance. The core elements, which are the most worrisome to the students, are public transportation transport (62%), buying food and buying study material (65.4%). These are three daily expenses in the life of every student at UFBA and it's possible to say that the financial resources provided by the program fulfilled its role of assisting the student to permanence in the university. Among the peripheral elements that generated concerns in the scholarship holders, which are not present every day, but have an significant meaning in their lives, appeared housing costs (19,8%), health insurance (28,1%), and extra-curricular activities, such as participating in courses, conferences, seminars etc. (35,7%).

Although they are attending the university, it is concerning to note that the scholarship holders could not afford to include in their expenses more cultural activities. This could occur because the cultural activities come secondary as the scholarship meets their basic needs or because the value of the grant does not cover all students' needs, or perhaps for the weak relationship that students and the university itself make between academia and cultural life. The students also indicated in their responses the expenses that are part of their daily family life, including help with household expenses (water, electricity, and telephone); buying food for the family and help their parents with health care expenses.

## Final Considerations

The *ProgramaPermanecer* was the first step towards the improvement of conditions of permanence of students from UFBA. Nevertheless, UFBA's administrators need to be aware that their student population had change significantly over the last decade. However, the first cohort of students that were beneficiaries of the *ProgramaPermanecer* was already in the middle of their majors when they started to receive financial aid from the university. Another main issue is the fact that a substantial number of students still need to work or is seeking for work during at the same time they are performing their universities studies.

To credit the success of higher education only to the exceptional qualities of students, without considering the students' trajectories and the challenges that they have to face to earn their degrees is a mistake. Initiatives such as the *ProgramaPermanecer* had demonstrated that, with the right support, students from lower-income families could be as competitive as other students, who had a privileged background.

Although the survey presented in this journal indicated some of the main social characteristics of the first cohort of *ProgramaPermanecer*' student population, more research can be conducted and should be stimulated by UFBA. One major point that should be explored by researchers is the emotional experiences of students from lower-income families during their time at university, especially what they experience during difficulties times and what strategies they use to overcome these moments. Monitor the students' academic life conditions is an important task and universities should provide support to the students, so they can overcome their main difficulties.

The *ProgramaPermanecer* scholarship holders devote twenty hours per week for project activities, and, at the same time, they need to attend all classes and be approved for all the courses they are enrolled. Moreover, the program should look for ways to improve the quality of life of students from lower-income families, through a model that integrates the various services offered by the university in an attempt to minimize academic life difficulties. The program should also improve its online platform in a way to use more resources currently available by new tools from ICT in education. A better online platform would help the program's students to achieve more practical skills and other important abilities in academic life. A more intensive use of ICT in education tools could improve students' academic skill and maximize student retention.

Although the affirmative action programs were a step forward, Brazil needs a more comprehensive strategy regarding access to higher education. Improving online programs and make more knowledge available to students through online platforms would also increase the student's accessibilities to new skills required in modern life. Therefore, focus on permanence and, at the same, working on new tools that can transform academic life is of extreme value to universities. Brazil is on the right path but still needs constant development.

# Chapter 2

# Utilising ICT in Education: Focus on Distance Education

✎ **Simon-Peter KafuiAheto**
*University of Cape Coast, Ghana, Africa*

## Preview at a Glance

This study explores how ICTs are utilised in the deployment of Distance Education in Ghana. The College of Distance Education, University of Cape Coast in Ghana was selected as a case, because, it is currently the leading provider of Distance Education in West Africa. Analyses of data were made in two folds to cover students' and staff perspectives on the use of ICTs to enhance Distance Education. The research design made use of numeric and narrative analyses of data. A number of 21 participants made up of seven staff and 14 students were involved in the study. The study found 31 ICTs categorised into five that are utilised by both students and staff of the College. The ICTs ranged from mobile phones, WhatsApp, Biometric clocking to radio cassettes. There were 18 ICTs that were utilised by both groups. However, an aspect the staff also considered is Monitoring and Security devices as another dimension that are virtually not mentioned as tools that aid Distance Education deployment. Both students and staff said they stored data on their mobile phones. Nevertheless, students also used their cameras and microchips as storage devices. One of the recommendations from this study is that the University of Cape Coast should collaborate with other educational and research institutions to get hooked up onto shared and distributed Internet wireless networks such as Eduroam. This will assist students who largely own digital devices less cost and the proximity to Internet wireless access.

## Introduction

Within the last decade, there has been a dramatic growth towards Distance Education (DE) in Ghana. This growth started slowly and made used of less digital technologies.

Providers basically used print based approaches to deliver their lectures where course facilitators meet their students on regular basis (Koomson, 2009; Keegan, 1980). With the advancement of technology as time evolved, various Information and Communication Technologies (ICTs) have been used in the deployment of DE (Simone, Smaldino and Zvacek, 2015) in a developing country such as Ghana. Unfortunately, there is poor documentation of the details on which kinds of ICTs aid the proper delivery of Distance Education in Ghana. The University of Cape Coast Distance Education was purposively selected for this study because it is a leading Distance Education institution in Ghana and West Africa in terms of infrastructure, personnel, students and recognition. This year alone, a total of 17, 182 comprising of 15, 780 and 1, 402 undergraduate and postgraduate students respectively were admitted into the university as fresh students (Ampiah, 2018). This number exceeds the total number of students who were admitted to study through the regular stream made up of 5230 which includes 555 postgraduate students (Ampiah, 2018). It is also interesting to note that the institution could only admit 5230 (less than 50%) out of a total of 13,188 applicants to the regular stream. A number of factors will determine why ICTs are used. The factors can also include gender, Internet and access in terms of cost or proximity.

According to BECTA (2008) females use ICT more for school work than males. The findings are likely to be possible reasons accounting for systematic population increases in some programmes in Distance Education. One important factor in the deployment of Distance Education today is the Internet. According to the International Telecommunication Union (ITU) report 2017, Africa recorded the lowest percentage of internet access from work, schools and universities and shared public connections out of homes. But positively, Africa was also recorded to have the highest proportion of youth aged, 15-24 of internet users (37%) in the world. This may be informed by the rate mobile phone penetration in developing countries (Mahenge and Sanga, 2016). A number of Distance Education students are no longer elderly people. A greater portion constitute of the youth (including students and staff of Distance education) are affected by the above statistics. On this note, identifying the various technologies used is likely to help improve the quality of Distance Education and to take advantage of maximising learning opportunities.

## *Objectives of the study*

The study was guided by the following objectives:
1. The extent to which utilization of ICTs differ between students and staff of Distance Education at the University of Cape Coast?
2. The extent to which students' enrolment on Distance Education programme is affected by ICT utilisation by the institution?

The study sought to answer these research questions:
1. To what extent is the rate of admission of Distance Education Students affected by ICT utilisation?

2. To what extent is students' enrolment on Distance Education programme affected ICT utilisation by the institution?

## University of Cape Coast's College of Distance Education

Formerly known as the Centre for Continuing Education when it was established in 1997, College of Distance Education is one of the five colleges in the University of Cape Coast in Ghana, West Africa. The centre attained the status of a College on the August 1st, 2014. This upgrade brought in a number remarkable changes such us the College weaning itself from the then Faculty of Education. Positions such as Director and some co-ordinators changed to Provosts and Heads of Department. For the students, what it meant for them was quicker responses and less bureaucratic system (CoDE, UCC website, 2017).

The vision of the 'new' college is "to position the college as the leading provider of quality distance and continuing education in Ghana and beyond." The centre which started with 27 students across the 10 regions of Ghana currently has more than 50, 000 students across more than 80 study centres in Ghana just about the same number of study centres for The Tanzanian Open University. However, the student population (both undergraduate and postgraduate) is dominated by professional teachers or under-training teachers. There are programmes also offered in the Businesses (CoDE, UCC website, 2017).

The college has over the years used technology to drive its activities. It started slowly with modules but now it has an E-Learning project that is currently rolling to students' learning, facilitation and some aspects of administration. The centre has modules for each of the undergraduate subjects written by lecturers who teach students on the regular stream. This is to adhere to the university's commitment to quality and equity. This is to ensure that no student is disadvantaged on the basis of mode of studies, hence the value of certificate is awarded to graduates on distance Education programme is the same as those on the regular stream. This approach is known as the dual mode of Distance Education (Bates, 1990). Students follow the same curriculum prescribed the university but take their facilitation or lectures or examinations from any of the centres bi-monthly. At Distance Educational centres, and in between the face-to-face periods, a number of ICTs are utilised for the benefit of Distance Education (Anderson and Dron, 2011). ICTs are key components of any 21st Century Distance Education. In effect, ICTs cannot be taken out of Distance Education delivery (Moore and Kearsley, 1996).

This study is motivated by the reason that it appears that studies in Distance Education largely focus on social media use or performance appraisal via technologies in education (Englund, Olofsson and Price, 2017; Wang and Cranton, 2017). It appears that little or no work has been done to map out the utilisation of ICTs in Distance Education from the perspective of Staff and Students.

## Methodology

The research design made use of numeric and narrative data collection and analyses (Plowright, 2011). The College of Distance Education, University of Cape Coast in

Ghana was purposively selected as a case because it is currently a leading Distance Education provider in West Africa. A total number of 21 participants made up of seven staff and 14 students were involved in the study. The participants were sampled randomly from the College and the staffs include 3 academic and 4 administrative members who have worked within the ranges of five to 10 years at the College. Literature materials on Distance Education, Statistics on the Colleges intake and graduation and the university's website (specifically for news items) were consulted. High ethical standards were followed. Permission was sought from the College to undertake this study. To protect the identity of the participants; names used for participants in this report are pseudonyms. Again among others, participants had the opportunity to pull out from the interview sections anytime they so wished during the process.

## Results and Discussions

### To what extent does utilization of ICTs differ between students and staff of Distance Education at the University of Cape Coast?

Research question 1 is answered with the help of Table 1 and some findings from the interviews. The kind of ICTs used and how they differ between the students and staff of Distance Education in the university are presented and discussed below. Table 1 gives an overview of the various ICTs used by students and staff in Distance Education.

Table 1: ICTs utilised by Distance Education Students and Staff

| | Category and ICT | | Staff | Student |
|---|---|---|---|---|
| **Category 1** | **Communication and office devices** | | | |
| | 1 | Camera (still) | ✓ | ✓ |
| | 2 | Camera (video) | ✓ | ✓ |
| | 3 | Computer (Desktop and Laptops) | ✓ | |
| | 4 | External Hard drive | ✓ | |
| | 5 | Flash/pen drive | ✓ | |
| | 6 | Internet | ✓ | ✓ |
| | 7 | Internet modem | ✓ | ✓ |
| | 8 | Microphone | ✓ | ✓ |
| | 9 | Mobile phone | ✓ | ✓ |
| | 10 | Photocopier | ✓ | ✓ |
| | 11 | Pointer | ✓ | |
| | 12 | Printers (for paper and Identification cards) | ✓ | |
| | 13 | Projector | ✓ | ✓ |
| | 14 | Public address system | ✓ | |
| | 15 | Recorder | ✓ | ✓ |

# Utilising ICT in Education: Focus on Distance Education

|  |  | Category and ICT | Staff | Student |
|---|---|---|---|---|
|  | 16 | Risograph printer | ✓ |  |
|  | 17 | Scanner | ✓ | ✓ |
|  | 18 | Server | ✓ |  |
|  | 19 | Tablet/IPad | ✓ | ✓ |
| **Category 2** |  | **Social media** |  |  |
|  | 1 | Facebook | ✓ | ✓ |
|  | 2 | WhatsApp | ✓ | ✓ |
|  | 3 | LinkedIn |  | ✓ |
| **Category 3** |  | **Software and Platforms** |  |  |
|  | 1 | Moodle | ✓ |  |
|  | 2 | Software (open source) | ✓ | ✓ |
|  | 3 | Software (proprietary) | ✓ | ✓ |
| **Category 4** |  | **Monitoring and Security devices** |  |  |
|  | 1 | Biometric clock | ✓ |  |
|  | 2 | Closed-Circuit Television (CCTV) | ✓ |  |
| **Category 5** |  | **Storage devices** |  |  |
|  | 1 | Camera (still) |  | ✓ |
|  | 2 | Camera (video) |  | ✓ |
|  | 3 | Cassette |  | ✓ |
|  | 4 | Cloud | ✓ | ✓ |
|  | 5 | Computer (Desktop and Laptops) | ✓ | ✓ |
|  | 6 | External hard drive | ✓ | ✓ |
|  | 7 | Mobile phone | ✓ | ✓ |
|  | 8 | Microchip |  | ✓ |
|  | 9 | Pen/flash drive | ✓ | ✓ |

Source: Interviews, 2018

According to Table 1, a total of 31 ICTs were identified as tools utilised by students and staff in the deployment of Distance Education. These tools were categorised into five, based on their functions. The categories are Communication and office devices, Social media, Software and Platforms, Monitoring and Security devices and Storage devices. Table 1 also reveals that the staff of Distance Education used more ICT tools than the students and a total of 18 tools were identified as tools utilised by both the staff and students. It is interesting to note that one of the current students who were part of the pioneer class of Distance Education in the university used cassette to record for her notes. According to Student Akua, she said, *"...hmm in those days, the cassette recorder was just a saviour. That was the best way to store lectures from my module. It was a bit tiring getting the text onto tapes but it helped me and I could pass is onto friends who also found good use for it."* Her experience also shows clearly how technology use in Distance Education has evolved.

Both students and staff also agreed that the mobile phone cannot be left out in rolling out distance education. Since a lot of young people own and use mobile phones (ITU, 2017) it is not surprising that mobile phone penetration affects Distance Education since it is the commonest way of communicating between students and students and staff and staff. Staff Roland said that the mobile phone was used to communicate with colleagues on the official *"WhatsApppage especially during examinations. In some cases, we need to convey quick decisions and these decisions are broadcasted on our phones* [sic] *a call on the field saves you from some troubles."*

Under Category 4, the staff mentioned Biometric clocking and Closed-Circuit Television (CCTV). The Biometric clock ensures the punctuality of staff and serves as a record or database of staff attendance. In most cases, categories like this are ignored but the staffs think that this system is a quality assurance measure in deploying Distance Education. *"I have no problem with the biometric clocking system. It only protects me by keeping a database of my attendance over time* (Staff Caro)." For the CCTV, it is a security measure. A staff (Staff Beauty) had this to say *"because of the numbers that come around for Face-to-Face lectures, it is prudent that management put in place some sought of surveillance to monitor life and property."*

Moodle platform is also used to deploy some e-learning courses (postgraduate coursesespecially). At the postgraduate level, our lecturers share with us course materials via the Learning Management System (LMS). *"I am able to download materials to from the LMS for our group discussions at homes* (Student Derrick)." From the submissions of Student Derrick, it can be seen that students also use their LMSs as a repository.

Internet was also mentioned by both students and staff as a key tool for teaching, learning and administration. *"As a distance education student, my only worry is the cost of buying data to access some course materials or to even connect with colleagues. Once you are out of the main campus and you are at any of the hired Study Centres, accessing university internet becomes a very big challenge* (Student Jo)."

## To what extent is the rate of admission of Distance Education Students affected by ICT utilisation?

Tables 2 and 3 give an overview on the distribution of students admitted to the University of Cape Coast Distance Education programmes in 2016/2017. The two tables support discussions that answer research question 2.

Table 2: Distribution of Diploma/Bachelor Distance Education Degree Students by Programme, Year and Gender 2016/2017

| Programme | Year 1 | | Year 2 | | Year 3 | | Year 4 | | Total | | Total |
|---|---|---|---|---|---|---|---|---|---|---|---|
| | M | F | M | F | M | F | M | F | M | F | |
| Dip. in Mgt Studies | 337 | 403 | 336 | 498 | 375 | 291 | | | 1,048 | 1192 | 2,240 |
| Dip. in Commerce | 371 | 158 | 362 | 209 | 301 | 163 | | | 1,034 | 530 | 1,564 |
| Dip. in Basic Education | 2,913 | 3,225 | 4,195 | 4,132 | 5,165 | 4,836 | | | 12,273 | 12,193 | 24,466 |
| Dip. in Psychology & Found. of Educ. | 1,697 | 1,251 | 1,731 | 931 | 1,359 | 646 | | | 4,787 | 2,828 | 7,615 |
| Dip. in Math & Science | 126 | 10 | 133 | 8 | 135 | 7 | | | 394 | 25 | 419 |
| Bachelor of Science in Marketing | | | | | 324 | 212 | 310 | 189 | 634 | 401 | 1,035 |
| Bachelor of Mgt. Studies | | | 56 | 60 | 307 | 534 | 463 | 656 | 826 | 1,250 | 2,076 |
| Bachelor of Commerce | | | | | 1127 | 507 | 1250 | 517 | 2377 | 1,024 | 3,401 |
| Bachelor Degree in Basic Education | | | 65 | 62 | 336 | 422 | 575 | 530 | 976 | 1,014 | 1,990 |
| Bachelor Degree in Psychology & Found. Education | | | | | 1364 | 836 | 1277 | 523 | 2,641 | 1,359 | 4,000 |
| Bachelor of Math & Science | | | | | 22 | 5 | | | 22 | 5 | 27 |
| Total | 5,444 | 5,047 | 6,878 | 5,900 | 10,815 | 8,459 | 3,875 | 2,415 | 27,012 | 21,821 | 48,833 |

Source: Students Records and Management Information Section of UCC (2017) (p. 32)

Generally, the population of students from Table 3 fluctuates and differ in terms of programmes. Table 3 presentsa distribution of Postgraduate Distance Education Degree Students by Programme, year and Gender 2016/2017.

**Table 3: Distribution of Postgraduate Distance Education Degree Students by Programme, Year and Gender 2016/2017**

| Programme | Year 1 | | Year 2 | | Total | | Grand Total |
|---|---|---|---|---|---|---|---|
| | M | F | M | F | M | F | |
| M.A. (Admin. Higher Education) | 25 | 7 | 17 | 17 | 42 | 24 | 66 |
| M.A. (Guidance and Counselling) | 9 | 2 | 15 | 4 | 24 | 6 | 30 |
| M.ED (Admin. in Higher Education) | 38 | 46 | 23 | 37 | 61 | 83 | 144 |
| M.ED. (Educational Psychology) | 24 | 26 | 15 | 17 | 39 | 43 | 82 |
| M.ED. (Guidance and Counselling) | 9 | 8 | 26 | 19 | 35 | 27 | 62 |
| M.ED. (Measurement and Evaluation) | 15 | 9 | 4 | 3 | 19 | 12 | 31 |
| MBA (Accounting) | 82 | 30 | 79 | 24 | 161 | 54 | 215 |
| MBA (Finance) | 196 | 76 | 157 | 56 | 353 | 132 | 485 |
| MBA (Human Resource Management) | 50 | 99 | 48 | 69 | 98 | 168 | 266 |
| MBA (Marketing) | 37 | 29 | 47 | 16 | 84 | 45 | 129 |
| Total | 485 | 332 | 431 | 262 | 916 | 594 | 1510 |

Source: Students Records and Management Information Section of UCC (2017) (p. 33)

Table 3 clearly indicates a higher population of female students in M.ED (Admin. in Higher Education), MBA (Human Resource Management), M.ED. (Educational Psychology). The findings are consistent with report from The Open University of Tanzania (2017). It is possible that females in these fields of study are established workers who may be holding responsible positions where they cannot leave for school but use ICTs to enhance their work (Olatokun, 2017). It is possible however such students have also benefited from ICT trainings encourage and empower females to use ICTs at work and for their studies (BECTA, 2008). One student compared her daily use of ICT to attitude towards a LMS. *"it is a daily routine for me to use my computers in the office. As a Human Resource Manage in my firm, I use the computer to monitor work targets so I have no problem using any online learning platform at all* (Student Stella). The story is the same in Table 2 for Bachelor of Management Studies and directly opposite for Bachelor of Commerce.

## Conclusion and Recommendations

While the staffs focus more on ICTs in the deployment of quality Distance Education students also leverage on similar tools to enhance the learning. The differences come about based on the individual roles played in Distance Education. One key finding is that both students and staff said they stored data on their mobile phones. All the same, students also used their cameras and microchips as storage devices. Further studies need to be conducted on the details of how the ICTs are used especially for ICTs that were utilised both staff and students. Since the College of Distance Education has over 80 centres across the country, it is also recommended that university collaborates with other educational and research institutions to get hooked up onto shared and distributed Internet wireless networks such as Eduroam. This will enable both students and staff to enjoy and have access to constant wireless Internet services when they visit other institutions either for personal studies, Face-to-Face and or library services.

# Chapter 3

# ICT: New Paradigms for Old Problems

### ⌦ Renato Bulcao de Moraes

*UniversidadePaulista, Sao Paulo, Brazil, South America*

## Preview at a Glance

Brazil has new legislation of Distance learning. After almost fifteen years trying to mimic traditional education, distance learning is free to put in place the results of pedagogical research. But what is the philosophy behind ICT that could set the base for a new education, and what are the targets we should consider pursuit?

## Introduction

The educational legislation of Brazil establishes that it is the exclusive responsibility of the Union the accreditation of distance learning courses. Although this principle is unconstitutional, the Brazilian constitution defines that the federal government decides who has the right to operate higher programs (Santos Jr., 2017). The K-12 education has their permissions granted by the state governments.

It must be said that wealthy people in Brazil, pay for the K-12 education, but the best universities in the country were until recently public with absolutely no fees or tuitions. On the other hand, poor people go to public schools but have very few chances to get to the higher education. They never get the necessary grades to become public universities students.

Some forty years ago, private universities were opened to give the poor students an opportunity of better education. Today, in the big towns of Brazil, lower-middle-class students go to private institutions where they pay between US$ 1.200,00 to US$ 3.600,00 annually to learn.

Distance learning is making this cost more affordable, offering courses around US$ 960,00. For the ruling class, it is just not possible to provide an education for that amount of money. Because the Brazilian state is not efficient, and the cost per student in public universities is well above that, civil servants believe that Distance Education courses are just diploma mills. The good thing about that is that all private higher education institutions are strictly controlled every year! In such environment, either they improve or close doors.

Of the 16 million Brazilians between the ages of 15 and 18, only 9.2 million (58%) attend secondary school. Of these, 91% performed less than expected in math. Just 16.8% or 1.5 million students enrol in higher education (Silva, 2016). Because of this scenario, distance learning is the way higher education is expanding; with technological parallel where mobile phones are the way lower classes get access to the Internet.

## The Old Paradigm

Distance Learning in Brazil developed under the Military Dictatorship (1964-1985) offered already a MOOC like system. The classes were broadcast to everybody and the ones in need of a certificate could find local schools or even licensed teachers to buy the books and get serious help to understand the curricula. This gave the government the idea that you may broadcast as many hours of useful classes, but at the end of the day, if there is no face to face interaction, there is no learning.

This led to a distance learning model where you transmit the classes thru live streaming or on demand, give them slides with the content facilitated by topics, asked them to read an introduction book on the matter, call the tutor free by telephone and as many times you need it, and according to a specific calendar, find an examination centre because someone else could be willing to do it for the student. But yes, at the examination centre you could also visit a small library that should complement the virtual library with thousands of books.

This model endured for the last 10 years since the beginning of higher education market in Brazil, in 2007. Every institution had to obey the law, and there was no alternative model to be adopted. The model has a flaw because private schools in Brazil are not only schools but also commercial enterprises. Thus, private schools must follow not only the educational regulation but also the consumer legislation. In other words, a student became a consumer and may complain and even sue a Higher Education Institution for their lousy services. And very soon smart students started to sue the institutions every time they felt hindered by the federal law.

Even with the catch, distance learning grew in numbers, and one in every five undergraduates attends an e-course (Silva, 2016). The completion rate of distance education is today better than the traditional face to face courses. The model succeeds when it obliges the students first to watch and listen to the information of the content, then understand its logic with the slides that resume the video class. Now they can understand the introduction book which will be the base from where the exams will be prepared. It is a nice model to teach anything you should learn by heart, and forget.

Well, that's precisely the same problem we have in Brazil with the traditional schooling model: just after passing the exams, the students forget what was all that about, and move on to the next obstacles they must to get a diploma (Horton and

Freire, 1990). The question is, do we have a weak philosophy of education or the distance education regulation was built to mirror the traditions of Jesuit education, the mainstream in Brazil until 1960?

## Developing Ideas towards a New Paradigm

As a researcher in distance education since 1995, is very tempting to applaud the new regulation which states that there are no rules: since June 2017, we may develop our own standards and adopt any technology to build new courses that will be replacing the old ones in 2019 (Jair, 2017).

And the government just allowed K-12 schools to adopt the technology. Nobody is openly talking about distance learning for children, but adolescents are already digital natives and may handle a smartphone or even a computer better than adults. So why not give it a try?

First, when talking about Information and Communication Technologies, we should start categorizing what helps to inform, and what we should inform, and what is there only to communicate? What is the difference between text on a smartphone screen, on a laptop screen or on a television screen? Does the PDF document change it content when it is displayed on different screens? Is the context of the text message anyhow disturbed when traveling through various devices or inside a book (Guerin, 2013)? My guess is that text is text has a specific way of coding and for centuries the understanding of text surpassed clay tablets, parchments, books and just arrived on screens, but Plato's Republic is still the victory of ideas over things. Or do the forms change when the media change? This leads us to the question if teaching and learning still must be based on the text?

Second, why are video images important? Do they mimic reality so well, that we are just reproducing a specific context previously offered by the classroom? Why most of the videos only register a teacher talking and redundantly showing slides with precisely the same words he's speaking? Are we trying to expand Vygotsky's zone of proximal development broadcasting or streaming the moving images with sound? If so, then it is time to let students communicate while watching the class, using their favourite app on their smartphone. If teachers participate in the same group, waiting to be asked about some difficult issues, they would be better mentors (Bozkurt et al., 2016). And why only one teacher, maybe two or three could interact better with the audience. And should attendance be mandatory and all communication is synchronous, or do asynchronous contact has the same end effect?

Last, is all technology disruptive for the classroom? What is the big difference between an electronic whiteboard and the traditional blackboard? Is traditional teaching endangered by those gadgets? Really? Is there any difference of sending a warning to the parents written on the old paper notebook or by WhatsApp? With the capacity of big data, now we know how to measure how much did a student understood any proposed content. Assessments should become a help for the student, not a punishment or a filter. With technology, we are able to understand why one or more students stopped reading at page 8, or read page 20 six times. We may get more learners achieving their grades by merely asking them 'Have you got it?' or 'Try to explain it to me, now.' Old Socrates back to the game, which could be the way of training robots as personal tutors to replace the Skinnerian model of teaching machines.

The question is if future education is about knowing or about understanding. Because I know a lot of things that I don't understand. There are a lot of drivers who don't understand how the engine works, but they drive. Lots of passengers don't understand why an airplane flies, but they keep on traveling. Do we have to know everything, or only understand things that may be useful to engage us in society and help us to exchange goods and services to collaborate in our chosen community (Cormier, 2008)? How does education should help the future generation to weave a global nation? Do we need laws for this new way of teaching? In such a world, is texting from Shanghai to Mumbai, or conference call with a smartphone from Moscow to New York, not a perception of here and now? Isn't time and space relative?

Chapter

4

# ET for Higher Education: Innovative Practices at Global Level

✎ **Ramesh C. Sharma\* and Maria Antonia Lima Gomes\*\***

*\*Wawasan Open University, Malaysia, Asia &*

*\*\*Da Universidadedo Estado da Bahia,Brazil, South America*

## Preview at a Glance

Information and communication technologies have greatly transformed all sectors of our life. Over past few decades, technology in its simple or complex form has brought grand changes in the way the instruction and learning is designed and delivered. Expansion of Internet has been a big catalyst for such transformation. New tools and technologies offer ways to learning-facilitators to plan, design, deliver and evaluate teaching and learning. This chapter discusses innovations and global practices of comprehension-focused digital technologies and its implications for teaching and learning in the digital society.

## Introduction

'We are at the beginning of a global transformation that is characterized by the convergence of digital, physical, and biological technologies in ways that are changing both the world around us and our very idea of what it means to be human. The changes are historic in terms of their size, speed, and scope. This transformation—the Fourth Industrial Revolution—is not defined by any particular set of emerging technologies themselves, but rather by the transition to new systems that are being built on the infrastructure of the digital revolution. As these individual technologies become ubiquitous, they will fundamentally alter the way we produce, consume, communicate, move, generate energy, and interact with one another' (Schwab, 2016). These changes have revolutionized the educational sphere too. Moving from simple technology like overhead project and transparencies and radio to complex technologies of today like

Virtual Reality and Artificial Intelligence, Internet has played a great role. ICT is the backbone of developments. We are now living in digital era where user generated content dominates. With the help of social media individuals are contributing to knowledge generation or replication. Robbins (2016) predicted that by 2020, there will be over 26 billion Internet-connected devices and over 4 billion global Internet users. He further notes that, 'every day, Exabyte of new data are created and transported over IP networks. In 2016 the world has entered the 'zettabyte era': global IP traffic will reach 1.1 zettabytes, or over 1 trillion gigabytes. By 2020 global IP traffic will reach 2.3 zettabytes. This data growth is fueling economies, sparking innovation, and unleashing waves of creativity.'

With so much of the data being generated, our communication, interactions, teaching and learning are being altered. New tools and technologies are being invented and thus those who adopt and implement them stand out separately from those who do not use and tend to lag behind. World Economic Forum publishes 'The Global Information Technology Report' examining the state of networked readiness of countries using a Networked Readiness Index (NRI). This report also looks at the role of information and communication technologies (ICTs) in driving innovation in the Digital Economy. The networked readiness framework is based on six principles: (1) a high-quality regulatory and business environment is critical in order to fully leverage ICTs and generate impact; (2) ICT readiness, as measured by ICT affordability, skills, and infrastructure, is a pre-condition to generating impact; (3) fully leveraging ICTs requires a society-wide effort: the government, the business sector, and the population at large each have a critical role to play; (4) ICT use should not be an end in itself. The impact that ICTs actually have on the economy and society is what ultimately matters; (5) the set of drivers, the environment, readiness, and usage, interact, co-evolve, and reinforce each other to form a virtuous cycle; and (6) the networked readiness framework should provide clear policy guidance (Baller, Dutta andLanvin, 2016, p. xi). The Global Information Technology Report 2016 examined the data on four main categories / sub indexes (Environment, Readiness, Usage and Impact); 10 subcategories (pillars) and 53 individual indicators (Political and regulatory environment, Business and innovation environment, Infrastructure, Affordability, Skills, Individual usage, Business usage, Government usage, Economic impacts, and Social impacts) related to 139 countries. The key findings of the report are: (a) change in the nature of innovation due to digital revolution, for example digitization of existing products and processes, distributed manufacturing, block chains and suberized activities in various sectors including education; (b) Increasing pressure to innovate continuously as digital technologies become the winner-decider. Those who have high level of ICT adoption and usage stand out from others in economic and digital innovation impact; (c) A growing digital population creates more demand for digital products and services, but businesses and governments are not fast enough to offer matching innovative digital solutions, and (d) emergent need for innovations in governance and regulation because right kind of governance and regulatory frameworks would ensure sustainability and would bring in digital transformation of industries and societies.

Developments and innovations in digital products and processes have transformed the education sector too. Globally there are some common challenges the higher education sector faces: challenge of numbers, of relevance, of Quality, of access, of costs and of speed. These challenges can tackled by a number of disruptive innovative solutions, which include inculcating self-learning (building on meta-cognition), measuring learning, collaborative and co-operative learning, personalization of learning and learning analytics. However, in addition to new systems or technologies, we need a fundamental change of perspective. Education is seen as the responsibility of the State and the system is based on authority and licenses and permissions to allow education to be transacted in modern times this is unlikely to work. As Henry Maine had said ' as society progresses, it moves from status to contract'. So must the educational system build contractual relationships between the learner and providers of learning as more important than statutory authority? Some of the very promising technological and pedagogical models that has received a lot of attention during the last few years and adoption have been MOOCs, flipped classroom, social media in education, gamification, augmented reality and virtual reality etc.

Sharples *et al.* (2016) identified ten innovative pedagogies which might transform education: (1) Learning through social media (Using social media to offer long-term learning opportunities); (2) Productive failure (Drawing on experience to gain deeper understanding); (3) Teach back (Learning by explaining what we have been taught); (4) Design thinking (Applying design methods in order to solve problems); (5) Learning from the crowd (Using the public as a source of knowledge and opinion); (6) Learning through video games (Making learning fun, interactive and stimulating); (7) Formative analytics (Developing analytics that help learners to reflect and improve); (8) Learning for the future (Preparing learners for work and life in an unpredictable future); (9) Trans-language (Enriching learning through the use of multiple languages); and (10) Block chain for learning (Storing, validating and trading educational reputation). This report highlights new science of learning, wherein the research outcomes from neuroscience, cognitive sciences, educational and social sciences are integrated for understanding the dynamics of how we learn. The NMC Horizon Report (Adams Becker et al., 2017) identifies blended learning designs and collaborative learning as a key trend accelerating higher education technology adoption as a short term while growing focus on measuring learning and redesigning learning spaces as midterm trend. Blended learning design has been among the top trends for quite some time (p.4) along with other recent technology developments like games and gamification, flipped classroom, mobile learning, augmented and virtual learning, MOOCs, adaptive learning technologies and next-generation LMS among others. All these developments have significant implications for online pedagogy and course design. Let's have a look at some of the technology developments happening around us.

## *Real time communication tools*

Effective communication is the key to successful teaching and learning. Learning-facilitators and learners use synchronous and asynchronous tools for communicating. Real-Time communication tools have been found to be effective in sharing ideas among multiple users. These can be integrated with a LMS or through the institutional website. With the help of these tools, a learner can learn a subject offered by an institution in a different place or country all together by asking questions and interacting in real time with peer and learning-facilitators. Tools like WebRTC, Skype with now language translation facility enabled, and Slack etc. offer us the benefit of creating online presence, removing the feeling of distance, video conferencing, file sharing, social networking, gaming, screen sharing, and online education etc. For example, Curtin University is integrating Cisco Spark into its Challenge platform for team-based problem-solving and MOOC development on the Open edX platform. The 5th annual International Conference of Undergraduate Research (ICUR) involved the use of real time presentations delivered via live video links with institutions in the UK, Australia, South Africa, Japan, Indonesia, Singapore and the USA. The Pontificia Universidad Javeriana (PUJC) in Cali Colombia offers English-Spanish courses where the English part is taught by an American university and the Spanish part is taught by PUJC. So, each English speaker learner has a counterpart in Colombia. The first half of the course is based on questions in Spanish where the English learner has to solve using Spanish (getting the answers from the Colombian learner). The second part is the same but in English. More than 800 learners have taken these courses with excellent results. One interesting effect is that learners tend to continue in contact outside the classroom time. Given the reached success, several other Jesuit universities from AUSJAL (Latin America) and AJCU (USA) have joined the project. So far, more than 25.000 learners and 200 professors have participated (Reinoso, 2017).

## *Big Data and learning Analytics*

As the Internet traffic increases for our different online needs, a massive data is generated which provides insights into browsing behaviour and preferences of users. In case of educational institutions where online services are integrated for course delivery from admissions to examinations, such data can be very useful to identify at-risk learners, personalize learning, learner's choice and difficulties related to courses. The Western Governors University, Utah, USA uses big data to analyses all aspects of course delivery and learner performance so that University can bring fast and effective improvement in learner support services along with learner performance. The National University of Singapore has established a Data Analytics Consulting Centre to process data using advanced data analytics strategies serving economic, social and scientific community. Plymouth University, United Kingdom undertook a 'Stakeholder Engagement Project' to define impact by involving learners, staff, senior leaders and Board of Governors of the University. 'Learning Analytics strives to provide the right information, to the right person, at the right time. It also promotes greater transparency for staff and learners and casts light on factors currently hidden' (Witt, 2017). He cites the advantages of analytics technologies for the following:

- For Learners
    - Empowerment to be more reflective learners by being better informed
    - Awareness and better feedback on how they are doing

- Potential to input their own measures such as time spent reading
- Grade predictor

▸ For Personal Tutors
- Instant overview of how a learner is doing
- Early warning of signs that a learner is in need of extra support
- Increase engagement by forming a basis for conversations.

▸ For Module and Programme Leads
- A clearer picture about learners' and module performance
- Gauge impact of module changes on learner performance
- Comparing learner performance modules/programmes

▸ For Institutions
- Improve retention through early and consistent identification of 'at risk' learners across programmes, schools and faculties
- Monitor and enhance learner engagement
- Provide evidence to target resources and monitor longer term impacts
- Create best practice toolkit based on efficacy of interventions
- Help to implement institution-wide, and thus more consistent, approaches to learners in difficulty
- Remove information silos
- Contributing to improved learner satisfaction
- Better information for strategic planning
- Simplify the process of compiling metrics in existing and future statutory quality, monitoring and funding requirements

▸ For Governors
- Objective information to aid decision making if required

## *Artificial Intelligence*

According to Hammond (2015), artificial intelligence (AI) is the knowledge engineering that allows computers to simulate human perception, learning, and decision-making is based on access to categories, properties, and relationships between various information sets. Machine learning is a subset of AI, providing computers the ability to learn without being explicitly programmed. IBM Watson University Program is for those who wish to develop apps or work on cognitive technologies, building robots etc. These programs have implications for commerce, education, health, IoT, supply chain, Marketing and Financial services etc. The DFKI (German Center for Artificial Intelligence) is developing a 'Hyper Mind: The intelligent school book'. The learners would use intelligent school book via tablet and PC and innovative sensor technology, which detects and then analyses the reader's line of vision. This will quickly determine whether the pupil has understood the learning content and thus aid the individual learning progress.

College of Computing at the Georgia Institute of Technology, USA has an interesting example about AI where a course 'Knowledge Based Artificial Intelligence (KBAI)' is taught by Professor Ashok Goel every semester. This course is a core requirement of Georgia Tech's online masters of Science in computer science program. So every semester, his 300 or so learners post roughly 10,000 messages in the online forums which are somewhat difficult to manage by him or his teaching assistants. So he introduced another teaching assistant in 2016, named Jill Watson, which is a computer, a virtual assistant, based on IBM's Watson Platform. Initially the answers of Jill were not correct, but later she was answering with 97 percent correctness. Interesting fact is that the learners were not aware that they were interacting with a computer, the identity of which was revealed in April 2016.

## Internet of things (IoT):

According to Wikipedia, The Internet of things (IoT) is the network of physical devices, vehicles, home appliances and other items embedded with electronics, software, sensors, actuators, and network connectivity which enable these objects to connect and exchange data.

The ITU's Telecommunication Standardization Sector (ITU-T) defines Internet of Things as a global infrastructure for the information society, enabling advanced services by interconnecting (physical and virtual) things based on existing and evolving interoperable information and communication technologies. The University of Notre Dame is experimenting with various IoT devices, like low power beacons and bicycle sharing (Limabike). There is another research project where learners wear Fitbit-like devices that gather data on their exercise patterns. IoT is definitely relevant to the Higher Ed sector assuming privacy issues can be addressed as these devices scale up quickly on campus (Turner, 2017). Turner further informs about University of Notre Dame NIH Net Health research project which is an 'attempt to create a monitoring platform using both an app on the learners' smartphones and wearable monitoring technology, such as a Fitbit, to collect information'.

## Mobile learning

Mobile learning can be defined as the processes (both personal and public) of coming to know through exploration and conversation across multiple contexts amongst people and interactive technologies (Sharples, M. *et al.*, 2007). They focus more on context. MoLeNET (2010) provides a practical definition of mobile learning as which involves the 'exploitation of ubiquitous handheld hardware, wireless networking and mobile telephony to facilitate, support, enhance and extend the reach of teaching and learning.' The world has more mobile phone subscriptions than people, according to the International Telecommunications Union's Facts and Figures for 2017 (Sharwood, 2017).

## *Virtual and Augmented reality/3D simulation*

According to Wikipedia, Simulation is the imitation of the operation of a real-world process or system over time. The act of simulating something first requires that a model be developed; this model represents the key characteristics, behaviors and functions of the selected physical or abstract system or process. The model represents the system itself, whereas the simulation represents the operation of the system over time (https://en.wikipedia.org/wiki/Simulation). With the advances in web technologies, learning of scientific phenomena has taken a new dimension. Emergence of Virtual and Augmented reality has added a new dimension the way we learn a particular concept. These digital technologies provide us an opportunity to create representations of scientific, technical and historical phenomena. Lantz-Andersson, Linderoth, andSaljo (2009) found pictorial models effective in representing molecular reactions to explain concepts which involve invisible structures and dynamic characters. Chao et al. (2016) and OlympiouandZacharia (2012) suggested that a combination of virtual labs and physical experiments can enhance learners' conceptual understanding of scientific phenomena more than the use of virtual tools or lab experiments alone. An example is the São Joao da Bahia Virtual Museum, a project consisting of a three-dimensional (3D) modeling and imaging program as a means of ubiquitous and inclusive learning in a digital era. The 3D modelling of the Sao Joao da Bahia Virtual Museum has a great historical and cultural significance as it represents a heritage that existed during the 19th century and ended physically in the 20th century. The 3D computing environment was based epistemological principles with a socio-constructivist approach and with Dialogical bases. Chu (2007) found that online scenario-based learning provide an opportunity to the learners to virtually immerse in a scenario which can enhance their learning and knowledge. The three-dimensional (3D) modeling and imaging program of the Sao Joao da Bahia Virtual Museum provides such immersive environment where the visitor virtually experiences the culture and society of that period of time.

Anderson and Kanuka (2009) highlighted the use of Internet as it 'provides a new educational context or learning environment, such as a completely virtual education institution (e.g., virtual school or university, or private training organization) or augmentation of classroom-based schooling (so called blended-learning) with network mediated activities.' Anderson andKanuka further report that virtual learning environments (e.g., learning contexts build in Second Life and Active Worlds) can also be created using Internet in which the physical laws of nature can be transcended (2009). The scientific results proved that a Virtual Museum, or a 3D simulation, the Teatro Sao Joao da Bahia, Salvador, Brazil, from the nineteenth century, proved to be socio-constructivist and dialogical (Gomes, 2017) for ubiquitous and inclusive learning in a digital era. However, the challenges are numerous, although today we already have several programs, software, that allow a simulation as real as possible of the object modeled they still lack a greater malleability in terms of their configurations and dimensionalities and cheapen the costs when the software used is not free software. The implications are different, because through this Virtual Museum Teatro Sao Joao da Bahia with socio-constructivist Approach we find the meeting of people in different times, the dialogue, mediate in the virtual learning environment through the voices that emerge in the context of the Virtual Museum, The polyphony, because the subjects, the characters that are in it, did not tell us only stories, but they dialogue with and through them, the collaborative systems and networks, made possible by the creation of the Immediate Development Zones. In addition there are several possibilities of simulation within the domain of virtual museums that can be created and made feasible from the culture in which each person lives respected its principles, its roots.

## Conclusion

ICT is playing a significant role in all sectors of education. It is offering us new products and processes and learning-facilitators are now able to deliver instruction in a variety of ways. The learners have access to a plethora of resources as internet penetration increases and mobile telephony surpasses the landline telephones. There is need for capacity building of the learning-facilitators on effective use of tech tools for teaching and assessment.

Chapter 5

# ICT-based Evaluation of Professionals and Researchers

☙ **Vinod Kumar Kanvaria**
*University of Delhi, Delhi, India, Asia*

## Preview at a Glance

ICT has various facets for its usage and application. The current chapter tries to through light upon its application in evaluation at higher education and professional development level. With the easy access of ICT facilities like digital gadgets, equipment, internet facilities, software, apps and high speed internet, the application of the ICT has increased up to an exponential rate in higher education. The current chapter sees this education at the level of pre-service education in-service education. Beginning from the concept of application of ICT in higher education it goes up to using ICT for evaluation of assignments and papers in the higher education system written by scholars and faculty members. It is worth to mention here that now a day degrees, selection and promotion at higher education are closely linked with these assignments and papers. In the current study, the papers have been invited from the academics to present in the event. These papers were enlisted and put under preliminary screening for word limit and format. After that, these papers were put under plagiarism-check using Urkund as plagiarism-checking tool. The papers sent by the scholars and academics working at higher education level had been analyzed based upon their plagiarism percentage or similarity index. The selected papers have been discussed. Some quantitative discussions have been made to reach up to an evidential and logical conclusion. This conclusion paves a way for further discussion and opens a door for researchers for further investigation in this field. They can add further dimensions to the field and enrich the application of plagiarism-check in higher education.

## Introduction

ICT is being used for learning, teaching and evaluation in India too. Earlier private institutions and some premier institutions were famous for having ICT facilities for teaching and learning, but now almost every institution has ICT facilities irrespective of being private or government sector institution. If the facilities are not directly available with the institution, its learning-facilitators and learners have this facility available with them and they are using it. As a consequence, it can be said that almost every institution or its constituents are having access to ICT now a day.

Beginning from school level, the ICT facilities are increasing at higher education level too. At school level while various governments are helping for making available such facilities through policies and schemes like Policy on ICT and ICT@School scheme, at higher education UGC, NAAC, NCTE and various governments are playing a vital role to make such facilities available to the massive strength of learning-facilitators and learners. The learners and learning-facilitators are using too these facilities at mass level. While learners are using ICT facilities for developing and enriching their assignments, their learning-facilitators are using ICT for enriching their teaching, research and academic writing work for professional development.

ICT and its use are being supported by the excessive availability of the internet to the higher education level learners and learning-facilitators. Since the learning material is available at ease and at large on the internet, there are more possibilities for plagiarism and academic unethical practices by the both. Higher level learning-facilitators and learners write papers. The papers are meant for finding something new and communicate to this something new to the mass. Hence these papers are carrier of the researched work. The research demands a sort of novelty not only in its work but also in its writing and communication. And, due to various needs and policies of the stakeholders and institutional bodies, these papers are being made available on the internet, which can be accessed using ICT. The easy availability of research work on the internet, access to the ICT facilities at mass level, demands for the academic degrees, criteria for selection and promotion and laisse-faire nature of human being, this material is being copied and plagiarized by people at higher education level. This practice has become so high that the need of the plagiarism-check software has been felt by the stakeholders and institutions. And the result of this is that the most of the institutions have one or the other plagiarism-check software for checking and prohibiting such malpractice.

## Excerpts from University Grants Commission (Promotion of Academic Integrity and Prevention of Plagiarism in Higher Education Institutions) Regulations 2017 (Draft)

UGC (2017) takes a strict note on plagiarism and penalties attached to it in higher education institutions. Recommendations by the UGC (2017) clearly shares that though the similarity checks for plagiarism shall exclude all quoted work either falling under public domain or reproduced with all necessary permission and/or attribution, all references, bibliography, table of content, preface and acknowledgements, all small similarities of minor nature, all generic terms, laws, standard symbols and standard equations but there is a zero tolerance policy in core area/work and for this higher education institution shall impose maximum penalty. The core work shall include abstract, summary, hypotheses, observations, results, conclusions and recommendations. Rest of the areas will be treated as non-core areas.

For all other (non-core) cases, plagiarism would be quantified into various levels in ascending order of severity for the purpose of its definition i.e. similarities up to 10% - excluded, level 1: similarities above 10% to 40%, level 2: similarities above 40% to 60% and level 3: similarities above 60%.

The penalties for plagiarism are suggested as follows:

(a) Penalties for Learners

- Level 1: Similarities above 10% to 40% - Such learner shall not be given any mark and/or credit for the plagiarized script and shall be asked to submit a revised script within a stipulated time period not exceeding 6 months.
- Level 2: Similarities above 40% to 60% - Such learner shall not be given any mark and/or credit for the plagiarized script and shall be asked to submit a revised script after a time period of one year but not exceeding eighteen months.
- Level 3: Similarities above 60% - Such learner shall not be given any mark and/or credit for the plagiarized script and his/her registration for that course to be cancelled.

Special notes say that repeated plagiarism shall be punished for the plagiarism of one level higher than the previous level committed by him/her. In case where plagiarism of highest level is committed then the punishment for the same shall be operative. If plagiarism is proved on a date later than the date of award of degree or credit as the case may be then his/her degree or credit shall be put in abeyance for a period decided by the competent authority.

(b) Penalties for faculty, staff and researcher of higher education institution

- Level 1: Similarities above 10% to 40% - shall be asked to withdraw manuscript submitted for publication and shall not be allowed to publish any work for a minimum period of one year.
- Level 2: Similarities above 40% to 60% - shall be asked to withdraw manuscript submitted for publication and shall not be allowed to publish any work for a minimum period of two years and shall be denied a right to one annual increment and shall not be allowed to be a supervisor to any UG, PG, Masters, MPhil., Ph.D. learner/scholar for a period of two years.
- Level 3: Similarities above 60% - shall be asked to withdraw manuscript submitted for publication and shall not be allowed to publish any work for a minimum period of three years and shall be denied a right to two successive annual increments and shall not be allowed to be a supervisor to any UG, PG, Masters, M.Phil., Ph.D. learner/scholar for a period of three years.

Special notes say that in case level 3 offence is repeated then the concerned person shall be dismissed, if plagiarism is proved on a date later than the date of benefit or credit obtained as the case may be then his/her benefit or credit shall be put in abeyance for a certain period decided by the competent authority and if there is any complaint of plagiarism against the Head of an higher education institution, a suitable action, in line with these regulations, will be taken by the Competent Authority/Governing Board/ Governing Council.

The current chapter is a venture to look into this and to investigate the malpractice of plagiarism at higher education level. The chapter also gives hint that how many people read the instructions carefully or comprehend even a one page write-up clearly. The chapter discusses this issue based upon the factual data available.

## *Conceptual Framework*

- **ICT:** The popularly well-known term ICT (BECTA, 2002) stands for information and communication technologies. It is a combination of two technologies i.e. information technology and communication technology. The information technology while focuses upon creating the information into various formats, the communication technology deals with communicating the information to the mass or wherever it is required to be communicated. Hence, the combination of these two different technologies gives rise to a new technology i.e. ICT which deals with not only creating the information into various formats but also communicating it to the mass level. Some of the academic write it as information and communication technology, but in fact it is information and communication technologies as it's already a combination of two different technologies.

- **Evaluation:** Evaluation (Mertens, 2010) simply means adding value to an assessment or judgement. Though seems very small, but this term is very vast in its meaning, processes and outcome. Evaluation has a long process, long term outcomes and vast impact on the mass. While evaluation of learners decides their academic output, academic upgradation and future, the evaluation of the learning-facilitators decides their selection and promotion to the various posts with distinct designations.

- **Education:** Education now a day is not just overall development of mind, body and soul, but it's a more of sustaining in the current world in the rapidly changing scenario where the values have been drastically changed and a different sort of values are needed to sustain and grow in the current world. For an instance, though the medium of learning and education should not be an issue and equal degree holders should be counted as equivalent, but it's not so at present. Whatever be the level of knowledge of the learners, the English speaking learners are put at higher level and grab most of the top level positions. Hence, education has become more of sustaining in the current world.

- **Higher education:** Higher education (UGC, 2017) can be understood as the studies after school level. The various degrees and diplomas which need minimum school level completed for admissions in these can be termed as higher education. For a general understanding, the higher education level can be depicted as all those courses which require minimum class XII passed for the admissions. The UGC too defines this higher education in a well-defined manner with respect to degrees and diplomas.

- **Plagiarism:** Plagiarism (Kanvaria, 2013) is not merely copying and pasting someone's work, as it is understood at mass level, but in fact it is copying other's ideas too. Some academics think that paraphrasing alone removes plagiarism, but no it is the acknowledgement, referencing and citation which remove plagiarism. For removing plagiarism, not only paraphrasing is needed but also proper citation (Kanvaria, 2016) is required for the idea mentioned in the write-up. So, plagiarism is stealing someone's ideas word-by-word or line-by-line or in different set of words and not giving the proper credit to its author through citation.

- **Copied work and similarity:** Whenever a text existing in a source is re-written word-by-word or line-by-line by someone again, then it is called copied-work or similar work. Many of academics get confused with it saying it as plagiarism (Stolley, Brizee and Paiz, 2013). No, it's not complete plagiarism but a subset of plagiarism. Copied work or similar work also leads to the one of the kinds of plagiarism. The copied work is called similar work and this phenomenon is called as similarity. Most of the software and platform in fact tests the similarity. Similarity is a confirmed type of plagiarism if exceeds some limit.

## The Current Study

The current study is an objective-based well-planned venture to see into the issue of plagiarism and copied work. The study assumes that the plagiarism can be prohibited by researching in the field and making the research output available through an academic writing like this chapter to the mass. The readers after going through output of such formal research may be convinced that the plagiarism should be avoided in higher education level where research work is given more emphasis than that of the any other education levels.

The formal data of the research is also needed for the academics to refrain themselves from unethical academic venture like plagiarism and copy-paste work.

## Method

- **Sampling:** The sample was consisted of scholars and academics either working at higher education level or preparing learners for career in higher education. The sample selection was entirely random in the sense that there was no clue that who will send the papers for the event and who will be finally selected. It was further no pre-supposition or prediction that what will be job or occupation or designation or roles of the chapter senders.

- **Tools:** The tool used for the plagiarism-check was Urkund. This tool is an internet-based tool used for checking plagiarism in general and similarity in specific. The tool needs the write-ups to be emailed to a specific user email ID and in return it gives the report for each and every write-up about its similarity index.

- **Design:** The overall procedure included design for invitation, development of information brochure, dissemination of information for call for papers, collecting papers, pre-screening of papers, plagiarism-check of papers, final selection and analysis and discussion.
- **Data collection:** Data was collected by uploading the papers on Urkund platform for plagiarism-check. The plagiarism percentage or similarity index was obtained from the reports generated by Urkund.

## Findings and Analysis

Initially around 200 proposals/papers were received. And after summarily rejecting those on the criteria like with only abstract, lesser word count, only proposal, improper formatting, not original, published, double authored etc., around 71 papers were left. These 71 papers formed the formal sample for the study.

This data depicted that around 129 academics out of 200 (64.5%) were not able to comprehend even one page of guidelines very clearly. They were not bothered about issues of abstract, chapter, word count, formatting, originality, publishing, number of authors, etc. Either they took the guidelines very casually or were not able to even comprehend them clearly. These 129 write-ups or proposals were summarily rejected. This data depicts the seriousness of academic fraternity on the issues of conference papers, which is an essential part of higher education research degrees, selection and promotion.

The remaining 71 papers underwent plagiarism-check and similarity check.

### *Preliminary Collection of Papers after Preliminary Screening*

Table 1: Category of Designation or Role

| S. No. | Designation | No. of Papers |
|---|---|---|
| 1. | Faculty/Professionals | 42 |
| 2. | Research Scholars | 16 |
| 3. | UG/PG learners | 13 |
| Total | | 71 |

Table 2: States

| S. No. | State | No. of Papers |
|---|---|---|
| 1. | Delhi | 21 |
| 2. | Uttar Pradesh | 7 |
| 3. | Tamil Nadu | 5 |
| 4. | Punjab | 5 |

| | | |
|---|---|---|
| 5. | Rajasthan | 5 |
| 6. | Haryana | 4 |
| 7. | Odisha | 3 |
| 8. | Maharashtra | 3 |
| 9. | Bihar | 2 |
| 10. | Karnataka | 2 |
| 11. | Himachal Pradesh | 2 |
| 12. | West Bengal | 2 |
| 13. | Andhra Pradesh | 2 |
| 14. | Kerala | 1 |
| 15. | Gujarat | 1 |
| 16. | Uttarakhand | 1 |
| 17. | Meghalaya | 1 |
| 18. | Nagaland | 1 |
| 19. | Madhya Pradesh | 1 |
| 20. | Jharkhand | 1 |
| 21. | Jammu and Kashmir | 1 |
| **Total** | | **71** |

Table 3: Similarity Index

| Range of Similarity Index | No. of Papers |
|---|---|
| 0-20 | 43 |
| 20-40 | 14 |
| 40-60 | 8 |
| 60-80 | 3 |
| 80-100 | 3 |
| **Total** | **71** |

## *Final Collection of Papers after Entire Selection Process*

Table 4: Category of Designation or Role

| S. No. | Designation | No. of Papers |
|---|---|---|
| 1. | Faculty/Professionals | 23 |
| 2. | Research Scholars | 7 |
| 3. | UG/PG learners | 10 |
| **Total** | | **40** |

Table 5: States

| S. No. | State | No. of Papers |
|---|---|---|
| 1. | Delhi | 19 |
| 2. | Uttar Pradesh | 4 |
| 3. | Rajasthan | 3 |
| 4. | Odisha | 3 |
| 5. | Tamil Nadu | 2 |
| 6. | Punjab | 1 |
| 7. | Maharashtra | 1 |
| 8. | Bihar | 1 |
| 9. | Karnataka | 1 |
| 10. | Himachal Pradesh | 1 |
| 11. | West Bengal | 1 |
| 12. | Kerala | 1 |
| 13. | Madhya Pradesh | 1 |
| 14. | Jharkhand | 1 |
| 15. | Jammu and Kashmir | 0 |
| 16. | Andhra Pradesh | 0 |
| 17. | Gujarat | 0 |
| 18. | Uttarakhand | 0 |
| 19. | Meghalaya | 0 |
| 20. | Nagaland | 0 |
| 21. | Haryana | 0 |
| Total | | 40 |

Table 6: Similarity Index

| Range of Similarity Index | No. of Papers |
|---|---|
| 0-20 | 40 |
| 20-40 | 0 |
| 40-60 | 0 |
| 60-80 | 0 |
| 80-100 | 0 |
| Total | 40 |

## Discussion

The highest number of papers were received from the faculty members and lowest were from UG/PG learners. The difference between faculty member and research scholars is much more than that of the research scholars and UG/PG learners. It depicts that faculty members are more research-based career oriented than that of the others. Research scholars seem to be completing minimum requirement only for their degrees. The biggest surprise is about UG/PG learners. Though it's not their necessary requirement for their degree or promotion, still they are also doing research and sending their papers for presentation events.

The data depicts that rate of plagiarism or similarity in the papers of research scholars is more than that of the faculty members i.e. research scholars' papers are more vulnerable to this unethical practice. The reason can possibly be that they are having lesser time for real research work than that of the faculty members as might be doing other academic tasks also in addition to the research. Hence, they can devote lesser sincere time for the research work.

The data depicts that the practice of plagiarism among research scholars is also not less than 55%. This high level of plagiarized papers is an alarming situation for the academia and research guides. They must guide and make aware their research scholars about issues and consequence of plagiarism. And, if research work has such a big amount of plagiarism then, research guides and institutions should make clear policies about plagiarism and copy-pasted work. A proper orientation is a must during research guidance to the research scholars about this unethical issue.

The data depicts that the highest number of papers have been received from Delhi. This can be due to the reason of proximity of the venue of the event. But the highest number of selection after the plagiarism-check shows that the plagiarism is lowest in papers from Delhi. As per the data provided by Urkund reports, highest rate of plagiarism or similar work was observed in the papers from Andhra Pradesh, Gujarat, Uttarakhand, Meghalaya, Nagaland, Jammu and Kahmir and Haryana.

Initially papers received from Tamil Nadu, Punjab and Rajasthan were equal and the second highest in numbers. This depicts that the distance did not matter among chapter senders for this event.

The data depicts that the researchers, learning-facilitators and learners from Delhi, Uttar Pradesh, Rajasthan and Odisha are very much aware of the plagiarism issues or are the good researchers. Their papers had least number of plagiarized works and least similarity index. The final selection of the papers from the preliminary list after the plagiarism-check through Urkundsupports this argument.

## Conclusion

The current study collected papers from all over the India. The data collected is quite random in nature. The papers depict that the issue of plagiarism is very high and vulnerable to the system of higher education. The plagiarism among faculty members/professionals (more than 45%) and research scholars (more than 55%) are in danger zone. While the rate of plagiarism is higher in research scholars, it is lesser among faculty members. The possible reason can be spending lesser time for research by the research scholars than that of the faculty members. But this excuse can't work because the onus of real research lies upon the faculty members as they are research guides and research supervisors too and are actually responsible for researches of their research scholars. The research depicts that either faculty and research scholars are not aware of the concept of plagiarism, hence unknowingly doing plagiarism, or they are habitual of plagiarizing text from the Internet websites or they do not take the plagiarized work seriously as there is no strict consequence of it upon them. The research further depicts that even UG/PG learners can also execute the research work and write non-plagiarized papers, if guided properly.

The data depicted that around 64.5% academics were not able to read and comprehend even one page of guidelines properly. They were not bothered about guidelines and issues of complete chapter, word count, formatting, originality, publishing, number of authors, etc. Either they took the just one page guidelines very casually or were not able to even comprehend them clearly. This data points out towards the seriousness of academic fraternity on the even basic issue like reading guidelines properly of conference papers, which is an essential part of higher education research degrees, selection and promotion.

The data obtained during this research depicts that the researchers, learning-facilitators and learners from Delhi, Uttar Pradesh, Rajasthan and Odisha are very much aware of the plagiarism issue or are the natural researchers. Most of the papers sent from these states were finally selected for the presentation event. Highest rate of plagiarism or similar work, as depicted by Urkund reports, was observed in the papers received from Andhra Pradesh, Gujarat, Uttarakhand, Meghalaya, Nagaland, Jammu and Kashmir and Haryana. Depending upon plagiarism-check, none of the papers out of the received could be selected from these states.

The issue of plagiarism is very sophisticated and must be dealt carefully in higher education. Faculty members and research scholars are highly vulnerable to this unethical academic issue. They should be made aware and oriented properly for the concept of plagiarism and how to avoid plagiarism. If research and its communication are to be new, the plagiarism has to be nullified up to the extreme level.

Chapter

6

# Educational Technology: A Tool for Facilitating Learning

**A. Subramanian**
*University of Madras, Chennai, TN*

## Preview at a Glance

Past twenty years, the use of ICT has fundamentally changed the practices and procedures of business and governance, education. Now-a-days ICT in education is becoming more important to grow and develop in the 21st century. ICT defines learning as neutral, social, active, linear or non-linear, integrative, and contextualized, based on ability and strength of learners. Use of ICT in teaching-learning environment can bring a rapid change in society. It has the potential to transform the nature of education i.e., where and how learning takes place and role of learners and learning-facilitator in the process of learning. It is essential that learning-facilitators must have basic ICT skills and competencies. It is for the learning-facilitator to determine how ICT can best be used in the context of culture, needs and economic conditions. Educational reforms include successful designing and implementation of ICT in teaching learning process, which is the key to success. It involves use of computers, computer software and other devices to convert, store, and process, transmit and retrieve information and includes the services and application associated with them. ICT has become an important factor for effective teaching learning. It has brought a revolution in the teaching learning process. And all this has positively affected the learning of the learners as the learners show great enthusiasm in learning through ICT. But there are certain factors which help in the acceptance of ICT in teaching learning by the learning-facilitators and these factors should be motivated in one way or the other. This chapter is to study the Educational Technology as a tool for Teaching Learning.

## Introduction

Information and communication technologies (ICTs) are a diverse set of technological tools and resources used for creating, storing, managing and communicating information. For educational purposes, ICTs can be used to support teaching and learning as well as research activities including collaborative learning and inquiring. One of the main applications of the ICTs in education is teaching and learning based on these new technologies. This is concentrated on the obstacles, facilitators, and the risks of using these technologies in teaching and learning in the field of education.

Recently, Information and Communication Technology (ICT) for education, initiative by UNESCO, conducted an extensive consultation to identify the competencies that learning-facilitators should develop to use technology effectively in the classroom. It is basically an umbrella term that encompasses all communication technologies such as Internet, wireless networks, cell-phones, satellite communications, digital television computer and network hardware and software; as well as the equipment and services associated with these technologies, such as videoconferencing, e-mail and blogs etc. that provide access to information.

Today, ICT applications permeate all human activities like education, health, agriculture, community development, livelihoods activities, entrepreneurship development, governance, emergencies, to name a few. Interventions across these sectors lead to prosperity of social, economic, cultural and political at large in that entails wider ramifications for human development at large.

The rapid growth in Information and Communication Technologies (ICT) has brought remarkable changes in recent years. ICT is becoming increasingly important in daily lives and in educational systems. As the learning-facilitator plays an essential role in the management of learning, learning-facilitators should equip themselves with ICT competencies to design new learning environments using the most modern technologies in the field of education.

## Information

It covers the topics such as meaning and value of information, how information is controlled, and the limitations of ICT, legal considerations how data is captured, verified and stored for effective use, the manipulation, processing and distribution of information, keeping information secure and designing networks to share information.

## Communication

It is the networks of sending and receiving equipment, wires and satellite links. (a) Internal networks: Local Area Network (LAN), (b) External networks: Wide Area Network (WAN)

## Technology

It is the collection of techniques, knowledge of how to combine resources to produce desired products, to solve problems, fulfil the needs or satisfies wants, it includes technical methods, skills, processes, techniques, tools and raw materials. The Ministry of Human Resource Development (MHRD), Government of India and the Indian Span Research Organization (ISRO) took a path breaking policy decision to launch a dedicated educational satellite, in which the use of ICTs can make substantial changes both in teaching and learning.

## Objective of the Study

The objective of the present study is to find out the Educational Technology as a tool for Teaching Learning.

## Methodology

This present study is based on the secondary sources like Books, Articles, Journals, Thesis, University News, Expert opinion and also from websites. The method used is Descriptive Analytic method.

## Information and Communication Technology

ICT (Information and Communication Technology or Technologies) is an umbrella term that includes any communication device or application, encompassing radio, television, cellular phones, computer and network hardware and software, satellite systems and so on, as well as the various services and applications associated with them, such as videoconferencing and distance learning.

Heeks defined Information and Communication Technologies (ICT) as 'electronic means of capturing, processing, storing and communicating information. ICT may be computer hardware, software and networks. They also include intermediate technologies like radio and television, literate technologies like books and newspapers and organic technologies based on human body like brain and sound waves'. Hamelink classifies ICT according to five distinct functionalities

Capturing Technologies: Input devices, which collect and convert the information into digital form, come under this category. Such devices include keyboards, mice, trackballs, touch screens, voice recognition systems, bar code readers, image scanners and palm-size camcorders.

Storage Technologies: Devices to store and retrieve information in the digital form, among these are magnetic tapes, floppy disks, hard disks, RAM disks, optical disks (such as CD-ROMs), erasable disks and smart cards (credit-card sized cards with memory and processing capacity for financial transactions or keeping medical data).

Processing Technologies: Creating the systems and applications software that is required for the performance of digital ICT.

Communications Technologies: Producing the devices, methods and networks to transmit information in digital form, They include digital broadcasting, integrated services digital networks, digital cellular networks, local area networks (LANs), wide area networks (WANs, such as the Internet), electronic bulletin boards, modems, transmission media such as fibre optics, cellular phones and fax machines and digital transmission technologies for mobile space communications (the new Low Earth Orbit satellite voice and data services).

Display Technologies: To create a variety of output devices for the display of digitized information. Such devices include display screens for computers, digital television sets with automatic picture adjustment, set-top boxes for video on demand, printers, digital video discs (which might replace CD-ROM drives and audio CD players), voice synthesizers and virtual reality helmets.

## Educational Technology

Technology in education is defined as an array of tools that helpful in advancing learner learning and measured in how and why individuals behave. Educational technology is the study and ethical practice of facilitating e-learning, which is the learning and improving performance by creating, using and managing appropriate technological processes and resources in terms of technology of education and technology in education (Kanvaria, 2014). Educational Technology relies on a broad definition of the word 'technology' which significant the tools and the sources to enhanced, to develop the skill of the Education.

## Basic Skills of ICT

The transmission of Basic skills and concepts that are the foundation of higher order thinking skills and creativity can be facilitated by ICTs through drill and practice. Educational television Programmes can use repetition and reinforcement to teach the alphabet, numbers, colours, shapes and other basic concepts. Most of the early uses of computers were for computer-based learning or computer-assisted instruction that focused on mastery of skills and content through repetition and reinforcement.

Enhancing learning-facilitator training, ICTs have also been used to improve access to and the quality of learning-facilitator training. ICT supported education can promote the acquisition of the knowledge and skills that will empower learners for lifelong learning.

- Active learning
- Collaborative learning
- Creative learning
- Integrative learning
- Evaluative learning

## ICT Teaching and Planning

ICT Teaching includes teaching aims and learning objectives, possible teaching strategies, assessment opportunities, pupil's prior knowledge, structuring lessons, sequencing activities and providing variety, the relevance of context, the important of recap and review, pace and timing, exceptions for pupil's achievement and specific target, progression in pupil's learning. ICT Planning includes identifying aims and objectives, selecting teaching strategies, identifying assessment opportunities.

## ICT and Convergence Technologies

Information and Communication Technologies (ICT) acts as a powerful tool in bringing out radical change in the society. ICTs are a diverse set of technological tools and resources to create, disseminate, store, bring value-addition and manage information. ICT does not include only the internet but a gamut of other tools, which could be used individually or in convergence with each other to catalyse the process of change in a manner which reduces the skew in knowledge distribution between rich and poor, educated and uneducated, rural and urban, men and women. The convergence technologies include community radios, Internet radios, local area networks, tele-centres, information kiosks, mobile phones, Tablets, WAP applications etc. They often enhance the reach and penetration of the ICT.

## Technologies Included In ICT

ICT helps to keep pace with the latest developments with the help of different technologies included in it. Technologies included in ICTs are Radio and Television, Telephone, Computers and Internet, Video, Cameras, cell phones, personal digital assistants. Some of the services available through ICT are:

1. **WWW:** www stands for World Wide Web which is one of the most important and widely accepted services like IRC, E-mail etc. of the Internet. Its popularity has increased dramatically, simply because it is very easy to use colourful and rich content.

2. **E-Learning:** E-Learning is also known as online learning. E-learning encompasses learning at all levels both formal and non-formal that uses an information network like the Internet, an Intranet (LAN) or extranet (WAN). The components include e-portfolios, cyber infrastructures, digital libraries, and online learning object repositories. All the above components create a digital identity of the user and connect all the stakeholders in the education. It also facilitates inter disciplinary research.

3. **Group Discussion:** Internet Relay Chat (IRC) is among the popular Internet service people mostly use for live chatting. Group of people with common interest can exchange views/opinions with each other instantly through Internet. Description of the Internet technologies required to support education via ICTs (www, Video Conference, Teleconference, Mobile Conference, CD Database, Word-Processor, Intranet, Internet etc.)

4. **E-Modules:** Modules written are converted and stored into digital version into a computer using word processor accessible by the user through Internet.

5. **Trust and Security:** Existence of six main components of a commerce site suggests trustworthiness as Seals of Approval, Brand, Navigation, Fulfilment, Presentation and Technology. As for security there are also six issues to look namely Integrity, No repudiation, Authenticity, Confidentiality, Privacy and Availability.

6. **Teleconferencing:** Teleconferencing refers to 'interactive electronic communication among people located at two or more different places'. There are four types of teleconferencing based on the nature and extent of interactivity and the sophistication of technology that is Audio-Conferencing, Audio- Graphic Conferencing, Video-Conferencing and Web-Based Conferencing.

## Audio-Conferencing

It involves the live (real-time) exchange of voice messages over a telephone network when low-band width text and still images such as graphs, diagrams or picture can also be exchanged along with voice messages, then this type of conferencing is called audio-graphic. Non-moving visuals are added using a computer keyboard or by drawing/writing on graphics tablet or whiteboard.

## Video-Conferencing

Video Conferencing allows the exchange not just of voice and graphics but also of moving images. Video Conferencing technology does not use telephone lines but either a satellite link or television network (broadcast/cable).

## Web-Based Conferencing

Web-based conferencing as the name implies, involves the transmission of text and graphic, audio and visual media via the Internet, it requires the use of a computer with a browser and communication can be both synchronous and asynchronous.

## ICT Infrastructure and/or Hardware

- Interactive whiteboard
- Classroom computers
- Learner laptops
- Data projector
- IPods
- Digital Camera
- DVDs
- Videos and video clips
- Webcams
- Hand-held voice recorders

## Programs/Software

- **Microsoft Office programs:** PowerPoint, Word, Excel, Access and Publisher
- **Educational:** Classtools.net, Spellodrome, Interactive games, Interactive mathematics programs, Maths 300 and Mathletics

- **Graphics editing:** Photoshop, Illustrator, Paint, Google Sketch Up, GIF animator and Flash
- **Video/audio editing:** Windows Moviemaker, Premier Elements, Final Cut Pro, Audacity, Photo Story, Animoto, Podcasts and Cartoon Story Maker
- **Web-authoring:** Dreamweaver
- **Presentation software:** Prezi
- **Other:** OneNote, Geographic mapping programs and Hot Potatoes
- **Intranet:** Moodle and Click view
- **Websites:** Websites, E-learning interactive websites, Google, Wikipedia and YouTube
- **Social networking websites:** Face book and Myspace
- **Online applications:** Email, Hyperlinks, Blogs, Wikis, Interactive games and Online testing applications
- **Other communication applications:** Short Message Service (SMS)

## Educational Technology as a Tool of Teaching

There are various types of Educational Technologies currently used in classrooms. These are as follows:

### Computer in the Classroom

Having a computer in the classroom is an asset to any learning-facilitator. With a computer in the classroom, learning-facilitators are able to demonstrate a new lesson, present new material, illustrate how to use new programs, and show new information on websites.

### Class Blogs and Wikipedia

There are a variety of Web 2.0 tools that are currently being implemented in the classroom. Blogs allow for learners to maintain a running dialogue, such as a journal, thoughts, ideas, and assignments that also provide for learner comment and reflection. Wikipedia, an online encyclopaedia, are more group focused to allow multiple members of the group to edit a single document and create a truly collaborative and carefully edited finished product.

### Wireless Classroom Microphones

Noisy classrooms are a daily occurrence, and with the help of microphones, learners are able to hear their learning-facilitators more clearly. Learners learn better when they hear the learning-facilitator clearly.

### Mobile Devices

Mobile devices such as tablet or smart phone can be used to enhance the experience in the classroom by providing the possibility for professors to get feedback.

## Interactive Whiteboards

An interactive whiteboard, that provides touch control of computer applications. These enhance the experience in the classroom by showing anything that can be on a computer screen this not only aids in visual learning, but it is interactive so the learners can draw, write, or manipulate images on the interactive whiteboard.

## Digital Video on Demand

Digital video eliminates the need for in-classroom hardware and allows learning-facilitators and learners to access video clips immediately by not utilizing the public Internet.

## Online Media

Streamed video websites can be utilized to enhance a classroom lesson.

## Online Study Tools

Tools that are motivate studying by making studying more fun or individualized for the learner.

## Digital Games

The field of educational games and serious games has been growing significantly over the last few years. The digital games are being provided as tools for the classroom and have a lot of positive feedback including higher motivation for learners.

## Benefits of ICT in Education

Use of ICT in education presents a unique opportunity to solve multitude of challenges quickly as well as at low rate. Here is an overview of advantages of an online system.

## Improve Quality of Education

- Support collaboration among learners, learning-facilitators and institutions
- A reliable grading system to measure and assign rank to Learners, Learning-facilitators, Schools and Universities
- All round development of learners
- Promote educational ideas
- Continuous improvement by feedback

## Improve Accessibility

- Accessible anytime from anywhere to everyone
- Bring the books and other resource within reach of learners
- Promote education in rural areas
- Provide online courses to learners.

- 24×7 schooling system for those learners who cannot attend regular schools during daytime

## *Reduce the Cost of Education*
- Provide services at lower cost through online solutions
- Promote learn yourself and community learning via online system, etc.
- Assist learning-facilitators for conducting exam and offer courses material
- ICT opens the doors for girls to get education from home for e.g. online learning if social and cultural reasons are preventing them.
- ICT promote vocational courses as well as self-paced learning for the adults
- ICT bring culturally diverse India on a common learning platform which is offered in all languages

## *General Benefits of ICT*
- Enable grater learner autonomy,
- Enable tasks to be tailored to suit individual skills,
- Enable learners to demonstrate achievement in ways which might not be possible with traditional methods,
- Unlocks hidden potential for those with communication difficulties.

## *ICT Benefits for Learners*
- Learners using voice communication aids gain confidence and social credibility at school in their communities,
- Increased ICT confidence amongst learners motivates them to use the Internet at home for schoolwork and make their curiosity fulfil
- Computer can improve independent access for learners to education,
- Learners with profound and multiple learning disabilities can easily communicate more,
- Visually impaired learners using the internet can access information along their sighted peers.

## *ICT Benefits For Learning-facilitator, Non-Teaching Staff*
- Using the ICT gadgets learning-facilitators can easily represent their lecture.
- Learning-facilitators make interesting and fruitful their teaching by using ICT.
- Non-teaching staff easily store the recodes in computers.
- Reduces isolation of learning-facilitators working in special Educational needs by enabling them to communicate electronically with colleagues.
- Enhances professional development and the effectiveness of the use of ICT

with learners through collaboration with peers.
- Improving the skills of staff a greater understanding of access technology used by learners.

## ICT Benefits for Parents
- Not only learners, learning-facilitators, non-teaching staffs but also parents to have higher expectations of children's sociability and potential level participation may occur by ICT.
- Parents also have updated themselves by using ICT.

## E-Learning Tools and Technologies
- Content creation tools are Tools for creating avatars, Course and lesson authoring tools, E-book tools, Graphics and animation tools, Image galleries and sound effects libraries, Assessment tools, Pdf tools, Video and simulation tools, Web page authoring tools, Survey and polling tools.
- Delivery and distribution tools are Podcasting tools, RSS tools, Web casting and streaming tools, Presentation tools and Mobile learning tools.
- User Tools are Operating system, Browsers, Media Players, Plug INS, Pdf reader and Word processor.
- Communication and Collaboration Tools are Discussion boards and forum tools, E-mail tools, live support tools, Meeting and teleconferencing tools, instant messaging and chat tools, Social book marking and file sharing tools and Wiki tools.
- E-Learning Systems are Content management, Learning management systems and Course management systems.
- Hardware Tools are Personal Computer, laptop, net book, Smart phones, palmtop computer, Printer, Scanner, Speaker, Microphone and web.
- Other input Devices are Trackball, Light Pen, Touch Screen, Joystick, Digitizer, Scanner, Optimal Mark Reader (OMR), Bar Code Reader (BCR), Optical Character Reader (OCR), Magnetic Ink Character Reader (MICR) and Voice-Input Devices.
- Output Display Storage devices are Hard Disk, Floppy Disk, Compact Disk, Digital Versatile Disk and Pen Drive.

## Conclusion
ICT play vital role as a strong agent for change among many educational practices i.e. conducting on line exam, pay on line fees, accessing on line books and journals. Thus the developments of ICTs in education have a strong impact on. Thus ICT in education improves teaching learning process, provides the facility of online learning to thousands of learners. Technology can reduce the tremendous effort given by learners to gather number of printed book and journals for acquiring knowledge and

increase learners focus on more important knowledge gathering process. Equally important, technology can represent education in ways that help learners understand latest concepts and ideas. The Education Technology also enables learning-facilitators to integrate project based learning. With guidance from effective learning-facilitators, learners at different levels can use these tools to construct knowledge and develop skills required in modern society such as presentation skills and analytical skills. In the present time the learning-facilitator's role in teaching is facilitator. The learning-facilitator has to facilitate the learning by providing learners with access to educational technology.

Chapter

7

# Learning through Social Networking

≥ **Bharti Nagpal**
*University of Delhi, Delhi*

## Preview at a Glance

Social networking means being in connection with other people with the help of social network service (Deka, 2015). It has been in trend from last few decades. It has become more common now-a-days to be in contact with the friends and family (Zaidieh, 2012). This chapter focuses on the understanding the concept of social networking. The aim of the chapter is on how social networking can be understood, how it is being used by the females of age group 18-25 years, what are perception of the females of age 18-25 years regarding the social networking sites and its usage for educational purposes. For this purpose, the data had been collected from the participants through questionnaire. The chapter depicted that social networking is used a lot now-a-days, and how it affects the teens and their education. The result of the study reveals that social networking can become a useful tool that can be used in education sector. There are various benefits and challenges of social networking which can be faced by the learners if social networking sites are used learning. Hence, it should be wisely used for educational purposes. The study also highlights social networking sites are used by all the participants and Facebook is mostly used social networking site. It had also being seen that main purpose of using social networking sites is entertainment. With the help of the current study the facilitators and learners can get the understanding about how social networking can be used for their learning and things they need to avoid while using it for their learning. The study also gives opportunity to further explore about how social networking is currently being used by the learners and facilitators at different levels of education sector i.e. school and higher education.

## Introduction

Social networking is recent trend which is very much talked about, not only in personal life of people but also in researches especially in education and its implementation in teaching and learning process (Santos, Hammond, Durliand Chou, 2009). But before talking about the social networking and other aspects related to it, first it's important to understand what social networking is. To understand social networking understanding what 'social' and 'networking' means is important.

'Social' refers to the interactivity between the living organisms including humans (Wikipedia, 2017); interaction among individuals (Merriam-Webster, n.d.); being with the other members of community rather than being alone (Collins English Dictionary, 2012a); festive gathering (Wiktionary, 2017). Hence, it can be said that social means being in connection with human beings.

'Networking' refers to the connectivity within group (Collins English Dictionary, 2012b); a process that helps in exchanging and sharing of ideas and information (Investopedia, n.d.); transferring of information and services among individuals and group (Merriam-Webster, n.d.). Hence, it can be said that networking means connection through which the information and ideas can be shared between the individuals.

Social networking refers to making connection through social media (Rouse, 2016); using internet based social media to interact and connect with other people (Investopedia, n.d.); knowing and communicating with people through internet (Nations, 2017). Thus it can be said that social networking is when we connect and share information with others through internet social media.

The researches had shown that social networking sites have numerous impacts on the learners. These can be positive as well as negative, depending on the way social networking sites are being used (Asiedu, 2017). This chapter is an attempt to explore the perspective of females from different background regarding social networking sites in education.

## Review of Related Literature

### *History of Social Networking*

Social networking initially started in 1971, with the invention and beginning of e-mail. Then in 1978, BBS or Bulletin Board System was invented. It helped the people to be connected with each through Internet. Initially it was very slow, but it was good step towards the connectivity between the people. After BBS, in 1994 the first ever social networking site was started. The name of the site was Geocities. It provided the facility to create or customize their websites and based on the content of the websites they were grouped into 'cities'. After the launch of the Geocities, following year TheGlobe. com was launches, in which the individual had the opportunity to connect with people of their own interest and also talk to them and share the content through publishing option.

After its launch few years later other social networking sites were also launched, which allowed the users to create their profile and have chats with their friends.

At initial stage the social networking sites that we know today was Friendster. Then after sometime, Myspace came into place, which had more specifications as compared to Friendster and hence it became popular very soon. Its customization facility was much enriched as per that time. In 2003, LinkedIn was launched, which gave social networking a new dimension of using it for business and professional purposes. Then in 2004, Facebook was launched, in initial period the access to it was limited. In 2008, Facebook became popular among the people and was at first position among social networking sites (Web designer, 2016; Digital trends, 2016; Walker, 2013; Boynand Ellison, 2007).

## Research on Usage of Social Networking Sites in Education

The aim of the study was to explore how academic relations with peer and facilitators effect with the use social networking sites. The results of the study reveals that there was a positive impact on the relationship with the use of social networking sites and the leaners and facilitators had formed online academic identity with the use of social networking site (Rambbe, 2009).

Prasad (2015), in his/her research on social networking sites which had the aim to study the impact of social networking on pre-university learners in an urban settings, obtained that there is a significant difference in usage and impact of SNS based on gender, income status.

## Objectives

- ▶ To analyse the usage of social networking sites among the females of age group 18-25 years.
- ▶ To study the perceptions of females of age group 18-25 about the usage of social networking sites in education.

## Hypothesis

- ▶ Social networking sites are used by all the females of age group 18-25 years.
- ▶ Usage of social networking sites for educational purposes is rare among the females of 18-25 years of age group.

## Rationale of the Study

The social networking sites are largely being used by people in their day-to-day life. There are several reasons for which the females are using these social networking sites. The need of this was to examine for what purposes the females of 18-25 years of age group are using social networking sites and what are their views about the use of social networking sites for educational purposes.

## Methodology

- ▶ **Sample:** The females of age group 18-25 years old were the participants of the current study.
- ▶ **Tool for data collection:** The questionnaire was used for data collection. Open as well as close ended questions were included in the questionnaire.

- **Procedure for data collection:** On the basis of the review of related literature the theoretical background was formed by the researcher and four parameters were identified. Then, the questionnaire was formed on the basis of those four parameters. Then the data was collected with the help of the questionnaire being formed by the researcher.

## Findings and Results
### Engagement in Social Networking Site
- All the participants are the member of some or the other social networking sites.
- Out of all the social networking sites, Facebook is the most used social networking site. Facebook is used by 80% of the participants. After Facebook, YouTube is other mostly used social networking site accessed by 66.7% of the participants. After these two mostly used social networking sites comes the Twitter, Instagram, Hangout and others.
- All the participants access social networking sites through their smartphones. Out of all the participants, 46.7% participants use Laptops too for accessing social networking sites. 26.7% participants also use PC along with their smartphones to access social networking sites.
- All the participants were using social networking sites from more than a year.

### Usage of Social Networking Sites by Them
- 73.3% participants uses social networking sites just for being in connection and communicate with their existing friends, 20% participants use it for gathering information or learn something from those sites, whereas rest of the 6.7% participants use it for just to pass their times.
- Several participants use the social networking sites for differentiated communication purposes, 40% participants use it for entertainment, education and information, 26.7% participants use it for entertainment only, 13.3% participants use it for entertainment and information, 6.7% participants use it for educational purposes, 6.7% participants use it for educational and information and rest 6.7% participants use it for entertainment, educational, informational and anything new and of interest.

### Views on Use of Social Networking Sites for Educational Purposes
- 53.3% participants had neutral views about usage of social networking for teaching and learning in school/colleges, 20% participants had agreed for the use of social networking for teaching learning in school/colleges, 13.3% participants had strongly agreed for the use of social networking for teaching learning in school/colleges, 6.7% participants had strongly disagreed for the use of social networking for teaching learning in school/colleges, remaining 6.7% participants had disagreed for the use of social networking for teaching learning in school/colleges.

- 71.4% participants often used social networking sites in educational capacities whereas rest of the 28.6% participants rarely used social networking sites in educational capacities.
- 53.3% participants believed that social networking sites have neutral effect on teaching and learning, 40% participants believed that social networking sites have positive effect on teaching and learning remaining 6.7% participants believed that social networking sites have very positive effect on teaching and learning.
- 46.7% participants often used social networking sites to discuss educational work, other 46.7% participants rarely used social networking sites to discuss educational work and remaining 6.7% participants never used social networking sites to discuss educational work.

## Benefits and Challenges of Using Social Networking for Educational Purposes

The participants have mentioned several benefits and challenges of using social networking for educational purposes, which are as follows:

### Benefits
- Learners will have opportunity to learn beyond the course material.
- It will lead to development in education system along with development in other sectors of our country.
- Latest and relevant information can be acquired through distinguished pages that one can subscribe on social networking sites.
- An individual comes across several issues, policies and news more frequently through social networking sites as compared other sources.
- Gives opportunity to learn new things through different views.
- Through it knowledge is disbursed in a better way.
- One remains updated with the knowledge. As it can be accessed anytime and anywhere if the Internet connectivity is there.
- It helps in being connected with the people and being socially active.

### Challenges
- Cyber security is a major issue now-a-days. It is the most challenging challenge for the learners if they use social networking for their learning.
- Social networking sites can be very distractive.
- Age inappropriate content can also be there and hence a facilitator needs to be there always to keep the check on the content that learner is watching.
- There is privacy issues related to use of social networking.
- Over and misuse of social networking sites by the learners can be there in place of its educational use.

- Limited one to one interaction between learner and facilitator through social networking sites.
- Accessibility of technology to all is a biggest challenge.

## Discussion and Analysis

From the findings of the study it could be inferred that social networking is popular among the females of age group 18-25 years. All the females of this age group have personal account on one or the other social networking site.

Although majority of them used social networking for just being in connection with their friends, but they also held neutral views regarding the use of social networking in teaching and learning.

Like is it wisely said that every coin has two faces, use of social networking in educational settings has its own pros and cons. The majority of the females believed that social networking sites can help the learners to go beyond the learning material that they get from the institute and learn on their own. But they feared about the cyber security and learners' tendency to be distracted by other inappropriate content on the Internet.

Hence, they believed that there is no issue in the usage of the social networking sites for learning but the elder's at home and facilitators at institutes like schools and colleges need to direct the learner to be focused on the right path.

## Conclusion

The chapter talks about various aspects related to the social networking and how it has become part of life of females of age group 18-25 years old. There are various advantages of using social networking in general and specifically for the educational purposes. It would have been a better idea if these sites and apps will be used for betterment of the education sector in our country. As with social networking a personal link between the learners and facilitators and other stakeholders of the education sectors can be maintained. The social networking helps to learn in interesting manners and hence learners will be motivated to learn numerous things at whenever they access the social networking sites.

Chapter 8

# Web 2.0 Technologies in Learning-Facilitator Preparation through Educators

✎ BinulaIK. R.

*Mount Tabor Training College, Pathanapuram, Kerala*

## Preview at a Glance

The unprecedented development in the field of digital technology, both in the case of software and hardware has created a need and urge to utilize these in the process of teaching and learning. Earlier, during the era of web 1.0, the users are only the consumers of information and nowadays it became the creators of knowledge or information. That is the learners and the learning-facilitators became the creators of information and knowledge; where they can also contribute to, collaborate on and edit that information. Web 2.0 technologies enable the users to achieve in this. Applications of web 2.0 hold profound potentials in education because of their open nature, ease of use and support for effective collaboration and communication. The investigator, as a learning-facilitator educator felt the need for a thorough study of the present problem. Major purpose of the study is to investigate the perception of learning-facilitator educators towards the use of Web 2.0 technologies in their learning-facilitator preparation. The importance of the present study is that by determining whether the learning-facilitator educators have positive perception in using web 2.0 technologies. Descriptive research design of the survey type was adopted for the study and a sample of 85 learning-facilitator educators were selected for the present study. Results of the study revealed that the learning-facilitator educators have positive perceptions in using web 2.0 technologies. And the most often used tools by the learning-facilitator educators were social networking and blogging and micro-blogging. It is also inferred from the study that a significant proportion of the learning-facilitator educators use these online applications as educational tools for their content enrichment.

## Introduction

Dynamic changes in the era of information and communication technology contributed to shape the pattern of teaching and learning and created a paradigm shift in the learning environment. In the past, the web 1.0 technologies are only the knowledge providers or they are the information repositories. The unprecedented development in the field of digital technology, both in the case of software and hardware has created a need and urge to utilize these in the process of teaching and learning. Earlier, during the era of web 1.0, the users are only the consumers of information and nowadays they became the creators of knowledge or information. That is the learners and the learning-facilitators became the creators of information and knowledge; where they can also contribute to, collaborate on and edit that information. Web 2.0 technologies enable the users to achieve in this. Applications of web 2.0 hold profound potentials in education because of their open nature, ease of use and support for effective collaboration and communication. Web 2.0 is an online application that elicits participation, collaboration and interaction. Lenke *et al.* (2009) has noted that 'creation and sharing of intellectual and social resources by end users' is an important characteristic of web 2.0 applications. Web 2.0 applications promote communication between learners and learning-facilitators within and between classes. Using an online discussion forum or a social network, learners and fellow learning-facilitators can ask questions, make comments as well as get instant feedback. Since these social platforms can be accessed anywhere and at any time, learners and learning-facilitators can have more opportunities to interact with each other.

## Web 2.0 Technologies

Web 2.0 technologies are generally associated with a variety of meanings that include emphasis on user generated content, information sharing, collaborative efforts, new ways of interacting with Web-based applications as well as the use of the Web as a social platform for creating, editing and consuming content. These include social networks, blogs, micro-blogs, wikis, discussion boards, bookmarking, media sharing and RSS.

- **Social Networks:** Social networks are defined as web-based services, platforms or websites that enable individuals to communicate, interact and share ideas, messages, comments, photos, videos or any other content with a network of friends on the site or with a much wider audience over the Internet. The main aim of social networking sites is to provide an online virtual community that not only promotes the individual, but also emphasizes the individual's relationships within this community.

- **Wikis:** Wikis are collaborative websites that anyone within a community of users can contribute to or edit. Wikis can be open to a global audience or can be restricted to a specific network or community. A Wiki can cover a specific topic or subject area. The largest and most popular wiki is Wikipedia, a user-contributed online encyclopaedia currently hosting millions of articles.

- **Discussion forums:** A discussion forum is a platform in which participants can get engaged in an exchange of information about a particular topic. It provides a venue for questions and answers and is usually monitored by a moderator to keep the content appropriate. Discussion forums can also be used in asynchronous mode. That means the participants need not be logged in at the same time but can read and post comments or answers to others' messages whenever convenient.
- **Blogs:** A Blog is a weblog that allows users to share a running log of events and personal insights on a particular issue, event or topic with online audiences. Blogs are usually written and maintained by a single person and are updated on a regular basis with entries displayed in reverse chronological order. Visitors to the blog can comment on the entries made or respond to comments made by other visitors.
- **Micro-blogs:** A Micro-blog provides a similar function as a traditional blog, but with a much stronger focus on brevity. A micro-blogging website enables users to write short text messages and publish them in real-time so that they could be viewed either by anyone or by a restricted group chosen by the user.
- **Media sharing:** Media sharing sites enable users to upload and share their multimedia content (photos, videos and audio) with others on the web so that other users can view and download these media files.
- **RSS:** RSS (Really Simple Syndication), an XML-based format for sharing and distributing regularly changing Web content. RSS is a common component of many Web 2.0 platforms as well as of most news related sites. It allows these platforms to distribute their updated and dynamic content as feeds to users' devices as soon as it is published. Therefore, instead of consulting a website regularly, subscribed users to RSS feeds can have all the news and content they desire right at their fingertips.

Thus the web 2.0 technologies can work in three domains such as, Social networking, content sharing and Content creation and editing.

## Rationale of the Study

Information communication technology is a broad term that refers to the electronic or digital tools that people can use nowadays. As far as education is concerned, these digital tools are used by educators to enhance teaching and learning. These tools range from computers to the internet. Recent trends in the web technologies indicate that the learning-facilitators are getting more opportunities for learning-facilitator preparation. They depend on these web technologies for their content enrichment as well as for online collaboration. Web 2.0 technologies incorporates social networking, wikis, discussion forums, media sharing, blogging and micro-blogging, etc. in the professional preparation of learning-facilitators. The popularity of these virtual tools paved the way to numerous researches on the impact of using web 2.0 technologies in teaching-learning. Though a lot of research studies have demonstrated that these web tools have educational benefits, many educators are questioning the usefulness and validity of using these tools in education. On this outset, the investigator, as a learning-facilitator educator felt the need for a thorough study of the present problem.

In light of these facts the present study can be stated as learning-facilitator educator's perceptions towards the use of web 2.0 technologies in the learning-facilitator preparation. The important keywords used in the problem are perception, web 2.0 technologies and learning-facilitator preparation. Learning-facilitator preparation in the present study indicates the act of preparation of teaching learning materials as well as the content enrichment by the learning-facilitator educators. The importance of the present study is that by determining whether the learning-facilitator educators have positive perception in using web 2.0 technologies.

## Overview of the Studies Already Done

Davis (2007) argues that 'in both real and virtual classrooms, wikis have a number of potentially exciting applications for hypertext/web essays and writing projects, particularly those encouraging collaboration among learners'.

Zakaria, Watson and Edwards (2010) conducted a study 'Investigating the use of Web 2.0 technology by Malaysian learners' to investigate the learner's use of ICT technology for learning with a focus on how the learners would perceive the use of Web 2.0 for learning. Results of the study revealed that learners are comfortable with ICT, online and Web 2.0 tools.

Harinarayana and Raju (2010) conducted a study 'Web 2.0 features in university library web sites'. The main purpose of the study was to explore recent trend in the Web 2.0 applications, types of technologies applied in the university website and purpose of implementation of these tools. The results of the study depicted that the emergence of dynamic applications of web 2.0 technologies is utilized by the users through university library websites.

Haneefa and Sumitha (2011) conducted a study 'Perception and Use of Social Networking Sites by the Learners of Calicut University' with an objective to investigate the perception and use of social networking sites by the learners of Calicut University, Kerala. The study revealed that 79 (58.9 percent) got information from their friends when they were asked about the source of information about Web 2.0 tools. It is also observed that 68 (50.7 percent) learners spent less than 2 hours, 40 (29.8 percent) 2-4 hours, 11(8.2 percent) 4-6 hours and 9 (6.7 percent) more than 6 hours. Their opinion about social networking sites were also analysed which revealed that 68 (50.7 percent) opined that these are helpful for easy communication.

Virkus and Bamigbola (2011) conducted a study 'Learners conceptions and experiences of Web 2.0 tools'. Study supports the incorporation of Web 2.0 in higher education, especially its inclusion in LIS education. They stated that Web 2.0 tools can be used as professional tool, multi-purpose tool, and communication and education tools. Skype, Yahoo, Messenger and Facebook were preferred tools.

Batsila *et al.* (2014) evaluated the learning-facilitators' opinion on the use of web

2.0 Edmodo tool in their classrooms. Results of the survey concluded that web 2.0 applications present many educational advantages for learners.

## Purpose of the Study

The major purpose of the study is to investigate the perception of learning-facilitator educators towards the use of Web 2.0 technologies in their learning-facilitator preparation.

## Research Questions

Which type of web 2.0 applications is preferred by the learning-facilitator educators to their learning-facilitator preparation?

What are the perceptions of learning-facilitator educators on the use of web 2.0 technologies in learning-facilitator preparation?

## Methodology

Descriptive research design of the survey type was adopted for the study. The instrument used for collecting data was a self-designed questionnaire which sought information on perception of learning-facilitator educators on the use of web 2.0 technologies in learning-facilitator preparation. A sample of 85 learning-facilitator educators from six learning-facilitator education colleges affiliated to University of Kerala was selected for the present study. The questionnaire was distributed to the sample during the centralized valuation camps and data were collected.

## Major Results of the Study

Major results are given in the following heads:

(a) Personal Information Analysis

▶ Most of the learning-facilitator educators participated in the survey was female learning-facilitators which is 69 (81.2 %) and male of 16 (18.8 %). Among the respondents 39 (45.9%) are in the age group of 25 to 35 years, 27 (31.8%) of the learning-facilitator educators are between the age group 35-45years and 19 (22.3%) are of the senior learning-facilitators (above 45 years of age). It is also identified from the personal information analysis that among the learning-facilitator educators 28 (32.9 %) are of 0-5 years of teaching experience and 8 (9.4%) are having more than 20 years of teaching experience. All other learning-facilitators that are 49 (57.6%) are having 5 to 20 years of teaching experience.

(b) Learning-facilitator Educators' primary preference of use of Web 2.0 technologies

▶ The primary preference of learning-facilitator educators, in the use of web 2.0 technologies has been studied and the results are depicted in the Table 1.

**Table 1: Preference of Learning-facilitator Educators**

| S. No. | Criterion | Percentage |
|---|---|---|
| 1. | Wikis | 5 |
| 2. | Blogging and Micro Blogging | 35 |
| 3. | Media Sharing | 12 |
| 4. | R.S.S. | 6 |
| 5. | Discussion Forum | 7 |
| 6. | Social Networking | 35 |

From the pie-diagram, it is observed that majority of the learning-facilitator educators prefer social networking and blogging as one of the means of web technologies for the learning-facilitator preparation. It may be due to the reason that for learning-facilitator preparation or collaboration, the educators are utilizing social networking applications including Edmodo and blogging platforms of web 2.0 technologies. It is also evident from the pie chart that learning-facilitator educators are using these facilities to interact with the learners.

(c) Frequency of usage of Web 2.0 technologies

▸ The frequency of usage of web 2.0 technologies by the learning-facilitator educators are is given in the following table.

**Table 2: Frequency of Usage of Web 2.0 Technologies**

| Web 2.0 tools | Never | Rarely | Sometimes | Often | Very Often |
|---|---|---|---|---|---|
| Wikis | 0 (0 %) | 13 (15.2%) | 36 (42.4%) | 12 (14.1%) | 24 (28.3%) |
| Blogging and Micro Blogging | 2 (2.4%) | 12 (14.1%) | 5 (5.8%) | 10 (11.8%) | 56 (65.9%) |
| Media Sharing | 5 (5.8%) | 4 (4.8%) | 49 (57.6%) | 12 (14.1%) | 15 (17.7%) |
| R.S.S. | 51 (60%) | 12 (14.1%) | 13 (15.3%) | 6 (7.1%) | 3 (3.5%) |
| Discussion Forum | 42 (49.3%) | 36 (42.4%) | 2 (2.4%) | 3 (3.5%) | 2 (2.4%) |
| Social Networking | 1 (1.2%) | 0 (0%) | 3 (3.5%) | 22 (25.9%) | 59 (69.4%) |

From table 1, it is revealed that 42.4% of the learning-facilitator educators are using the wiki's applications such as Wikipedia, whereas majority of the learning-facilitator educators (65.9%) are make use of blogging and micro blogging facilities for their professional preparation. 57.6% of the educators are sharing images, animations and videos in blogs and social networking sites and thereby utilizing the media sharing facilities in web 2.0 platforms.

In the case of feeds, that is RSS, majority of the learning-facilitator educators are not utilizing properly. It may be due to the lack of awareness regarding the same. It is the same in the case of discussion forums too. Around 50% of the learning-facilitator educators are not using the discussion forum facilities. In the case of social networking nearly 70% of the learning-facilitator educators are using very often, in preparation of contents and sharing and collaboration with other fellow educators.

(d) Perception of learning-facilitator educators towards the use of web 2.0 technologies

▸ The perception of learning-facilitator educators was measured using the perception scale and detailed percentage analyses were carried out. It is shown in the table 2.

**Table 2: Percentage, mean and standard deviation of the responses on Perception scale**

| S. No | Scale Items | Agree % | Neutral % | Disagree % | Mean | Standard Deviation |
|---|---|---|---|---|---|---|
| | The use of Web 2.0 technologies | | | | | |
| 1. | Leads to update the teaching contents | 62.2 | 21.1 | 16.7 | 2.46 | 0.77 |
| 2. | Helps the access of course information easier | 74.2 | 15.7 | 10.1 | 2.88 | 1.12 |
| 3. | Aids in evaluating learner's performance by giving online assignments or conducting online tests | 64.5 | 20.8 | 14.7 | 2.76 | 0.89 |
| 4. | Contributes to the enhancement of browsing skills/search strategies | 100 | 0 | 0 | 3.0 | 0 |
| 5. | Provides more opportunities to interact with fellow learning-facilitators | 81.4 | 18.6 | 0 | 2.92. | 0.84 |
| 6. | Strengthens social relations among fellow educators | 100 | 0 | 0 | 3.0 | 0 |
| 7. | Helps to follow academic discussions through discussion forums | 66.2 | 32.7 | 1.1 | 2.64 | 0.54 |
| 8. | Integrates collaboration though social networking platforms | 72.8 | 12.6 | 14.6 | 2.80 | 0.89 |
| 9. | Motivates to share the ideas or concepts through blogs or micro-blogging platforms | 65.0 | 15.0 | 20.0 | 2.62 | 0.92 |
| 10. | Develops autonomy in one's own professional preparation | 100 | 0 | 0 | 3.0 | 0 |
| 11. | Gives a platform to share one's opinions, experiences and ideas | 80 | 5.0 | 15.0 | 2.90 | 0.81 |
| 12. | Allows to upload the images or videos through media sharing platforms | 100 | 0 | 0 | 3.0 | 0 |
| 13. | Facilitates communication and feedback between learning-facilitators and learners | 100 | 0 | 0 | 3.0 | 0 |
| 14. | Promotes critical reflection by working through one's own ideas | 90.0 | 10.0 | 0 | 2.91 | 0.42 |
| 15. | Encourages content creation rather than content reception. | 85.0 | 12.8 | 2.2 | 2.82 | 1.32 |

From table 2, it is revealed that the learning-facilitator educators have positive perceptions on the usage of web 2.0 technologies. It is also revealed from the table that the major use of web 2.0 technologies helps in, enhancing searching skills (100%), accessing course information (74.2%), encouraging content creation (85%), facilitating social interaction (81.4%), sharing content/blogging (85%), fostering academic discussions ( 66.2%).

## Conclusion

The extensive use of ICT in classroom has many promises because it provides enormous amount of open educational resources for the learning-facilitators. Web based platforms provide link to connect the learning-facilitator with global network of learning-facilitators. Also they increase the opportunities for collaboration and thereby updating their current knowledge. In the present study, the investigator focused on the specific features of web 2.0 technologies. Web 2.0 technologies are widely used by the learning-facilitator educators for sharing their teaching resources and also in content management, for example through Edmodo. Results of the study revealed that the learning-facilitator educators have positive perceptions in using web 2.0 technologies. And the most often used tools by the learning-facilitator educators were social networking and blogging and micro-blogging. Moreover, it is worth to mention that the results of the study are quite useful in the digital era, as these technologies given us an insight in the promises of ICT in order to enable effective learning-facilitator preparation. It is also inferred from the study that a significant proportion of the learning-facilitator educators use these online applications as educational tools for their content enrichment. Given these facts, it can be recommended that these web based technologies, for example the learning management system such as Edmodo should be made use of.

Chapter

9

# Social Media for Learning: Perception of Pre-University Learners

✎ **Devaki T. C.**
*Bangalore University, Bangalore, Karnataka*

## Preview at a Glance

Education being a social process that can happen formally, informally or non-formally within a group, is no more restricted to happen only in school that is considered a miniature society. We have noticed that the emerging social media is preferred over this miniature society gradually by the learners to socialize, get information and collaborate for their learning needs. Not only are the learners, even the learning-facilitators are observed to be relying on them for many academic related activities. In this empirical study the social media usage among the PU college learners and their perception towards social media usage is determined and analysed. It was hypothesized that the social media users would have a higher score in positive perception towards the usage as compared to the non-users. For this purpose a descriptive survey was made among 290 PU college learners of Bangalore city. The Social Media Usage Questionnaire was administered to the sample and the descriptive statistics was used to analyse the data. The results indicated that mean scores of perceived effects of social media usage among social media users is slightly greater than that of the social media non-users. However, as the difference is not statistically significant, the data collected may be considered as inconclusive and the researcher opines to repeat the study with a larger representative sample in future.

## Introduction

ICT plays an important role in shaping the new global economy and producing rapid changes in the society. It also has changed the whole education system in the areas of administration, teaching, learning and evaluation. Computers and smart phones with access to internet are functioning as a major socializing and change agent for the learners. The use of social media has diffused widely in everyone's life with recent statistical data showing high penetration rates into adolescents' life (Lenhart, 2009). Social media is a new form of ICT that has changed the way people communicate. These are the computer mediated tools that allow people to create, share or exchange information, ideas, pictures / videos in virtual communities and networks.

Social media is defined as a group of Internet based applications that build on the ideological and technological foundations of web 2.0; and that allow the creation and exchange of user generated content. Social media is best understood as a group of new kinds of online media, which share most of the characteristics like Participation, Openness, Conversation, Community, and Connectedness.

## Basic Forms of Social Media

These are some of the basic forms of social media known now, though innovation and change are common:

1. **Social networks:** these sites allow people to build personal web pages and then connect with friends to share content and communication. The biggest social networks are Myspace, Facebook, and Twitter.
2. **Blogs:** perhaps the best known form of social media; blogs are online journals, with entries appearing with the most recent first.
3. **Wikis:** these websites allow people to add content to or edit the information on them, acting as a communal document or database. The best-known wiki is Wikipedia, the online encyclopaedia which has over 2 million English language articles.
4. **Podcasts:** audio and video files that are available by subscription, through services like Apple iTunes.
5. **Forums:** areas for online discussion, often around specific topics and interests. Forums came about before the term 'social media' and are a powerful and popular element of online communities.
6. **Content communities:** communities which organize and share particular kinds of content. The most popular content communities tend to form around photos (Flickr), bookmarked links (del.icio.us) and videos (YouTube).
7. **Micro blogging:** social networking combined with bite-sized blogging, where small amounts of content ('updates') are distributed online and through the mobile phone network. Twitter is the clear leader in this field.

A good way to think about social media is that all of this is actually just about being human beings. Sharing ideas, cooperating and collaborating to create art, thinking and commerce, vigorous debate and discourse, finding people who might be good friends, allies and lovers – it's what our species has built several civilizations on. That's why it is spreading so quickly, not because it's great shiny, dashing new technology, but because it lets us be ourselves – only more so. And it is in the 'more so' that the power of this revolution lies. People can find information, inspiration, like-minded people, communities and collaborators faster than ever before. New ideas, services, business models and technologies emerge and evolve at dizzying speed in social media.

Social media has become the buzz word around the world in almost all spheres of adolescents' life despite its destructive effects being highlighted. According to The Telecom Regulatory Authority of India (TRAI), more than 165 million among the wired Indian teens and learners are using social media websites. Youngsters are exchanging ideas, feelings, personal information, pictures and videos at an astonishing rate. Social media is considered a boon to us with its benefits like accessibility, scope for both formal and informal learning. It can also be a bane in the sense of misuses leading to cyber-crime, inaccessibility in rural areas and internet barriers. If the above mentioned barriers are rightly addressed, no doubt social media can be one of the effective means of learning tool.

## Need for the Study

Learners of this digital age are already using social media for various purposes. The extensive diffusion of social media into the learners' life has led to the new opportunities for learning. This in turn observed to have great potential for knowledge dissemination. Social media usage for learning can elicit positive attitude among the learners. In the present scenario, all learning-facilitators of all level need to be sensitized to learn a minimum use of social media for teaching purpose. Hence appropriate incorporation of social media into education is the need of the hour.

Studies also show that the learners feel it apt for a learning-facilitator to use Facebook and interact with their learners by this means despite the fact that there are gloomy perceptions about the possible effects of social media usage on learners' academic performance. They also believe that these tools allow them to share knowledge related to their academics (Baran, 2010). Regardless of the challenges faced in using social media as an educational tool, experts still remain optimistic in this regard.

The advantages of social media usage in teaching-learning include their potential to engage learners in self-learning, to enable interactive learning through collaboration and to instruct personally to meet the divergent needs of learners. A study by Churchill (2009) depicted that the use of blogs in education facilitated a practical learning. So we need to understand the aspects driving learners towards the use of social media in order to prepare a new generation of learners who can effectively use this new tool for learning.

## Objective

The purpose of this study is to explore the social media usage, the perceived effects of social media usage by the PU college learners of Bangalore city.

## Methodology

The study was conducted by descriptive survey method. The sample comprised of 290, 1st PU adolescents randomly drawn by the stratified technique from arts, science and commerce stream located in different areas of Bangalore. The data was collected by using the social media usage questionnaire (SMUQ) prepared by the researcher for the purpose of this study. The questionnaire comprises of two parts to get the information related to their perceived effects of social media usage on their academics and their social media usage status. The data obtained was analysed using percentages.

## Analysis

The data collected are statistically analysed and the results of the descriptive statistics on the perceived effects among social media user and non-user adolescents based on gender and stream of study are discussed in the following passages.

### Stream wise analysis of the SM User and Non-User Adolescents

The analysis reveals that science learners (65.22%) outstand in social media usage status with their counterparts from arts (48.75 %) and commerce (64.54 %) stream in social media usage. Adolescents from arts stream are the least social media users while good numbers of commerce learners are also observed to be using social media.

### Perceived effects of social media usage and their usage status

The analysis reveals that 68.57% of the social media users have positive perception on the effect of usage on their academics and 63.48% of non-users also are observed to be having positive perception.

### Gender wise analysis of the SM User and Non-User Adolescents

The analysis of the obtained data shows that 60.34% of 1st PU learners are using social media. Among them 68% are male users and only 32% are female users. 78.81% of male learners are users while only 40.29% of female learners are users.

## Discussion of Result and Conclusion

The study revealed that the perceived of effects of social media usage among Social Media User and Non-User adolescents based on gender and stream of study are positive. Thus it can be interpreted as the learners perceive that the social media usage can have positive effects on their academics irrespective of their usage status. This may be attributed to the fact that the sample comprised of only 1st PU College learners who have just come out of a disciplined school environment and fascinated by the social media usage.

Still it has to be noted that more than half of the sample studied (60.34%) are using social media irrespective of their stream of study within few days of their entry to PU College. There are other factors like family environment unlike in foreign countries that can influence their perception and usage status. So, this result can be further tested by conducting a similar study on the same sample over a period of time along with other variables like family environment. Also science stream learners' stands top on the list of social media users followed by commerce and arts stream learners. Only further studies can reveal the reasons for this difference in the social media usage pattern.

The main aim of education is transmission and transformation of the society for the betterment of humanity. In view of this, it is essential to maintain a healthy balance between virtual and real world in contemporary society to bring about social transformation. Adolescents of today need to be properly educated and empowered with right, adequate and update knowledge of social media usage. They need to be properly trained/ educated when to connect and disconnect with social media as a virtual reality. Also teach them how to secure their digital identity as most of the Internet users, especially children are exposed to cyber threats due to weak and easy-to-guess passwords in spite of India being second largest Internet population in the world.

Most teens surveyed who are regular media users have lots of friends and get along well with their parents, and are happy at school (Rideout, 2010).This is evident in the present study where the social media users perception on the effects of social media usage is in par with that of the non-users. The Telenor India's Web Wise survey done in 13 cities covering 2,700 learners depicted that 83.5% children between 6 to 18 years are active on social media. It also revealed that 15.74% shared that they have received inappropriate messages.

Youth of today need to be involved in social realities with social interactions so that they connect with society at large. They are also to be educated with digital literacy to update their knowledge to solve social problems. The present world is becoming increasingly empirical, worldly, secular, humanistic, pragmatic, utilitarian, contractual and hedonistic. More and more decisions are being made by fewer and so called highly educated individuals. In this era of turmoil, scientific and technological knowledge is the base for bringing about social transformation.

In this digital age, there has been transformation of human mind with alterations of the chemistry of our brains. Verbal skills will be affected by the available means of sending skills via technological links and electronic impulses. Our technical equipment can now create added values to our messages. With all these around, learning styles will be influenced by the network interactions. Such networks will have learners of future thinking more multidimensional and creatively, utilizing visual, computer and communication tools to enhance the way they process and utilize information.

The study concludes that social media being a virtual world, has both merits and demerits attached to its usage. Many studies in future will think and process information in ways that may challenge and even differ from their learning-facilitators who might still rely on traditional thinking patterns. It is very much possible that future learners think more future oriented than their learning-facilitators. Thus today, youth should be able to adapt to the world of optical fibres, lasers, chips and electronics much easier than the older generations.

# Chapter 10

# Awareness of OER at Higher Education

✎ **Dinesh Maharana**
*Ravenshaw University, Cuttack, Odisha*

## Preview at a Glance

Open educational resources (OER) are recent trend in the era of ICT. Open educational resources (OER) refers to free and open access to digitized materials that are accessible to academics, learners and self-learners researcher, learning-facilitators etc. OER material includes textbooks to curricula, syllabi, lecture notes, assignments, tests, projects, audio, video and animation learning applications, online text book, software etc. The basic principles of OER material is one can legally and freely copy, use, adapt and re-share them. The main stakeholders of higher education are learning-facilitators and learners. In this study attempts have made to find out the awareness level of learning-facilitators and learners of higher education about OER. The objectives of the study were to study the awareness of Learners of Higher Education about Open Educational Resources in relation to their gender and stream of study and to study the perception of Learners and learning-facilitators of Higher Education about Open Educational Resources. Descriptive survey research design was followed to conduct to study. On the basis of Stratified sample technique the researcher has taken 30 learning-facilitators and 70 learners from affiliated colleges of Utkal University and Ravenshaw University as Sample of study. Data were collected through self-developed awareness test and perception test and analysed through the help of statistical techniques like Mean, standard deviation, t-test and Chi-square test. The study revealed that the awareness level of both male and female learners of higher education is below average. The awareness level of both science and arts learners is below average.

## Introduction

The OER movement originated from developments in open and distance learning (ODL) and in the wider context of a culture of open knowledge, open source, free sharing and peer collaboration, which emerged in the late 20th century The term 'open educational resources' was first adopted at UNESCO's (2002) Forum on the Impact of Open Courseware for Higher Education in Developing Countries as 'teaching, learning and research materials in any medium, digital or otherwise, that reside in the public domain or have been released under an open license that permits no-cost access, use, adaptation and redistribution by others with no or limited restrictions.'

Open educational resources (OER) are recent trend in the era of ICT. It is used in every level of education that is higher, secondary, and elementary, learning-facilitator education, distance education etc. It makes teaching learning meaning full, live, resource full etc. Generally Open educational resources (OER) refers to free and open access to digitized materials that are accessible to academics, learners and self-learners researcher, learning-facilitators etc. OER material includes textbooks to curricula, syllabi, lecture notes, assignments, tests, projects, audio, video and animation learning applications, online text book, software etc. The common features of OER materials which distinguish from other materials that are given below. The features of OER are:

- Open access
- Open source
- Reuse
- Revise
- Remix
- Redistribute

## Rationale of the Study

Open Educational Resources (OER) are teaching and learning materials that are freely available online for everyone to use, whether an instructor, learner or self-learner. OER as teaching learning material is useful to everyone. It is assumed that the main users of open educational resources are learning-facilitators and learners of both face-to-face mode and open distance learning mode. Learning-facilitators of higher education have moderate level of awareness towards OER (Ahmad, 2012). Most of the learning-facilitators of higher education are not familiar with the term OER, but had a clear notion of what it meant. They were familiar with open content repositories within the university but not externally (Rolfe, 2010). Similarly, most of the learners of higher education only heard about OER and some are not aware about OER (Hurt, 2013). Study conducted by (Ganapaty and Peiwei, 2015) shows that majority of learning-facilitators said that they have heard about at least two types of OER. Further, it describes that respondents have high tendency sharing OER. Study conducted by (Olufunke and Adedun, 2014) indicates that the levels of OER awareness among undergraduate learners are moderate. The level of usages of OER was high. Further, it describes that OER have great impact on the quality of education. Open educational resources are largely developed by learning-facilitators who expect to share them with and see them (re)used by other learning-facilitators (Lane, 2012). Many claims are made as to how this gifting culture will support learning-facilitators and educational institutions to provide learners with teaching resources that cost less and/or are of higher teaching quality through that shared endeavour, either done alone or through formal collaborations. Half of the undergraduate learners used OER to either or great extent, 2.75% respondents reported that it was either very important or very important for them to know which institution creates OER contents (Hew and Cheungs, 2013).

The investigator came across very few studies in the area of open educational resources in India (Venkaih, 2006; Ghosh 2006; Ahamad, 2012) etc. The investigator did not find any research studies conducted in Odisha in the area of OER.

From the above analysis, following questions may be raised:

- To what extent the learners and learning-facilitators of higher education in Odisha are aware about Open Educational Resources?
- What is the perception of learners and learning-facilitators of higher education about Open Educational Resources in relation to motivation, teaching learning process, value and flexibility?

So there is a need to have a study on the awareness and perception of learners and learning-facilitators of higher education about open educational resources. Hence, an attempt has been made to see the awareness and perception of learning-facilitators and learners on the basis of variable like gender and streams, so that steps may be taken to improve the educational process

## Objectives of the Study

The objectives of the present study were:

- To study the Awareness of Learners of Higher Education about Open Educational Resources in relation to their Gender and Stream of study.
- To study the Perception of Learners of Higher Education about Open Educational Resources.
- To study the Perception of Learning-facilitators of Higher Education about Open Educational Resources.

### Hypotheses

On the basis of above objectives following hypotheses were formulated:

- **H01:** There exists no significant difference in awareness about Open Educational Resources between Male and Female learners of higher education.
- **H02:** There exists no significant difference in awareness about Open Educational Resources between Science and Arts Learners of higher education.

### Operational Definition of Key Terms

- Open Educational Resources:

Open Educational Recourses are freely accessible, openly licensed documents and media that are useful for teaching, learning, and assessing as well as for research purposes.

- Awareness about OER:

It refers to the basic knowledge about Open Educational Resources such as, accessibility, licensing, assessing, purpose, types, uses, importance, features and scope.

- Perception about OER:

It refers to interpretation of sensation according to one's own experiences such as utility, impact, value, motivation, flexibility etc.

## Delimitations of the Study

The study was delimited to the following:
- The sample was taken from two Universities i.e. Utkal University and Ravenshaw University.
- Sample has been taken from Arts and Science stream.
- Unstandardized self-developed tools were used for present study.
- Delimited to only Liberal courses.
- Delimited to Cuttack and Bhubaneswar city.

## Methodology

The present study focused to find awareness and perception of learning-facilitators and learners of Higher Education about Open Educational Resources. So the present study came under descriptive survey research design. In this study survey method has been followed to collect data about awareness and perception of learners and learning-facilitators about Open Educational Resources. In the present study the researcher has taken all the Learning-facilitators and Learners of Higher Education from Cuttack and Bhubaneswar city as the population of the study. The researcher has taken 30 learning-facilitators and 70 learners from the affiliated colleges of Utkal University and Ravenshaw University as Sample of study. Further the researcher has taken 15 learning-facilitators and 35 learners from each of the University. The technique of selecting sample was Stratified sample technique. This technique was followed due to the accessibility of sample. The distribution of sample is presented below.

### Distributions of Samples

| | | 15 Learning Facilitators |
|---|---|---|
| | Utkal University | 35 Learners |
| Higher Education Institutions | | |
| | Ravenshaw University | 15 Learning Facilitators |
| | | 35 Learners |

In the present study the researcher has used three tools viz. awareness test for learners (self-developed) Perception Scale for learners (self- developed) and Perception Scale for learning-facilitators(self-developed). The researcher had gone to affiliated colleges of Utkal University and Ravenshaw University for data collection as the sample of study. The researcher has personally collected data from the learning-facilitators and learners and for this purpose researcher has given enough time to the samples to respond to the items. The data has been analysed by the researcher applying quantitative techniques like

- Mean Standard deviation
- t-test
- Chi-square test

Mean, Standard deviation, t-test was used for objective no1 and Chi-square test was used for objective numbers 2 and 3.

## Analysis and Interpretation

### Awareness about OER with regards to Gender

Under this dimension the investigator has analysed the awareness about OER among the male and female learners of higher education which has been presented in the following table:

Table1: Significance difference of means of male and female learners in relation to awareness about OER

| Category | N=70 | Mean | SD | Df | t Value | Remarks |
|---|---|---|---|---|---|---|
| Male | 37 | 14.35 | 3.831 | 68 | 0.348 | Not Significant |
| Female | 33 | 14.06 | 3.061 | | | |

From the above table, it is observed that the mean awareness score about OER of male and female learners are 14.35 and 14.06 respectively. The computed value of t is (0.348) which is less than the table value at 0.05 level of significance with df 68. Hence, the null hypothesis 'There exists no significant difference in awareness about Open Educational Resources between Male and Female learners of higher education' is retained.

### Awareness about OER with regards to Stream of study

Under this dimension the researcher has analysed the difference between science and arts learners of higher education institutions in relation to awareness about OER. The detail analysis is presented in the following table 1.2:

Table 2: Significance difference of means of science and arts learners in relation to awareness about OER

| Category | N=70 | Mean | SD | Df | T | Remarks |
|---|---|---|---|---|---|---|
| Science | 32 | 14.16 | 3.143 | 68 | 0.128 | Not significant |
| Arts | 38 | 14.26 | 3.761 | | | |

From the above table, it is observed that the mean awareness score about OER of science and arts are 14.16 and 14.26 respectively. The computed value of t is (0.128) which is less than the table value at 0.05 level of significance with df 68. Hence,

the null hypothesis, 'There exists no significant difference in awareness about Open Educational Resources between Science and Arts Learners of Higher Education is retained.

## Perception Analysis of Learner Respondents

To study the perception learners respondents about Open Educational Resources a self-made perception scale was developed by the researcher having five points like Strongly Agree(SA), Agree(A) Undecided(UD), Disagree(DA), Strongly Disagree(SD). The test of significance to each item was tested by using Chi-square test of significance and interpreted below. The number of item was 30.

N = 70

| S. No. | Statements | SA | A | UD | DA | SDA | Chi-square value |
|---|---|---|---|---|---|---|---|
| 1. | I enjoy learning in an environment that incorporates OER | 26 (37.14%) | 35 (50%) | 5 (7.14%) | 4 (5.71%) | 0 | 68.7 significant at 0.01 level of significance |
| 2. | I would describe OER as interesting. | 24 (34.28%) | 40 (57.14%) | 2 (2.85%) | 3 (4.28%) | 1 (1.42%) | 86.41 significant at 0.01 level of significance |
| 3. | OER make me feel more engaged with learning. | 31 (44.28%) | 30 (42.87%) | 6 (8.57%) | 1 (1.42%) | 2 (2.87%) | 65.84 significant at 0.01 level of significance |
| 4. | If given choice, I prefer learning using OER. | 23 (32.58%) | 25 (35.71%) | 13 (18.57%) | 9 (12.85%) | 0 | 30.27 significant at 0.01 level of significance |
| 5. | OER directly improve the quality of my learning experience. | 25 (35.71%) | 30 (42.58%) | 8 (11.58%) | 5 (7.14%) | 2 (2.85%) | 45.55 significant at 0.01 level of significance |
| 6. | I would like curriculum which includes OER. | 20 (28.57%) | 32 (45.71%) | 13 (18.57%) | 4 (5.71%) | 1 (1.42%) | 44.99 significant at 0.01 level of significance |
| 7. | OER materials helps me to understand the content matter easily | 20 (28.57%) | 32 (45.71%) | 11 (15.71%) | 6 (8.57%) | 1 (1.42%) | 42.99 significant at 0.01 level of significance |
| 8. | I am very active when OER used in class room | 22 (31.42%) | 32 (45.71%) | 6 (8.57%) | 9 (12.85%) | 1 (1.42%) | 58.35 significant at 0.01 level of significance |
| 9. | OER makes teaching learning interactive | 30 (42.87%) | 20 (28.57%) | 8 (11.42%) | 10 (14.28%) | 2 (2.87%) | 34.67 significant at 0.01 level of significance |
| 10. | OER materials is of less value to me because any one can access this materials | 11 (15.71%) | 20 (28.57%) | 16 (22.85%) | 15 (21.42%) | 8 (11.42%) | 6.13 (not significant) |
| 11. | OER are not good as purchased textbook | 11 (15.71%) | 12 (17.14%) | 20 (28.57%) | 19 (27.14%) | 8 (11.42%) | 7.89 (not significant) |
| 12. | OER saves me from high cost on textbook | 18 (25.71%) | 35 (50%) | 11 (15.71%) | 5 (7.14%) | 1 (1.42%) | 51.13 significant at 0.01 level of significance |

contd...

## Awareness of OER at Higher Education

| |  | | | | | | |
|---|---|---|---|---|---|---|---|
| 13. | OER materials are very useful to me | 18 (25.71%) | 40 (57.14%) | 9 (12.85%) | 2 (2.85%) | 1 (1.42%) | 73.55 significant at 0.01 level of significance |
| 14. | OER used learning purpose | 23 (32.85%) | 33 (47.14%) | 5 (7.14%) | 7 (10%) | 2 (2.87%) | 51.12 significant at 0.01 level of significance |
| 15. | OER is not used for entertainment purpose | 5 (7.14%) | 29 (41.42%) | 14 (20%) | 8 (11.42%) | 14 (20%) | 24.42 significant at 0.01 level of significance |
| 16. | OER materials helps for intellectual development | 24 (34.28%) | 30 (42.87%) | 9 (12.87%) | 4 (5.71%) | 3 (4.28%) | 42.98 significant at 0.01 level of significance |
| 17. | OER is substitute of traditional materials | 11 (15.71%) | 20 (28.57%) | 23 (32.85%) | 11 (15.71%) | 5 (7.14%) | 15.41 significant at 0.01 level of significance |
| 18. | OER help me understand topics better than textbook. | 8 (11.42%) | 33 (47.14%) | 14 (20%) | 9 (12.87%) | 6 (8.57%) | 34.7 significant at 0.01 level of significance |
| 19. | One use OER materials for better understanding of materials | 12 (17.14%) | 38 (54.28%) | 7 (10%) | 12 (17.38%) | 1 (1.42%) | 57.27 significant at 0.01 level of significance |
| 20. | OER material creates confusion regarding contents matter | 6 (8.57%) | 12 (17.14%) | 18 (25.71%) | 23 (32.87%) | 11 (15.71%) | 12.41 significant at 0.05 level of significance |
| 21. | OER does not offer any advantage to me | 2 (2.85%) | 12 (17.14%) | 6 (8.57%) | 30 (42.87%) | 20 (28.57%) | 35.98 significant at 0.01 level of significance |
| 22. | OER can cater to the need of every individual | 12 (17.14%) | 26 (37.14%) | 23 (32.87%) | 6 (8.57%) | 3 (4.28%) | 29.55 significant at 0.01 level of significance |
| 23. | OER is helpful for creating a knowledge society | 32 (45.71%) | 22 (31.42%) | 12 (17.14%) | 4 (5.71%) | 0 | 36.11 significant at 0.01 level of significance |
| 24. | Every institution should use OER | 28 (40%) | 30 (42.58%) | 8 (11.42%) | 3 (4.28%) | 1 (1.42%) | 55.56 significant at 0.01 level of significance |
| 25. | OER materials help for creation of knowledge | 24 (34.28%) | 35 (50%) | 6 (8.57%) | 5 (7.14%) | 0 | 62.99 significant at 0.01 level of significance |
| 26. | OER helps me creating new knowledge in my own pace | 17 (24.28%) | 37 (52.87%) | 12 (17.17%) | 3 (4.28%) | 1 (1.42%) | 53.1 significant at 0.01 level of significance |
| 27. | One can read OER materials in own pace | 16 (22.85%) | 33 (47.14%) | 12 (17.14%) | 6 (8.57%) | 3 (4.28%) | 39.55 significant at 0.01 level of significance |
| 28. | OER promotes individual learning | 32 (45.71%) | 23 (32.85%) | 7 (10%) | 5 (7.14%) | 3 (4.28%) | 46.84 significant at 0.01 level of significance |
| 29. | OER materials save time for learning | 28 (40%) | 24 (34.28%) | 13 (18.57%) | 4 (5.71%) | 1 (1.42%) | 40.42 significant at 0.01 level of significance |
| 30. | OER materials are easily available | 29 (41.42%) | 23 (32.85%) | 14 (20%) | 3 (4.28%) | 1 (1.42%) | 42.56 significant at 0.01 level of significance |

## Perception Analysis of Learning-facilitator Respondents

To study the perception of Learning-facilitators respondents about Open Educational Resources a self-made perception scale was developed by the researcher having five points like Strongly Agree(SA), Agree(A) undecided(UD), Disagree (DA)and Strongly Disagree(SD). The test of significance to each item was tested using Chi-square test of significance and interpreted below. The number of items was 30.

N = 30

| S. No. | Statements | SA | A | UD | DA | SDA | Chi-square value |
|---|---|---|---|---|---|---|---|
| 01 | Use of OER in curriculum is possible | 18 (60%) | 12 (40%) | 0 | 0 | 0 | 46.00 significant at 0.01 level of significance |
| 02 | OER content needs localization | 12 (40%) | 13 (43.33%) | 3 (10%) | 2 (6.66%) | 0 | 24.32 significant at 0.01 level of significance |
| 03 | OER materials are easy to understand | 10 (33.33%) | 18 (60%) | 0 | 2 (6.66%) | 0 | 41.32 significant at 0.01 level of significance |
| 04 | The coverage of OER are not adequate | 6 (20%) | 13 (43.33%) | 6 (20%) | 3 (10%) | 2 (6.66%) | 12.32 significant at 0.05 level of significance |
| 05 | The content of OER needs frequently updating | 16 (53.33%) | 13 (43.33%) | 1 (3.33%) | 0 | 0 | 40.98 significant at 0.01 level of significance |
| 06 | OER is easily accessible | 10 (33.33%) | 13 (43.33%) | 1 (3.33%) | 6 (20%) | 0 | 20.80 significant at 0.01 level of significance |
| 07 | OER saves time of the learning-facilitator | 6 (20%) | 20 (66.66%) | 0 | 4 (13.33%) | 0 | 45.32 significant at 0.01 level of significance |
| 08 | OER requires higher skills on computer | 6 (20%) | 14 (46.66%) | 2 (6.66%) | 8 (26.66%) | 0 | 17.48 significant at 0.01 level of significance |
| 09 | Some OER web links are not accessible | 9 (30%) | 13 (43.23%) | 2 (6.66%) | 5 (16.66%) | 1 (3.33%) | 16.64 significant at 0.01 level of significance |
| 10 | Learners use OER for learning | 11 (36.33%) | 12 (40.23%) | 5 (16.66%) | 2 (6.66%) | 0 | 18.96 significant at 0.01 level of significance |
| 11 | OER promotes collaboration approach | 6 (20%) | 16 (52.33%) | 6 (20%) | 2 (6.66%) | 0 | 14.91 significant at 0.01 level of significance |
| 12 | Adaptation of OER will improve the image of institutions | 7 (23.33%) | 14 (46.66%) | 5 (16.66%) | 4 (13.33%) | 0 | 20.52 significant at 0.01 level of significance |
| 13 | OER enhance personal reputation | 3 (10%) | 7 (33.33%) | 6 (20%) | 14 (46.66%) | 0 | 18.32 significant at 0.01 level of significance |
| 14 | OER can help to build partnership with college and university world wide | 10 (33.33%) | 16 (53.33%) | 2 (6.66%) | 1 (3.33%) | 1 (3.33%) | 30.3 significant at 0.01 level of significance |

|  |  | | | | | |  |
|---|---|---|---|---|---|---|---|
| 15 | OER helps one identifying recent innovation in Education | 9 (30%) | 20 (66.66%) | 0 | 0 | 1 (3.33%) | 50.32 significant at 0.01 level of significance |
| 16 | One should be update with OER movements | 11 (36.33%) | 18 (60%) | 0 | 1 (3.33%) | 0 | 44.32 significant at 0.01 level of significance |
| 17 | OER helps in better learner's achievements | 10 (33.33%) | 14 (46.46%) | 4 (13.33%) | 4 (13.33%) | 2 (6.66%) | 16.28 significant at 0.01 level of significance |
| 18 | OER are useful making teaching learning effective | 8 (26.66%) | 16 (53.33%) | 4 (13.33%) | 2 (6.66%) | 0 | 26.64 significant at 0.01 level of significance |
| 19 | OER materials make teaching learning process live | 6 (20%) | 19 (63.33%) | 0 | 5 (16.66%) | 0 | 40.32 significant at 0.01 level of significance |
| 20 | Learners actively respond when OER is used | 6 (20%) | 12 (40%) | 4 (13.33%) | 8 (26.66%) | 0 | 13.32 significant at 0.01 level of significance |
| 21 | OER materials helps to adopt different strategies by learning-facilitators | 10 (33.33%) | 18 (60%) | 1 (3.33%) | 1 (3.33%) | 0 | 40.98 significant at 0.01 level of significance |
| 22 | OER increases learner's participation | 5 (16.6%) | 14 (46.46%) | 4 (13.33%) | 7 (23.33%) | 0 | 17.64 significant at 0.01 level of significance |
| 23 | Learners are motivated by using OER | 8 (26.66%) | 18 (60%) | 3 (10%) | 3 (10%) | 0 | 33.66 significant at 0.01 level of significance |
| 24 | OER creates interest among learners to learn | 8 (26.66%) | 18 (60%) | 1 (3.33%) | 3 (10%) | 0 | 36.82 significant at 0.01 level of significance |
| 25 | OER material needs ICT facilities to access | 10 (33.33%) | 17 (56.66%) | 2 (6.66%) | 1 (3.33%) | 0 | 35.64 significant at 0.01 level of significance |
| 26 | OER helps for searching research materials | 11 (36.32%) | 18 (60.66%) | 0 | 1 (3.33%) | 0 | 44.32 significant at 0.01 level of significance |
| 27 | OER helps for publishing Research work | 8 (26.66%) | 15 (50%) | 2 (6.66%) | 5 (16.6%) | 0 | 22.98 significant at 0.01 level of significance |
| 28 | OER helps for updating knowledge | 13 (43.33%) | 15 (50%) | 1 (3.33%) | 1 (3.33%) | 0 | 35.98 significant at 0.01 level of significance |
| 29 | OER is not essential for research work | 1 (3.33%) | 6 (20%) | 2 (6.6%) | 16 (53.33%) | 5 (16.6) | 23.64 significant at 0.01 level of significance |
| 30 | OER is useful for professional development | 10 (33.3%) | 18 (60%) | 1 (3.33%) | 1 (3.33%) | 10 (33.3%) | 40.98 significant at 0.01 level of significance |

## Major Findings of the Study

Followings were the major findings of the study:

▶ There is no significant difference in awareness about Open Educational Resources between male and female learners of higher education.

- There is no significant difference in awareness about Open Educational Resources learners between science and arts learners of higher education.

Significant proportion of learner respondents was strongly agreed to the following:

- OER makes teaching learning interactive.
- OER is helpful for creating a knowledge society
- OER promotes individual learning
- OER materials saves time for learning
- OER materials are easily available

Significant proportion of learner respondents was agreed to the following:

- I enjoy learning in an environment that incorporates OER.
- I would describe OER as interesting.
- OER make me feel more engaged with learning.
- If given choice, I prefer learning using OER.
- OER directly improve the quality of my learning experience.
- I would like curriculum which includes OER.
- OER materials help me to understand thecontent matter easily.
- I am very active when OER used in class room.
- OER saves me from high cost on textbook
- OER materials are very useful to me
- OER used learning purpose
- OER is not used for entertainment purpose
- OER materials help for intellectual development.
- OER help me understand topics better than textbook.
- One use OER materials for better understanding of materials
- OER can cater to the need of every individual
- Every institution should use OER
- OER materials helps for creation of knowledge
- OER helps me creating new knowledge in my own pace.
- One can read OER materials in own pace

Significant proportion of learner respondents was undecided to the following:

- OER is substitute of traditional materials
- OER are not good as purchased textbook
- Significant proportion of learner respondents were disagreed to the following:
- OER materials are of less value to me because any one can access these materials.

- OER material creates confusion regarding contents matter.
- OER does not offer any advantage to me

Significant proportion of learning-facilitator respondents was strongly agreed to the following:

- Use of OER in curriculum is possible.
- The content of OER needs frequently updating.

Significant proportion of learning-facilitator respondents was agreed to the following:

- OER content needs localization.
- OER materials are easy to understand.
- The coverage of OER are not adequate
- OER is easily accessible.
- OER saves time of the learning-facilitator
- OER requires higher skills on computer.
- Some OER web links are not accessible.
- Learners use OER for learning.
- OER promotes collaboration approach.
- Learner's adaptation of OER will improve the image of institutions.
- OER can help to build partnership with college and university worldwide.
- OER helps one identifying recent innovation in education.
- One should be update with OER movements.
- OER helps in better learner's achievements
- OER are useful making teaching learning effective.
- OER materials make teaching learning process live.
- Learners actively respond when OER is used.
- OER materials helps to adopt different strategies by learning-facilitators
- OER increases learner's participation.
- Learners are motivated by using OER.
- OER creates interest among learners to learn.
- OER material needs ICT facilities to access
- OER helps for searching research materials.
- OER helps for publishing research work.
- OER helps for updating knowledge.
- OER are useful for professional development.

Significant proportion of learning-facilitator respondents was disagreed to the following:

- OER enhance personal reputation.
- OER are not essential for research work.

## Educational Implication of the Study

The mean awareness score of male and female learners about OER is 14.35 and 14.06 respectively out of 30 and the mean awareness score science and arts learners about OER is 14.16 and 14.26 respectively out of 30. This shows that the awareness level among learners is below average. So measures should be taken to promote awareness among learners about OER.

- The higher education institutions should organize awareness program, in service training, seminar, lectures, workshops to orient learners and learning-facilitators of higher education.
- ICT should be an integral part of curriculum in every course in higher education.
- School curriculum should be added with ICT to orient learners from lower level.
- Though ICT is recently introduced in learning-facilitator education program but, learners need to be more oriented about OER.
- Finally Govt. should have adequate financial provisions, policy, guidelines for it.

# Chapter 11

# Psycho-Utopianism among Learning-facilitators and ICT

### Divya Rajkumar Panjwani
*Integral University, Lucknow, UP*

## Preview at a Glance

With the fast changing technology it becomes need of an hour for a human being to update with latest gadgets. As every aspect of society be it culture, economy, politics, family life, etc. is affected how can a teaching-learning situation not be affected. Being considered as a new concept since years ICT has emerged as a necessity. A descriptive study was done by surveying the learning-facilitators of CBSE School. Population consists of all the learning-facilitators of CBSE School of Lucknow City. Purposive sampling, area wise selection of school was done. 10 schools were taken as sample from Lucknow city. 50 learning-facilitators from each school were taken comprising of 500 learning-facilitators in total. The findings revealed that there is use of ICT in classroom, learners are more active then learning-facilitators while using technology, there is reluctance from the part of many learning-facilitators for using technology in proper sense and there is a need to develop a sense of using technology judicially and in such a manner that integrated ICT approach is followed.

## Introduction

### Background of the problem

Information and communication technology itself has, of course, changed significantly: There is more of it; it is more influential; it is quicker; it is cheaper; it is available to masses; and mostly people know how use it in their daily lives. Tools basically for connections between learning-facilitators and learners across national borders have enhanced a lot, but that doesn't mean that it is easy to really make and keep up such relations over time in ways that are useful and sometimes even stimulating.

The concept of linking world need to connect learning-facilitators and learners globally so that they can be engaged for enriching collaborative learning projects together to encourage global peace and understanding and develop 21st century skills and competencies'. To the extent it might be of interest to anyone that there should be computers and Internet. Using computers and the Internet has become a vital part of our daily lives. Effective use of technology and continuous learning is the greatest vehicles for the 21st century. Peoples' lives are affected by increasing communication, mounting educational services, and increasing quality along with personal interaction. Seeking, evaluating, organizing using and sharing information with others are emphasised more. The Internet is the greatest source for information and the best way to quickly share and exchange information with others, the Internet sharpens one's ability to search and analyse information (Tutkun, 2011).

As Technology is now all around it is increasingly becoming work lives. School needs to be reconsidering their organizational climate so as foster a healthy learning environment for learning-facilitators and learners both. Technology will not play a major role in learning-facilitators' professional learning until such an environment is fostered which includes learning-facilitators having more 'say' in the development of technologies to support their learning.

Numbers of researches are done on the favourable effect of the use of new technologies on a learning process in terms of its facilitation and enhancement (Allen and Seaman, 2011; Graham, 2006). Studies related with some constraints and limitations of the use of ICT in education are also done (Fadde and Phu Vu, 2014). And still the question remains: Does the use of IT really matter in education? Should IT by definition be used in education nowadays? Does it always work? What are the gaps between learning technology between learners and learning-facilitators? The scope of attitudes is very broad: from very enthusiastic ones of ardent supporters, completely 'converted into a new religion', to irreconcilable opponents and even 'rejecters' of any didactic value of ICT.

As usual there exist not only advantages but also disadvantages, which can be discussed both from the point of guarantors/ learning-facilitators/ instructor / tutors and learners. All the following, more detailed issues of ICT exploitation in teaching and learning are based on research and own experience with on-line tuition in the Czech Republic (Cech and Klimova 2003; FrydrychovaKlimova 2011; Hubackova 2011; Semradova 2011 & Poulova 2005).

At coaching (face to face) learners usually talk about the problems they come across when doing variety of tasks or writing assignments. There are options of regular classes and e-courses also which are used as reference courses (i.e. learners can once again read the information obtained in class and do some additional exercises to practise their knowledge) for further self-study or revision of the lecture.

For producing quality teaching learning outcomes one of the critical components required is learning-facilitator professional learning. Professional learning is necessary for learning-facilitators throughout as there is diversity of learning-facilitators' awareness, experience and training, The major reason being this is that learning-facilitator's career occurring along a continuum from initial undergraduate education, through school practicum, internship, induction, to ongoing lifelong learning (DEST, 2003; Ramsey, 2000).

Learners today live in a very technological world. Texting, social networking, and web surfing are usually used by many learners. Learners feel these technologies as useful and extremely enjoyable. These very same learners that are accustomed to these types of technologies will relate to using technology at school. If their 4 learning environment mirrors the ways in which they engage with the world, they will excel in their education (Christen, 2009). Technology can transform the classroom into an interactive learning environment

Learning-facilitators should model the use of technology in support of the curriculum so that children can see the appropriate use of technology and benefit from exposure to more advanced applications that they will use independently when they are older (DePasquale, McNamara, and Murphy, 2003).

Here comes the need to know that is there any serious psycho-utopian thoughts going on at present? To clarify things it is necessary to differentiate 'utopia' and 'utopianism.' Utopia involves definite and detailed descriptions of an allegedly ideal social order, whereas utopianism is a more vague 'social dreaming' about the future (Sargent, 1994). Starting from this distinction, today utopianism seems more prevalent than utopia. Disregarding the possibly utopian elements in various New Age movements (Hammer, 2001), perhaps Skinner was the last psychological thinker who actually spelled out an ideal—albeit small scale—social order and whose ideas really had an impact beyond a narrow circle of believers. Furthermore, there is always a hope that science of psychology can be the basis for effective psycho-technological applications in child rearing or education seems to have decreased a great deal and perhaps completely disappeared. There is, however, a new kind of utopianism emerging in connection with the rapid developments of information and communication technology (ICT), called by Coyne (1999) 'digital utopias'. Its impact on education and educational thinking is evident, considering present educational discourse and practice. There have been many claims about how computers and ICT 'will bring about a free, better and enlightened world' (Coyne, 1999), especially by their employment in schools. Coyne quotes one U.S. social scientist: 'These technologies can support learning-facilitators in fostering learner engagement with peers and outsiders, and construction of projects that contribute to a better world. These approaches also promote each learner's self-worth while learning the subject material. I believe that as learning-facilitator effectiveness increases and learning becomes interactive, creation generates satisfaction, process and product become entwined, and cooperation builds community.'(Schneiderman, as quoted in Coyne 1999). As Coyne comments, these sentiments echo the Enlightenment educational project of fostering the reason of the individual in order to create freedom and cooperation between peoples. Thus, the belief is that by employing ICT in education human nature will become more reasonable, and this in turn will create a better society. This is a kind of psycho-utopianism, and weak sort. A further example of how computers and ICT are regarded as a positive and important factor for human and social development is the notion of Homo Zappiens presented by Professor Wim Veen (Head of the Centre for Education and Technology at the Deft University of Technology, The Netherlands). According to Veen (2004), the 'e-generation' of Homo Zappiens is involved in 'Brain based Learning.' By using multiple ICT-technologies they develop four skills crucial for present and future society: (1) integrated scanning skills, (2) ability to multi-task, (3) ability to process discontinued information and deal with discontinuity (e.g., through TV-zapping), and (4) nonlinear approaches to problem solving. In developing these capacities, they are building on a (presumed) fundamental agreement with the use of the ICT-technologies and the way the human brain operates. In a small Swedish magazine called The Computer in Education, started by ICT-enthusiastic learning-facilitators, Veen's ideas about the 'screenagers' of the e-generation are presented with the following ingress: 'They are young. They seem inattentive. They do seven things at the same time. They communicate continuously. They are Homo Zappiens' (Naslundh, 2001). These psychic abilities of Homo Zappiens are further pictured as necessarily belonging to the 'creative society' (Naslundh 2001, 14), which has already arrived, but presumably will be even more realized in the future.11 Learning-facilitators and schools are advised to consider the importance of the potentials of these youngsters, implying a reconsideration of their possible negative attitudes towards them (they only seem inattentive!). Although the ideas espoused by Veen and his adherents do not constitute a coherent vision of a future Utopia, they obviously contain an element of psycho-utopianism.

Here comes an important point to note that the transformative human development envisioned here is not primarily that of the mind, but of the brain (cf. the expression 'brain based learning'). The brain of learners and not of learning-facilitators is developed simply by the use of the new ICT. The content of the software seems to be only of marginal importance. Nevertheless, because 'the mind is the brain,' according to hard-core materialists such as the famous Daniel Dennett (1991), transformation of the brain presumably equals transformation of the mind.

Warwick (2003) claims that Cyborgs which can be said as human–computer alliances that will decide whether to let the human race continue or not. By merging their brain and nervous system with computer information processors, human beings will achieve an extra ordinary enhancement of their mental powers.

Now these extraordinary enhancement of the mental powers of the human race have more number of learners if we assume that there are two groups namely learners and learning-facilitators.

## Need of the Study

Here becomes important to study about the deficiency of psycho-utopianism among learning-facilitators. It can be understood by the following points:

- ▶ Learning-facilitators need to at par to learners so a learning-facilitator can control them as and when required.

- Learning-facilitator should be aware of the latest technology to adjust with change in learner learning-facilitator roles.
- For self-Esteem.
- To learn new technical skills so as to gain confidence about being able to learn new tools that will support.
- To accomplish more complex Task so that they can be with ease.

## *Variable Used*

- Psycho-Utopianism denoting the notion that the ideal society presupposes a 'new man,' that is, the psychological nature of man must change before society can change. Here Psycho-Utopianism among learning-facilitators reveal that society has changed, schools has changed but learning-facilitators need to accept psychologically that they need to change the mind-set for using Information and Communication Technology in classroom for effective teaching learning.
- Vulgarization Of Technology: Using the technology to the fullest.

## *Research Questions*

Q. To what extent traditional teaching technology is replaced by ICT?

Q. To what extent ICT is user friendly?

Q. Why Learners are more vibrant in using ICT than learning-facilitators?

Q. To what extent the missing human element in ICT is a barrier for effective Teaching-learning?

## Objectives

1. To find out the elements of ICT which are overpowering the traditional teaching technology
2. To find out the ways through which these gaps can be resolved
3. To find out the factors which provokes the reluctance in using technology among learning-facilitators
4. To find out the reasons why learners are more advanced than learning-facilitators in using technology
5. To enhance Psycho-Utopianism among learning-facilitators

## Delimitations

- The study is conducted in Lucknow City only.
- The sample is taken from CBSE.

## Research Methodology

- **Type of Research:** Descriptive research will be used in the study
- **Method of Research:** Survey Method will be used in this study. Data can be collected from the learning-facilitators
- **Approach of Research:** Quantitative and Qualitative approach will be used.
- **Population:** Uttar Pradesh one of the largest states of India and is having good economy also so this state is being selected for study. Lucknow city is the capital of Uttar Pradesh and all the CBSE Schools of Lucknow City are taken as a population.
- **Sample:** Non-probability or convenience sampling was used because questionnaires were taken from selected school whose selection was done area wise of the city. Not every CBSE school had an equal chance of being included in the sample. Out of the total CBSE schools of Lucknow the researcher will first of all select the sample each of from East, West, South, North and central of Lucknow city. Thus it will comprise of in total 10 schools. A sample of 10 CBSE Schools is taken. From each school 50 learning-facilitators are selected randomly. So in total there will be 500 learning-facilitators.
- **Tools used:** Self-constructed questionnaire is designed by the researcher to get data from learning-facilitators regarding the use of ICT in schools for teaching-learning.

## *Findings and Analysis*

1. To find out the elements of ICT which are overpowering the traditional teaching technology.

The data collected from learning-facilitators through questionnaire reveals that there are many elements in teaching through ICT which proves the transformation of education. The traditional approach of teaching consists of Learning-facilitator-centred learning, one pace applied to all, and studies during school hours through textbooks and emphasis on facts and recitation. Against this introduction of technology allowed teaching to be focused on individual learner needs, flexibility of place, time and pace of learning, immediate feedback, absenteeism of learning-facilitator is allowed, etc.

2. To find out the ways through which these gaps can be resolved.

Collected data from learning-facilitators revealed many ways through which the gaps between traditional teaching and teaching through ICT can be resolved. Though there are many advantages in teaching through ICT but still it does not hold the position where we can replace it with traditional teaching. It has its own disadvantages also which shows the importance of teaching through traditional measures. Out of them few are lack of personal contact (especially for language teaching), time-consuming for learning-facilitators, costly for learners, absence of emotions. The above drawback of ICT can be removed by combining traditional teaching with modern one in a reciprocal manner. Teaching through ICT can be done by considering psychological theories. The benefits which are received by teaching through ICT can be mentioned as issues of autonomous learning which can make learning effective as autonomy involves learners being aware of their own ways of learning. They need to utilize their strength and weaknesses where they use intrinsic motivation.

3. To find out the factors which provokes the reluctance in using technology among learning-facilitators.

From the data collected the researcher observed that there is an element of fear of letting go things out of control, a belief that they don't know the right skills, concerned about privacy or cyber-bullying, low efficacy in believing their own ability to produce tech-integrated classes, consumerist mentality is observed among elder learning-facilitators as learning-facilitators themselves have only used computers for entertainment and social interaction, lack of leadership, comfort with instructional strategies which learning-facilitators used for their learning and finally as it is always kept optional.

4. To find out the reasons why learners are more advanced than learning-facilitators in using technology.

The collected data revealed that the there are many reasons why learners are more advanced than learning-facilitators in using technology. One of the major reasons among them is that children have had technology in their lives since they were born. They are used to deal with ever-changing gadgets and so they manage to accept in easier ways. The ways through which the information is being processed in the minds of learners is different as they are getting information is totally different way. The dealings with problems, projects and learning are different as they get information in an easy way. To find out the ways through which the gaps in usage of technology by learners and learning-facilitators can be resolved

It becomes a need of the hour for learning-facilitators to figure out to what extent tech is disrupting their lives the least

Learners are very experimental and really push boundaries on the other hand learning-facilitators tend to be more cautious and so because of this confidence learners tend to know more than their learning-facilitators.

5. To enhance Psycho-Utopianism among learning-facilitators.

It is revealed from the data that constant changing in pattern of teaching makes difficult for learning-facilitators for implementing.

The wants and needs of the learning-facilitators should be made open and alert by providing the help as and when they require

Adoption of technology should be systematic at classroom level.

Training days for hesitant learning-facilitators should not be in the middle of the year.

Encouraging learning-facilitators to have a tool at home which will remove the pressure of performing under an alert situation and also allow them learn things at their own pace. This can help them to have tool awareness. To enhance Psycho-Utopianism learning-facilitators should be encourage treating their school tools as their personal tools.

## Suggestions

- Learning-facilitators should treat the adoption of technology as part of lesson planning.
- Use online education portfolio to evaluate learners.
- Though the tool that is used may be superior, but the level of comfort should be the matter of concern.
- Teaching the technology to learning-facilitators using peers to train and model can be more fruitful.
- For technology to also support in the professional learning process for learning-facilitators, it needs to become infused into their work habits.
- An infrastructure is required for ongoing workplace learning accompanied with more time to make it possible.
- Importantly, technology needs to be developed with learning-facilitators, not for learning-facilitators.
- And last but not the least: there should be an adequate academic policy, administration support of using technologies in education as one of the 'pillars' of efficient learning (Moore, 2002).

Chapter

# ICT: Learning in Own Way

 **Dolly Pachouri**

*Indian Convent School, Delhi*

## Preview at a Glance

Information and Communication Technology has become an integral part of everybody's life now-a-days. People are using it for several purposes and education is one of the main purposes for which ICT is being used. Facilitators and learners of every level are using ICT for teaching and learning purposes. The learners of secondary school are the digital natives; we cannot deprive them from using ICT. This study is an attempt to understand how the secondary school learners are using ICT for their learning. The aims of this study are to analyse the usage of ICT by secondary school level learners and what are the benefits and barriers that are being faced by them in the usage of the ICT for their learning. For the current study the researcher had formed questionnaire based on the review of the literature. Then the google form was made and mailed to the secondary school level learners for data collection. The data collected revealed that learners like using ICT for their learning but the learners are not able to access Internet in the school. Mostly, interactive white board are being used in the classroom space for teaching and learning purposes. The learners have stated that the major benefit of using ICT for learning is concretizing the concepts. Lack of accessibility of the technology is the major barrier in the usage of the ICT by the learners. This study opens up the further avenue for the researchers to examine the role of ICT in teaching by the facilitator.

## Introduction

Information and Communication Technology computes the infrastructure and components in a modernised way. It is basically an umbrella term that includes all technologies. It records information through different mediums like paper, magnetic tape, CD and DVD, flash memory, pen drive etc. (Rouse, 2005, as cited in Kulkarni 2016).

Information and Communication does not stand on its own. Information and Communication both has to go with the technology hand in hand and hence they cannot exist independently. If we view clearly that what is Information, Communication and Technology, then, the 'Information' is the data which is in the paper format or can say the electronic format. 'Communication' is done in person or electronically such as through E-mails, in writing, by voice or through telecommunications. A person may broadcast his or her views as well which he or she wants to communicate. 'Information Technology' is all about Software, Hardware and electronics whereas 'Communication Technology' is the thing which includes Software, Hardware and Protocols (Giles, 2017). The individuals need to be aware about one thing that technology is not only about what it is and how to use it but it also comprises the information related various aspects which is communicated through (Player-Koro, 2012). ICT although is a short form but it is itself a broad term (Information Communication and Technology) in terms of telecommunication, broadcast media, management system, audio visual processing, network based control system, transmission system and monitoring other functions as well (Techpedia, 2018).

ICT has given a new vision to the world by which we have created a global scenario which includes communication across the world who are living miles away but feels like living next door. ICT is a great invention through which we can modernize our world and it affects the society in a positive manner (Christensson, 2010).

If we look at the ICT tools for education, it can be infer through various researches that ICT can lead to better teaching methods and improved learning of the learners. ICT has a significant role in creating positive impact over the learners' achievement especially in terms of knowledge, comprehension, practical skill and presentation skill. For example in subjects like Mathematics, Science and Social Studies, ICT has played a vital role in combining all these aspects and providing a clear view to the learners to learn better (Kanvaria, 2015). If we look at the advantages of the ICT tools for education then we can say that with the use ICT and visuals a facilitator can teach in an effective manner and it can also improve the retentive memory of the learners. ICT helps the facilitator to explain the complex topics with better instructions. It also helps the learners to comprehend well whatever is taught by the facilitator. ICT helps in creating the interactive classrooms and making the lessons more joyous and enjoyable. Through ICT one can ensure the good attendance of the learners and we can expect the better concentration of the learners regarding the same (Mohanty, 2011; Nagpal, 2017).

There are also disadvantages of ICT tools for education. If someone is setting up the devices then that can be very troublesome and can consume a lot of time. It might not work sometimes and the person may lose the patience. The setup of the ICT can be expensive or say very expensive to afford by some institutions. Those who lack the experience of using the ICT tools may find it difficult to work with. It may be therefore hard for the facilitators to use if they lack experience for the same (Elco, 2012).

In the current study the researcher has tried to analyse the status of usage of ICT for learning at secondary school level and what are the benefits and challenges of using it according to secondary level learners.

## Objective
- To study the usage of ICT by secondary level learners for their learning inside as well as outside the school.
- To examine the benefit and barriers of usage of ICT as per secondary school learners.

## Review of Related Literature
Webb (2005), in his study had identified four effects of using ICT for learning. According to his study ICT promotes acceleration of cognitive domain, it helps the learners to relate the text with their real life experiences and hence learn in better manner, self-management by learners enhances and help learners in better presentation of their ideas.

Shraim and Khlaif (2010) in their study had identified that although ICT has been perceived to be a very useful in the teaching and learning by facilitators as well the learner, respectively. But the facilitators and learners face various challenges in the usage of ICT for teaching and learning. They are also not confident about the usage of ICT for teaching and learning practices.

Furlong and Davies (2012) in their study found out that usage of ICT in informal setups makes learning experience better for the learners and helps learners to understand things in much better way. ICT provides them to be in connection with different people for their learning at any place they are.

Ferguson, Faulkner, Whitelock and Sheehy (2015) in their study related to use of ICT in formal and informal settings, found out that the usage of ICT differs with respect to the settings and age of the learner. In formal settings, the usage of ICT is limited, whereas the learners use more ICT for learning in informal settings.

## Hypotheses
- ICT has been used by secondary school learners, outside as well inside the school for their learning.
- ICT usage is more outside then inside the school.

## Rationale
ICT is evolving with time and no one has been deprived of it. The learners of every level are it School or Higher education are using ICT for some or the other purposes. This study was done to analyze how the learners of secondary school level are using ICT for their learning purposes and what are the advantages and disadvantages of using ICT according to them.

## Methodology
- **Sampling:** The learners of secondary school level were chosen as sample.
- **Sampling techniques:** Convenient sampling technique was used for choosing the participants for the current study.

- **Method:** Survey method was used for data collection.
- **Tool for data collection:** Questionnaire was used for data collection from the learners of secondary schools.
- **Procedure of data collection:** Based on the review of related literature a questionnaire was formed. A google form was made for doing the survey. The form was sent to several secondary school learners for data collection.

## Results and Findings

- 80% of like usage of ICT for their learning but 20% do not like usage of ICT for their learning.
- Usage of ICT by learners for different purposes is given below.

| Purpose | Never | Rarely | Sometimes | Often | All the Time |
|---|---|---|---|---|---|
| Do homework on the computer | 20% | 10% | 2% | 30% | 20% |
| Search the Internet for home and school work | 00% | 20% | 20% | 30% | 30% |
| Check school websites for announcements etc. | 30% | 10% | 20% | 20% | 20% |

- 70% learners accessed Internet in their school in last 6 months, whereas rest 30% didn't access Internet in their school in last 6 months.
- All the learners have access any of the following, desktop computer, laptop, tablet PC, in their school in last 6 months.
- Usage of ICT tools for learning purposes by the learners are given below.

| ICT Tool | Never | Rarely | Sometimes | Often | All the Time |
|---|---|---|---|---|---|
| Desktop computer with no Internet | 60% | 30% | 10% | 00% | 00% |
| Desktop computer with Internet | 60% | 00% | 10% | 20% | 10% |
| Interactive white boards | 30% | 20% | 00% | 50% | 00% |
| Laptops, smartphones, tablets with no Internet | 10% | 60% | 30% | 00% | 00% |
| Laptops, smartphones, tablets with Internet | 00% | 10% | 10% | 20% | 60% |

- Confidence of doing several things with ICT.

| Task | None | A Little | Somewhat | A Lot |
|---|---|---|---|---|
| Producing a text using word processing programmer | 60% | 20% | 00% | 20% |
| Edit digital photographers or other images | 20% | 30% | 20% | 30% |
| Email a file to someone | 30% | 30% | 10% | 30% |
| Install software | 30% | 30% | 30% | 10% |

- Agreement on benefits of using ICT for learning.

| Benefits | Strongly Agree | Agree | Don't Know | Disagree | Strongly Disagree |
|---|---|---|---|---|---|
| Interaction and sharing enhances | 50% | 30% | 10% | 10% | 00% |
| Concretizing the concepts | 40% | 60% | 00% | 00% | 00% |
| Easy and convenient communication | 50% | 50% | 00% | 00% | 00% |
| Improves self-esteem of the learner | 60% | 30% | 10% | 00% | 00% |
| Motivation enhance | 60% | 30% | 00% | 10% | 00% |

- Agreement on barriers of using ICT for learning.

| Barriers | Strongly Agree | Agree | Don't Know | Disagree | Strongly Disagree |
|---|---|---|---|---|---|
| Illiteracy related to technology | 30% | 40% | 30% | 00% | 00% |
| Lack of accessibility of technology | 20% | 70% | 00% | 10% | 00% |
| Curriculum restrictions | 40% | 30% | 20% | 10% | 00% |
| Lack of time in classroom | 40% | 50% | 10% | 00% | 00% |
| Cost effective | 50% | 40% | 00% | 10% | 00% |

## Discussion and Analysis

From the above data it can be analysed that more than half of the learners like to use ICT for their learning but rest of them do not like to do so. If we consider the purpose of using ICT then there was not even a single learner who opted 'never' to search the Internet for home and school work. Although we could find that those students who searched the Internet for their work do not use it to check their school websites for announcements which shows that they did not like to use it for such purposes. Using Internet in the school was not common but using the desktop computers, laptops, etc. was common for 'all' the learners in the last 6 months. Hence this shows that the school also focuses on the ICT tools for education and provides the same to the learners for their benefit. There was not even a single student who said that he or she had never use the laptops, smartphones, tablets with Internet. Majority or more than 50% learners are there who had use laptops, smartphones and tablets with Internet. There were more than 50% learners for the confidence of using word processing programmer and there was near about 30% ratio each for confidence of using ICT to install software or to email a file to someone. No single student agreed that interaction and sharing do not get enhanced by the use of ICT. They agreed that it concretize the concepts, makes the communication easy and convenient. It also improves self-esteem as per their views. Although the learners also agreed that illiteracy related to technology is the barrier for ICT learners and the major barrier in using ICT for learning found was cost effectiveness. Curriculum restriction, lack of time in classrooms, lack of accessibility and Technology were also the barriers according to the learners. Not even a single student disagreed to any one of these barriers. Thus it can be said that ICT is one of the important or say vital tool for learning. Without ICT, they could feel helpless. ICT helps them a lot in their homework, learning, understanding, communicating, and concretizing the concepts and many other things. It also helps in easy and convenient communication. ICT can be one of the best tools for learning if the barriers like illiteracy related to technology or cost-effectiveness will be reduced. We can have ICT across the world for the betterment of the learners. If we support this system and would encourage learners to read and learn more with the help of ICT then we can have the best education facility provided to the learners.

## Conclusion

The ICT has been playing role in education from many years. But at this era of technology no one is deprived of its usage in some or the other way. Many researchers have worked on the field of usage of ICT by the learners at different levels in education and it has been found by them that ICT plays very important role in their learning. At present the Indian school system is divided into five levels, out of these five levels the current study focused on the usage of ICT by the learners of secondary level of school education. It has been found out that the learners use ICT for their learning in different ways but they face barriers in its usage. It has also inferred that the learner of this age use ICT more at their home place as compared to school. It can be said that usage of ICT in informal setting is more as compared to the formal setting. Infrastructure and accessibility to the resources are the major barriers faced by them. But since the usage of ICT benefits them in several ways like concretizing their understanding and convenient communication, so some how they manage to use it and do their work with its help.

Chapter

13

# Perception of School Learners towards ICT in Science Learning

✎ **Geetika Nidhi**
*Integral University, Lucknow, UP*

## Preview at a Glance

Electronic technologies such as television, audio-video and computers have capability of revolutionizing the quality, productivity and availability of education. Ambivalent attitude towards ICT could be deterrent to using computer in learning environment. It seems likely that learners attitude towards acceptance of communication technology may be important in integration of electronic technologies in classroom. Thus to investigate the existing picture this study was conducted to find out the perception of learners towards the use of ICT in learning science in Lucknow city. This is a qualitative study of descriptive survey type which was employed to see the attitude of learners and learning-facilitators towards the changing technologies. A sample of 200 learners was taken from secondary schools of Lucknow city. A structured questionnaire titled ICT Attitude Test using four point scale was used to collect data. The result of findings depicted that most of the learners had positive perception towards use of computers and information technology in learning science but they lacked support from the learning-facilitators. They believed use of computers in the class can help them perform better if they get sufficient support from the learning-facilitators indicating that information and communication technology can be instrumental in improvising learning of learners.

## Introduction

Electronic technologies such as television, audio-video and computers have capability of revolutionizing the quality, productivity and availability of education. ICT as a term encompasses a range of human-devised hardware, software and telecommunications technologies that facilitate communication and sharing of information across boundaries and which may be used to generate arts experiences and objects. The use of ICT in education offers new opportunities to deliver information and for enhancing learning processes. In order to best utilise ICT, digital and information competency are required to access and utilise e-learning and online materials, and to appropriately select and operate digital materials and technologies With expanding arena of teaching and learning efforts are made to make learning effective through use of inclusion of ICT. The impact of using it will be more if the attitude of learners are known as human –computer interaction is a complex phenomenon and feelings involved with the relationship are difficult to identify.

Ambivalent attitude towards ICT could be deterrent to using computer in learning environment. It seems likely that learners attitude towards acceptance of communication technology may be important in integration of electronic technologies in classroom. Before education incorporates the new electronic media educators need to discern what is different about it and this process may lead to better consensus though the exploration of attitude of learners towards it. This study is an effort to investigate the perception of secondary school learners towards use of information and communication technology in learning and specifically in science subjects as it includes a range of topics and age level and can play a major role in enhancing and extending practical work.

## Review of Literature

The studies conducted all over the world show that the understanding, knowledge and comprehension skills of the learners can be improved by including changing technologies in teaching learning environment This process requires multidisciplinary approaches involving learning-facilitators, researchers, technologists, developers and learners (Hartley, 2007). Among them, learning-facilitators play a pivotal role in creating ICT-mediated learning environments (Lim, 2007). In a study of ICT integration in Singaporean schools, Lim (2007) analysed the necessary and sufficient conditions for effective integration of ICT in the classroom and the supporting context of the school. These conditions include classroom management issues, availability of ICT tools, establishment of disciplinary and educational rules, division of labour among learning-facilitators, learning-facilitator assistants and learners, and supporting school policies. Suwana (2004) conducted a study on primary learners and observed that learner favoured use of computers in classroom. Jayraman (2006) in his study revealed that learners had positive attitude towards use of computers.

Patel(2008) in his study shares that it seems to be that an early age is a highly relevant factor for the learning-facilitators who have a positive attitude towards the incorporation of ICT (Shaunessy, 2007; Aduwa-Ogiegbaeni, 2008) because those who are young have more teaching experience with ICT and therefore, they feel more involved with their use than older learning-facilitators (Hammond *et al.*, 2008a) observed that both learners and learning-facilitators had favourable attitude towards study using computers. Noor and Jeyavany (2012) in their study observed that learners had positive attitude towards use of computers but learning-facilitators were not well versed to use it.

## Research Methodology

### Purpose of the Study

Success of an endeavour resides in the perceptual ground provided to it thus this study was undertaken. The purpose of the study was to investigate the perception of secondary school learners of Lucknow city towards the use of information and communication technology in learning science.

### Research Questions

1. What do the secondary school learners feel towards using of information and communication technology in learning science?
2. What is the attitude of learning-facilitators towards use of Information and communication technology in learning science?
3. What is the status of facilities provided by the school for use of information and communication technology in schools?

### Objectives of the Study

1. To examine the perception of secondary school learners towards use of information and communication technology in learning science.
2. To study the support of learning-facilitators in using Information and communication technology to learn science.
3. To investigate the facilities provided by the schools for the use of information and communication technology in learning science.

### Research Design

Since this study involves the projection of learners perception of learners towards the use of information and communication technology in learning and the support provided by the learning-facilitator and the school therefore the research design for this study was a qualitative study of descriptive survey type as the of learners of the learners need to be analysed on attitude scale. The survey method is chosen as it gathers data from the relatively large number of cases and brings about the existing picture of the conditions that prevail

### Population

The population of the study are the secondary school learners studying science.

### Sample

The sample comprises of 200 learners of secondary schools of Lucknow city. There were 118 males and 82 female learners. Six schools of urban area were taken in which two schools was government and four were private which had the facility of computers in their school. The learner were of standard seventh and eighth. This included learners in the age group of twelve to fourteen years.

## Tool

Tool proves to be instrumental in collection of data. As the researcher had to study the perception of the learners towards information and communication technology so a questionnaire was made by the researcher to study it. The tool used to collect data was an information and communication technology perception Questionnaire constructed by the researcher. It consists of 18 items, first 10 items to observe perception of learners, 4 items to study the support of learning-facilitators and 4 items to observe the facilities provided in the school. The responses were to be marked on four point Likert scale of strongly disagree, disagree, agree and strongly agree which provided the perception of learners towards use of computer, support of their learning-facilitators and the facilities provided by the school.

## Data Collection

Data if not collected with precautions may not give the correct picture. So, all the efforts were made to get genuine responses from the learners. The institutions were coordinated before the collection of data. A cordial environment was created to get the responses of the learners before the administration of the questionnaire. The data was collected by administering the questionnaire on the learners. The respondents were given proper instruction by the researcher before taking their responses related to the questionnaire. They were assured that the information they were giving would be kept confidential so they should respond to best what they feel like. The test was administered for 30 minutes and after that completely filled copies were taken back from the learners. Their responses were analysed using the frequency and percentage of the learners showing their response towards each of the item. The observationswere taken on the basis of their responses and inferences were drawn.

## Limitations

The study was conducted only in Lucknow city, only secondary school learners of science stream of seventh and eighth standard were considered.

## Analysis

Objectives of the study were observed using the items of the questionnaire on the responses of the learners. The responses observed were divided into three categories their perception towards use information and communication technology in learning science, support of learning-facilitators for use of computers and the facility provided in school and analysed accordingly as shown in the tables. Frequency of response and percentage was used to analyse the data collected which is shown in the tables shown below

Objective 1: To examine the perception of secondary school learners towards use of information and communication technology in learning science.

# Perception of School Learners towards ICT in Science Learning

Table 1

| S. No. | Item | S.D F | S.D % | D F | D % | A F | A % | SA F | SA % |
|---|---|---|---|---|---|---|---|---|---|
| 1. | I enjoy use of Internet while studying. | 12 | 06 | 22 | 11 | 86 | 43 | 80 | 40 |
| 2. | I study effectively with use of ICT. | 00 | 00 | 24 | 12 | 94 | 47 | 82 | 41 |
| 3. | I feel comfortable when I study through Internet and computers. | 04 | 02 | 36 | 18 | 90 | 45 | 70 | 35 |
| 4. | I find studying science interesting using ICT. | 12 | 06 | 38 | 19 | 116 | 58 | 34 | 17 |
| 5. | I am less embarrassed when I use ICT to study. | 00 | 00 | 04 | 02 | 140 | 70 | 56 | 28 |
| 6. | I remember the content for longer time when I study through ICT. | 18 | 09 | 34 | 17 | 88 | 44 | 60 | 30 |
| 7. | I would like to attend classes which use ICT to teach. | 12 | 06 | 40 | 20 | 92 | 46 | 56 | 28 |
| 8. | I support the use of ICT in the classroom. | 18 | 09 | 48 | 24 | 80 | 40 | 54 | 27 |
| 9. | I prefer learning with ICT than learning-facilitator. | 38 | 19 | 40 | 20 | 60 | 30 | 62 | 31 |
| 10. | Learning through ICT makes me confident. | 18 | 09 | 32 | 16 | 84 | 42 | 66 | 33 |

The first objective was to study the perception of learners towards learning through use of ICT. On the analysis of responses it was seen that 83% of learners enjoyed the use of Internet and computers while learning while 17% did not enjoy its use. 41% of learners strongly agreed that they learn efficiently using computers. 80% of the learners were comfortable when they used ICT to study; only 20% of them were not comfortable in using computers to study science. 58% of learners agreed that they observed learning through ICT interesting while 17 % strongly agreed to it. 98% of the learners said that they were less embarrassed when they used ICT to study. 78% of learners like to attend classes using ICT while 22 % of them disagreed to attend the classes using ICT for learning. 27% of learners strongly supported the use of internet and computers in classroom. 61% of learners preferred to learn through ICT than learning-facilitators. 75% of them said that learning through ICT makes them confident while 16% of them did not agree to this.

Objective 2: To study the support of learning-facilitators in using information and communicationtechnology to learnscience.

The table 2 shows us the responses regarding the support learning-facilitators provide in using ICT to learn science.

Table 2

| S. No. | Item | SD | | D | | A | | SA | |
|---|---|---|---|---|---|---|---|---|---|
| | | f | % | F | % | f | % | F | % |
| 11. | My learning-facilitators make use of computers and Internet while teaching. | 58 | 29 | 50 | 25 | 52 | 26 | 40 | 20 |
| 12. | The learning-facilitators are always ready to explain us content using Internet and power point presentations. | 32 | 16 | 62 | 31 | 80 | 40 | 26 | 13 |
| 13. | Our learning-facilitators regularly take us to computer lab to teach other subjects. | 68 | 34 | 64 | 32 | 40 | 20 | 28 | 14 |
| 14. | Learning-facilitators are always ready to fulfil our queries regarding computers. | 20 | 10 | 94 | 47 | 50 | 25 | 36 | 18 |

The second objective was to study the support of learning-facilitators to the use of ICT in classroom. 20% of the learners strongly agreed that their learning-facilitators used computers and Internet while teaching, 54% of the learners gave negative response regarding this. 40% of the learners reported that their learning-facilitators were always ready to explain the content using ICT while 31% of the learners disagreed to this. 66% of the learners reported that their learning-facilitators do not take them regularly to computer laboratory to study. Only 14% of the learners strongly agreed that their learning-facilitators regularly take them to the computer laboratory. 57 % of the learners confirmed that their learning-facilitators were not ready to fulfil their queries regarding ICT.

Objective 3: To investigate the facilities provided by the school for the use of information and communication in learning science.

Table 3

| S. No. | Item | SD | | D | | A | | SA | |
|---|---|---|---|---|---|---|---|---|---|
| | | F | % | F | % | f | % | F | % |
| 15. | Computer laboratory in my school is well equipped with Internet. | 14 | 07 | 44 | 22 | 80 | 40 | 62 | 31 |
| 16. | The number of computers in the laboratory is appropriate. | 62 | 31 | 94 | 47 | 34 | 17 | 10 | 05 |
| 17. | There are smart boards in my class are used while teaching. | 60 | 30 | 70 | 35 | 44 | 22 | 26 | 13 |
| 18. | We are always appreciated for using ICT to study in school. | 28 | 14 | 52 | 26 | 82 | 41 | 38 | 19 |

On analysing the responses of learners 71% of learners said that their computer laboratory was well equipped they did not have regular Internet connection. 78% of the learners observed that the numbers of computers in the laboratory was inappropriate. 65% of learners said that learning-facilitators did not use the smart boards in the classroom. 60% of the learners observed that they were appreciated for using computers in the school.

## Discussion

The responses of the learners are intended ensure the effective utilization of information and communication technology in learning in future directions. It shows that learner is receptive towards use of newer technologies like ICT in learning. They feel comfortable when they are taught using computer aided instruction. It also makes their learning effective and long lasting. They remain emotionally stable when they learn through Internet and computers. They become confident and interested when they learn through ICT. Though the support from learning-facilitators and the facilities was not sufficient be benefitted from, their inclination towards the science increased, when they learnt the subject using information and communication technologies. Some of the schools and learning-facilitators depicted support to learning of science through information and communication technologies.

## *Findings*

The major findings of study are:

- Majority of the learners enjoyed use of ICT and observed learning through it interesting.
- Most of the learners were less embarrassed when the used ICT for learning of science
- Most of the learners felt that they were more confident on learning through ICT.
- Support for using ICT while learning was shown by the learners.
- It was seen that support of learning-facilitators was not appreciable and the lacked in the knowledge of ICT.
- Some schools were well equipped in the resources of ICT but they were not properly utilized.
- Most of the learners said that the school preferred the use of computers and Internet while learning.
- The schools promoted the use of ICT in learning in some of the schools

## *Educational Implications*

From the present study it can be seen that learner find learning through ICT interesting its use can make learning effective.

- The learning-facilitators need to increase their knowledge to properly utilize the resources of the school.

- The use information and communication technology can be effective in motivating learners and increasing their learning abilities.
- Learning environment can be improved by the use of ICT in learning other subjects also.
- The quality of learner performance can also be improved with the use of information and communication technology in school.
- Inclusion of ICT in schools initially should be done at lower level and then increased
- Proper utilization of the resources and technology can be taught to the learners.
- Learning-facilitators should be trained to make optimum utilization of emerging technologies.

## Conclusion

The study brings about the perception of learners towards the use of ICT in learning science. It was observed that most of the learners observed the use of ICT interesting and felt that they can learn better using ICT the study also indicated that the support of learning-facilitators in using ICT was not much there need to be more support by the learning-facilitators. Although the institutions had proper infrastructure but proper direction is required to make complete use of available resources. Thus we can conclude that learner perceive ICT as vital tool towards learning. The learning-facilitator and institutional resources are to be adeptly employed so that the learning conditions can improve in the schools.

# Chapter 14

# ICT Mediated Pre-Service Learning-Facilitator Training

> **KartikeswarBehera**
> *Special B.Ed. College, Ganjam, Odisha*

## Preview at a Glance

The use of Information and Communication Technology (ICT) for quality education in both pre-service learning-facilitator education and in-service learning-facilitator education is considered vital for which it is gaining wider ground day by day. Appropriate application of ICT provides the learning-facilitator with desired inputs in the direction of building their capacity in relation to teaching competency. The chapter focuses on integrating ICT into class room process at secondary stage pertaining to English Prose, Poetry and Grammar lessons of class IX. At the outset the needs of the learner learning-facilitators were identified basing on their prioritize needs like preparation of power point presentation, animation, preparation and display of Audio cassette with required sound effect, and delivery of dialogues with proper modulation of voice etc. Then they were trained in the technique of content analysis in relation to prose and poetry lesson and the ways of concept mapping in respect of English Grammar lesson. They were also made aware of how to write instructional objectives in terms of pupil behaviour. They prepared content based visuals with integrating ICT during class room transaction. Accordingly Interventions were planned and extended for a period of two weeks based on a time-table. They were also acquainted with integration of visuals and pre-recorded audio cassettes containing songs and dialogues with sound effect which were used during presentation of lessons. As it was a single group pre-test design, the pre assessment and post assessment results were compared and it was observed that there was considerable improvement among the learners pertaining to knowledge and skill in the presentation of lesson plans with ICT integration.

## Introduction

Use of ICT has brought about a momentum in the use of materials in the teaching-learning process both in School Education and Learning-facilitator Education. Introduction of SMART class BLENDED Learning have been profitably used by the learning-facilitators and learning-facilitator educators. Integration of ICT into class room process has turned over a new leaf in the 21$^{st}$ century. Computer Based Instruction (CBI) and Computer Added Learning (CAL) are often used terms at present. A number of studies have been conducted across the states and the findings of the study reveal that. Both the pre-service and In-service learning-facilitators have been imparted training on the use of ICT in the class room and their knowledge and skills have been upgraded in that direction. Research studies revealed that the learning-facilitators were observed deficient in the use of computer due to lack of practice, improper training of learning-facilitators, days functional computers, software (Iqubal, Z 2016). Further it was reported by the RIE, Bhopal that the pre-service pupil learning-facilitators the pre-service learner are neither exposed or they use multimedia packages based on the observation (Kanvaria, 2009). Kanvaria,there, further stated that it is a felt need 'to orient the pupil learning-facilitators to develop educational multimedia presentation in Mathematics during Pre-service T.E. Programmes'. The Researcher of the present study capitalizing the above observations made by two prominent Researchers attempted to do something vital for the larger interest of the Pre-service learners learning-facilitators of special B.Ed. college, Kodala in Ganjam district of Odisha.

It is an established fact that methods and materials go together in the teaching learning process and if there is any deficiency in both the aspects, the teaching-learning process will tend to failure in achieving the objectives of the lessons. The Researcher has some experiences that when teaching-learning materials are appropriated used in the class the learner take interest in observing the activities going on in the class. Hence the Researcher felt ardently that the learner-learning-facilitators of special B.Ed. class should be oriented about the integration of the ICT into class room process.

ICT facilitates quick access to information, communicating networking teaching-learning and research work. Thus it has two major functions, communication and access. While communication includes use of net, internet, chatting and browsing, access encompasses information, resources, materials and databases.

## Role of ICT in Education

- ICT can be taken an agent of change pertaining to pedagogical shift in respect of latest methodology.
- ICT tends to enhancing quality education.
- It also enriches Educational Management
- It paves the way for content enrichment
- It facilitates research and development
- It enriches the learning environment
- It enhances professional development and administration.

# ICT Mediated Pre-Service Learning-Facilitator Training

## Rationale

The learner-learning-facilitators of B.Ed. class perform badly while delivering practice lessons without taking the help of ICT. The Researcher experienced in course of in house seminars that they requires support in various aspect like browsing, Internet, preparing Power Point etc. to fulfil their needs, the Researcher conducted a study title 'Effectiveness of ICT mediated Learning-facilitator Training Programme in the Pre-Service B.Ed. Class'.

## Objectives of the Study

The objectives of the study were:

- To identify the specific needs of the learner-learning-facilitators regarding technicalities of ICT integration into classroom process.
- To familiarize them with the techniques of integrating ICT in the class room.
- To demonstrate model lessons using lesson plans and related materials.
- To examine how far the learners-learning-facilitators are able to prepare model lesson plans with the help of ICT.
- To assess their competency in the use of ICT during transaction of lessons.
- To assess the achievement of the learners of both the group in the field as an effect of intervention of ICT mediated learning in language classes.

## Hypotheses

- There will be improvement in the performance of the learner-learning-facilitators in integrating ICT into class room process.
- There exist no significant difference between the post-test Mean Achievement Scores of Experimental Group and Control Group of the school learners.

### Delimitation of the Study

The study concentrated on the following aspect.

- The prose and poetry lessons of Class-IX were taken into account for the study which included
- One prose lesson (The Swimmer Who Does not Use Her Legs)
- One poem i.e. Home and Love
- One Grammar lesson i.e. Article (Determiner)
- The learning-facilitator teaching English in Class-IX was selected as mentor who has adequate knowledge in the content-cum-methodology.

## Methodology

- **Design:** It was single group pre and post assessment experimental design with intervention in between for the learner learning-facilitators. Again it was a pre-test post-test control group design for the learners of class-IX.

## Sample

Purposive sampling technique was adopted for selection of 35 learner learning-facilitators of B.Ed. class.

- **Tools:** Need Identification Questionnaire, Pre and Post Assessment Questionnaire, Feedback analysis Format, Observation Schedule were used.
- **Statistical Techniques:** Calculation of percentage, Mean, SD, t-value were used for analysis and interpretation of data.

## Procedure of the Experiment

At first the learner-learning-facilitators were trained to prepare lesson plans and how to present the same through power point on completion of the model teaching learning process. They were made aware of developing observation schedule and how to use them (some learners and learning-facilitator educators were treated as observers having some expertise in the content-cum-methodology of English and use of ICT). Then they were assigned to prepare lesson plans other than the lessons demonstrated by the Researcher having adequate knowledge and skill in preparing lesson plans and use of ICT. The learners were asked to work in small groups (3-4) while preparing lesson plans integrating ICT. The group leader was asked to present on behalf of the group. In the second phase individual learner-trainees (short listed learner learning-facilitator) were asked to present the lesson with the use of ICT. During group work the Researcher and the mentor monitored the work and provided on-site support in the way of addition and deletion.

Then six sessions were devoted for presentation followed by observation using observation schedule with a 5-point rating scale. Observations were shared among the learner-learning-facilitators of both section of B.Ed. class. The Researcher specifically and overly assessed the performance of the learner-learning-facilitator with the help of another learning-facilitator-educator/ mentor.

It was a two way assessment i.e. process assessment and product assessment. At first the learner-learning-facilitators performance in the use of ICT integration class room was assessed.

Then the performance of the learners pertaining to comprehension (prose and poetry) grammar and vocabulary were assessed in order to know the effectiveness of the ICT mediated learning. Out of 24 learners in Class-IX, they were divided into two groups on the basis of the pre-test and in each group learners were taken. As the learners-learning-facilitators extended intervention on prose, poetry, vocabulary and grammar, these areas were assessed after intervention. The test items were on reading comprehension use of vocabulary and functional grammar. Test items carried 30 marks, 10 marks in each sub-skill viz. comprehension, vocabulary and grammar. Then the performance of learners were assessed in relation to above sub-skills and compared between the Experimental group and Control group.

# ICT Mediated Pre-Service Learning-Facilitator Training

## Task Analysis

- At the out-set a content analysis exercise was undertaken on the prose and poem lesson.
- For teaching and learning of Grammar (use of Article) concept mapping exercise was undertaken.
- They were acquainted with the techniques of preparing power point highlighting main idea, supporting ideas followed by comprehension questions.
- Objectives of the lesson in behavioural terms.
- Dividing the prose lessons into SGPs (Sense Group Paragraphs) and clubbing the stanzas of the poem (as an example one prose, one poem and one Grammar lesson was included for demonstrate and that got place in the power point.
- Preparing visuals, check lists and observation schedule using rating scale.

## Classroom Process

- Class: IX
- Subject: English (Prose)
- Topic: 'The Swimmer Who Does not need Her Legs!'

Lesson Objectives: After transaction of the lesson the learners will be able to;

- Skim and scan the text and comprehend the same
- Make use of the language items like unbelievable, marathon, in spite of, at a stretch in sentences.
- Write a composition using the central theme of the text.
- Class: IX
- Subject: English (Poem)
- Topic: 'Home and Love'

Lesson Objectives: On completion of the lesson, the learners will be able

- To answer how sweetness of home link up with love.
- To answer why it is say Home and Love are very wide and gracious.
- Appreciate the beauty of the poem and recite the lines rhythmically
- Use the vocabulary items like bitterness, tenderly, gracious, hand and gloves, divine etc.
- Class: IX
- Subject: English (Grammar)
- Topic: Article

Lesson Objectives: On completion of the lesson, the learners will be able

- Identify the articles Indefinite and Definite Article
- Used the articles a, an (Indefinite Article) the (Definite Article)– in the appropriate places

## Concept Mapping (English Grammar-Teaching Point Article)

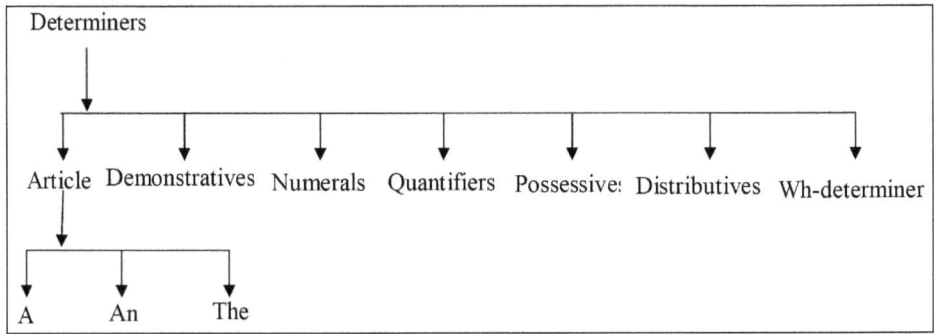

## Sample of a 5E Model Lesson Plan (Constructivist Approach)

| Steps | Learning-facilitator's Activity | Learner's Activity |
|---|---|---|
| Engagement | A the participants to look at it carefully and answer the following questions.<br>1. What is man doing in the picture?<br>2. Does he look physically normal like us?<br>3. What abnormalities do you mark?<br>4. How could he do the work without legs?<br>5. What shall we call him?<br>   a) Disabled<br>   b) Differently abled<br>6. Do you know his name?<br>Asks-<br>Q. 1. Could you name some differently abled persons who were highly successful in their lives?<br>Let's read a lesson and see how a differently abled girl became successful in her life. The lesson is in your text and it is 'The Swimmer who does not need her legs!' | Bhima Bhoi, Helen Keller Rabindra Jain read the paragraphs They identify the words like handicapped, unbelievable, convey, at a stretch, coach etc.<br>HukeHar (Ammerica) |
| Exploration | Asks learners to read first four paragraphs silently and try to know the dream of Janaki and how she prepared herself to fulfil her dream. After the silent reading is over, the researcher divides the whole class into seven groups as per feasibility of the class and gives each two groups one sense group to read and locate the unfamiliar words and expressions and try to guess their meaning in the context in order to understand the theme of the text. | Read the SGPs silently, discuss among themselves in the groups and explore the main idea/ theme and the key language items. |

# ICT Mediated Pre-Service Learning-Facilitator Training

| | | |
|---|---|---|
| Explanation | Asks the following questions to the learners to help them understand the text. She/he ask global, local, inferential questions and questions beyond the text to take the learners to the reflective level. Moreover, questions should be so framed that the learners are able to relate the text to their real life. Asks different groups and creates opportunities for the other groups to react. | Members of the group respond.<br><br>Note the key points written on the BB. |

Group 1and 2

Q. 1. What is the 1st paragraph about? (Global)
Q. 2. Who is C. N. Janaki? (factual)
Q. 3. Which channel did she cross? (factual)
Q. 4. What is described as 'unbelievable' in the Para?
Q. 5. Janaki is a handicapped person. Why is she called handicapped? (Read last Para of 'Lead in')
Q. 6. A handicapped person like Janaki could swim across the English channel. How? (inferential) (If the learners do not answer it the learning-facilitator tells- Let's read the next paragraphs to get the answer to this question).

Group 3and 4

1. What is the 2nd paragraph about? (global)
2. When did Janaki get the idea of swimming the English Channel? (factual)
3. Read the text and try to guess the meaning of 'convey' (clue- our proposal to go on a picnic and we convey this to the Hm.)
4. Read the third line of the second paragraph. 'So she conveyed this-----' what does it refer to here? (Factual)
5. What did Janaki do to fulfil her wish? (factual)
6. What was the reply of the academy? (factual)
7. What was the first condition? (factual)
8. What was the 2nd condition? ( factual)
9. By acquiring skill in marathon swimming what did the Association want Janaki to do?
(clue- Read the last two lines of 2nd condition)

Group 5 and 6

1. What is the third Para about? (global)
2. What did Janki do to fulfil the conditions? (factual)
3. What was she able to do after four years of teaching? (factual)
4. What is the word used in the paragraph which means 'at a stretch' (clue: read the last two lines of the 3rd paragraph)
5. He had seen me swim. Who had seen and whom? (referential)

6. Was the training in Bangalore sufficient for her? Why do you think so? (factual/ referential)
7. What is NIS? (clue: see the glossary)

Group 7and8

1. What is the fourth Para about? (global)
2. What did she do with the help of Thimaiah National Academy of Adventure? (factual)
3. Who was her couch there? (factual)
4. What did she learn there? (factual)
5. Why did she choose Arabian Sea to take the training of swimming? (clue: read condition)

General Questions:

1. How did Janki become successful in her attempt? (factual)
2. What qualities did Janki possess? (Global)
3. Why is it difficult to swim across the English Channel? (predictive)

(write the key words/expressions on the BB)

Read aloud (if necessary) to demonstrate the pronunciation/ intonation pattern of some sentences/ words for the learners. The slow learners are asked to read a line or two for encouraging them to take part and improve. Help learners to use language to read and speak, listen to others and interact. Goes into the text, analyses the text and goes beyond the text. (On the whole a language context of learning L1/L2 needs to be created. The learners will be encouraged to ask Questions.)

| | | |
|---|---|---|
| Elaboration | Language Work: | Members of the group respond. |
| Evaluation | Distribute language activity work among the groups. Write one example with use of suffix to the root word. Learners may add 'suffix' to the given words to get some new words. | Note the key points written on the BB. |

Group 1 and 2

Nation + al = National

National + ity = Nationality

National + ise= Nationalize

Exercise: i) continue

ii) Believe

iii) Success

Group 3 and 4

# ICT Mediated Pre-Service Learning-Facilitator Training

| | |
|---|---|
| Asks the learners to write some sentences using the following phrases 'in spite of', at a stretch', 'struck by'. | Add appropriate suffixes to the words as shown in the examples. |
| Group 5 and 6 | |
| Asks the learner to identify the sentence in which 'be able to, is used. (Para 1to 4) | Courage, allow, similar, learn, successful. |
| Now write some sentences thinking of what you are able to do in some situation like this. | |
| Example: I am a bowler in the team but able to score some runs. | Learners write or take part in oral discussion |
| Group 7 and 8 | |
| Asks the participants to find out the words (locate by scanning) that take prefixes to or opposites. (unbelievable (Un-) | |
| Learners are further encouraged to find out other words which can take the prefixes like – 'in' 'dis' 'un' etc. | |
| (Give these activities to different groups to do in work sheets, Discusses the activities of each group in the class.) | |
| Here the learning-facilitator focuses on exercises for application of the theme in different situation | |
| Diagram | |
| Janaki | |
| Struck by polio | |
| Handicapped by legs | |
| Dreamt to swim the English channel | |
| Reported to English channel swimming association | |
| Kept two conditions | |
| to spend 10 hours in water to do marathon swimming | |
| began training in Bangalore began training in Arabian sea | |
| become able to swim for learn to spend long hour in water | |
| 10 hours | |
| Ques. Write a paragraph using the above diagram. | |
| Home Task: | |
| Some differently abled learners of your school want to write a letter to the collector to help them. Write the application. | |

## Results and Discussion

(The observers are required to circle the number corresponding to the statements showing indicators)

**Table1: Performance ofLearnerLearning-facilitators before Intervention**

N= 35

| Sl. No. | Indicators | Before Intervention % | |
|---|---|---|---|
| | | Could do | Could not do |
| 1. | The presenter stated the objectives in behavioural terms. | 20 | 80 |
| 2. | Lesson plan was in completed form | 30 | 70 |
| 3. | Power Point presentation | 15 | 85 |
| 4. | Use of Visuals | 25 | 75 |
| 5. | Use of Dialogues | 25 | 75 |
| 6. | Recitation of the poem using Audio cassette | 20 | 80 |
| 7. | Concept mapping | 15 | 85 |
| 8. | Interactive question answer using interactive video CD | 22 | 78 |
| 9. | Presentation of the concerned observation schedule in filled in form | 25 | 75 |

The above table shows that the learners are very weak in power point presentation, concept mapping, and formulating instructional objectives and in operating computers. They have no knowledge and skill of using ICT in classroom process.

**Table 2: Performance ofLearnerLearning-facilitators after Intervention**

N = 35

| Sl.No. | Indicators | After Intervention % | |
|---|---|---|---|
| | | Could do | Could not do |
| 1. | The presenter stated the objectives in behavioural term. | 60 | 40 |
| 2. | Lesson plan was in completed form | 75 | 25 |
| 3. | Power Point presentation | 55 | 45 |
| 4. | Use of Visuals | 70 | 30 |
| 5. | Use of Dialogues | 50 | 50 |
| 6. | Recitation of the poem using audio cassette | 60 | 40 |
| 7. | Concept mapping | 50 | 50 |
| 8. | Interactive question answer using interactive video CD | 65 | 35 |
| 9. | Presentation of the concerned observation schedule in filled in form | 76 | 24 |

# ICT Mediated Pre-Service Learning-Facilitator Training

The above table shows that there is considerable improvement in relation to formulating instructional objectives, concept mapping, use of visuals and power point presentation etc. They are able to use the knowledge and skills of using ICT in classroom process. As it was only two weeks intervention substantial improvement could not be attained, however some improved was marked. Hence learnerlearning-facilitators need support the help of ICT expert can do better. If it could be taken up on a continuous basis the learnerlearning-facilitators may show desirable progress in ICT integration in the context of classroom process.

**Table 3: Comparison of Post-test Achievement Mean Scores ofExperimental Group and Controlled Group**

| Groups | N | Mean | SD | Value of t | Level of Significance |
|---|---|---|---|---|---|
| Experimental | 12 | 15.66 | 1.77 | 4.63 | 0.01 |
| Controlled | 12 | 12.50 | 2.06 | | |

It is clear from the above table that the Post-test Achievement Mean Scores of Experimental and Control group are presented in Table-3. Mean Scores of post achievement test for Experimental and Controlled groups are 15.66 and 12.50 respectively. The Obtained t value is 4.63 which are significant at 0.01 levels. Thus, the null hypothesis is rejected. Results show that there is significant difference in Post-test Mean Achievement Scores of Experimental Group and Control Group. The t value obtained is observed higher than the table value. Thus the experiment proved effective due to ICT mediated intervention in the classroom.

## Findings

### Phase-I

On the basis of collected data, analysis and interpretations were done as mentioned in the table above. At the pre-test stage knowledge and skills pertaining to the indicators above has fixed and reflected on the table. From the need assessment it was observed that only 15% of the learnerlearning-facilitators knew the art of operation of computers. Only 25% of the learnerlearning-facilitators knew how to integrate ICT in class room process. Again only 10% of the learnerlearning-facilitators were acquainted with the power point presentation and synchronization. They had minor knowledge about multimedia approach. After intervention it was observed that 60% of learnerlearning-facilitators were able to prepare power point including ICT into classroom process. 40% of learnerlearning-facilitators need special training on integrating ICT in classroom process.

### Phase-II

As an effect of ICT mediated classroom transaction the experimental group learners proved better than the control group who were not given any treatment on ICT integration. The experimental group proved better result because the clarity was made better than the control group. Concept mapping exercise helped them to understand the basics of Determiner to which Article is a part and they were clarified on the use of a, an and the.

## Educational Implications

In all the subjects, pre-service learnerand learning-facilitators, in-service learnerand learning-facilitators can apply these strategies. In the practice schools they can use power points where electricity facilities are available. They can develop lessons adopting 5E Model in other subjects and can have power point presentation during classroom transaction. Besides power point presentation, they can use animation technique and simulation during presentation of lessons in the schools. They can apply their creative talent in the preparation of lessons integrating ICT to make the teaching learning process interestingly and appealing.

## Suggestions

The learnerlearning-facilitators need to be widely acquainted with the use of ICT in respect of power point presentation, animation, reflecting visuals etc. It should be compulsory that each learnerlearning-facilitator to take help of the ICT during presentation of lessons. They should more acquaint with the art of synchronization while presenting the lesson. Learnerlearning-facilitators should be aware of preparing observation schedule and the techniques of using them. The learners who are not at home in preparation of lesson plan with integration ICT need to be well trained.

# Chapter 15

# ICT for Learners and Educators

✍ **Lovish Raheja**
*PCGE, Jaipur, Rajasthan*

## Preview at a Glance

This research work titled 'ICT for Learners and Educators' is mainly aimed to analyse the concept of Information and Communication Technology for Education from learning perspective through its current usages and further possibilities of advancements.'Information and Communication Technology is the biggest turnabout of the present pace',was quoted by one of the research participants. Thus contemplating over this turnabout is our compulsion, for which the research work is done. The major work was done with the help of answers of 2 types of questionnaires: Expert's and Learners' Questionnaire. The learners I included were those graduate and undergraduate learners, who had a basic understanding of ICT. The research work raises important issues and concerns thatcannot be ignored while thinking of its implementations. Though the probable problems are really serious but the futurepossibilities of technical developments give solutions to big spectra of the problems. The benefits of the system motivate its development and continuous improvements keep it going. I have also analysed the satisfaction of learners towards the efforts of government, which is also an interesting part of the research, where I observed the satisfaction level almost 50:50. At last, for making the pace of development in technical advancements, establishment of the 'Pace Setting Unit' is proposed. And overall the research tries to explore the futurepossibilities, through the points discussed: concept, usefulness, current status, govt. efforts and problems of the system.

## Introduction

This research work is done for increasing helpfulness of ICT for learners and educators. ICT is a method of learning and teaching effectively by the help of audio-visual aids which makes education easier and helpful to learning-facilitator and learners both perspectives. ICT is used at a much larger scale today than the past by learners and educators, more generally, learners, but still possibilities of development never end. They keep on growing and growing by the time. This research chapter is also prepared for finding out the possibilities through the study of its concept and its current usages status, so that we would be able to open our minds for thinking the possibilities. As, we here are talking with special reference to learners, then the research work automatically contains a big spectra of innovative ideas and possibilities.

The research work also discusses the problems faced, the benefits enjoyed and the side-effects of using the system as without discussing these, we cannot grow in a positive way.

## Objective
To find, how ICT can be more useful for learners and educators.

## Research Questions
1. What is ICT?
2. Why is ICT proposed to be used so preferably in the educational field?
3. What are the current usages of ICT for learners and educators?
4. What is the possibility of further advancements and their Implementation?

## Research Methodology
- The required information was collected from primary and secondary sources.
- Primary Sources:
- Primary sources were the answers of 2 types of subjective questionnaires- Expert and Learners Questionnaire, prepared for this research work by me.
- Secondary Sources:
- The secondary sources were:
- Internet
- Oxford Dictionaries
- Business Dictionary

**Participants:** A number of graduate and undergraduate learners who had a basic understanding of ICT and one ICT expert

## General Meanings and Concept
To understand the concept of Information and Communication Technology, let's first divide the entire term in parts: Information, Communication and Technology

And then try to analyse the meaning of Information and Communication Technology and understand its concept.

Information: According to Oxford Dictionaries [1] - Information is- 'Computing data as processed, stored, or transmitted by a computer.'

Communication: According to Business Dictionaries [2] - Communication is a 'Two-way process of reaching mutual understanding, in which participants not only exchange (encode-decode) information, news, ideas and feelings but also create and share meaning.

Technology: According to Oxford Dictionaries [3] - Technology is 'the application of scientific knowledge for practical purposes, especially in industry.'

Analysis of the meaning of Information and Communication Technology as a whole:

As per the above discussion information and communication technology is the application of the knowledge of computing the data and its exchange. More generally, computation of the data refers to the process in which data is interpreted for the user and the two-way process communication is exchange of this interpretation.

According to Goswami, ICT refers to the technologies that provide access to the information through telecommunications but focuses primarily on communication technologies.

## ICT's Usefulness in Educational Field

Information and Communication Technologies are essentially useful in educational field. It is very helpful to satiate the knowledge bank and opening the minds. The basic purposes of education are physical, mental, social and moral development of the learner. ICT plays a big role from mental and socio-perspective. Social awareness is a big aspect that is achieved at a high level with its help. At mental level, it helps in visualising the constructive ideas. ICT is also useful in quality upgradation of the education. Moreover, it is a single window method whereas traditional methods needs multitasking- fully inevitable in this fast-growing world. Thus fast learning takes place with ICT.

## Current Status

### *Positive aspects:*
- Learners gain free and accessible information that causes permanent impression on their mind.
- Better Conceptualization of subject related problems. A big role in this is played and will be played at a higher level in future by virtual reality, you don't need to think much and waste your time, see its visuals and then everything is clear. Nicely animated online lectures from experts also help in effective learning and improvement in score. A learner can understand a single concept in various ways that helps a lot.
- It is an entertaining medium of learning.
- Telecommunication is a useful tool for open and distance learning.

- ICT allows flexible, self-paced learning where learners, to an appreciable extent are able to choose what they would like to focus on and spend variable amounts of time on it based on the perceptions of their learning needs.

## *Negative aspects:*
- According to our expert current status of ICT is very poor as people are still not aware about the computer knowledge.
- Lack of ICT's awareness. In today's modern world, where ICT is used in each and every field, people still do not understand the meaning of ICT. Current status of ICT is very poor for a common man. Learning-facilitators are not enough trained for technology, they have lack of adequate technical support for education.
- Technical issues like improper setup of audio-visual aids, operational problems and also sometimes setting up the devices is very troublesome.
- Irrelevant facts and non-standardised information is presented that create illusions and confusions.
- According to one participant in our research, 'It takes time to understand this system in initial stages.' Thus, understanding this system is time consuming. When someone spends the time on learning, how to use the system, that is the time they are not devoting to learning the content of their subject field.
- The tools of this system are expensive those are unaffordable for the poor.
- The biggest problem is learners are taking this as a medium of entertainment at much higher level rather than taking it as a medium of knowledge, though both can be together because ICT makes study entertaining but still negative use is observed at a larger scale.
- Learners are copying the content from internet without giving them a touch of understanding. In other words, learners are enforcing their brain to eat ripped food.
- One reason for the above point is the role of language. One understands the content better written in one's own language. Content available currently is mainly in English, it should be available also in regional languages, and so that people of remote areas be able to access it easily. So, language plays an essential role.

## Possibilities for Further Advancements

Before getting the possibilities known, let's first recognise the efficiency of the efforts of Indian Government, as political system and political will affects the development of each and every area.

When I asked the learners that, are they satisfied from the efforts of government I got almost 50:50 result. Half were satisfied while the other half were not contented with the current efforts, some of the important answers about their satisfaction are given below:

# ICT for Learners and Educators

| Learners' level | Satisfied (Yes/No) | Statement (Translated into English) |
|---|---|---|
| Graduate | No | Information publishing is not controlled, that may cause communal riots. |
| Graduate | Yes | Government on his behalf is doing many advancements in sector of ICT i.e., it is possible to think about digital India |
| Graduate | No | At this time efforts made by government for ICT is very poor. On the basis of today's government school, it is negligible because for government school ICT is like a dream not real thing in the world so nope for government efforts. |
| Undergraduate | No | Government needs to apply more effort. |
| Undergraduate | Yes | It is sufficient if we properly read/understand the things/material. |
| Undergraduate | Yes | There are a lot of big concerns in the country more important than the development of ICT which require much hard work. So government is doing its best. |
| Graduate | - | Government creates the plans and try and enforces the implementation partially but get success when targeted people participate actively. |
| Undergraduate | Yes | Somehow they are sufficient but follow ups and lagging. |
| Graduate | No | Government should focus on proper infrastructure for ICT in remote areas too. |

Thus, from above discussion, we can analyse that government is trying by providing free training programmes and through the concept of Digital India but still remote areas and poor are untouched with ICT. Awareness' is not at that level, which it should have been.

So, now, the further possibilities are needed to be discussed and those are here:

## *Possibilities*
- Bookless and bugless system i.e., Eco-friendly Education: The system of paperless education is an essential need today, as environment pollution is increasing day by day, so with the help of ICT, this big concern can also be dealt.
- Home Education: Learners will be able to learn by themselves as conceptual understanding will be easier. Quantity of engaging content will have

increased.
- Technical Procedures will be easier: Learners will easily be able to deal with technical issues in computer setup. There are two reasons for this :
1. Easiness that will be caused by technical expertise.
2. Every new generation brings advancements with itself; they will learn the setup more easily than us.
- Increase in cost-effectivity: less money investment and high level knowledge profit.
- Smart classes will have a new meaning. Virtual reality will come into existence and learners will be exploring the new world of knowledge in a different way. E-learning will reach a new level.
- Future books will be IPAD/Computer books.
- Research and theory presentation will also reach at higher level due to virtual reality.
- The future is about access, anywhere learning and collaboration, both locally and globally. Also it suggests the idea of 24x7 availability of the educators which means learners will be able to learn anywhereand anytime.
- As known, ICT is a powerful medium, if we use this tool to eradicate the social evils to accomplish the purpose of education, it will be very useful.

## Implementation

Before its implementation, we need to consider its drawbacks, some of them we have seen in the negative aspects of current status of ICT and some other harmful effects of promoting this system are:

1. Increased level of frustration and tension from continuous working on computer
2. Eye-sight weakness
3. Cybercrimes
4. Privacy problems
5. Back-pain due to continuous sitting
6. Weakness in imagination and explanation power: traditional system requires and emphasises on good imagination and explanation capability of the learner but ICT gives the learner everything with ease that affects the mental development.
7. ICT lacks 'Do and Learn Method'
8. Content from every field due to which distractions take place (Though, it depends much on user)

All points mentioned above hold an important significance. So for overcoming them, here are the recommendations and suggestions:

- ICT awareness should not only include what is ICT and how computer is operated, but also, how to use the system in ethical and proper manner including the breaks/rests while using the computer.
- Some technologies related to making the computer system and mobile system, eye-friendly are under the process of development, so that will happen by the time soon.
- Security will always remain the issue in my eyes because hackers and security maintainers, both are developing themselves together, but still as awareness will spread, security level will automatically enhance.
- Lifestyle teaching through ICT is also possible, that can help us live a modernised and decent life at the same time.
- Playing Memory enhancing, imagination developing and Brainstorming games.
- ICT alone will not work, as some shift into reality from virtuality will always be needed for practical purposes.
- To deal with technical issues, a setup tour must be taken by the experts initially.
- Proper training programmes and workshops should be conducted for learning-facilitators' training.
- Guidelines for the control of the government on the abusing and porn content should be issued recalling Indian moral values.
- Content should be tried to be translated in regional languages as much as possible.
- Making technical procedures easier.
- Parental control should be there even for mature people.
- Every educational institution should be enforced to use the basic ICT tools in the classroom, because now is the time to consider projectors, OHP and other tools as the basic requirement for schools and equivalent to blackboard and chalks.

Thus, implementing the above suggestions and recommendations will help ICT reach a good level of quality in Education.

One important thing told by one of the participants is stated as follows -

'Every year there is something new in ICT that schools are expected to deal with, hence it is better to look for an approach that is facilitating the uptake.'

These words suggest an idea that a 'Pace Setting Unit' should be set up at national level whose work will be to provide guidance and show a proper technical model infrastructure of ICT to the educational institutions, so that they would adopt the system as per their financial capabilities. This will help increasing the quality level of education.

## Objective of the Pace Setting Unit

As clear from the name, it will try to keep up the country's educational institutions with the contemporary advancements in the field of ICT by showing them technical models and giving them financial wherever and whenever possible.

## Proposed Structure of the Pace Setting Unit

It should be established as a government operated institution. Initially, it may be in the form of a central board consisting of limited number of members. The board will be consisting of Computer and Software Engineers, Economists, Educationists, Health Experts, Psychologists, Communication experts and Manager's guides whose qualification will be MBA degree. Later on, this may be decentralised as per the requirements of educational institutions.

## Work Division

Computer and Software Engineers: The team of computer and software engineers will work on developing the models of ICT, adopting the new changes taking place globally, developing artificial intelligences and doing own innovations concerning proper security of the system.

Economists: The team of economists will analyse the financial aspects of the implementation of the innovations done and the adoption of the changes. To which extent, the adoption is possible practically taking in the account country's financial status and all that will be its major concerns.

Educationists: The team of educationists will be the backbone of this board. They will recognise the needs of learners, organise the subject specific contents, helping engineers giving a proper direction. As this team will have the most ground level approach, most nearest to learners and that is why this team may be treated as an advisory panel. In this team there will be some number of Computer Science learning-facilitators/lecturers/professors who will be playing major role.

Health Experts: The team of health experts will analyse the health related aspects of the implementable system, how it will be affecting one's physical and mental health and suggesting what should be done for avoiding the harmful effects, even including the factors that may cause effects on IQ.

Psychologists: The team of psychologists will concern upon the psychological effects on learners of the system to be implemented. How, learners will be dealing with that when we imply such-and-such concepts of ICT into their studies, either this concept will make them lazy or it will encourage them to put more efforts into their studies and all that. Moreover, this group will also play a major role in admitting new members into the board by interviewing.

Communication Experts: The team of communication experts will have the role of communicating with other countries to learn and asking for the new information and advancements whenever needed. This team will be given a special training of ICT before their joining, so that they would understand the technical talks better.

# ICT for Learners and Educators

Manager's Guides: As cleared earlier, this MBA degree holder group will guide the educational institutions' managers to deal with ICT resources management.

## The Board as a Financial Supporter

For some of the important implementations, this board will work as a fund provider organisation. By 'Important', I mean the implementations those are the compulsion for the country to stand before the world such as basic ICT reach till rural areas. In this form of the board economists' role will be crucial.

## Decentralisation in Later Stages

As I said earlier, initially it may be established as a central unit but later on, as the time goes by, the need of its decentralisation will be realised. So, it is proposed that the unit should gradually keep decentralising itself except doing it all suddenly.

As soon as the unit will start decentralising itself, its approach will go into more depth and at last it will reach till the most deprived community of the society. Thus the objective taken will be fulfilling.

## Why is Establishment of Such Unit Proposed?

Our world is growing rapidly in all aspects, including technological advances. This growing up has become a race among the countries, due to which some countries are ahead and some are lagging. On the counterparts, this board, with the help of communication experts, sets up coordination between countries. And such coordination is a need of today otherwise heavy difference will be seen in technical advancements in different-different countries.

Field Work: Directed and distant communication regarding research questions through two types of subjective questionnaires.

## Conclusion

Thus the research done concludes the important results about the Implementation of further advancements in ICT. ICT is the unexcelled need of the era. Its usages are in every field but specifically talking from learning perspective, we discuss quality, quality that increases through visualisation, deep understanding of the concepts and exploring new ideas. Due to its so many benefits most of us become negligent about its untechnical drawbacks that are what I have not done because these are the drawbacks that cannot be ignored like weakness in imagination power and problems in memory. I have also suggested their solutions with a bit of contemplation and through the research work.

At last I have also tried to tell about a Pace Setting Unit's need for today's system. This unit is a compulsion not only for India, but for every country because ignited minds can be observed anywhere, those have new ideas which may need rapid implementations and that implementation can be done more effectively with the help of coordination that this unit will make.

So the objective taken 'increasing ICT's usefulness' has been tried to get accomplished by dealing with major usages, that opens the path of further possibilities and later on, discussing the major problems in the implementation of the advancements.

# Chapter 16

# ICT Integration in Teaching and Learning

✎ **M. Satheeshkumar**
*University of Madras, Chennai, TN*

## Preview at a Glance

Information and communication technologies (ICT) have become commonplace entity in all parts of life. Across the past twenty years the use of ICT has fundamentally changed the practices and procedures of business and governance, education. The role of ICT in education is becoming more and more important and this importance will continue to grow and develop in the 21st century. Use of ICT in education field leads to more learner-centred. Education is the life long process of acquiring new knowledge and skill through formal exposure of information, ideas and experiences. These can be done in the schools by way of systematic planning of instruction. In turn it needs proper method or technology to adopt in teaching the concepts of the subjects in the school. Now a day they call it as an educational technology which implies a behavioural science approach to teaching and learning, in trait, it makes use and pertinent, scientific and technological sociology, communicating linguistics and their related fields. Educational technology has grown as a result of technological devices in the use of practices with the explored psychological of teaching, learning and behavioural modification. There are many means by which effective instruction can be imparted in the classroom. The use of Computer Assisted Instruction (CAI) in schools is gaining momentum. Now days, more and more schools are having computers, so use of technology enhances effectiveness of a learning experience. This chapter highlights the integration of information communication technology in teaching learning.

## Introduction

Information and Communication Technology (ICT) for education, initiative by UNESCO, conducted an extensive consultation to identify the competencies that learning-facilitators should develop to use technology effectively in the classroom. It is basically an umbrella term that encompasses all communication technologies such as internet, wireless networks, cell-phones, satellite communications, digital television computer and network hardware and software; as well as the equipment and services associated with these technologies, such as videoconferencing, e-mail and blogs etc. that provide access to information.

Integrating Information and Communication Technology (ICT) into teaching and learning is a growing area that has attracted many educators attention in recent years. Learning-facilitators need to be involved in collaborative projects and development of intervention change strategies, which include teaching partnerships with ICT as a tool. Learning-facilitator perceptions are a major predictor of the use of new technologies in instructional settings. Early studies have indicated that blended learning can be as successful as either online or face-to-face instruction, particularly in learning-facilitator preparation programs. Blended learning can lead to improved training, increased access and flexibility, and better cost-effectiveness.

Education has a great role for a country. It is the grass root level for any country. Any type of failure in this stage may become a country backward. Government of India has taken many programmes and schemes for Education. In modern society ICT plays a remarkable role in Education. ICT in schools provide lots of opportunities to learning-facilitators to transform their practices by providing the learners with improved educational content and more effective teaching and learning methods. ICT improves the learning process through the provision of more interactive educational materials that increase learner's motivation and facilitate the easy acquisition of basic skills.

## Operational Definition of Key Terms

Information and Communication Technology (ICT) - any technology that allows for the creation, storage and display of information in all its forms or communicate with others over a distance such as computers, computer, networks, television, cell phones, radio, cassette players, DVD and CD players.

E-maturity - when educational institutions make strategic and effective use of ICT to improve educational outcomes

Digital learning environments - learning environments that make use of computers and computer related technologies, such as the Internet, interactive whiteboards for teaching and learning.

Embedded ICT - when ICT use is incorporated in all or most activities related to teaching and learning delivery, record keeping, planning, communication, administration, assessment

Multimedia rooms - rooms equipped with a full range of information and communication technologies designed to support the delivery of the curriculum using a variety of methods.

# ICT Integration in Teaching and Learnings

## Objectives of ICT Implementation in Education
- To implement the principle of life-long learning/education.
- To increase a variety of educational services and medium/method.
- To promote equal opportunities to obtain education and information.
- To develop a system of collecting and disseminating educational information.
- To promote technology literacy of all citizens, especially for learners.
- To develop distance education with national contents.
- To promote the culture of learning at school

## Technology
Technology is the making, modifications, usage and knowledge of tools, machines, techniques, crafts, systems and methods of organization, in order to solve a problem, improve a pre-existing solution to a problem, achieve a goal, handle an applied input/output relation or perform a specific function. It can also refer to the collection of such tools, including machinery, modifications, arrangements and procedures.

## Planning For Technology Integration in Education
In 1998, Levine proposes the following components of ay integration plan in Schools
- Formulating a planning team
- Collecting and analysing data
- Formulating the visions, goals and objectives
- Exploring available technology
- Determining training and staffing needs
- Determining a budget and funding sources
- Developing an action plan
- Implementing the plan
- Evaluation

## Integration of ICT in Teaching Learning
### *Technology Literacy*
Basic digital literacy skills to use technology, ability to select and use appropriate software available including internet in computer laboratories or with limited classroom facilities to complement standard curriculum objectives, assessment approaches, lesson plans and didactic teaching methods, able to use ICT to manage classroom data and support their own professional development.

### *Knowledge Deepening*
Ability to manage information, structure problem tasks, integrate open-ended software tools and subject specific applications with learnercentred teaching methods

and collaborative methods and collaborative projects in support of learners deep understanding of key concepts and their application to solve complex world real problems, use network resources to help learners collaborate, access information, communicate with experts to analyse and solve their selected problems and use ICT to create and monitor individual group plans.

## Knowledge Creation

Design ICT-based learning resources and environments use ICT to support the development of knowledge creation and critical thinking skills of learners, support learner's continuous reflective learning, and create knowledge communities for learners and colleagues.

## Impact in Classroom

Opportunities to deploy innovative teaching methodologies and to deploy more interesting material that create an interest in the learners, enable better management of classroom and learners thereby improving the productivity of the tutor as well as the taught, enables the learning-facilitator to concentrate on other tasks such as research and consultancy, enables optimum utilization and sharing of resources among institutions thereby reducing the cost of implementing ICT solution and to find appropriate online resources that can be used offline or converted to a chapter based resource. Ex-NRICH website offers enrichment materials for mathematics to pupils of all ages.

## Steps Taken To Integrate ICT

- Eleventh Five - Year Plan (2007-2012) importance of ICT in education has been emphasized.
- 'National Curriculum Framework (2005)' emphasized the judicious use of technology to increase the reach of educational program, facilitate management of the system as well as address specific learning needs and requirements.
- Government of India has set up a national task force on information technology and software development to universalize computer literacy.
- Intel Teach to future program is a world wide effort to integrate technology in classroom.

## Motivating Learner through ICT

ICT such as videos, television, and multimedia computer software that combine text, sound, and colourful, moving image can be used to provide challenging and authentic content that will engage the learner in learning process. Interactive radio likewise makes use of sound effect, songs, comic skits and other performances convention to compel the learner to listen and become involved in lesson being delivered. Moreover so than any other type of ICT, networked computer with internet connection can make the learner more motivate to his/her learning. One type of ICT combines the media richness and interactive to other ICT with the opportunity to connect with real people and to participate to real world events.

Through ICTlearners can experience various stages of learning, such as critical thinking, problem solving, guided instruction, extra connect, cooperative learning and group monitoring.

- Simulations-provide excellent opportunities for learning-facilitators to create settings where learners are led through critical thinking stages.
- Guided instructions-allows learners to submit pieces of a project step by step, allowing for a rich feedback interaction between learners and instructor. A problem like Textra connect or lotus notes allow draft essays to be submitted and returned.
- Cooperative learning-websites provide ready sites for discussions, cooperative groups are designed and assigned to do the activities by monitoring these groups, and the instructor can introduce timely prompts to redirect the conservation, posing problems that challenge the quo.
- Acceleration-children can be accelerated within their own class working independently, often with some additional support.
- Extension-moving outside the syllabus normally not covered in the curriculum.
- Enrichment-extending learners understanding and applying them to other situations and problems to develop higher level problem solving and communication skills.

## Benefits of Technology Integration
- Increased Learner Motivation and Engagement
- Improved Classroom Organization
- Improved Ability to Monitor Individual Learner Progress
- Practice for Upcoming Statewide Assessments
- Creation of Improved Final Products
- Improved Communication with Parents

## Types of Networking
- Main Network Types are Ethernet, FDDI, Token Ring, ARCnet and AppleTalk.
- Other Network Type is Fibber Channel and Gigabit Ethernet.

### *External Networks*

Often you need to communicate with someone outside your internal network in this case you will need to be part of a Wide Area Network (WAN). The internet is the ultimate WAN - it is a vast network of networks.

## Internal Networks

Usually referred to as a Local Area Network (LAN), this involves linking a number of hardware items together within an office or building. The aim of a LAN is to be able to share hardware facilities such as printers or scanners.

## Advantages of Networking
### File Servers
- Users can access their work from any workstation connected to the network.
- Users can easily exchange work with colleagues.
- Users can easily co-operate on tasks.
- Backing up is centralized and can be placed under the control of experts who will follow the correct procedures.

### Printer Servers
- Instead of having printers attached to each computer, printers only need to be purchased for the print servers. This results in financial savings.
- As there are fewer printers to look after there is lower maintenance.
- As for fewer printers need to be purchased better quality printers with advanced features can be purchased.

### Application Servers
- Software only needs to be installed on the applications server instead of each workstation.
- The software is configured in the same way for all users.
- Upgrading of software only needs to be done on the server.
- Cost of licensing software for an applications server is less than the cost of many stand-alone versions.

### Internet Connection Sharing (Proxy Servers)
- Proxy Servers contain a repository of Internet sites recently visited and cached for quicker access at a future date.
- Proxy Servers can be configured with firewall software. This helps protect the network from attack by hackers.
- Files can be filtered for computers viruses before being passed onto the network.
- Organizations can control access of users to outside sites.
- Since there is only one point of communication there is a large saving online cost.

## ICT in Everyday Life

ICT is a part of our everyday life and using ICT devises such as computers and tablets in the classroom motivate learners in the English language classroom. The use of ICT in the classroom is becoming more and more convenient and there are many different ways a learning-facilitator can use it as a pedagogical tool. ICT is an abbreviation of Information and Communication Technology. ICT is a wide concept, however, the focus on ICT in this study is tools that can be located and used in a classroom, such as computers and tablets.

Tools are now available on the Internet to assist both learning-facilitators and learners to manage writing assignments to detect and avoid the pitfalls of plagiarism and copyright violations. One of the great benefits of ICTs in teaching is that they can improve the quality and the quantity of educational provision. ICT in everyday life as follows that

- ICT in Business
- ICT in Financial Services
- ICT in Entertainment
- ICT in Public Service
- ICT in Education

## *Application of ICT in Education*

The Applications in ICT Educations are Blogs, Learning Management Systems, Survey Systems, Online Image/Video Sharing, and Video-conferencing/Chat/File Sharing Applications, Online collaborative Work Spaces, Online Whiteboards, Virtual Worlds, Mind Maps, Learning-facilitator's Role, Administrative, Design, Facilitation, Evaluation and Technical.

## *New Digital Technologies*

The new digital technologies are not single technologies; they are combinations of hardware and software, media, and delivery systems. They are evolving and converging rapidly, as seen in PCs, laptops, notebooks, and digital cameras that are both video and single-image; local area networking; the World Wide Web; CD-ROMs and DVDs; application software, such as word processing, spreadsheets, and simulations; email; digital libraries; and computer-mediated conferencing, videoconferencing, and virtual reality. They also have a capacity to integrate with older analogue technologies from print, and through audio and video, make it possible to retrieve information stored in older technologies and to develop synergies between the old and the new. There are excellent reviews of the older analogue technologies, which still have tremendous value, especially in many developing countries and their educational systems.

ICTs for teaching and learning range from those that rely on ubiquitous low-cost technology, such as the stand-alone PC, to those deployed for specific purposes at higher cost, such as the electronic classroom. Decisions on the choice of technologies are subject to many considerations and constraints, ranging from constancy of power supply to availability of skilled technical and managerial support to maintaining the technological infrastructure. Assuming these are available, then questions of pedagogical strategies of the system, accessibility, scale, and cost will play a role in the choice. Some of the newer IC technologies available and used today are discussed below.

## E-Mail

Increasingly, e-mail is becoming the most widely used medium, ranging in function from exchange of gossip, to serious dialogue and collaborative research. It also has become an important supplement to classroom teaching. Bulletin board services extend the classroom beyond fixed timetables; list serves bring communities of learners together; and assignments and term papers are beginning to be channelled routinely through e-mail. On-campus education is being enriched by e-mail facilities, and off-campus education is made more personal and interactive. In economically developed countries, e-mail is almost as common as the telephone. In many cases, connections are free of charge, appliances are provided at low or no cost, and training is available for neophyte users. In poor economies, e-mail has yet to make its presence felt throughout society, but is increasingly available at community service centres such as libraries, tele-learning centres, and cyber cafes.

## Presentational Software

PowerPoint and similar programs are already commonplace among academics and other professionals. While a simple slide presentation requires little skill to develop, the increasing sophistication level of such a presentation requires higher-level training.

## World Wide Web

Many on campus instructors are beginning to use the Web to make their lecture notes available to learners at any time. The Web also has the advantage of providing access to primary sources of information in most media like print, graphics, photographs, audio, and video through streaming. This technology requires good organizational and pedagogical skills to profit from its enormous potential, and faculty training in its use will be essential. Bates considers the Web to be a low-cost technology for several reasons: the existence of simple computer languages such as HTML and intermediary course authoring systems such as the WebCT and Blackboard; it uses the Internet as a transport vehicle that involves no direct charge for independent packets of information, and pricing is by volume and not by time or distance; the Web's ability to combine media, thereby increasing its range of applications; access to high-quality learning resources inexpensively; it allows asynchronous interpersonal communication through e-mail, bulletin boards, and discussion forums; and it enables cross-cultural, international, collaborative learning.

## Multimedia, CD-ROM, DVD

Multimedia, CD-ROMs and DVDs are very exciting learning tools. Their development costs can be very high, especially those at the very high end that can carry large quantities of data in a variety of formats, such as audio and video clips, Internet connections to other databases, large amounts of information, and built-in simulation and other enrichments. Putting all these together in user-friendly packages will require teams of experts, from media producers to content experts. The reproduction cost of CDROMs can be reduced considerably if large numbers are burned. Consequently, this medium is a consideration only when enrolments are large enough to justify the development expense. However, there is a strong case for developing the medium when the course can be used by a consortium of institutions working together.

## *Satellite Broadcasting*

Satellite broadcasting for educational purposes has a long history. Countries such as India and China, and such regional universities as the University of the West Indies and University of the South Pacific have long used satellites to deliver audio- and video-based lectures to all corners of their region. Satellites serve as good vehicles to carry lessons, and, by marrying satellites to ground facilities, it is possible to build a two-way learning environment.

In addition, their digital technologies allow for further sophistication to be built into the learning systems. However, because of their high start-up cost, satellites value for educators is limited. Recent developments sponsored by private enterprises such as World Space have combined satellite technologies with digital ones to broadcast voice and data directly to specially design digital receivers over very large geographic areas. While this venture is driven by and for commercial interests, special provision for educational purposes allows educational providers to reach very remote and isolated parts of the world. World Space eventually expects to reach an audience of some 3 billion people. While satellite technology has some significant advantages in terms of reach and low unit cost, for it to be truly effective as a learning technology requires extensive local support on the ground, either on an interpersonal basis or through telephony, the Internet, etc. Ground support will cause costs to increase considerably, thereby reducing the economic benefits. As Bates concludes, well designed printed texts can be more educationally cost-effective than real time or even recorded satellite lectures.

## *Video Conferencing*

In the late 1970s, multi-campus postsecondary institutions began experimenting with videoconferencing to distribute their education and training services and lectures in real time. With the decreasing costs of telephony, videoconferencing has become relatively popular, especially in Australia and the United States. This technology, an amalgam of telephony and computer-compressed technologies, reduces the amount of time instructors and learners spend travelling from campus to campus to deliver and receive lessons. It also saves instructors from having to repeat lectures. The traditional culture of classroom teaching is preserved, and no new skills have to be learned by learners or learning-facilitators. It is not a flexible system of learning, however. New innovations incorporating videoconferencing technologies with the Internet and Web technologies offer new opportunities, notwithstanding some concerns about the visual and voice quality of such arrangements.

## Conclusion

One of the many challenges facing developing countries today is that of preparing their societies and governments for globalization and the information and communication revolution. The rapid growth in Information and Communication Technologies (ICT) has brought remarkable changes in recent years. ICT is becoming increasingly important in daily lives and in educational systems. ICT has become an important factor for effective teaching learning. Thus Integrating Information and Communication Technology (ICT) into teaching and learning is a growing area that has attracted many educators attention in recent years.

# Chapter 17

# ICT in Administration of Higher Education Institutions

✎ **Manju Gupta**
*Meerut College, Meerut, UP*

## Preview at a Glance

The present study is a Descriptive survey to explore the infrastructural facilities and ICT facilities of the higher education institutions. The population of the study consists of Principals of the institutions, directors, deans, and head of the departments of higher education institutes of Meerut Districts. Purposive sampling technique was used to select the sample. Size of the sample was 50 administrators. Self-made questionnaire and inventories solicited for information of ICT facilities, Extent of using ICT and the level of Basic ICT skills and proficiency used by the administrators for the administrative purposes. Data was collected in frequencies and analysed by simple percentage to describe the studied variables and $x^2$ test was used. The results indicated that there are inadequate ICT facilities in the institutions; the extent of ICT usage by the administrators is very low. The study further depicted the low level of Basic ICT skills and proficiency among the administrators. Recommendations are suggested that the government and the management should fund the institutions generously in general and ICT in particular to make the dream of Digital India come true. It should be made mandatory for the administrators to acquire Basic ICT skills/ proficiency for administrative purposes through workshops, refresher courses, special technical courses.

## Introduction

Higher Education Institutions are regulated by the apex bodies like, NCTE, AICTE, BCI and many others which have their own norms and directives which every institution needs to fulfil for recognition. Besides the apex bodies, the institutions are affiliated to Central or State Universities as per their regulation book. The administration of these institutions totally depends on the College Principal/ Directors and management. Administration goes a long way to determine the success of these Government/ Government Aided or Self Financing institutions hence is seen as critical by the stakeholders. College administration manages and regulates the major issues like finances, admission, examination, scholarship distribution, disciplinary environment, social- physical environment. The most important activities of the colleges like curriculum planning, execution of teaching learning process, formative evaluation, co-curricular and extra-curricular activities are planned and administered by the dean/ Head of the Department to provide instructional leadership and the associated learning-facilitators as the educational administrators / functional leaders to execute teaching learning process in the classrooms to establish, attain the educational goals.

On the basis of various literature reviews, the three main areas of administration were identified to manage the higher education institutions:

**General Administration:** Use of ICT in making time table, salary of teaching and non-teaching staff, and maintenance of budget, need based allocation of funds, to establish rapport with apex regulatory bodies and concerned university; maintenance of Archives, facilities like Library, Laboratory, field, offices, seminar rooms, multipurpose halls, sports and play grounds, researches and publications should be uploaded on website of the institution for its public image and reputation.

**Staff Administration:** Recruitment, work allotment as per academic calendar, administrative role given in various management committees, their attendance and leave management, performance appraisal uploaded on institutional website speaks about the richness of the college. Inter-faculty , inter- disciplinary exchange of thoughts and ideas on emails, WhatsApp, Tweeters, LinkedIn, Facebook help in processing of voluminous records in a quick, meticulous and impeccable manner thereby making innovation in education.

**Learner administration:** it involves admission, registration, course selection and allotment, attendance, examination, scholarships, counselling, hostel accommodation, transportation and their participation in curricular, co-curricular and extra- curricular activities. These can be uploaded on institutional website and can be retrieved as and when required. Parents/ guardian - learning-facilitator association, Alumni Association, Learner union, Grievance Redressal cell, Women cell in-charge and their e-mails and mobile numbers should be uploaded on the websites as learner support system.

The effective administration depends on how effectively and efficiently the links between the administrator and the various agents like administrative staff, heads of the organization, learning-facilitators and learners are maintained. This requires effective communication and transmission of information from one part to the other. To make the institutions more functional, accurate and effective, use of Information and Communication technologies could be seen as engine for growth and tool for empowerment. Information and Communication Technologies (ICT) include computers, mobiles and telephones, LCD projectors, Cameras, internet, satellite, cable data transmission, and computer assisted equipment that could be used to process, store, preserve, access, retrieve, and disseminate information with ease. The knowledge of computer application software such as spreadsheet, Excel, computer based design and data base are basic and important skills which enables administration towards quality assurance, growth and transformational development of the institution.

On the basis of review of Literature of Iweand Ike (2009) and many others, ICT was categorized on the basis of its use as below:

**Sensing Technologies:** Scanners, sensors, keyboards, mouse, and electronic pen, barcode readers, touch of digital boards, voice recognition system are used to gather and record data to do computation very rapidly and accurately. These are used in recording attendance through thumb impression, barcodes on admission and examination forms, checking of OMR sheets and recording results in one click for entrance tests and annual examination, preparing merit lists for admissions or giving scholarships.

**Communication technologies:** Facsimile machines (FAX), teleconferencing on telephones, WhatsApp, messengers on mobiles, , electronic bulletin board, CCTVs, electronic mails, Facebook, LinkedIn, Tweeter on computers, Television programmes, radio telecasts are various technologies used for transferring the information overcoming the barrier of speed and distance.

**Display technologies:** Computer screen, printer, television, mobile screen are the display technologies to form the interface between sensing, communication and analysing technologies and human users i.e. open to public, researchers, learners, learning-facilitators, parents for getting the information about the institution.

**Analysis Technologies:** Use of software like Microsoft Office (use of Access, Excel, Word, Power point), and other simple applications to collect, store and analyse the data like SPSS (Statistical Package for the Social Science) may provide information to the administrator for taking decisions or further communication to the apex bodies.

**Storage Technologies:** Optical discs, memory card, pen drives facilitate the efficient and effective storage of information.

'In an institution, administration has been extended as a service activity or tool through which the fundamental objectives of the institutional process may be more optimize efficiently when allocating human and material resources as well as to make the best use of existing resources' (Liverpool and Jacinta, 2013). Liverpool andJacinta (2013) stated the role of ICT in administration of higher education institutions as follows:

**Organization of Information:** to collect the information regarding learning-facilitators, learners, supportive staff and categorize them by sex, level, demographic data, socio- economic status, performance etc. This will help to take the decisions in taking admissions, granting scholarships and awards, appointment of teaching and non-teaching staff.

**Computation and Processing of Chapter Work:** In mapping out different activities like academic calendar, internal assessment, examination, results, stipulated scheme for teaching practice and Learner-learning-facilitators' School Internship work Scheme (SSIWS). Microsoft Access, Office, Excel can be used for collecting, tabulating and keeping the records.

**Enhancement of Effective Communication:** Computers, internet, Wi-Fi, dish channels, telephone lines, fax etc. make institutional administration easy for transferring information, growing, receiving and understanding of message within the network of independent relationship across international frontiers to develop global understanding. Dissemination of information can be done through e- circulars among learners, learning-facilitators, and staff. Websites Emails, WhatsApp, messaging through mobiles, strips display on CCTV can be used easily for dissemination of information at one click.

**Enhancement of Planning:** College Administration can use ICT to plan and make decisions regarding finance, budget on the basis of collected facts. It may plan to replace old furniture/ equipment and repair/ renovate the labs, library, classrooms, and offices fields as per need of the hour or construct the new ones.

**Improvement of Monitoring:** CCTVs in classes, offices, field for continuous monitoring of institutional system, social environment and disciplinary tone of the institution. It may help in storing and analysing educational indicators like the learning-facilitators' efficiency and involvement with the learners, learners' performances, infrastructural facilities etc.

**Management Instructions:** Administrator may use ICT in taking the decisions on the basis of first-hand information gathered through various technologies.

On the basis of existing institutional scenario and after reviewing various researches and studies, the following research questions were formulated by the researcher:

Q1: What are the ICT facilities available in the institutions for administrative purposes?
Q2: What is the level of ICT skills/ ICT proficiency among the institutional administrators?
Q3: To what extent do institutional administrators use these ICT for administrative purposes?

## Hypotheses

In order to find the answers for these three research questions, the researcher formulated the following directional hypotheses:

H1: Availability of ICT technologies in the institution will enhance the ICT proficiency among institutional administrators.

H2: ICT proficiency will enable the institutional administrators to use ICT for effective administration

# ICT in Administration of Higher Education Institutions

## Methodology

Descriptive survey method is used. The population of the study consists of Principals of the institutions, directors, deans, and head of the departments of higher education institutes of Meerut Districts. Purposive sampling technique was used to select the sample. Size of the sample was 50 administrators in number.

A self-made questionnaire was used to elicit information on 'Use and Application of ICT for Institutional Management. 'It consisted of two sections. Section I was focused to gather general information of the respondent to collect the demographic data. Section II contained 25 questions with yes/ no responses to provide information about the infrastructural facilities and availability of ICT facilities in the institution. Inventory 1 was made which contained 41 questions in 5 sections with never/ sometimes/ always responses to explore the level of Basic ICT skills/ proficiency for using ICT for institutional administration. Inventory 2 was developed to know the extent of use of ICT facilities for institutional administration. Test- retest method was used to establish the content validity of the questionnaire and Inventories respectively. Reliability coefficient was established by using KR 21 and it was calculated to be .89 for the questionnaire, .81 for Inventory 1 and .79 for Inventory 2. The questionnaire and Inventories were administered personally and through emails to ensure hundred percent responses. Data was collected and analysed. Analysis of Data was done using simple percentage, frequency counts, chi squire test and results were interpreted.

## Collection of Data

Table 1: Designation of Respondents

| Designation | Number of Respondents | Responses in % |
|---|---|---|
| Dean | 3 | 10% |
| Principal | 12 | 20% |
| Director | 5 | 10% |
| Head of the Department | 30 | 60% |
| Total | 50 | 100 |

Table 1 describes the position and designation of the respondents.

Table 2: Gender of the Respondents

| Gender | Number of Respondents | Responses in Percentage |
|---|---|---|
| Male | 34 | 68% |
| Female | 16 | 32% |
| Total | 50 | 100 |

Table 2 shows that 68% respondents were male heading the institutions / departments while only 32% respondents were females. This attributed to the dominance of males among the institutional administration.

**Table 3: Questionnaire to explore the Availability of Infrastructural facilities and ICT facilities for Administrators of the institution/ department**

| S. No. | Response Items | Alternative Responses | No. of Respondents | % of responses |
|---|---|---|---|---|
| 1 | Do you have full-fledged office? | Yes | 38 | 76% |
|   |   | No | 12 | 24% |
| 2 | Do your institution/ department have committee room? | Yes | 12 | 24% |
|   |   | No | 38 | 76% |
| 3 | Do you have computer in your office? | Yes | 42 | 84% |
|   |   | No | 08 | 16% |
| 4 | Do you use personal laptop/ tablet for office use? | Yes | 11 | 22% |
|   |   | No | 39 | 78% |
| 5 | Do you have the website of your institution/ department? | Yes | 50 | 100% |
|   |   | No | 00 | 00 |
| 6 | Do you have your email address? | Yes | 48 | 96% |
|   |   | No | 02 | 04% |
| 7 | Do your colleagues/ staff have their email address? | Yes | 48 | 96% |
|   |   | No | 02 | 04% |
| 8 | Do you use ICT to prepare electronic form of timetable/ class schedule/ exam schedule/ curricular/ co-curricular/ extra-curricular activities? | Yes | 22 | 44% |
|   |   | No | 28 | 56% |
| 9 | Do you use ICT to communicate academic growth of learners to their parents? | Yes | 06 | 12% |
|   |   | No | 44 | 88% |
| 10 | Do you use electronic media for learners' admission online? | Yes | 50 | 100% |
|   |   | No | 00 | 00 |
| 11 | Do you use inter- comm. in your office/ department? | Yes | 09 | 18% |
|   |   | No | 41 | 82% |
| 12 | Do you have land line phone in your office/ department? | Yes | 42 | 84% |
|   |   | No | 08 | 16% |
| 13 | Do you have public address system connected with all departments/ class rooms? | Yes | 04 | 08% |
|   |   | No | 46 | 92% |
| 14 | Do you use your mobile for office work? | Yes | 50 | 100% |
|   |   | No | 00 | 00 |

| 15 | Do you have LCD projector in your office/ committee room? | Yes | 04 | 08% |
| --- | --- | --- | --- | --- |
| | | No | 46 | 92% |
| 16 | Do you have smart boards in your office/ committee room? | Yes | 02 | 04% |
| | | No | 48 | 96% |
| 17 | Does the institution have any electronic examination management system/ database? | Yes | 11 | 22% |
| | | No | 39 | 78% |
| 18 | Do you apply Bio-matrix for automation of attendance and leave management of staff and learners in your institution/ department? | Yes | 16 | 32% |
| | | No | 34 | 68% |
| 19 | Do you apply electronic media for performance appraisal in your institution/ department? | Yes | 12 | 24% |
| | | No | 38 | 76% |
| 20 | Do you send e- circulars for learning-facilitators/ learners/ parents and staff regarding official matters? | Yes | 34 | 68% |
| | | No | 16 | 32% |
| 21 | Do you have computers/ Wi-Fi/ printers and scanners in library management? | Yes | 28 | 56% |
| | | No | 22 | 44% |
| 22 | Do you have facility for learners to pay their fee online? | Yes | 31 | 62% |
| | | No | 19 | 38% |
| 23 | Do you have e-payments for salary of learning-facilitators and other staff? | Yes | 36 | 72% |
| | | No | 14 | 28% |
| 24 | Do you ask learning-facilitators to develop question bank in each subject and for each class to make examination chapter? | Yes | 18 | 36% |
| | | No | 32 | 64% |
| 25 | Do you have voice/ video recorders/ cameras for reporting documents and evidences? | Yes | 27 | 54% |
| | | No | 23 | 46% |

Responses on the questionnaire depicted that most of the institutions had administrators' office equipped with computer, websites, emails, land line phones. The majority of institutions did not have rich ICT facilities. On the basis of availability of ICT facilities, these institutions were classified as: Institutions well equipped with ICT facilities and Institutions less equipped with ICT facilities.

**Inventory I: To identify the Level of Basic ICT Skills among the Respondents**

The ICT skills based inventory was given to each respondent and on the basis of their responses as yes/no, level of Basic ICT skills and proficiency was roughly estimated.

On the basis of their acquired scores, they were categorized as highly proficient, moderately proficient and less proficient.

| S. No | Basic ICT Skill based items | Responses Yes/ No | Scores 1/ 0 |
|---|---|---|---|
| A | Basic Knowledge of Computers | | |
| 1 | Understand basic computer hardware components and terminology | | |
| 2 | Understand the concepts and basic functions of a common computer operating system | | |
| 3 | Start up, log on, and shut down a computer system properly | | |
| 4 | Use a mouse pointing device and keyboard | | |
| 5 | Use Help and know how to troubleshoot routine problems | | |
| 6 | Identify and use icons (folders, files, applications, and shortcuts/aliases) | | |
| 7 | Minimize, maximize and move windows | | |
| 8 | Identify common types of file extensions (e.g. doc, docx, pdf, html, jpg, gif, xls, ppt, pptx, rtf, txt, exe) | | |
| 9 | Check how much space is left on a drive or other storage device | | |
| 10 | Back up files | | |
| 11 | Download and install software on a hard disk | | |
| 12 | Understand and manage the file structure of a computer | | |
| 13 | Check for and install operating system updates | | |
| B | Proficiency in Using Productivity Software | | |
| 14 | Create documents of various types and save in a desired location | | |
| 15 | Retrieve an existing document from the saved location | | |
| 16 | Select, copy, and paste text in a document or desired location | | |
| 17 | Print a document | | |
| 18 | Name, rename, copy and delete files | | |
| 19 | Understand and know how to use the following types of software programs: | | |

| | | |
|---|---|---|
| 2 | | Word processing (example: MS Word, Google Doc, Writer) |
| 2 | | Presentation (example: PowerPoint, Impress) |
| 2 | | Spreadsheet (example: Excel, Calc) |
| 2 | | PDF reader (example: Acrobat Reader, Preview) |
| 2 | | Compression software (example: WinZip, StuffIt, 7-Zip) |
| C | | Electronic Communication Skills |
| 20 | | Email, using a common email program (example: MS Outlook, Gmail, Apple Mail) |
| 21 | | Compose, Send, Reply, Forward messages |
| 22 | | Add attachments to a message |
| 23 | | Retrieve attachments from an email message |
| 24 | | Copy, paste and print message content |
| 25 | | Organize email folders |
| 26 | | Understand what an electronic discussion list is and how to sign up and leave one (example: Listserv, Listproc) |
| D | | Internet Skills |
| 27 | | Set up an Internet connection and connect to the Internet |
| 28 | | Have a working knowledge of the World Wide Web and its functions, including basic site navigation, searching, and installing and upgrading a Web browser |
| 29 | | Use a browser effectively, including bookmarks, history, toolbar, forward and back buttons |
| 30 | | Use search engines and directories to find information on the Web |
| 31 | | Download files and images from a Web page |
| 32 | | Understand and effectively navigate the hyperlink structure of the Web |
| 33 | | Understand how keep your information safe while using the Internet |
| E | | Moving Files |
| 34 | | Transfer files by uploading or downloading |
| 35 | | View and change folder/document security settings |
| 36 | | Copy files from hard disk to storage devices and vice versa |

**Table 4: Classification of Respondents on Inventory 1 to explore Basic ICT skills and proficiency among Administrators**

| Respondents scores on Inventory 1 | Number of Respondents | % of Respondents | Classification of Administrators |
|---|---|---|---|
| Above 25% scores | 26 | 52% | Tech Savvy |
| Middle 50% scores | 13 | 26% | Semi Tech Savvy |
| Below 25% scores | 11 | 22% | non- Tech savvy |

Table 4 shows that 52% respondents were highly proficient in using ICT skills, 26 % respondents were moderately proficient while 22% respondents were less proficient.

On the basis of their independent responses on acquisition of basic ICT skills, the institutional administrators were classified into Tech savvy administrators, semi tech savvy administrator and non-tech savvy administrators.

Inventory 2: 'To know on Extent of using ICT' for administrative purposes by the institutional administrators

| S. No | Response Items | Always | Some times | Never |
|---|---|---|---|---|
| 1 | Use computer for automation of attendance and leave management of staff | 10 | 00 | 40 |
| 2 | Use computer for learners' registration/ enrolment and for attendance records | 10 | 00 | 40 |
| 3 | Use internet for administrative purposes | 38 | 08 | 02 |
| 4 | Use mobiles for SMS/ WhatsApp to communicate with the staff and learners | 35 | 12 | 03 |
| 5 | Sending emails/ e-circulars for official work | 21 | 24 | 05 |
| 6 | Use ICT to communicate academic details of learners to their parents | 10 | 12 | 28 |
| 7 | Use ICT to prepare electronic form of timetable/ class schedule | 04 | 15 | 39 |
| 8 | Use ICT for performance appraisal | 01 | 13 | 36 |
| 9 | Use ICT for collecting the fee online | 10 | 00 | 40 |
| 10 | Use ICT for giving salaries to the staff and keeping the record | 18 | 00 | 32 |
| 11 | Use ICT for budget making/ implementation | 10 | 04 | 36 |
| 12 | Use ICT for question banks for examination | 12 | 08 | 30 |
| 13 | Use ICT for scheduling/ allocation of duties of invigilators/ examiners | 34 | 15 | 01 |
| 14 | Use ICT for the processing and display of learners' results | 32 | 04 | 14 |

| 15 | Use computer for staff recruitment and work allotment | 02 | 02 | 46 |
| 16 | Use mike address system for management | 34 | 06 | 10 |
| 17 | Use website for the information | 24 | 02 | 24 |
| 18 | Use cameras/ videos for spreading information/ maintaining records for disciplinary action | 12 | 12 | 26 |

Inventory 2 depicted that institutional administrators were using frequently ICT facilities for keeping the records of attendance, examination, timetable/ schedules. They also used ICT for sending the information and getting the information from apex bodies. There were more than 50% administrators who did not use ICT for salary/ fee/ budget details. ICT were not used for seminars/ guidance / updated information. Learners' attendance/ results were not communicated to parents online.

On the basis of their responses on the Inventory 2 'To know the Extent of using ICT for administrative purposes ', the institutional administrators were classified as using ICT always, some times and never.

## Analysis of Data

Simple statistical techniques were used like frequency, Chi square test to analyse the data and Hypotheses were tested one by one.

Hypothesis($H_1$): Availability of ICT facilities in the institution will enhance the ICT skills and proficiency among institutional administrators.

**Table 5: 2 X 3 table on Availability of ICT facilities and Administrators equipped with ICT Skills**

| Variable 1 \ Variable 2 | | Administrators equipped with ICT Skills | | |
|---|---|---|---|---|
| | | Tech Savvy | Semi Tech Savvy | Non Tech Savvy |
| Availability of ICT facilities in the Institutions | Well equipped with ICT Facilities | 20 | 09 | 04 |
| | Less equipped with ICT Facilities | 08 | 05 | 04 |

The Analysis of Chi- square ($x^2$) values for Hypothesis ($H_1$):

| $x^2$ Calculated | $x^2$ Table value | df | **Level of significance** | **Decision** |
|---|---|---|---|---|
| 9.11 | 5.99 | 2 | .05 | $H_1$ Accepted |

The calculated Chi-square value is 9.11 which are higher than the table value (5.99) at 2 degree of freedom and at .05 level of significance. Therefore $H_1$ is accepted which stated that the institutions well equipped with ICT facilities enhances the ICT skills and proficiency among the administrators making the tech savvy, thus rejecting the Null Hypothesis ($H_0$).

Hypothesis ($H_2$): ICT proficiency will enable the institutional administrators to use ICT for effective administration.

**Table 6: 3 X 3 table on Extent of use of ICT facilities and Administrators equipped with ICT Skills and Proficiency**

| Variable 2 / Variable 1 (Administrators equipped with ICT skills) | Extent of use of ICT Facilities by the Administrators | | |
|---|---|---|---|
| | Always | Some times | Never |
| Tech Savvy | 15 | 08 | 03 |
| Semi Tech Savvy | 04 | 04 | 05 |
| Non- Tech Savvy | 02 | 05 | 04 |

The Analysis of Chi- square ($x^2$) values for Hypothesis ($H_2$):

| $x^2$ Calculated | $x^2$ Table value | Df | Level of significance | Decision |
|---|---|---|---|---|
| 12.54 | 9.49 | 4 | .05 | $H_1$ Accepted |

The above table shows that the calculated $x^2$ value is 12.54 at degree of freedom 4 and at level of significance .05 which is much higher than the $x^2$ table value (9.49). Therefore the hypothesis II that states that ICT based skills and proficiency enable the institutional administrators to make best use of ICT facilities available for effective administration, thus rejecting the Null Hypothesis.

## Conclusion

From this study, it is concluded that in higher education, still the ICT facilities are not adequate to meet out the challenges of 21st century where everyone is talking about Digitalization of education. The situation in government institutions is really pathetic where the administrators and staff are highly qualified, tech savvy but do not have the well-equipped offices/ committee rooms or ICT facilities. Private institutions have the different scene where the ICT facilities are adequate but the administrators are not tech savvy or have control of management to use ICT selectively. This study revealed that administrators use computers and mobiles just to communicate information through e-mails / e-circulars. Most of the websites of the institution were non-functional or updated. Information uploaded was outdated. Private institutions did not provide the current status of the faculties/ staff, learners' intake, fee or salary. The gender of administrators had no bearing on their basic ICT skills and proficiency and use of ICT facilities in effective administration of the institutions. The study also revealed that some of the senior administrators did not want to cross their comfort zone and were happy working with chapter work and files. There were some of the administrators who were tech savvy, had the adequate ICT facilities in their institutions and used ICT in best possible ways for effective administration. Use of ICT helped them to achieve the goals by reducing complexities and establishing rapport with the apex bodies, regulatory bodies, management, learning-facilitators, learners, supportive staff and the community at large.

## Recommendations

**The following recommendations are suggested:**

The Government and the management should provide adequate infrastructural facilities andS ICT facilities for the administrators.

It should be mandatory to have workshops and in service training for the administrators also to equip them with latest technologies, apps and programmes.

There should be free internet/ Wi-Fi connection for administrators, learning-facilitators, learners and staff to have access of information for smooth administration.

There should be proper maintenance of ICTequipment to increase the life span of these gadgets.

There should be solar systems/ invertors/ generating systems for alternative electricity source.

Chapter 18

# Computer Phobia towards Using ICT among B.Ed. Learning-facilitators

✍ **Mohit Dixit**
*Parishkar Institute of Education, Jaipur, Rajasthan*

## Preview at a Glance

This study was conducted to find out the computer phobia of B.Ed. College learning-facilitators and their attitude towards using new technology .The sample was consisted 120 B.Ed. college learning-facilitators from Jaipur district of Rajasthan state. Computer phobia scale and an attitude towards using new technology scale were used to collect the data. The statistical techniques used were the mean, standard deviation, T-test. The results depicted that the factors like locality of the school, gender, marital status influence computer phobia and their attitude towards using new technology. Thus the results concluded have significant implications in educational field as today is the era of Information and Communication Technologies, where computer can be a medium of deep understanding and better conceptualization of the content for the learners as well as a boon for administrative purposes learning-facilitators are not using this because of lack of knowledge and later on, due to a hidden fear of damage of computer called computer phobia.

This research work motivates B.Ed. learning-facilitators to change their attitude towards using new technology as negative relationship is being observed between Computer Phobia and Attitude towards using new technology. Hereby, the research work is essentially helpful for policy framers and educators.

## Introduction

The current education scenario in India is an information age where there is knowledge explosion and skills essential for living have become increasingly complex and interdependent. Information and communication technology can be an extremely powerful enabler in efforts to bring positive and sustainable development to countries around the globe. Today almost a full decade into the 21st century, we live amidst an unprecedented revolution in the advancement of ICT.

Computers are influencing every aspect of life such as social, economic and education. In most of the task there is involvement of both human being and computer interaction. Computer literacy is seen to the more and more positively related with our success. Only a minimum percentage of people are regularly using the computer and many do not use computers for various reasons .Even many of the learning-facilitators have this irrational fear for the use of computers. This irrational fear towards computers is known as 'computer phobia'. If a learning-facilitator gets rid of the computer phobia and becomes a computer friendly, he/she can make use of computer during his/her teaching process without any inhibition and make the teaching learning process effective.

## Need and Significance of the Study

Education technology and computer play an important role in education. It is essential for all learners, present and future learning-facilitators to use and understand the computer and implement technology in order to be successful in their present and future careers. Teaching and learning activities have a huge impact on educational technology. The way learning-facilitators view technology, how they respond to it? How they present it? And how it helps to accomplish their vision of teaching and learning will affect the future implementation of educational technology.

Information of basic knowledge of computer is essential for learning-facilitators. Computer phobia and attitude towards using new technology of learning-facilitators are an important factor of determining his/her progress and development in the field of education. In the present scenario many a time the computer knowledge of the children is more than that of the learning-facilitators. Therefore it is the need of the hour that the learning-facilitators make use of the advance technology to hold the interest of the learner. Therefore there is a need to study the computer phobia and attitude towards using new technology of B.Ed. college learning-facilitators.

## Review of Related Research and Literature

**Diamantis(1982)** in his article on micro phobia contains suggestion on how learning-facilitators can prepare themselves for using computer in their classroom. In-service workshop practicing on machine and reading about computer are among the activities suggested.

**Davidson (1994),** in his work regarding removing computer phobia from the writing classroom, discusses the use of computer with learners of English as a second language focusing on a pilot programme that utilize computer word processing in ESL writing classes.

**Bailey (1994)** has examined the role of building administrator in helping staff cope with change various phobias and described appropriate treatments considered including a fear of change, fear of computer, fear of technology, fear of electronic open spaces, and fear of new learning methods.

**Reed (2000)** uses discourse on computer phobia and computer addictions to describe the cultural work involved and marketing strategies used between 1960-1990 regarding management of computer fear. Draws on popular discourses, advertisement and advice to explore how the personal computer was successfully connected to middle class family ideals and was transformed from a (cold) war machine into a socially friendly machine.

**Viji(2000)** conducted a study on computer self-confidence and computer experience in relation to computer related attitude and commitment to learning among Higher Secondary learners.

**Sivakumar (2000)** investigated computer awareness among higher secondary school learners. The study revealed that there is no significant difference between the boys and girls in computer awareness. The learners studying computer science had more awareness than the learners who are studying other courses.

**Dennis (2009)** has reported that as many as 50% of adults, including first year university learners, have some sort of computer related phobia. This report demonstrates that the use of computer still has unpleasant side effects despite the internet bloom in past decade.

**Sai (2010)** has reported that the factors like locality of the school gender types of school management do not influence computer phobia of 9$^{th}$ standard learners and their attitude towards computer usage in Education.

**Magre (2011)** reported that 30% degree college learning-facilitators have the computer phobia and there is a significant difference in the computer phobia of science and arts learning-facilitators.

**Mehra (2011)** observed that country type and interaction between country and faculty had significant effect on university learner's computer anxiety scores.

**Gihar (2012)** observed that there was no significant difference between government and private organization prospective learning-facilitators on computer phobia scale. A sharper variation wasobserved between the science and art stream prospective learning-facilitators on personal failure dimension of computer phobia.

**Tzu(2013)** investigated that the learning-facilitators who frequently used computer shoed lower computer phobia. It is evidenced that computer phobia is negatively associated with computer self-efficacy.

After reviewing these studies the researcher felt the need to undertake this study.

## Statement of the Problem

Study of Computer Phobia and Attitude towards Using New Technology among B.Ed. College Learning-facilitators on the Basis of Locality, Gender and Marital Status

## Objectives

The study was carried out with the following objectives:
- To investigate the level of computer phobia and attitude towards using new technology among B.Ed. College learning-facilitators.
- To investigate the computer phobia and attitude towards using new technology among B.Ed. College learning-facilitators in terms of
    1. Locality of the college
    2. Gender
    3. Marital Status

## Hypotheses

In ordered to achieve the above said objectives of the study the investigator formulated the following hypotheses:

1. Computer phobia of B.Ed. college learning-facilitators is high.
2. Attitude towards using new technology B.Ed. College learning-facilitators is Neutral.
3. There is no significant difference in the computer phobia of Urban and Rural B.Ed. College learning-facilitators.
4. There is no significant difference in the computer phobia of Male and Female B.Ed. College learning-facilitators.
5. There is no significant difference in the computer phobia of Married and unmarried B.Ed. College learning-facilitators.
6. There is no significant difference in the attitude towards using new technology of Urban and Rural B.Ed. College learning-facilitators.
7. There is no significant difference in the attitude towards using new technology of Male and Female B.Ed. College learning-facilitators.
8. There is no significant difference in the attitude towards using new technology of Male and Female B.Ed. College learning-facilitators.
9. There is no significant relationship between computer phobia and attitude towards using new technology among B.Ed. college learning-facilitators.

## Delimitations

**The following were the limitations of the present study:**
- The study was delimited to Jaipur District of Rajasthan only.
- The study was delimited to B.Ed. college learning-facilitators.
- The study was delimited to 120 B.Ed. college learning-facilitators only.

- The study was delimited to 60 Urban and 60 Rural B.Ed. college learning-facilitators only.
- The study was further delimited to 60 Male and 60 Female Married/Unmarried B.Ed. college learning-facilitators only.

## Methodology

In the present descriptive survey method was employed in order to know Computer phobia and Attitude towards using new technology of B.Ed. college learning-facilitators of Jaipur District of Rajasthan. Relationship between these variables was calculated by Pearson's Product Moment Method of correlation. In order to know the significant difference between the mean score of both variables, the statistical technique t-ratio was employed.

## Sample

The present study was conducted on random sample of 120 B.Ed. college learning-facilitators of Jaipur District of Rajasthan. The study was equally balanced between 60 Urban and 60 Rural B.Ed. college learning-facilitators. The study was further equally categorized between 60 Male and 60 Female Married/Unmarried B.Ed. college learning-facilitators

## Tool Used

The instrument employed for the exploration of new field is called tools. The selection of suitable tools and their applications is an important step in the collection of data after the research problem has been selected, defined and delimited. The collected data should be following tools were used:

Computer Phobia Scale by Rajasekar and Vaiyapuri Raja (2006)

Attitude Towards Using New Technology Scale by Rajasekar (2006)

## Statistical Techniques

Mean, Standard deviation, Standard error, t-value andcorrelation.

## Data Analysis

Hypothesis 1: Computer phobia of B.Ed. college learning-facilitators is high.

Here the data was analysed in three levels of computer phobia -

1. High computer phobia
2. Low computer phobia
3. No computer phobia

**Table 1: Showing the Percentage of Computer Phobia of 120 B.Ed. College Learning-facilitators**

| S. No | Computer phobia level | N | Percentage |
|---|---|---|---|
| 1. | High computer phobia | 66 | 55% |
| 2. | Low computer phobia | 24 | 20% |
| 3. | No computer phobia | 30 | 25% |
| | Total | 120 | 100% |

From table 1, it is observed that that 55% B.Ed. learning-facilitator reported high computer phobia, 20% reports no computer phobia and 25% B.Ed. learning-facilitator reported low computer phobia.

Hence the hypothesis 1, 'Computer phobia of B.Ed. college learning-facilitators is high' is accepted.

Hypothesis 2: Attitude towards using new technology B.Ed. College learning-facilitators is Neutral.

Here the data was analysed in three levels of attitude towards using new technology -

1. Unfavourable
2. Neutral
3. Favourable

**Table 2: Showing the percentage of level of attitude towards using new technology of 120 B.Ed. college learning-facilitators**

| S. No | Attitude Level | N | Percentage |
|---|---|---|---|
| 1. | Unfavourable | 54 | 45% |
| 2. | Neutral | 30 | 25% |
| 3. | Favourable | 36 | 30% |
| | Total | 120 | 100% |

From table 2, it is observed that 45% B.Ed. learning-facilitator reported unfavourable attitude towards using new technology. 25% B.Ed. learning-facilitators reported neutral attitude and 30% B.Ed. learning-facilitators reported favourable attitude towards using new technology.

Hence the hypothesis 2, 'Attitude towards using new technology B.Ed. College learning-facilitators are Neutral' is rejected.

Hypothesis 3: There is no significant difference in the computer phobia of Urban and Rural B.Ed. College learning-facilitators.

From table3, it is observed that t-value of computer phobia of 60 Urban and 60 Rural B.Ed. college learning-facilitators is 2.71 which non-significant at 0.05 level of significance. Hence there is no significant difference in computer phobia of Urban and Rural B.Ed. college learning-facilitators.

**Table 3: Mean, S.D., S.E. and t-ratio of computer phobia of 60 Urban and Rural B.Ed. college learning-facilitators**

| Locality | Number | Mean | S.D. | S.E. | t-value | Level of Significance |
|---|---|---|---|---|---|---|
| Urban | 60 | 73.06 | 13.78 | 2.71 | 1.826 | Non- significant difference at 0.05 level of significance |
| Rural | 60 | 68.11 | 15.82 | | | |

Significance Level 0.05 df =118

Hence the hypothesis 3, 'There is no significant difference in the computer phobia of Urban and Rural B.Ed. College learning-facilitators' is accepted.

Hypothesis 4: There is no significant difference in the computer phobia of Male and Female B.Ed. College learning-facilitators.

**Table 4: Mean, S.D., S.E. and t-ratio of computer phobia of 60 Male and Female B.Ed. college learning-facilitators**

| Gender | Number | Mean | S.D. | S.E. | t-value | Level of Significance |
|---|---|---|---|---|---|---|
| Male | 60 | 83.65 | 12.06 | 2.43 | 3.266 | Significant difference at 0.05 level of significance |
| Female | 60 | 75.71 | 14.46 | | | |

Significance Level 0.05 df = 118

From table4, it is observed that t-value of computer phobia of 60 Male and 60 Female B.Ed. college learning-facilitators is 3.266 which is significant at 0.05 level of significance. Hence there is significant difference in computer phobia of Male and Female B.Ed. college learning-facilitators.

Hence the hypothesis 4, 'There is no significant difference in the computer phobia of Male and Female B.Ed. College learning-facilitators' is rejected.

Hypothesis 5: There is no significant difference in the computer phobia of Married and unmarried B.Ed. College learning-facilitators.

**Table 5: Mean, S.D., S.E. and t-ratio of computer phobia of 60 Married and Unmarried B.Ed. college learning-facilitators**

| M. Status | Number | Mean | S.D. | S.E. | t-value | Level of Significance |
|---|---|---|---|---|---|---|
| Married | 60 | 73.65 | 14.78 | 2.58 | 4.303 | Significant difference at 0.05 level of significance |
| Unmarried | 60 | 84.76 | 13.47 | | | |

Significance Level 0.05 df =118

From table 5, it is observedthat 't' value of computer phobia of 60 Married and 60 Unmarried B.Ed. college learning-facilitators is 4.303 which significant at 0.05 level of significance. Hence there is significant difference in computer phobia of Married and Unmarried B.Ed. college learning-facilitators.

Hence the hypothesis 5, 'There is no significant difference in the computer phobia of Married and Unmarried B.Ed. College learning-facilitators' is rejected.

Hypothesis 6: There is no significant difference in the attitude towards using new technology of Urban and Rural B.Ed. College learning-facilitators.

Table 6: Mean, S.D., S.E. and t-ratio of Attitude towards using new technology of 60 Urban and Rural B.Ed. college learning-facilitators

| Locality | Number | Mean | S.D. | S.E. | t-value | Level of Significance |
|---|---|---|---|---|---|---|
| Urban | 60 | 118.75 | 10.73 | 2.22 | 3.664 | Significant difference at 0.05 level of significance |
| Rural | 60 | 110.58 | 13.52 | | | |

Significance Level 0.05 df =118

From table 6, it is observed that t-value of Attitude towards using new technology of 60 Urban and 60 Rural B.Ed. college learning-facilitators is 3.664 which is significant at 0.05 level of significance. Hence there is significant difference in Attitude towards using new technology of Urban and Rural B.Ed. college learning-facilitators.

Hence the hypothesis 6, 'There is no significant difference in the Attitude towards using new technology of Urban and Rural B.Ed. College learning-facilitators' is rejected.

Hypothesis 7: There is no significant difference in the attitude towards using new technology of Male and Female B.Ed. College learning-facilitators.

Table 7: Mean, S.D., S.E. and t-ratio of Attitude towards using new technology of 60 Male and Female B.Ed. college learning-facilitators

| Gender | Number | Mean | S.D. | S.E. | t-value | Level of Significance |
|---|---|---|---|---|---|---|
| Male | 60 | 109.05 | 11.74 | 2.01 | 1.196 | Non- significant difference at 0.05 level of significance |
| Female | 60 | 105.08 | 10.30 | | | |

Significance Level 0.05 df =118

From table 7, it is observed that t-value of Attitude towards using new technology of 60 Male and 60 Female B.Ed. college learning-facilitators is 1.196 which non-significant at 0.05 level of significance. Hence there is no significant difference in Attitude towards using new technology of Male and Female B.Ed. college learning-facilitators.

Hence the hypothesis 4, 'There is no significant difference in the computer phobia of Male and Female B.Ed. College learning-facilitators' is accepted.

Hypothesis 8: There is no significant difference in the attitude towards using new technology of Male and Female B.Ed. College learning-facilitators.

From table 8, it is observed that t-value of Attitude towards using new technology of 60 Married and 60 Unmarried B.Ed. college learning-facilitators is 2.839 which significant at 0.05 level of significance. Hence there is significant difference in Attitude towards using new technology of Married and Unmarried B.Ed. college learning-facilitators.

**Table 8: Mean, S.D., S.E. and t-ratio of Attitude towards using new technology of 60 Married and Unmarried B.Ed. college learning-facilitators**

| M. Status | Number | Mean | S.D. | S.E. | t-value | Level of Significance |
|---|---|---|---|---|---|---|
| Married | 60 | 118.25 | 11.69 | 2.59 | 2.839 | Significant difference at 0.05 level of significance |
| Unmarried | 60 | 125.63 | 16.39 | | | |

Significance Level 0.05 df =118

Hence the hypothesis 8, 'There is no significant difference in the Attitude towards using new technology of Married and Unmarried B.Ed. College learning-facilitators' is rejected.

Hypothesis 9: There is no significant relationship between computer phobia and attitude towards using new technology among B.Ed. college learning-facilitators.

**Table 9: Showing the co-efficient of co-relation between Computer phobia and Attitude towards using new technology**

| S. No | Variable | N | Co-efficient of Co-relation | Level of Significance | Result |
|---|---|---|---|---|---|
| 1. | Computer phobia | 120 | -0.67 | Non-significant difference at 0.05 level of significance | Negative Correlation |
| 2. | Attitude towards using new technology | 120 | | | |

Significance Level 0.05 df =238

Table 9 represents the co-efficient of co-relation of computer phobia and Attitude towards using new technology of B.Ed. college learning-facilitators. It comes out to be -0.67 which is non-significant at 0.05 level of significance. Hence there is negative relationship between computer phobia and attitude towards using new technology of B.Ed. college learning-facilitators.

Hence the hypothesis 9 'There is no significant relationship between computer phobia and attitude towards using new technology among B.Ed. college learning-facilitators' is accepted.

## Findings

On the basis of results obtain after the Interpretations of Objectives and Hypotheses the following findings has been drawn:

- ▶ The level of computer phobia is high.
- ▶ The attitude towards using new technology is unfavourable.
- ▶ There is no significant difference in the computer phobia of Urban and Rural learning-facilitators.
- ▶ There is a significant difference in the computer phobia of Male and Female learning-facilitators.

- There is a significant difference in the computer phobia of Married and Unmarried learning-facilitators.
- There is a significant difference in attitude towards using new technology of Urban and Rural learning-facilitators.
- There is no significant difference in attitude towards using new technology of Male and Female learning-facilitators.
- There is no significant difference in attitude towards using new technology of Marriedand Unmarried learning-facilitators.
- There is no significant relationship between computer phobia and attitude towards using new technology among B.Ed. college learning-facilitators.

## Conclusion

The main finding of the study is that both urban and rural B.Ed. college learning-facilitators are affected by their computer phobia. So the teaching working in urban and rural area must be given computer literacy. Training in computer must be given by government especially for female learning-facilitator's .The government must ensure that all the colleges have the infrastructure facilities to have computer labs. Learning-facilitators should attend seminar, webinar and workshop related to ICT.

## Educational Implications

Teaching is one of the most challenging and crucial professions in the world. Learning-facilitators are critical in facilitating learning and in making it more efficient and effective; they hold the key to success of any education reform; and they are accountable for successful human development of the nation and for preparing the foundation for social and economic development.

The present inquiry has accessed to computer phobia among prospective learning-facilitators. In this technological era with the help of computers we can improve the class room teaching also. By using computers, in the class we can give the number of information to the learners. It is also helpful for the learning-facilitators in keeping the records. It also benefited for our society and educational environment. But mostly learning-facilitators are not using the computers due to the lack of knowledge or a hidden fear of damage of computer called computer phobia. As computer phobia is concerned. The educational planners and administrators can take clue from following revelations of study.

The investigator observed Negative relationship between Computer Phobia and Attitude towards using new technology. The present will give immense help to motivate the B.Ed. college learning-facilitators to change their attitude towards using new technology by this they are able to come out from Computer phobia.

The Present study will help the B.Ed. college learning-facilitators in development favourable attitude towards using new technology.

This result will also give immense help for policy framer in the formation of Educational Policies and Curriculum Construction for B.Ed. college learning-facilitators.

The present study helps the learning-facilitators in developing new methods of learning and teaching based on ICT.

These results have practical implications in the field of Learning-facilitator Education.

This problem has practical implications. Thus it can play a pivotal role in the nourishment of harmonious and all round personality of B.Ed. college learning-facilitators.

Chapter 19

# ICT Integration in School for Technological Teaching and Learning

✍ **Pramod Kumar Gupta**
*S. S. S. B.Ed. College, Bokaro, Jharkhand*

## Preview at a Glance

Over the previous decade India governments have put essentially in digital education, making a solid base as far as technological framework, advanced assets and support for learning-facilitators training. In the meantime, the Digital Education Revolution (DER) activity has encouraged school authority in the utilization of digital technology. The test now confronting schools is to expand on this limit, utilizing further enhancements by moving the concentration far from the securing of new technologies to the utilization of these new apparatuses as empowering influences of inventive, testing and connecting with methods for learning and teaching. By moving to the following stage, schools will prepare learners and learning-facilitators to address the difficulties of a quickly evolving world.

## Introduction

Information and communication (ICT) is a power that has changed numerous parts of the way we live. If one something equates to look at such fields as medication, tourism, travel business, law, managing an account, building and engineering, the effect of ICT over the previous a few decades has been massive. The way these fields work today is not same as the ways they worked previously. Be that as it may, when one takes a gander at training, there appears to have been an uncanny absence of impact and far less change than different fields have faced. Various people have endeavoured to investigate this lack of action and impact. There have been various elements hindering the extensive approval of ICT in training over all areas. These have included such factors as a lack of financing to help the buy the technology, an absence of preparing among built up showing experts, an absence of inspiration and need among learning-facilitators to adopt ICT as educating devices. Be that as it may, as of late, factors have developed which have reinforced and urged moves to adopt ICTs into classrooms and learning settings.

ICT can be utilized as a part of different ways where it helps the learning-facilitators and learner to find out about their individual subject knowledge. An technology based instructing and learning offers different fascinating ways which incorporates educational recording, mind-mapping, incitement, guided disclosure, the use of databases, brainstorming, music, storage of information, World Wide Web that will influence the figuring out how to process all the more satisfying and significant. Then again, learner will profit by ICT joining where they are not limited to the restricted educational modules and assets, rather hands-on exercises in an innovation based course is intended to help them to animate their comprehension about the subject. It likewise encourages learning-facilitators to outline their lesson designs in a viable, innovative and intriguing methodology that would bring about learner' dynamic learning. Past explores demonstrated that utilization of ICT in educating will upgrade the learning procedure and augments the learner' capacities in dynamic learning.

## *Impact of ICT on How Learners Learn*

Similarly as technology is impacting and supporting what is being learned in schools and colleges, so too is it supporting changes to the way learner are learning. Moves from content-focused educational program to competency-based educational program are related with moves far from learning-facilitator focused types of conveyance to learner focused structures. Through innovation encouraged methodologies, contemporary learning settings now urge learner to assume liability for their own learning .In the past learner have turned out to be exceptionally agreeable to learning through Tran's missive modes. Learner has been prepared to give others a chance to present to them the data that structures the educational modules. The developing utilization of ICT as an instructional medium is changing and will probably keep on changing a large number of the procedures utilized by the learning-facilitator and learner in the learning procedure. The accompanying section portrays specific types of learning that are prominence in colleges and schools around the world.

## *Learning-facilitator' Belief on Technology Based Teaching and Learning*

With the advancement of learning technology in the late twentieth century, education framework has changed quickly. This is because of the capacity of technology to give a proactive, simple access and comprehensive educating and learning condition. These days, Ministry of instruction in everywhere throughout the world has provided lot of facilities and training keeping in mind the end goal to improve the utilization of cutting edge advances in the nations' instructing and learning process. A high spending plan has been put in request to give the hardware required by learning-facilitators to enhance the education framework. In spite of the considerable number of endeavours,

# ICT Integration in School for Technological Teaching and Learning

the greater part of the nations is confronting comparable issue whereby the learning-facilitators are not amplifying the utilization of the innovation gave. This has turned into a genuine issue the same number of past explores have demonstrated the utilization of ICT in educating and learning procedure could enhance learner' accomplishment. Numerous, analysts have required a push to investigate the elements that influencing learning-facilitators' acknowledgment of ICT use in the classrooms. It demonstrates that, the real hindrance of the execution was the learning-facilitators' conviction as the learning-facilitators are the individual who actualizes the adjustment in their teaching and learning process. Also, past research demonstrates that the relationship of learning-facilitators' conviction and the utilization of ICT are high. Learning-facilitator's part is getting more essential particularly in utilization of ICT in teaching method which could expand the accomplishment of the learner, their innovativeness and thinking aptitudes.

Be that as it may, learning-facilitators' viability in urban schools changes as the times of involvement of working and time of learners. It demonstrates that the learning-facilitators' adequacy is diminishing as the times of involvement and age increments yet some way or another the decline and the viability conviction rely upon the school administration. School administration here means the open doors for collegial communication, and the utilization of the instructional assets. Schools that could give chances to learning-facilitators to think about teaching and learning with their associates and for directors and learning-facilitators to team up and convey, and in addition bolster the utilization of learning-facilitators assets. From this exploration, the learning-facilitators adequacy conviction is rely upon the school administration and culture. Along these lines, if the school has dependably embed the way of life to change and learning-facilitators are constantly sent for training for upgrading themselves, and after that the coordination of ICT in classroom will be less demanding to be improved in the classroom.

## Methodology

### Research Design

In this research, computable methodology was used to gather and evaluate the data acquired from all the respondents. The researchers established the questionnaire and confirmed it before being circulated to the targeted group of respondents. Few sections on the questionnaire were designed specifically to address research objectives in respect with the efficiency of ICT integration for learners in learning and effective features of ICT integration in local public schools. Therefore, the questionnaire was circulated to get the data from the respondents.

### Sampling and Population

For the research the respondents are 90 learning-facilitators were selected from local public primary and secondary schools. The questionnaire was randomly circulated to the respondents with background of teaching irrespective of gender and teaching experience as well as maximum teaching experience. There are no likings set by the researchers as long as the respondents come with teaching background especially in public primary and secondary schools. Meanwhile the targeted respondents for this research are intended for people with teaching background, the researcher tried to get particularly learning-facilitators from public primary and secondary schools to the part of this research. Hence, the questionnaires are not equally circulated in numbers of primary and secondary learning-facilitators, the overall population as compared to learning-facilitators from primary schools and secondary schools.

## Data Collection Procedure

The researcher changed the survey before it is fact affirmed and disseminated to the objective gathering of respondents. The information was gathered inside 2 weeks through arbitrary conveyance. The respondents were given 3-5 days to finish the poll and afterward researcher has gathered the survey for information examination. Following 2 weeks, all the entire topped off surveys were accumulated and gathered for promote information examination by the specialist to get the yield and discoveries for the exploration.

## Procedure of Data Analysis

All the data accumulated from the respondents was amassed to be dissected using Statistical programming and Microsoft Excel. The examination fuses both enlightening and inferential examination. The scientist used clear examination to analyse the repeat and level of the all-inclusive community in the measurement establishment. Besides, it is similarly used to choose the mean, standard deviation, repeat and rate to recognize the reasonability of ICT consolidation for understudy in learning and also the suitable segments of ICT mix in educating in government funded schools.

## Finding and Results

The finding of this research will provide the output require by the researcher to answer the research required questions. The findings are completed as per the sections in the questionnaire and few inferential analyses.

**Table 1: Gender wise Distribution of the Respondent**

| S. No | Factor | Respondent | Percentage |
|---|---|---|---|
| 1. | Male | 25 | 27.78 |
| 2. | Female | 65 | 72.22 |
|  | Total | 90 | 100.00 |

**Source: Field Survey**

The above table describes the gender wise distribution of the respondent and has been observed that most of the respondent 65 (72.22) are female respondent from 90 respondent and remaining 25 (27.78) respondent are male respondent.

**Table 2: Teaching Experience wise Distribution of the Respondent**

| S. No | Factor | Respondent | Percentage |
|---|---|---|---|
| 1. | <1 year | 15 | 16.67 |
| 2. | 1 – 5 years | 30 | 33.33 |
| 3. | 5 – 10 years | 25 | 27.78 |
| 4. | >10 years | 20 | 22.22 |
| Total | | 90 | 100.00 |

Source: Field Survey

The above table 2 describes the teaching experience of the respondent and is been observed that 30(33.33) respondent having teaching experience between 1-5 years which is highest, the 25(27.78) respondent can have 5-10 years of teaching experience, 20(22.22) respondent can have greater than 10 years of experience and remaining 15(16.67) respondent can have less than 1 years of teaching experience.

**Table 3: School Type wise Distribution**

| S. No | Factor | Respondent | Percentage |
|---|---|---|---|
| 1. | Primary | 39 | 43.33 |
| 2. | Secondary | 51 | 56.67 |
| Total | | 90 | 100.00 |

From the above table 3 it is clear that researcher has selected 39 (43.33) primary school and 51 (56.67) are secondary school for the research study out of 90 schools.

**Table 4: Distribution of School Area**

| S. No | Factor | Respondent | Percentage |
|---|---|---|---|
| 1. | Urban | 69 | 76.67 |
| 2. | Rural | 21 | 23.33 |
| Total | | 90 | 100.00 |

Source: Field Survey

For the research study researcher has selected 90 schools from urban and rural area, in the above table 4 it is described that 69(76.67) schools are selected from urban area and 21 (23.33) schools are selected from rural area.

**Table 5: Distribution of Teaching Style Preferences**

| S. No | Factor | Respondent | Percentage |
|---|---|---|---|
| 1. | Traditional | 42 | 46.67 |
| 2. | Modern Technology (ICT) | 48 | 53.33 |
| Total | | 90 | 100.00 |

Source: Field Survey

The above table 5 describes the teaching style preferences given by the school and it has observed that out of 90 schools 42(46.67) are still giving the preferences to traditional type of teaching and 48 (53.33) are giving the preferences to modern technological teaching methodology that is ICT teaching methodology.

**Table 6: Distribution of Ability of Handling ICT teaching**

| S. No | Factor | Respondent | Percentage |
|---|---|---|---|
| 1. | High | 23 | 25.56 |
| 2. | Medium | 56 | 62.22 |
| 3. | Low | 11 | 12.22 |
| Total | | 90 | 100.00 |

Source: Field Survey

The above table 6 describes the respondents ability to handling ICT technology and it has observed that the 23 (25.56) respondent says that they can have high end ability to handle ICT teaching technology, 11 (62.22) respondent says that they can have very low end ability to handle ICT teaching technology and remaining 56 (62.22) respondent says that they can have medium ability to handle ICT teaching technology.

From the above table 7 it is observed that most learning-facilitators agreed that the use of ICT will definitely offer lots of prospects for an operative teaching as well as ICT maintained teaching makes learning more operative with the sharing mean of 24.9975 mean. This situation shows that learning-facilitators view the use of ICT in teaching and learning process as something positive where ICT is the assistance required by learning-facilitators to confirm the efficiency of both teaching and learning process.

Learning-facilitator's awareness and capability in managing ICT also obtained from the data where the mean of 33.33 shows that maximum learning-facilitators feel confident in learning new computer skills and they are able to use ICT to find teaching materials and resources. In this perspective, it indications that learning-facilitators are open towards the use of ICT in teaching, not actually strong and feels relaxed in learning new stuffs. Other than that, learning-facilitators consider that it is easier to teach by using ICT with the mean score of 22.435 but at the same moment, they still considers in the predictable way of teaching where learning-facilitators are the centre of learning and specified that they can still have an operative teaching without the use of ICT with recorded mean of 21.7475.

With other perspective, most learning-facilitators believe that the use of ICT assistances teaching and learning in numerous ways and saying that ICT integration is not a waste of time with total mean of 24.9975. Yet, there are also negative part of ICT integration where the result describes that classroom administration is out of control when ICT is used in teaching, followed by learners create no efforts for their lesson and learning procedure with score mean of 24.9925 and most learning-facilitators

# ICT Integration in School for Technological Teaching and Learning

agreed that the use of ICT in teaching only cause learners' to make less attention with the highest mean recorded of 27.27 which shows learning-facilitator's less recognition towards ICT integration due to learner's approach whom being too independent on ICT and not taking obligation for their own liberated learning which annoying and inadequate the learning-facilitators.

**Table 7: Learning-facilitator Perception of ICT integration in Teaching**

| S. No. | Items | Strongly Disagree | Disagree | Agree | Strongly Agree | Mean | SD |
|---|---|---|---|---|---|---|---|
| 1. | I can Confident learning new Computer Skills | 0 | 5 (5.55) | 63 (70.00) | 22 (24.45) | 33.33 | 3.937004 |
| 2. | I feel that it is easy to teach with ICT | 0 | 10 (1.11) | 62 (68.63) | 18 (20.00) | 22.435 | 1.658312 |
| 3. | I have knowledge that ICT provide great effective teaching | 0 | 2 (2.22) | 74 (82.22) | 14 (15.22) | 24.915 | 1.870829 |
| 4. | I feel that ICT supported teaching makes learning more effective | 2 (2.22) | 6 (6.67) | 46 (51.11) | 36 (40.00) | 24.9975 | 3.000 |
| 5. | I feel that ICT will help to improve the learning-facilitators teaching quality | 2 (2.22) | 9 (10.00) | 42 (46.67) | 37 (41.11) | 25 | 3.041381 |
| 6. | I think uses of ICT Improves the Teaching quality | 1 (0.11) | 8 (8.88) | 49 (54.44) | 32 (35.55) | 24.745 | 2.397916 |
| 7. | I have more time to provide to learners' need if ICT is used in teaching. | 0 | 35 (38.88) | 39 (43.33) | 16 (17.77) | 24.83 | 1.3228757 |
| 8. | I can effectively teach without ICT | 3 0.33 | 10 1.11 | 58 64.44 | 19 21.11 | 21.7475 | 1.5811388 |
| 9. | I think teaching with ICT is a waste of time. | 16 (17.77) | 36 (40.00) | 27 (30.00) | 11 (12.22) | 24.9975 | 3.6742346 |
| 10. | I know without ICT my learner can learn best | 9 (10.00) | 46 (51.11) | 23 (25.55) | 12 (13.33) | 24.9975 | 3.6742346 |
| 11. | Learner pay less attention when ICT is used | 13 (23.63) | 44 (48.88) | 25 (27.77) | 8 (8.88) | 27.27 | 3.6742346 |
| 12. | Learner cannot make any efforts for their lesson if teaching done through ICT | 21 (23.33) | 52 (57.77) | 10 (11.1) | 7 (7.77 | 24.9925 | 3.6742346 |

**Source: Field Survey**

## Conclusion

The result of this examination describes that technology based teaching and learning is more successful in contrast with traditional classroom. This is on the grounds that, utilizing ICTtools and material will set up a dynamic learning condition that is all the more intriguing and compelling for the learning-facilitators and learner. In any case, the greater part of learning-facilitator in this investigation concur that ICT enhances classroom administration as learner are all will make on and more engaged. Also, this examination demonstrated that learners take in more successfully with the utilization of ICT as lesson planned are all the more captivating and fascinating. Appropriately, the members concurred that coordinating ICT can develop learners' learning.

## Recommendations

It may be excessively regular for issues and difficulties of ICT reconciliation to be discussed about yet inside and out investigation of ICT incorporation in subjects in schools is minimum examined. It is great if additionally studies can be made in view of what obstructions educators are looking in utilizing ICT in their day by day classrooms in schools. Moreover, instead of simply centring in state funded schools, it is ideal if this examination can be led in 3 noteworthy schools we have in Malaysia that incorporates government funded schools, Chinese school and also Indian school. This is on account of a few schools may have all the more financing that makes ICT execution considerably quicker and less demanding. It is great if examination can be made between various schools in which it can take the great side as cases and make upgrades required from the imperfections distinguished.

To guarantee that the open issues and challenges are acknowledged, it will be imperative as it is in each other stroll of life to guarantee that the instructive innovative work dollar is supported so training everywhere can gain from inside and that encounters and exercises in various foundations and parts can educate and direct others without the consistent requirement for re-development of the wheel. By and by ICTs serve to give the way to quite a bit of this action to understand the potential it holds.

Chapter

20

# Functioning of ICT@School Scheme at Secondary Level

✎ **Ranjan Kumar Sahoo**
*University of Delhi, New Delhi*

## Preview at a Glance

Education is the most powerful instrument in the progressive transformation of a society. The Information and Communication Technology (ICT) in now a day plays a very strategic role in this transformation process. Thus government also tried to integrate ICT to teaching learning process. So in the year 2004, Govt. adopted its one of the ambitious program to revamp the secondary and higher secondary education sector in the country called as, the ICT@School Scheme. It is again revised in 2010. It is one of the creative evolutions which is being developed to boost secondary education sector in India by providing opportunities to learners to mainly build their capacity on ICT skills and make them learn through computer aided learning process. The present study has made an attempt to address the functioning of ICT@School Scheme with specific reference to the central query i.e. availability and integration of ICT in teaching learning and what are the perception of learners and learning-facilitators about prospects and problems of ICT use? For this purpose, descriptive survey method was adopted as the primary design of the study. Further, it delimited to Balasore district of Odisha and selected 6 secondary schools by using purposive sampling method. Data was collected from both learners and learning-facilitators and both two data base was compared to determine if there is convergence and difference. The investigator applied self-developed checklist for checking the availability of ICT resources, an observation schedule for integration of ICT in teaching learning process and also focus group discussion for perceptions of learners and learning-facilitators about prospects and problems of ICT use. The collected data was analysed by simple percentage analysis and thread wire discussion. The findings of the study revealed that almost all sampled schools were functioning ICT in teaching-learning process as our

ICT@School scheme stipulates. But overall picture on availability of resources like computers and peripheral hardware in all schools were not observed sufficient. High majority of learners and learning-facilitators were stated positively to integrate ICT in teaching-learning process.

## Background of the Study

Since the time of independence to this 21st century a remarkable change occurs in the teaching learning process. Learning process changed from learning-facilitator centric to learner centric, bookish to outer world. All the stakeholders of teaching learning process are now mostly depending on the Information and Communication Technology (ICT) world. So now there is a need of paradigm shift. Digitalization of education is the need of the society as well as of the individual. In order to satisfy this need to make classroom digitalize and to make future generation digitalize ICT@ School Scheme recognized by the Central Govt. It is one of the creative evolutions which is being developed to boost secondary education sector in India by providing opportunities to learners to mainly build their capacity on ICT skills and make them learn through computer aided learning process. The root of this project is so deep it started from as the scheme of Educational Technology (ET) was started in 1972 during the IV Plan. Then it leads to the Computer Literacy and Studies in Schools (CLASS) project for recognition of the importance of role of ICT in education during the VIII Plan. Then gradually the scope of this CLASS project widened to provide financial grants to educational institutions and also to cover new Government and Government aided secondary and higher secondary schools. Finally, in the year in the year 1998 in order to recognize the critical role of ICT in achieving the country's developmental and educational objectives, the National IT task force recommended the introduction of ICT infrastructure in schools and that 1 to 3% of the budget be spent on providing computers in secondary and senior secondary schools over the subsequent five years. The scheme stipulates that each school be provided with requisite infrastructure in the form of hardware and software like PCs and accessories like printers, projection systems, internet connectivity, power supply and computer labs etc. Following this recommendation, the Government launched its flagship ICT scheme for schools; 'The ICT@School Scheme' in 2004, to promote ICT literacy and ICT-enabled learning in Government and Government aided secondary and senior secondary schools (revised ICT@School Scheme).

Based on the implementation experience of the first six years, the government revised the ICT@School Scheme in 2010. The revised ICT @ Schools Scheme it is the mission to bring all government secondary and higher secondary schools under the ambit of the scheme with giving priority to educationally backward blocks and areas with concentration of SC, ST, minority and weaker sections. Now as per the 2011 census the population of India is 121.02 Cr. (Male 62.37cr, Female 58.65cr) with literacy rate 74.04% (Male 82.14% and Female 65.46%). The country has 2, 33,517 secondary schools and ICT@School: till date 85,343 schools have been approved and 62,917 schools are implemented under the scheme. 26,741 schools have already been completed their project period and 22,426 schools are yet to be implemented.

In order to address the functioning of ICT@School Scheme the investigator go through the review of related literature to the selected problem, in connection to availability of ICT resources some study revealed that most ICTs required for training were not available at all, and those were available are inadequate. It also observed that the available ICTs were being utilized to a very low extent and it was generally agreed that the given factors are indeed the ones affecting or hindering utilization of the available resources in schools (Obota, Beldina, andStanslous, 2015). Similarly, some study revealed on the positive side of availability of ICT resources that that many of learners learned how to use computer and other ICT facilities from home. Due to the availability of ICT resources teaches and learners both were get benefited in term of learning and teaching (GhwanmebandSameh, 2012). Then in relation to the dimension integration of ICT to teaching learning process it revealed that integration of ICT in teaching learning process created an effective and interactive platform both for learning-facilitators and learners (Keengwe,2007; Fatima, 2013; Natia, James andWassan, 2015). Then lastly on perception of learners and learning-facilitators about prospects and problems by the use of ICT revealed that learners were critical of their use of ICT; learning-facilitators are also make application of ICT in learning context but mostly used at home. Thus there observed a prevailing gap between home use and application in the classroom (Chigona, KayongoandKausa, 2010; Adesoji, Francis andFabunmi, 2012). It was also revealed that learners were positive, to an extent, about the application of ICT in the classroom. Further, there has a belief amongst learners that it could negatively impact their learning (Keengwe, 2007; Iyamu, OkhinedeandSumuel, 2016). Although the above review helped in making a concise idea on availability, integration of ICT in teaching learning process and perceptions of stakeholders about it but today after thirteen years of implementation of the ICT@ School Scheme in India there observed only few limited study on this scheme and especially in the context of Odisha. Thus the present study has made a humble attempt to have an insight about and address the functioning of ICT@School Scheme with specific reference to the central query i.e. availability and integration of ICT in teaching learning and what are the perception of learners and learning-facilitators about prospects and problems of ICT use at secondary school stage?

## Objectives of the Study

Keeping in view the requirement, the study focused on the specific objectives as mentioned below:

- To study the availability of ICT resources in secondary schools.
- To study the integration of ICT into teaching-learning process.
- To study the perception of learners and learning-facilitators about prospects and problems of ICT use.

## Methodology of the Study
### Design

Keeping in view the objectives of the study the investigator selected descriptive method for the study. The study was designed to obtain precise and pertinent information concerning both the learners and learning-facilitators from different government secondary schools of Balasore district of Odisha thus the investigator selected descriptive survey as the primary design for the study.

## Population and Sample

The target population for the present study was all the secondary school of Balasore district of Odishawhere ICT@School Scheme is functioning. Again the investigator has purposively selected six secondary schools of Balasore district as its sample.

## Tools Used

In the present study the following tools have been used to obtain information from the respondents. All the tools have been developed by the investigator.

Check list for objective no.1: A checklist was prepared by the investigator. It was classified under four heads; availability of hardware resources, software resources, interactive resources and human resources. The Hardware resources contained 36 items, software resources contained 17 items, interactive platforms contained 11 items and the last one the human resources contained 2 items only. Thus the checklist was consisted of overall sixty-six items. The investigator developed this tool with intension to check the availability and usability of ICT resources in selected secondary school.

Observation schedule for objective no.2: An observation schedule was also prepared by the investigator with the intention to observe ICT integration in teaching learning process in sampled schools. The investigator observed in 3 segments; integration of ICT with respect to subject, classroom environment by the use of ICT and learner's assignment through ICT.

Focus group discussion for objective no.3: The investigator also used FGD as a tool for the study. He conducted the FGD with intention to find out participants (both learning-facilitator and learner) perceptive about prospects and problems by the use of ICT.

## Analysis and Interpretation

### Availability of ICT Resources in Secondary Schools

The information obtained from the checklist revealed that in relation to first dimension the availability of hardware resources, cent percent of secondary school have been equipped with computers and other peripheral hardware (UPS, monitor, printer, scanner, internet connectivity) to support teaching-learning exercise but the quantity of the hardware resources are few. Most of the school didn't have CD/DVD player, audio and video cassette player and headphone but overall hardware resources were available in schools and it was smoothly running. Then in relation to second dimension availability of software it was observed that all school have internet connectivity and learning-facilitators in schools were using the internet for downloading the study materials and personal use. All school have also software like antivirus, word processor, spreadsheet, media player, pdf reader etc. but when come to other software like audio and video editing software, pdf editor etc. most of the school don't have it. So overall it was observed that most of the school have equipped with software resources. Further when it comes to interactive platform was observed thatthere were very poor interactive platforms functioning in the selected sampled schools. Lastly in relation to availability of human resources it was revealed that in all school computer learning-facilitators were available but no school have computer assistant.

### Integration of ICT in Teaching-Learning Process

The second purpose of this study was to identify how integration of ICT helps in teaching learning process. So the investigator further tried to addressed this objective under three head; integration of ICT with respect to subject, classroom environment by the use of ICT and learner's assignment through ICT. The results obtained are discussed below.

### Integration of ICT with Respect to Subject

The information obtained from the observation schedule with respect to first segment it was revealed that selected sampled schools were used ICT in teaching-learning process. They used both hardware and software resources in teaching-learning process. That class was very interesting due to the use of ICT. Learning-facilitatordepicted images and video player related to the chapter.Learning-facilitator applied ICT at minimum level in teaching-learning process due to its inadequate availability. Integration of ICT with respect to subject was very beautifully presented by the learning-facilitator. Further it was observed that mostly ICT used in social science and science subject. Though most of the school did not have any subject related software but the learning-facilitator was managed properly to the classroom. Sometimes learning-facilitator used personal laptop in teaching-learning process. Again for paying attention learning-facilitatordepicted video and images. Learning-facilitators had also depicted some interesting animation videos for understanding any concept.

Overall the integration of ICT with respect to subject was smoothly running in the class and due to its integration in class learner's participation increased and gained more interesting. Subject specific software also created special effects to learners in learning and it make learner easy to understand concept in short duration of time. The class was also more active due to its integration to subject.

### Classroom Environment by the use of ICT

In respect to classroom environment by the use of ICT it was observed from the observation schedule that the class room environments by using ICT in all the selected sampled schools were very stimulating. It creates a healthy classroom environment and gave new opportunity to build an effective learning in the classroom and make a strong interaction between learning-facilitator and learner. Further it was observed that learning-facilitator not only integrating ICT in teaching learning process but also applied constructivist methods of teaching like group discussion and presentation in the class. The playing of videos and showing pictures to learners make them more active in the class.

So overall the classroom environment was healthy, interesting and most effective due to the intervention of ICT in all the sampled schools only the negative point observed that learning-facilitators were not more competent in ICT skill.

### Learners Assignment through ICT

When it come to the segment, learner's assignment through ICT it was observed there was very alarming condition in all most all school. Only two schools out of six sampled school were giving home assignment to learners like collect pictures and audio and video clips which were chapter related and also downloaded some pdf documents for English writing. But in rest four schools' learning-facilitators were not dealing with home and class assignment to learners through ICT.

So overall it concluded that learnerassignments through ICT in all most schools are alarming and quite negligible.

### Perception of Learners and Learning-facilitators about Prospects and Problems of ICT Use

The information obtained from the FGD revealed thatICT integration can increase the learning quality in the courses by improving learning effectiveness and efficiency. Most participants remarked that ICT can 'empowers the learners to take the responsibility of learning on their own shoulder', 'provides greater opportunity for cooperative and collaborative learning among the learners and learning-facilitators', 'provides diverse learning situations to the learning-facilitators as well as learners', 'put their resources on line page by page, lesson plan by lesson plan so that other colleagues from the distance can access from anywhere, thus encourages collaborative work'. In addition to these, they argued that ICT can make instruction more enjoyable and increase concentration for the content of the course. They also noted that ICT can provide learner with access to a variety of ICT opportunities.

In relations to problem faced by learning-facilitators it was observed that learning-facilitators perceived 'shortage of hardware and other periphery materials (computer, printer, camera etc.).' as the most important problems in integration ICT in teaching learning process. The other key problems are 'lack of computer/internet access to the learners out of the school/class hour.', 'lack of in-service training particularly how to develop subject specific ICT lessons', 'lack of technical support within the school to operate the hardware' 'lack of knowledge how to handle minimum hardware operation problem' and 'absence clear-cut gridlines which portion of subject will be covered through ICT'. Thus overall it revealed, 'No availability of computer within the classroom', 'Frequent interruption of electricity', 'inadequate time', 'Overcrowded classroom' and 'Burden of syllabus coverage in stipulated time duration'.

Similarly in relations to problem faced by learners it was observed that learners perceived there both the positive and negative sides of ICT use. ICT was a just a tool for enhancing learners learning and effective teaching learning process. It met the all the requirements of different learning profile. All learners and learning-facilitators could access ICT at anytime, anywhere in the world. And at the same time it has some negative aspects like it slows down our thinking process and critical analysis and bad impact to eyes and fingers creates health issues.

## Major Findings of the Study

The major findings of the study revealed that almost all sampled schools were functioning ICT in teaching-learning process as our ICT@School scheme stipulates.

- All sampled school was not adequately and evenly equipped with peripheral hardware. Overall picture on availability computers and peripheral hardware in all schools were not sufficient enough for unlimited as well as multiple uses by the learners and learning-facilitators.
- None of the sampled school has hardware facilities for differently abled children.
- Cent per cent learning-facilitators denied their access of computer facilities in their classrooms.
- Access to computer by learning-facilitators was primarily provided in the dedicated computer room/computer lab. On the other hand, cent per cent learning-facilitators denied the access of computer facilities to their classrooms.
- All sampled school had only single computer learning-facilitators. Subsequently, majority of school had depended on contractual faculties for teaching ICT course; pedagogical support to the subject learning-facilitators and minor correction/reparation of hardware and software. Therefore, inadequate technical support and maintenance was observed to be a major impediment to the development of ICT in secondary school.
- Negligible Percentage of learners stated as ICT stops thinking and almost all stated as ICT gave a value-addition to their education system.
- Due to the integration of ICT tools in classroom it increased highly learners participation, paid attention and classroom environment was active and interesting. It created interactive environment by using ICT.
- From the perception of learning-facilitators, investigator observed that due to lack of ICT knowledge and competencies very lack number of learning-facilitators able to use it effectively in teaching learning process.
- From the perception of learners, it was again observed that high majority of learners were using ICT in study purpose. It kept touch with learning habits, and it was increased the study culture.

## Recommendations

The recommendations based on the results of the study are as follows:

- The study revealed that majority of the resources and facilities are not available adequately in all sampled schools, even those facilities are available in the schools are not used frequently. Hence it may be the recommendation of the study that the policy makers and headmaster of the school should consider this and make necessary arrangement for its improvement.

- All sampled school also facing the problem of ICT instructor, assistant only they have one computer learning-facilitator. Hence it may be recommendation of the study that the government and policy makers should look over this point and tries to remove this barrier.

- The findings of the study also revealed that cent per cent learning-facilitators denied the access of computer facilities to their classrooms. Hence it may be the recommendations of the study that the headmaster of all school should consider this and make necessary actions to avail this facility in classroom.

- There also observed very lack of ICT knowledge and competencies among secondary school learning-facilitators. Hence it may be the recommendations of the study that the government should make necessary arrangement of ICT training facilities for learning-facilitators as a result of which their ICT knowledge and competencies will be increased.

## Conclusion and Further Research Directions

The importance of ICT in education sector is being highlighted in many educational policies and exponents' speeches. In 21$^{st}$ century ICT brought a remarkable change in the teaching learning process. In relation to secondary education govt. of India implement ICT@School Scheme to make remarkable progress but today after thirteen years of implementation of the ICT@School Scheme in India there observed only few limited study on this scheme and especially in the context of Odisha. Therefore, the present investigation has opened up a new direction in this respect. The problems which have been identified by the investigator will give a proper direction to the authorities concerned in developing and modifying the programs regarding the use of ICT in classroom, subject of study, in assessment process etc. It also helpslearning-facilitators to have a clear cut idea and its utilization in classroom.

For further research, using the same methodology can be carried out in examining the ICT@School Scheme with respect to locality, type of schools etc. Further out of six schools of Balasore district of Odisha, the same studies can be undertaken of more than six schools and can be undertaken in other areas. In this present study learning-facilitators and learners were informers of the study. The same study can be conducted from policy makers and community members. The study can also be done with respect to the effectiveness and attitudes of stakeholders towards ICT@School Scheme. Comparative study will be useful in this domain. A comprehensive study would help to review the overall quality of secondary education in relation to its curriculum, lecturer, administration and facilities to improve service quality of the secondary education institutions.

Chapter 21

# Digital Games for Mathematics: Spatial Learning

✎ **Robin Sharma**
*UNESCO-MGIEPSD, Delhi*

## Preview at a Glance

Twenty first century learners daily consume digital content in different forms and the time spent on digital platforms and devices by school learners is increasing every day. But what if this digital content, which is enjoyed so much by learners, could also yield some kind of meaningful learning at the same time? National Curriculum Framework (2005) talks about providing enjoyable experiences to learners as one of the goals of mathematics education and also lays emphasis on enriching learning-facilitators with a variety of mathematical resources.This chapter presents one such example of a self-developed single player computer game aimed at learners of secondary grades and aligned with constructivist theory of learning. The third person, open world game was built through Unity (an open source development engine). The specific learning objective behind the game is to reinforce coordinate geometry skills among learners and inculcate a sense of spatial awareness and geometric intuition in the player. It can be used to introduce learners to the idea of Cartesian plane; it can be used to present some real-life application of Coordinate Geometry in a relatable and fun context.The said computer game was tested on a single group of 16 learners of Grade IX employing a pre-test post-test based quantitative and qualitative experimental research methodology. The results exhibit significant positive improvement in performance and learners demonstrate enhanced spatial reasoning and application skills as well. The research opens new domains for further investigation into effective integration of digital games into the curriculum.

## Introduction

The face of the education system has changed drastically over the past few decades. New domains and research fields have emerged, like education management, ICT (Information Communication Technologies) integration, learning-facilitator capacity building and whatnot. Developing resources, supporting learning-facilitators and their development has been identified as a significant mandate by educational councils around the world and can be seen as one of the key research and development areas in the Indian education scenario as well (NCF, 2005). As digital platforms and experiences are invading our lives, many educationalists think that there lie huge opportunities to harness these energies to assist and facilitate meaningful learning.

One component of using these digital pedagogies is the use of digital games. Game based learning has proven its strength form the learner's point of view (Ketamo, 2013). Modern learners spend an enormous number of hours on their devices and the stats keep increasing day by day. According to a report on Mobile Games trend by Newzoo, in 2011, mobile gaming took 13% of all time spent on games worldwide, totaling more than 130 million hours a day, and 9% of total money spent on games. The number of people using console for Gaming is also expected to grow to 40 % by end of 2017 as against 31% in 2013. Handheld gaming is projected to increase due to the success of tablets, which enrich the playing experience due to larger touch screen. Given this scenario, the potential of ICT in terms of digital games for enabling lifelong learning is enormous.

The 'designed experience' afforded by the immersive multimodal environment allows the learner to experience of ways of knowing, doing and being that closely resembles the way people learn in real world situated (Brown, 1989). While gaming is a largely a commercial market and education being largely a social one, it has been difficult to find and develop games with specific educational objective and application. Educational games either become too boring for learners and commercial games lack the sound educational and pedagogical aspect. Empirical studies that have actually attempted to use commercial games in educational contexts have thrown up a host of problems (Brown, *et al.*). Commercial off the shelf games either turn out to be too complex for teaching purposes or learning-facilitators have a hard time to fit them easily into a traditional one or half hour classroom lesson, as studies by BECTA have shown (Computer Games in Educational Report, 2001).

The incapability of commercial games to achieve desirable learning objectives calls for game developers and educationists to come together to work together. We need well designed, well planned educational games which catch the attention of learners, have elements of a good game imbibed in them, are enjoyable and are educationally sound as well. Good video games incorporate good learning principles, principles supported by current research in Cognitive Science (Gee, 2003). At a deeper level, however, challenge and learning are a large part of what makes good video games motivating and entertaining. Humans actually enjoy learning, though sometimes in school you wouldn't know that (Gee, 2003).

# Digital Games for Mathematics: Spatial Learning

This chapter is an effort to demonstrate a possible solution to the problem with an example. It presents a computer game specifically designed with the educational objectives it wants to achieve and features of game design in mind. It is designed for learners of grades IX and X, who have been introduced to the concept of two-dimensional coordinate geometry and the idea of Cartesian plane and its coordinates. It features a good background story which is observed intriguing by many learners from the target audience, which is one of the most critical features of a good video game. The chapter also talks about the implementation of the game in a classroom setting and supports the claim with research results.

## Objectives

Digital resources specifically designed for mathematics education are scarce in number. We mostly use different platforms and services which are designed for some other purposes and try to incorporate them in our classrooms in the name of ICT. When it comes to gaming, there are hardly any digital games out there, mobile or PC, which are specifically designed for mathematics education and trying to inculcate mathematical ideas among learners through games. Gamification of classroom teaching though has some background, but not in terms of digital pedagogies. The objectives of this research were as follows:

- To develop a computer based game focused on coordinate geometry and spatial skills for secondary grade learners.
- To test effectiveness of the developed game in classroom setting.
- To identify different ways to harness the potential of digital games to encourage actual learning among learners.

## Method and Procedure

The idea of developing a focused educational computer game arose when the researcher was a part of the M.Sc. Mathematics Education program at JamiaMilliaIslamia's AJK Mass Communication and Research Centre and undertaking a course on gaming. While digital gaming was identified as a promising domain to engage learners in learning, it was also realized that there were not many games specifically designed for school level mathematics. When the researcher looked even deeper, it was also observed that games designed for the Indian context were far scarcer. Whenever there is talk about digital and computer games which are also educational at the same time, some feel that this might neglect a certain section of learners who are not well versed with computers and modern devices. But at the same time there are researches which show that computer literacy and comfort level with digital devices do not play a role in biasing the situation. When talking even more specifically about games for mathematics education, research titled 'Effects of computer games on mathematics achievement and class motivation: An experimental study' (Kebritchi, 2008)' noted that mathematics computer games have positive effects on learning as well as motivation among learners from different backgrounds. It also indicated that prior mathematics and computer knowledge did not play a significant role in achievement and motivation indicating that computer games provide an unbiased and equal platform to learners. Overall research results indicate that mathematics games are effective teaching and learning tools to improve mathematical skills of learners. Kebritchi (2008) also observed one of the learning-facilitators stating: 'This is definitely the way that we have to go to teach mathematics in the future.'

The game discussed here too, has been developed for educational purposes and specifically to reinforce geometry skills among school learners of Grade IX and X. Position Paper on Teaching of Mathematics (NCF, 2005) has pointed out the requirement of mathematics pedagogy that is enjoyable for every child and engages learners in the process. National Curriculum Framework, 2005 also identifies aims of teaching geometry to learners as developing spatial awareness and geometric intuition among learners. The focus game of this research, titled Dimension Destination, aims to engage learners with a sense of success while offering conceptual challenge at the same time. The idea is to offer scope for abstraction and visualization of Quadrants, grid lines and points (on the Cartesian plane) and the complete coordinate system.

## About The Treatment: The Game

This third person interactive game places the player in the body of Rohan, the humanoid, who is left stranded on an unknown world and his oxygen tank is draining. In order to progress in the game, the player must ensure that Rohan timely collects jewels placed across the playing region. For the player to be able to collect the jewels, he must find their location with help of coordinates he is provided with. The player experiences the world as Rohan. The game's interface maps the interaction Rohan has with the environment to a third person interactive audiovisual display. The game takes place in an interactive simulation of the unknown world. More regions/parts of the world become accessible for the player as he/she progresses in the game. It caters to domain of mathematics education, dealing with concepts from secondary school mathematics. Dimension Destination only runs on computers with Windows platform. It is specifically designed keeping learners of Grade IX and X in mind. The game has a definite objective of reinforcing coordinate geometry skills among learners and developing spatial awareness and geometric intuition.

## Gameplay and controls

Dimension Destination is single player, third person game designed in 3D environment.

The game begins with background story of the character Rohan that he is left stranded on an unknown, lifeless, weird, deserted world. The objective for the player is to save Rohan by activating the atmosphere. Rohan is running out of oxygen with time. His oxygen tank gets replenished the moment he collects a jewel. But this only provides a temporary solution to Rohan's problem. The player must collect all jewels to activate the atmosphere and make sure there is continuous supply of Oxygen for Rohan and he is not dependent on his tank. Cartesian plane with grid lines at unit distance is printed on the surface of the unknown world. There are hints and signs around the world as well to indicate the position of the player in terms of the quadrant

# Digital Games for Mathematics: Spatial Learning

he is in and the coordinate axis. In the game, for the player to find a jewel and collect it, the coordinates of the next jewel come up on the screen for the player to head to. The player must find the jewel with help of these coordinates and apply his geometry skills to find the jewel before his oxygen tank runs out. Good spatial awareness and well developed geometric intuition are an added advantage for a player in this game. The player experiences the alien world as Rohan, the humanoid, through third-person rendering. The player can move about freely in the world, where objects are subject to the physical laws and effects that dominate. Arrow keys and 'W', 'S', 'A', 'D' can be used for movement, Space Bar to jump and 'C' to crouch. Mouse can be used to look around by holding the 'Ctrl' Key and Right Mouse Button and moving to change camera angle in the horizontal plane. Points are gained throughout the game by collecting jewels. Collection of every jewel increases the score by 1 and completely fills the oxygen bar as well. The Oxygen bar keeps depleting with time as the player roams around the world to find the next jewel. The oxygen tank gets full when any jewel is collected. To pick up/collect any jewel the player has to run through it. The extra-terrestrial body which is the playing world of this game has grassy surface and a space sky-box to give the feeling of outer universe. Anything that can be interacted with in the world that is inanimate: rocks, structures, carts, plants, etc. Everything has a basic physical presence of touch. The unknown world is designed to look like a weird deserted place without any fauna. There is a graveyard, fences, temple, huts, house, some fauna, and carts among other things to give the world a weird, deserted look and feel. There are two levels in the game. In the first level the complete world (all four quadrants) is not accessible for the player. Jewels only appear for the player to collect in Quadrant I and II. The player enters Level 2 after collecting 4 jewels and then the complete world is accessible for the player and now he has to look for collectibles in the III and IV Quadrant as well.

## Procedure

It was recognized that empirical studies on effectiveness of computer games to teach mathematics to school learners were little and almost none in the Indian context. Informal interactions with various learners revealed that barely any digital game was being used to teach mathematics at school level. After reviewing some literature, it was decided to develop a computer game to support development of coordinate geometry and spatial skills among learners of secondary grades and also test its effectiveness on actual learning of learners and effects on motivation and classroom participation as well.

The learners in the study to test the effectiveness of the game were 16 learners from a mix of urban schools in New Delhi. The study employed a single group research design with quantitative and qualitative instruments. The learners were already taught the concept of coordinate geometry by the traditional chalk and duster method. A pre-test was done to test learners' knowledge of the Cartesian plane and their spatial awareness skills in terms of direction and movement with help of Cartesian coordinates, then the game was used as an intervention and the learners were given the game to play individually on desktop computers. After two sessions of one hour each with the game, the learners were administered using a pen and chapterpost-test. The independent variable in the study was the use of the game to give learners the opportunity to interact with the environment using their coordinate geometry skills and intuition and the dependent variable were learners' scores on the pre-tests and post-tests. The results were analysed for all the 16 learners.

Lesson plans in form of questions to be asked and instructions to be given while introducing learners to the game were also designed for the intervention. The lesson plans were fairly flexible and the intervention treatment, when the learners interacted with the game was mostly non-formal as well. Data to measure learners' performance was collected through self-developed pen-chapter quantitative tests on coordinate geometry and spatial awareness. The length of the post test was doubled to minimize the effect of practice. In addition to written post-test to collect quantitative data to measure learners' performance, a feedback form was also given to learners at the end of the study to collect their opinion and preference on use of computer game for teaching coordinate geometry.

## Data Analysis

The results were analysed using IBM's (International Business Machine) SPSS (Statistical Package for Social Sciences). The level of significance of difference of means between learners' performance in pretest and posttest was computed manually and using descriptive statistics from SPSS. The performance means were correlated (evaluated on the same group of learners) and therefore t test for correlated means was employed to test significance and hypothesis as explained by Garrett (2014). The results and inferences are reported in the next section.

## Results and Discussion

**The following research hypotheses were proposed in this study:**

There is no significant difference between the learners' performance from the experimental group, when they learn through computer games, versus the control group, when they do not receive the computer game approach.

In order to test the hypotheses, a single group experimental study was conducted on relevant sample of 16 learners. The mean score of the learners in the pre-test was 2.78 and in the post test was 10.27. There was a drastic increase. But at the same time the standard deviation in the post-test was also higher than the pre-test signifying a larger variation. It seems that though the intervention helped some learners significantly, it did not make much impact on the performance of a few other participants. The obtained t-statistics of 6.11 was far greater than 2.46 at 0.01 levels and hence can be considered highly significant. The results establish a high level of effectiveness of computer game based approach for teaching coordinate geometry and spatial awareness skills to secondary learners.

The feedback given by learners about the use of the computer games was highly positive. From the sample of 16 learners, 87.5% said that they liked and enjoyed

# Digital Games for Mathematics: Spatial Learning

learning through the game. Three-fourths said that they were able to visualize and 'imagine in their mind' where they were standing on the Cartesian plane. There was a high level of enthusiasm among the learners when they were involved in the game. They wanted an extended session with the game, if they could not complete it and find all the jewels. This is what computer games bring to the table, as modern twenty first century learners are more equipped to deal with complex systems and learn on their own through the use of digital devices and platforms, they also find it more interesting and engaging and want to willingly spend more time on it. Learners were observed developing a positive attitude towards geometry. The quantitative feedback given by the learners was also consistent with the quantitative measurements.

While the chapter talks about the game being implemented in a classroom setting, one of the benefits of such a digital media resource is that it can also be used in an informal or non-formal setting promoting learners to learn on their own and be their own guides. Play is regarded as one of the most ancient forms of learning and digital games like Dimension Destination also provide the learners with an opportunity to learn at their own pace and learn outside the classroom. The learning-facilitator can use the game to encourage learners to play it at their home, until they get good at it and are able to comprehend the space around them in terms of the coordinates. This kind of thinking develops higher spatial awareness skills among learners as shown by the research results.

The discussed game is only the first version of Dimension Destination. From the feedback received from learners and what was observed by the researcher, some improvements that can be made to the game, so it serves its purpose of being an educational game even better, are discussed below:

1. The game can be developed for hand-held mobile devices in order to increase its reach and usage. Also, it will make the game more accessible and user friendly.
2. The playing area/world which represents roughly a 10x10 grid can be increased in size to encompass a larger part of infinite nature of the Cartesian plane.
3. The coordinates for each jewel are hard cored into the game engine and code. Jewels appear on the same coordinates every time the game is played. This takes away the newness factor from the game when it is played over and over, again and again. This brings down level of motivation to play the game. Also, this limits the chance and possibility of enough practice of mathematical concepts reinforced through the game. The spawning of jewels can be randomized in order to keep the factor of exploration and adventure alive.
4. Since the game takes place in a world where coordinate grid is printed over the surface, it can be used to reinforce more concepts related to coordinate geometry and Cartesian plane. To find the coordinates or location of particular jewel the player can be asked to answer a particular question and then he will be able to locate the jewel only if he answers correctly.
5. The game can be developed in such a way that it is easier for the learning-

facilitator to inculcate the same in her lesson plan in the classroom and/or lesson plans can be developed in such a manner that they complement the game and can be used in the classroom. The game can be used for purpose of introduction to a concept, reinforcement of a concept and for assessment purposes as well. Williamson, Land, Butler and Ndahi (2004) have discussed how kids have a general interest in games and how learner achievement can be increased by linking this motivation with games in classroom.

6   Using the same approach, story and ideology a similar game can be developed to discuss 3D geometry and three-dimensional space. Position of octants and points in space will then come into the umbrella of concepts which can be reinforced using the game.

## Conclusion

Coordinate geometry is one of the fundamental topics in secondary school mathematics. Many concepts that learners learn in higher grades are laid on the foundation of coordinate geometry and spatial skills developed by the learners when they are first introduced to it in secondary grades. The main findings of this study indicate that computer games like Dimension Destination can prove to be beneficial assets in teaching the concept of coordinate geometry. They also favour the development of mathematical knowledge by acting as mediator to bridge the gap between learning-facilitators and learners. Learner centric tools shift the role of learning-facilitators to being facilitators, collaborators and catalysts. At the same time, they also pose a challenge for transformation of teaching experiences. Mathematics can be made more relevant and interesting for learners by providing enjoyable experiences to them and computer games do that.

Some contrasting learner performances also present new research questions. It is yet to be seen if such alternate methods and tools only motivate those who like using them. There is always a common notion that boys take more interest in computer games than girls. Some believe that such interventions can only be helpful with urban learners who have access to computers, mobiles and other digital devices. All these questions about the effectiveness of digital games depending on the socio-economical background of the user still need to be looked at from a keener point of view.

# Chapter 22

# ICT Embedded Experiential Learning Progression: Learning Outcomes

✎ **Sanjay Kumar**
*SCERT, Delhi*

## Preview at a Glance

Experiences are the results of inquiry. Inquiry is existential in nature. Human being starts accumulating experiences since conception to sustain existence. To enquire is natural so the human race learned what we are using in the form of inventions. Experiential learning can be simply defined as a process of learning where learner is part of learning process. Means to say is that the experiences what are acquired in involving the process of learning are of different value than the experiences acquired while learner is not a part of learning process. So the important is that there is difference between the quality of experiences the learner acquired within and without in the process of learning. The quality of experiences is directly proportional to quality of learning outcomes. Any experience which is enriched by maximum senses is undoubtedly leads to the learning outcomes which will be productive and progressive in the life ahead. Classroom learning is also directly related to the quality of experiences provided by the learning-facilitator in the classroom. This research study compare the richness of experiences in a progression of nature of learning experiences we are accumulating in the process of learning a concept in classrooms teaching learning processes and clearly observe the significance if ICTembeddedness in producing productive and progressive learning outcomes. Sample of the study includes 10 learning-facilitators of mathematics who taught mathematics at secondary level and 25 sixth grade learners who are studying in the classes of these learning-facilitators. Research Tool was 'ICT embedded experiential learning progression matrix' developed by the researcher for the study. The findings of the study clearly consolidates the hypothesis that experiential learning is the only learning that will bring the qualitative changes in the learners that an progressive educational system intended to bring and prosper. Finding clearly advocates that learners motivation, interest, own-ness, openness, reasoning skills and on the higher end life skills are directly influenced by the quality of experiential learning they got in their classroom teaching learning processes and of the experiences provided outside the wall, let it be structured or unstructured. Most of the learning-facilitators express that richness of experiences increases in the progression from abstract to concrete and concrete to ICT embedded experiential learning progression.

## Introduction

Human race moves towards development with the unique and important feature of learning and experimentation. This experimentation provide basis for advancement. Hence builds some experiences which strongly prove the point of advancement and learning. These Experiences are the results of inquiry. Inquiry is existential in nature. Human being starts accumulating experiences since conception to sustain existence. To enquire is natural so the human race learned what we are using in the form of inventions. Sometimes these inventions may be by chance but even then provides a lot of clues, understanding and learning of how and why it happened, which further add the experience regarding that particular incident and can further be ready to use it in other similar situations. Experiential learning can be simply defined as a process of learning where learner is part of learning process. Means to say is that the experiences what are acquired in involving the process of learning are of different value than the experiences acquired while learner is not a part of learning process. So the important is that there is difference between the quality of experiences the learner acquired within and without in the process of learning. The quality of experiences is directly proportional to quality of learning outcomes. Any experience which is enriched by maximum senses is undoubtedly leads to the learning outcomes which will be productive and progressive in the life ahead. Classroom learning is also directly related to the quality of experiences provided by the learning-facilitator in the classroom. Let's assume that learning-facilitator may be providing experiences in three possible ways:

1. Teaching learning experiences without concrete objects: Which means learners are getting the experiences in abstract form and hence in such situation the learner can be confused or understand the concept with difficulty especially the concepts which are not actually visible directly. This can be used for higher grade learners as their cognitive power for understanding abstract contents has been grown up but at some points even they don't feel comfortable in understanding of deep and complications of concepts.

2. Teaching learning experiences with concrete objects: This type of learning is generally used for primary class learners as their abstract thinking is not developed yet and is beneficial for concept clarity and understanding of concept. As in such type of learning; instructions, directions, explanations are used along with materials or models. Even activities and games can be a part of such type of learning. This type of learning is based on the principle of 'learning by doing'. Although each and every concept is not possible to be clear by this principle for example understanding about volume and capacity. It may sometimes looks as monotonous.

3. Teaching learning experiences with concrete objects embedded with ICT facilitation: This type of learning provides an insight to the learners in primary classes as well in high grades. It opens the room for each and every type of learner means caters individual differences. It has the benefits of understanding through concrete objects i.e. learning by doing and a visualize beyond that. In such type of learning learners involve in understanding the process and then do it by themselves and again ready for further explanation and exploration of the concepts and visualization of the concept in daily life use. It purely indicates the development of the learner according to the learning outcomes mentioned by education system which make the learner capable of grasping the concept and living it throughout his life.

Let's understand these three classroom teaching learning experiences with a concrete example:

Assume we are in class VI Mathematics classroom where learning-facilitator is providing the experiences related to the concept of triangle. Let take all the teaching skills like introduction, questioning, explanation, stimulus variation and closure as on high standards and same in all the three cases.

## Case 1
**Teaching learning experiences without concrete objects**

In this situation learning-facilitator is only using the display board to transact the concept of triangle by drawing the figures related to triangle and write what she thinks necessary to deliver the concept. Here primarily only audio visual senses are receiving the experiential inputs. This much of data is trying to make understand the mind to understand the concept of triangles with a hope to use it productively and progressively in future course of learning in particular and in life as general. Psychological and neural research studies says that mind understand patterns and visuals better which are associated with maximum number of sensual inputs. So this case experiential learning lacks what is required by mind to have a learning experience that is productive and progressive in any way.

## Case 2
**Teaching learning experiences with concrete objects**

In this situation learning-facilitator is using the display board supported by related and relevant concrete objects like cut-outs of triangles and origami techniques to transact the concept of triangle by drawing the figures related to triangle and write what she thinks necessary to deliver the concept and provide hands on experiences to support and facilitate her written and on spoken words and discussions. Here primarily audio visual and tackle senses are receiving the experiential inputs. This much of data is trying to make understand the mind to understand the concept of triangles with a hope to use it productively and progressively in future course of learning in particular and in life as general. Psychological and neural research studies says that mind understand patterns and visuals better which are associated with maximum number of sensual inputs. So in this case experiential learning added one more sensual experience but here also some sensual experience is lacking what is required by mind to have a learning experience that is productive and progressive in any way.

## Case 3
**Teaching learning experiences with concrete objects embedded with ICT facilitation**

In this situation learning-facilitator is using the display board, concrete objects and embedding ICT facilitations like displaying pictures of triangle with different shapes, sizes, colours, orientations and life connected context to transact the concept of triangle and do what she thinks necessary to deliver the concept. Here primarily all the senses are receiving the experiential inputs. This enriched data is enough to make understand the mind to understand the concept of triangles with a hope to use it productively and progressively in future course of learning in particular and in life as general. Psychological and neural research studies says that mind understand patterns and visuals better which are associated with maximum number of sensual inputs. So in this case experiential learning supports what is required by mind to have a learning experience that is productive and progressive in any way.

We can compare the richness of experiences in a progression of nature of learning experiences we are accumulating in the process of learning a concept in classrooms teaching learning processes and clearly observe the significance if ICTembeddedness in producing productive and progressive learning outcomes.

Table 1: **Experiential learning progression table (ELPT)**

| Richness of experiences | Senses used Humans have a multitude of sensors. Sight (vision), hearing (audition), taste (gustation), smell (olfaction), and touch (somatosensation) are the five traditionally recognized senses. | Nature of information processing in mind | Learning approach | Nature of experiences |
|---|---|---|---|---|
| Without concrete objects | Sight (vision), hearing (audition), | Symbolic | Cognitive | Temporary |
| With concrete objects | Sight (vision), hearing (audition), touch (somatosensation) | Visual | Behaviouristic | Short term memory |
| With concrete objects embedded with ICT facilitation | Sight (vision), hearing (audition), taste (gustation), smell (olfaction), and touch (somatosensation) | Visual Pattern association generalization | Constructive and meta cognitive | Long term memory productive progressive |

Keeping in view the importance of experiential learning progression and role of ICT facilitation in teaching learning processes, I am becoming very much interested in knowing the perspective of prospective learning-facilitators about the nature of experiences provided in the classrooms and role of ICTembeddedness in experiential learning progression.

## Objectives

1. To visualize the ICT Embedded Experiential Learning Progression this leads Processing towards Learning Outcomes.
2. To collect empirical views of learning-facilitators and learners about ICT Embedded Experiential Learning Progression

## Research Procedures

### Sample

1. Sample of the study includes 10 learning-facilitators of mathematics who taught mathematics at secondary level.
2. 25 sixth grade learners who are studying in the classes of these learning-facilitators.

## Research Tool

## Nature of data received

ICT embedded experiential learning progression matrix was filled up by the investigator on the basis of inputs received by the learning-facilitator by taking their semi structured interview .Simultaneously focus groups discussion were done on the basis of prepared guidelines prepared by investigator. The learners' inputs were recorded and filled in the matrix. The responses recorded in the matrix are prominent and frequent.

## Analysis

ICT embedded experiential learning progression matrix was prepared and analysed on the basis of nature of concept, degree of richness of experiences, senses used to obtain that experience, nature of information processing in mind, learning approach used, nature of existence obtain, responses of learning-facilitators and learners about the provided teaching learning processes.

The opinion of learning-facilitators and learners responses declares that the quality of teaching learning process when a learning-facilitator is only using the display board to transact the concept of triangle by drawing the figures related to triangle and writes what she thinks necessary to deliver the concept. Here primarily only audio visual senses are receiving the experiential inputs, becomes boring, not interesting , learner react as passive listener ,experiences provided had no connection with their life experiences ,academic work becomes burden, this process leads learner to Cramming ,learner is not Inquisitive , this is a exploiter process for learner, classroom is a stressor place ,learning-facilitator becomes authoritative ,Learning is neither productive nor progressive, no scope of team work, no scope of sharing, no scope for transfer of learning we never owns learning, no cooperative learning promises and class is not inclusive. Learning-facilitators is not aware about experiential learning processes, less prepared, follows passive process, provide no scope for questioning, explain less, never dialoguing, creates no scope for creativity. Learning-facilitator leads the class autonomously and learners are mere following without understanding.

**Table 2: ICT embedded experiential learning progression matrix**

| Concept | Richness of experiences | Senses used | Nature of information processing in mind | Learning approach | Nature of experiences | Opinion of learning-facilitator | Remarks based on FGD with learners |
|---|---|---|---|---|---|---|---|
| Triangles and its type | Without concrete objects | Sight (vision), hearing (audition), | Symbolic | Cognitive | Temporary | Details given below in findings | Details given below in findings |
| | With concrete objects | Sight (vision), hearing (audition), touch (somatosensation) | Visual | Behaviouristic | Short term memory | Details given below in findings | Details given below in findings |
| | With concrete objects embedded with ICT facilitation | Sight (vision), hearing (audition), taste (gustation), smell (olfaction), and touch (somatosensation) | Visual Pattern association generalization | Constructive and meta cognitive | Long term memory productive progressive | Details given below in findings | Details given below in findings |

## Case 1

**Table 3: Teaching learning experiences without concrete objects**

| Opinion of learning-facilitator | Remarks based on FGD with learners |
|---|---|
| Not aware about experiential learning | Boring |
| Less prepared | Not interesting |
| Passive process | Passive listener |
| No questioning | No connection with their life experiences |
| Less explanation | Academic work is burden |
| No dialoguing | Leads to Cramming |
| No creativity | No Inquisitiveness |
| Class work and home work is a burden | Exploiter process |
| No connection with life experiences | Classroom is stressor |
| No transfer of learning | Learning-facilitator is authoritative |
| No reasoning | Learning is nor productive nor progressive |
| Never owns learning | No team work |
| Not inclusive | No sharing |
| | Not cooperative |
| | Not inclusive |

## Case 2

**Table 4: Teaching learning experiences with concrete objects**

| Opinion of learning-facilitator | Remarsks based on FGD with learners |
|---|---|
| Less aware about experiential learning prepared but lack ICTembeddedness | Little Boring for some ones |
| | Sometimes interesting |
| Active process but lack rich sensual interaction | Less scope for Active listener |
| | Lack connection with their life experiences |
| less questioning | |
| Less explanation | Academic work is burden some time |
| Less dialoguing | Leads to understanding |
| Creative but no scope of manipulation | increase Inquisitiveness |
| Class work and home work is monotonous | less Exploiter process |
| connection with life experiences but lack reflections | Classroom is stressor for some ones |
| | Learning-facilitator is authoritative |
| less scope of transfer of learning | Learning may be productive and progressive |
| mild scope of reasoning | |
| less scope to own learning | Little scope of team work |
| lack inclusiveness | Sharing is not assured |
| | May be cooperative |
| | lack inclusiveness |

The opinion of learning-facilitators and learners responses declares that the quality of teaching learning process when learning-facilitator is using the display board supported by related and relevant concrete objects like cut-outs of triangles and origami techniques to transact the concept of triangle by drawing the figures related to triangle and write what she thinks necessary to deliver the concept and provide hands on experiences to support and facilitate her written and on spoken words and discussions. Here primarily audio visual and tackle senses are receiving the experiential inputs, becomes less boring, not so much interesting , less scope for Active listener ,experiences provided had not much connection with their life experiences ,academic work becomes burden sometimes, this process leads learner to understanding ,learner becomes little bit Inquisitive , this is less exploiter process for learner, classroom is a stressor place for some ,learning-facilitator becomes authoritative most of the times ,Learning may be productive and progressive ,little scope of team work, little scope of sharing , transfer of learning may possible but not sure, less scope for owning the learning , little cooperative learning promises and class is not fully promise inclusiveness. Learning-facilitator is less aware about experiential learning processes and lack ICTembeddedness, follow slightly active process, provide little scope for questioning, explain not so much, few dialoguing situations, tries to create no scope for creativity but fails most of the times. Learning-facilitator has no scope of manipulation here, Classwork and homework is monotonous in such settings.

## Case 3

**Table 5: Teaching learning experiences with concrete objects embedded with ICT facilitation**

| Opinion of learning-facilitator | Remarks based on FGD with learners |
|---|---|
| Fully Aware about experiential learning prepared in ICTembeddedness | Nothing Boring |
| | Interesting and motivating |
| Active process rich in sensual interaction | Active listener |
| Frequent questioning | Connections with their life experiences |
| Interactive explanation | Academic work is a thing of joy and consolidation |
| Prolonged dialoguing | |
| Creative with scope of manipulation | Leads to understanding |
| Class work and home work an enriching experience | Increase Inquisitiveness |
| | Salvatore process |
| connection with life experiences and cite reflections | Classroom is festive |
| | Learning-facilitator is democratic, facilitator and guide |
| Great scope of transfer of learning | |
| Good scope of reasoning | Learning is productive and progressive |
| Owns their learning | Great scope of team work |
| Inclusiveness promotes | Sharing is assured |
| | Promotes cooperative learning |
| | Inclusiveness promotes |

The opinion of learning-facilitators and learners responses declares that the quality of teaching learning process when learning-facilitator is using the display board , concrete objects and embedding ICT facilitations like displaying pictures of triangle with different shapes, sizes, colours, orientations and life connected context to transact the concept of triangle and do what she thinks necessary to deliver the concept. Here primarily all the senses are receiving the experiential inputs, nothing feels Boring , interesting and motivating, act as active listener, had connections with their life experiences ,academic work is a thing of joy and consolidation, leads to understanding, increase inquisitiveness,Salvatore process ,classroom is festive,learning-facilitator is democratic, facilitator and guide, learning is productive and progressive,great scope of team work, sharing is assured, promotes cooperative learning and promises inclusiveness. Learning-facilitator is fully Aware about experiential learning prepared in ICTembeddedness, provide active process rich in sensual interactions, do frequent questioning initiates interactive explanation, prolonged dialoguing, provide creative situations with scope of manipulations through ICT, class work and home work an enriching experience which had connection with life experiences and cite reflections , provide great scope of transfer of learning ,good scope of reasoning ,learners are ready to owns their learning and inclusiveness promotes and prosper.

## Findings

The findings of the study clearly consolidates the hypothesis that experiential learning is the only learning that will bring the qualitative changes in the learners that a progressive educational system intended to bring and prosper. Finding clearly advocates that learners motivation, interest, own-ness, openness, reasoning skills and on the higher end life skills are directly influenced by the quality of experiential learning they got in their classroom teaching learning processes and of the experiences provided outside the wall, let it be structured or unstructured. Most of the learning-facilitators express that richness of experiences increases in the progression from abstract to concrete and concrete to ICT embedded experiential learning progression. It is successful in dealing with our classroom needs of each and every learner which is different. They can cater the individual differences of learners and hence provide better learning and understanding of concept. Self-motivation automatically arose in the learners. A learning-facilitator can notice the developmental process of learning among the learners.

## Suggestions

ICT embedded experiential learning progression matrix may be a part of learning-facilitator's planner and lesson plans so that planned and structured ICT embedded experiential learning becomes productive and progressive for the learners.

Learning-facilitators should have proper knowledge of using this matrix for its optimum use.

Training should be provided to the learning-facilitators and follow-ups should be strictly done.

## Conclusion

Learning is the major expectation from both learning-facilitator and learners and everyone is working sincerely for it. But mere cramming formulas or definitions cannot solve our purpose. Our Government, policy planners, educationists etc. all are working on serious and sincere basis for the same purpose. For enhancing the quality of learning among the learners/learners learning outcomes are introduced which focuses on skills and processes. These learning outcomes can be easily assessable by the use of experiential learning which can be of a great support for both learning-facilitator and learner without actually burdening anyone of them. Progressive and productive learning outcomes are only possible through experiential learning. Such type of learning is long lasting and a way to success. Success lies in the classrooms which is full of rich and varied experiences. In this process of ICT embedded experiential learning outcomes becomes an enjoyable procedural journey towards self-confidence and promising happiness for learners.

Chapter

23

# ICT for Environmental Education and Sustainable Development

**Santosh Kumar Parida**
*RTE-SSA, Bhubaneswar, Odisha*

## Preview at a Glance

The study discusses the effectiveness of the information and communication technology (ICT) programme aimed at sustainability of the concepts of Environmental Education. In order to conduct the study a researcher selected 50 learners from two schools i.e. Rasulgarh UGUP School and Government Powerhouse colony UGUP School of Bhubaneswar Municipal Corporation. One group comprising 25 learners were treated as experimental group and the rest 25 learners were called controlled group. When the experimental group was dealt adopting new methodology through Computer Aided Learning (CAL) programme the controlled group was taught in conventional method. The intervention was extended over a period of five weeks and all sorts of TLMs pertaining to ICT were displayed to help the learners conceptualise the basic of sustainable development relating to environmental education. At the end of the experiment it was observed that the experimental group yielded better result at the post test stage i.e. the means score was 35 as against the post-test means score of the controlled group was 29. The t-ratio 4.28 justifies significance of difference at 0.01 level. Due to use of ICT based intervention. The study has wider implication in view of developing the concept of environmental education for the learner of Class-V. As future citizens of the society they can try to protect the environment for quality life.

## Introduction

The survival of human species on this planet earth is often questioned on account of the self-inflicted damages man has wrought on the Environment defacing it at places. The planet earth is like a spaceship where resources (that are global commons as per

Brundtland's Report, 'Our Common Future, 1987') are limited and to be consumed on a sustainable basis for continuation of all living species on the earth. Further, the by-products of consumption in the form of wastes should be such that they can be absorbed by the mother earth or transformed into/ recycled for human use by anthropogenic ingenuity and modern technological innovations. The 'Gaia' as James Lovelock has christened the living earth has to be preserved not only for the present generation but also for future generation. As Mahatma Gandhi the father of our nation has observed 'The earth can cater to everyone's need but not to everyone's greed'.

In the above context, the concept of Environment and Environmental Education must be understood in its proper perspective.

## Meaning of Environment

Etymologically the term environment has been derived from two words i.e. 'environ' and 'ment' meaning 'encircle' or 'surrounding'. Thus environment consists of bio-physical and manmade variables which surround man as well as all living organisms. The encyclopaedic definition of environment refers to the sum total of all conditions, agencies and influences, which affects the development, growth, life and death of organism, species or race. Environment is the source of life on earth. It not only directs but also determines the existence, growth and development of mankind and their activities. The Tbilisi Conference (1977) defined environment as a sum total of natural, artificial and social components of the material world which are or may be in direct interaction with mankind as a whole. Environment has two basic components (i) biophysical and (ii) socio-cultural. The bio-physical environment is the biotic and abiotic surrounding of an organism or population and includes those factors which contribute to survival, development and evolution of species. The scope of the biophysical environment is all that which is contained in the biosphere and which is that part of the Earth where all life occurs. A biophysical environment is the complex structure of biotic, climatic and edaphic factors that act upon an organism and determine its form, survival and morphs itself in the process. Ecosystems of numerous types form a defined part of the biosphere, collectively making up the whole of the biosphere. Within an ecosystem there are habitats in which an organism exists.

The biophysical environment extends in scale from microscopic to global. They can also be subdivided according to their attributes. Some examples of biophysical environment may be the marine, atmospheric and terrestrial environment. The socio-cultural factors consists of man's economic, social, political, technological intellectual and aesthetic activities and their products such as modes of production, industry, education, means of transport and commerce, culture, housing, bridges, dams and highways etc. Darwin's theory of evolution describes man's biological evolution to the present stage through a continuous process of interaction with the environment. Thus, the environment is to be viewed as a dynamic system in which subsystems are in constant interaction with each other and undergoing continuous change. Bronowski (1973) in his 'Ascent of Man' portrays the cultural evolution of mankind and its interaction with environment to reach the present level of culture and civilizations.

# ICT for Environmental Education and Sustainable Development

The total environment is dynamic and is always in a state of flux. Its ecosystem comprising the complex web of interaction between its biotic and abiotic components makes it self-balancing, self-adjusting and self-purifying. Ideally, there is no waste in a stable ecosystem. These substances are made available naturally through many bio-geochemical cycles like water, carbon oxygen, nitrogen, phosphorus, cycles etc. In the environment, plants, animals and micro-organisms thrive with only minor change in number.

## Genesis of Environmental Problem

The human civilization begins with the primitive man, eating wild fruits, hunting animals, raw fishes and who relied heavily on nature for his very survival. But as society developed human intervention on environment grew in scope and strength. Advent of modern science and technology, combined with man's greed and caprice to exploit the resources of the earth beyond point of redemption led to the creation of environmental crisis. The unprecedented growth in human population, advent of science, technology modern production and consumption processes, means of mass transport and last but not the least the change in human life style has brought serious havoc in the environment, upsetting its ecological processes and thereby endangering the health and even the very survival of humans on earth.

India is a developing country and like other developing countries is stuck with many environmental issues. Poverty among people being the major concern is caused due to lack of economic development leading to inadequate sanitation and problem of clean drinking water facilities. High growth rate of population leads to large scale depletion of natural resources and deforestation. Modern technological advancements, urbanization and industrialization play major role in disturbing natural environment causing water, air, noise and radio-active pollution. Though Government of India is paying attention to major environmental concerns of the nation and formulating environmental policies to keep pace with this alarming situation, yet efforts are not commensurate with the scale of the environmental crisis. Major environmental concerns of India may be categorized as follows:

- Population Explosion
- Air pollution
  - Acid rain
  - Smog
  - Greenhouse effect
  - Ozone layer depletion
- Noise Pollution
- Radioactive Pollution
- Water Pollution
- Deforestation

- Extinction of Species
- Depletion of Natural Resources
- Land Use
- Soil Erosion
- Energy Crisis
- Ecological Disruption
- Health Hazards

## Concept and Scope of Environmental Education

Environmental education is a process to promote the awareness and understanding of the environment, its relationship with man and his activities.Environmental education is education 'about' the environment, 'through' the environment and 'for' the environment. Education about environment means making environment a subject of investigation. It is based on a specific topic or a restricted area in which the main concern is to gain information and promote comprehension. It can be done in the classroom as well as in the field.Education through environment usually connotes using environment as a medium for study, the use of real life situations as the basis for learning and inquiry. It is essentially an approach or method of enquiry usually conducted through field work.Education for environment means education for conserving and improving the environment, a study of environmental problems and working for their prevention and solution. Problem solving, decision making, development of an environmental ethic and critical judgment are called for here. It is in this sense that Stockholm Conference recognizes the term environmental education.

The US Environmental Education Act (1970) defined environmental education in terms of relationships:

Environmental education means the educational process dealing with man's relationship with his natural and manmade surroundings and includes the relation of population, pollution, resource depletion and allocation, conservation, transportation, technology and rural and urban planning to the total human environment.

A more comprehensive definition involving understanding and skills is the one given by the 'US office of Education'.

Environmental education is the process that fosters greater understanding of society's environmental problems and also the process of environmental problem solving and decision making. It involves development of skills and insights needed to understand the structure, requirements and impact of interactions within and among various environmental entities, sub-systems and systems.

The above mentioned definitions do not give any emphasis to the affective aspects like values, feelings and attitudes. The following definitions arrived at the IUCN sponsored workshop on environmental education in school curriculum takes care of the affective components as well.

# ICT for Environmental Education and Sustainable Development

Environmental education is the process of recognizing values and clarifying concepts in order to develop skills and attitudes necessary to understand and appreciate the inter-relatedness among man, his cultural and bio-physical surroundings. Environmental education also entails practice in decision making and self-formulation of a code of behaviour about issues concerning environmental quality (IUCN Commission of Education, 1970).

From an analysis of all the definitions given above, it follows that environmental education involves:

- Knowledge and understanding of environment, its associated problems and future consequence.
- Understanding and appreciation of the subtle relationship between man and nature.
- Value clarification, development of attitude and interest concerning environment.
- Development of skills in environmental problem solving and decision making.

## Aims and Objectives of Environmental Education

**The goal of environmental education as contained in the Belgrade Charter is –**

To develop a world population that is aware of and concerned about the environment and its associated problems and which has the knowledge, skills, attitudes, motivation and commitment to work individually and collectively towards solutions of current problems and the prevention of new ones.

The environmental objectives encompassing this broad goal may be categorized under awareness, knowledge, attitude, skills, evaluation ability and participation from the instructional point of view.

1. Awareness: to help individuals and social groups acquire an awareness of and sensitivity towards the total environment and its allied problems.
2. Knowledge: to help individuals and social groups acquire basic understanding of the total environment, its associated problems and humanity's critically responsible presence and role in it.
3. Attitude: to help individuals and social groups acquire social values, strong feelings of concern for the environment and the motivation for actively participating in its protection and improvement.
4. Skills: to help individuals and social groups acquire the skills for solving environmental problems.
5. Evaluation ability: to help individuals and social groups evaluate environmental measures and education programmes in terms of ecological, political, economic, social, and aesthetic and education factors.
6. Participation: to help individuals and social groups develop a sense of responsibility and urgency regarding environmental problems and to ensure appropriate action to solve those problems.

## Guiding Principles of Environmental Education

The guiding principles of environmental education as per Tbilisi Conference 1977 are as follows.

## Environmental Education should

- Consider the environment in its totality natural and built, technological and social (economic, political, technological, cultural, historical, moral and aesthetic).
- Be a continuous life long process, beginning at the pre-school level and continuing through all formal and non-formal stages.
- Be interdisciplinary in its approach, drawing on the specific content of each discipline and in making possible a holistic and balanced perspective.
- Examine major environmental issues from local, regional and international points of view so that learners receive insights into environmental conditions in other geographical areas.
- Focus on current and potential environmental situations while taking into account the historical perspective.
- Promote the value and necessity of local, national and international co-operation in the prevention and solution of environmental problems.
- Explicitly consider environmental aspects in plans for development and growth.
- Enable learners to have a role in planning their learning experiences and provide an opportunity for making decisions and accepting their consequences.
- Relate environmental sensitivity, knowledge, problem solving skills and values clarification to every age but with special emphasis on environmental sensitivity to the learner's own community in early years.
- Help learners discover the symptoms and real causes of environmental problems.
- Utilize diverse learning environments and a broad array of educational approaches to teaching/learning about, from and for the environment with due stress on practical activities and first-hand experience.

Steps have also been taken to orient the primary school learning-facilitators on environmental education through different in-service learning-facilitator education programmers conducted under District Primary Education Programmed and SarvaSikshyaAbhijan.

## Concepts of Sustainable Development

Development that meets the needs of the present without compromising the ability of future generations to meet their own needs (i.e., development that nurtures the economy and improves the quality of life without undermining the natural resources and environmental integrity on which they depend)

# ICT for Environmental Education and Sustainable Development

## Information and Communication Technology (ICT)

Today's society is emerging as knowledge based society, right from the individual level to the level of nations, it has been accepted that the knowledge is going to be the only differentiating factor that decide strength of an economy. With the advent and existence of technology in our daily life, the whole equation of departing and getting knowledge has been changed. The impact of technology can also be seen in an area, which is directly related to knowledge i.e. teaching. Traditionally, for a learner, learning-facilitator is the only source of knowledge that is an again majorly bound by the 'information provided in the books. The viewpoint of the learners is generally ignored due to lack of supportive information. Exploration of new knowledge is not encouraged due to lack of resources. Now, the change has come and learning-facilitator is not the only source of knowledge for the learners. This happened because of fast paced technology. Technology has decentralized the knowledge source. Learners have many more resources from where they can supplement their viewpoint and many a times learners are more informed than a learning-facilitator. This situation poses a multi-faceted challenge for today's learning-facilitators. Now there as an acute need to facilitate training for learning-facilitator both at pre-service and in-service level. The training is required regarding ICT i.e. information and communication Technology.

Education and expansion of education have been the main task of any society. Owing to its heterogeneity and pressure from population of over one billion, India needs more rigorous attempts to elevate its educational status, information and communication ICT has become, within in very short time, one of the building blocks. ICT in education is a crucial tool for making leaning easy and concepts understandable. ICT is often perceived as a useful strategy to transform education systems and a means by which learners can develop basic competencies and skills needed for knowledge economy. Basically, ICT is defined, for the purpose of his primer, as a diverse set of technological tools and resources used to communicate and create, disseminate, store, and manage information. These technologies include computers the internet, broadcasting technologies and telephony. ICT is decreasing the burden of tasks of learners and learning-facilitators. ICT affect the delivery of education and enable wider access to the same. In addition, it will increase flexibility so that learners can access the education regardless of the time and geographical barrier. It can influence the way learner are taught and how they learn. This in turn would prepare the learners for lifelong learning. ICT is a crucial resource in education. ICT's has made an impact on education systems. ICT can be used to enhance school attraction and effectiveness. It can be used for capacity building of learning-facilitator. For educational administrators ICT can be working more effectively management of schools and management of the education system through e-governance. The education of the learning-facilitator in ICT not only facilitates improvement of school education by professionally competent learning-facilitators but functions as a bridge between school and higher education.

## ICT can be used as a tool in the process of education. It may act as an

- Informative tool-it provides vast amount of data in various formats such as audio, video and documents.
- Situating tools –it creates situations, which the learners experience in real life. Thus, simulation and virtual reality is possible;
- Constructive tools- to manipulate data and generated analysis;
- Communicative tools- it can be used to remove communication barriers such as that of time and space

Designing an ICT framework must follow few approached to make it a success; the approaches are related to the cultural and contextual diversity. As India is a diverse nation in terms of culture and these factor must be consider in infusing technology into the learning-facilitator education curriculum, it embraces the use of technology in culturally appropriate ways. Next is related to the requirement of both leadership and support from the administration of the learning-facilitator education institution. Infusing a feeling that education and learning doesn't end after school and it is an on-going process. Finally, acknowledging that change is inevitable and its acceptability results in good. These themes may be understood as a strategic combination of approaches that help learning-facilitator educators develop core competencies. The core competencies s may be seen as cluster of objectives that are critical for successful use of ICT's as tools for learning. These core competencies are:

- Pedagogy is focused on learning-facilitator's instruction practices and knowledge of the curriculum and requires that they develop application within their disciplines that make effective use of ICTs to support and extend teaching and learning.
- Collaboration and networking acknowledge the communicative potential of ICTs to extend learning beyond the classroom walls and the implication for learning-facilitator's development of new knowledge and skills.
- Technology brings with it new rights and responsibilities, including equitable access to technology resources, care for individual health, and respect for intellectual poverty included within the social issue aspect of ICT competence.
- Finally, technical issues is an aspect of the lifelong learning theme through which learning-facilitators update skill with hardware and software, as new generation of technology emerge.

## Role of ICT in bringing efficiency of delivery mechanism

Efficient delivery mechanism are an important component of overall school management. ICTs can provide the efficiency of delivery mechanism of educational services by supplementing conventional delivery mechanisms:

- Technology's capacity to reach learners in any place and at any time has the potential to promote revolutionary changes in the educational paradigm.

# ICT for Environmental Education and Sustainable Development

This means eliminating the premise that learning time equal classroom time. Learners can be encouraged to revisit the lesson/topics to reinforce learning without active intervention by learning-facilitators.

- Another illustration of efficiency is the domain of virtual laboratories. All school systems want to provide labs because science is empirical. But few schools have furnished them with equipment and supplies and fewer yet are willing to risk using them. Technology allows for video and digital demonstrations as well as digital.
- Simulation of laboratory activities in very real manner-but without the risks and cost associated with laboratory experiments. Simulations will not replace hands-on activity completely. Rather, they prepare the learner to conduct real-life experiments in the same manner as flight simulations prepare the learner pilot for rest flying.
- Multimedia-enabled learning modules can be developed by a group of master learning-facilitator and instructional designers, which can then be shared with all school to assure quality standards of learning delivery.
- Concerns about costs are always raised in discussions related to technology. Depending on the technology used, start-up costs can be high but economies of scale are significant. That is, the more the technology is used I.e. when more learners use the product, the unit costs of producing educational content ware decrease proportionately

## Rationale of the Study

Information and Communication and Technology (ICT) as a teaching tool is appreciated by majority of the learning-facilitators. Now-a-days as a useful tool it has been popularized in the schools and colleges that facilitate the process of learning by doing. It has been able to create interest among the learners as well as learning-facilitators. But due to some problems like insufficient computers (in comparison to the learners), less number of computer learning-facilitators, transfer of trained computer learning-facilitators to other schools and non-functioning of computers, teaching through computers sometimes becomes a problem.

## The objectives behind setting up the ICT are

- To improve academic learning levels,
- attract out of school children,
- provide child centric, joyful, interactive, self-paced learning,
- facilitate improvement of attendance of children.

At this juncture, it becomes pertinent to study the impact of this ICT program as on current date. This impact could be observed as to the current functioning of the ICT program as well as the impact it has had on the internal stakeholders within the school like the learning-facilitators, headmasters and children as well as the external stakeholders like parents.

Therefore, there is a need to undertake research in each aspect of the ICT programme to find out its effectiveness and shortcomings.

## Review of Related Literature

Kapadia's Ph.D. work (1992) was related to the impact of TV on learner learning. In contrast to Joshi(1987), the study reported that the TV group gained significantly more than the controlled group. Even retention scores of the experimental group were better. Seventy percent of the learners opined that TV programmes help them in self-learning.

Mohanty (1988) took up a study of the ETV programmes for primary school children and observed that children exposed to ETV programme has superior scholastic attainment as compared to children of the non-exposed group. The greatest achievement was in respect of 'language'.

Natarajanand Natesan (2004) studied the effects of competency based teaching of environmental science through video on learners' attainment at primary level and observed that teaching environmental science concepts through video cassettes is better than traditional method.

## Objectives of the Study

The objectives of the study were as follows.

- ▶ To assess the achievement of the learners in Environmental Education as an effect of ICT programme.
- ▶ To identify the strength and limitation of ICT programme.
- ▶ To study the Views of the SMC members, Parents, Learning-facilitators, Headmasters and PRI members on ICT programme.
- ▶ To suggest strategies for improving the ICT programme.

## Hypothesis

The Information and Communication Technology (ICT)programme has positive impact on the learners' achievement on Environmental Education with respect to experimental group.

## Scope of the Study
### Place of the study

The study was conducted at Rasulgarh UGP School and Govt. UP School Power House Colony under Bhubaneswar municipal corporation (BMC). Learners of class V were selected for this study.

## Design

Pre-test, post-test control group design was adopted to conduct the study.
  Concept dealt

  Class – V:

## Physical Environment
- Identification of main water region, land region, polar region in the globe
- locating India in the map of Asia
- Main crops, industry, tourist places of India
- contaminated disease
- Discharge of waste materials
- Adoption of animals and birds
- Forest, soil, river protection
- Air pollution
- Utility of natural resources

## Social Environment
- Central Government, State Government, Municipality
- Democratic Government
- Transportation, communication
- Industry
- Import and export
- Rapid population explosion and obstacles
- Census
- Freedom struggle
- Protection of our land

## Methodology
For the present study, the investigator used experimental and survey method.

## Sample
In this study, 50 learners were selected randomly for the purpose of the study out of which 25 of learners were tagged to control group and 25 learners were tagged to experimental group on the basis of their pre-test results as equated. The community members like, Parents, SMC members and PRI members were interviewed to know their Views regarding the parameters.

## Tools
To collect information from the sample selected, the investigator used the following tools for data collection. The tools were

i Learning-facilitator made achievement test: It was used to assess the performance of the learners of the class V of the sampled schools.

ii  School Profile: Through this tool, information were collected regarding the basic strength such as general information of the school, information about the learning-facilitators , facility available in the school and overall status of school regarding physic ICT, cognitive, organizational and social aspect.

iii Learner's schedule: To measure the impact of the ICTprogramme, the learners were interviewed on the content presented through ICT.

iv  Learners information schedule: In this schedule, teaching opinions were noted to know properly whether learning-facilitators liked ICT programme or not.

v   Interview schedule for Learning-facilitatorsand Headmaster: This schedule encompasses the enrolment and attendance, retention and their achievement-class and subject-wise.

vi  Interview schedule for Community members and Parents: Opinion of the community members such as chairman, members, parents etc. were measured through this tool to have an idea regarding Information and Communication Technology and the facilities available for the beneficiaries.

These tools were designed basically to assess the impact of Information and Communication Technology on the learner's attainment.

## Procedure of the Study

In the beginning a pre-test was administered on 50 learners of class V of the sample schools in Environmental Education. On the basis of the mark secured they were divided into two equi-standard group. One was treated as controlled group and other was treated as experimental group.

## Management of the Activities

The specific activities on the basis of the environmental education for the learners of class-V covered motivational and life skill activities like self-awareness, Empathy, Problem solving, effective communication, Critical thinking, Decision making and interpersonal relationship etc. and based on the environmental objectives comprising awareness, knowledge, attitude, skills, evaluation ability and participation from the institutional point of view for sustainable development.

## Results and Discussion

Table1: Means, S.D's and t-ratio for pre-test on achievement of Environmental Education in respect of Experimental group and Control Group

| Groups | No. of Learners | Mean | S.D | T-ratio |
|---|---|---|---|---|
| Experimental Group | 25 | 29.1 | 2.5 | 1.3 (N.S) |
| Controlled Group | 25 | 28.9 | 3 | |

N.S – Not significant

Table2: Means, S.D's and t-ratio for post-test and post-test of Experimental Group and Control Group

| Groups | No. of Learners | Mean | S.D | T-ratio |
|---|---|---|---|---|
| Experimental Group | 25 | 35 | 2.5 | 4.28** |
| Controlled Group | 25 | 29 | 6.6 | |

** - Significant at 0.01 level

It is revealed from the Table-1 that at the pre-test stage the mean achievement score of the experimental group and control group was nearly same and it was also observed not significant at t-value being 1.3

Consequent upon the intervention using the ICT, the experimental group improved substantially at the t-value (Table-2) was observed 4.28 which were significant at 0.01 levels. Thus it was proved that the Information and Communication Technology exerted positive impact on the learner's achievement in Environmental education. Thus hypothesis is retained.

## Major Findings

The major findings of the study regarding the impact of the ICT on the learners' achievement have been presented below.

1. The performance of the learners of experimental group and control group was same at the initial stage. But at the post-test stage these achievement of the experimental group was observed more than the control group.
2. The learners of experimental group work collaboratively.
3. There was proper group interaction among the learners of the group.
4. The learners who lagged behind they took the help of their peer who were ahead of them.
5. The learners derived pleasure out of the work.

Views of the Headmasters on usage of Information and Communication Technology programme in teaching process:

- ▶ As many as 75% of the Headmasters opined that Computer –aided education is an essential component of quality education in schools.
- ▶ It is observed that 84% of the headmasters were of the view that use of computer technology in teaching learning processes improves learner attendance.
- ▶ According to 96% of the Headmasters, use of computer technology in teaching learning processes improves learner performance.
- ▶ Computer education is appropriate for remedial teaching of under achievers (86%).
- ▶ Use of computer technology in teaching- learning processes makes it joyful (91%).

- Learning-facilitators can cope with the new role and responsibility and contribute for computer –aided education (89%).
- Computer provides only superfluous knowledge whereas; more than 40% of the Headmasters of Non-ICT== schools were in favour of usages of computer aided programme in curricular programme.
- The usages of computer aided programme in school curricular programme have the positive impact on the headmasters.
- Opinion of the learning-facilitators on usage of Information and Communication Technology programme in teaching process:
- As many as 94% of learning-facilitators viewed that computer is just a TLM and can be mastered through proper training and practice.
- Computer–aided education is an essential component of quality education in schools(87%).
- Use of computer technology in teaching learning processes improves learner attendance(89%).
- It is observed that 93% of the learning-facilitators were of the opinion that use of computer technology in teaching learning processes improves learner performance.
- Learning-facilitators can cope with the new role and responsibility and contribute for computer–aided education(90%).
- 88% of learning-facilitators' viewed that computer provides only superfluous knowledge.
- Opinion of the community members on implementation of Information and Communication Technology programme in teaching process:
- It is observed that more than 58.3% of the community members opined that they were aware that learners are educated through computer.
- It is observed that 78% of the learners have shown interest towards learning because of computer-aided learning.
- The learners are interested to go to school regularly because of computer-aided learning (86%).
- Community members in more than 60% of Non- ICT schools have shown interest towards Information and Communication Technology and they also opined that the learners will get benefit out of computer-aided learning.
- Opinion of the learners on implementation of computer aided education programme in teaching process:
- More than 66.6%of learners opined that their learning-facilitator teach through computer, they are interested to learn through computer.

## Suggestions

On the basis of the findings of the study, the investigator feels to suggest the following recommendations for effective implementation of ICT.

- The Non-ICT schools may be covered under ICTas far as feasibility.
- More number of learning-facilitators may be oriented under ICT programme
- More SMC members may be aware about ICT programme
- Frequently check-up may be done wherever the systems are facing trouble.
- Adequate number of contented CDs may be provided to make teaching learning process joyful.
- It may be suggested that frequently use of the computer in the curricular programme is essential.
- It may be suggested to provide Information and Communication Technology programme to the Non-ICT school as far as practicable.

## Implication

The study has wider implication in view of developing the concept of environmental education for the learner of Class-V. As future citizens of the society they can try to protect the environment for quality life.

## Conclusion

India has made impressive strides in the application of ICT in recent years and this is reflected in its vibrant and fast growing economy. However, the education sector particularly has lagged behind other sectors of the Indian Economy in benefiting from the fruits of technological development. For India to become a knowledge economy and society, it is essential to ensure that bulk of growing population has the capability to read and wrote, communicate and interact in modern economy. Especially, learners should be taught by using ICT so that their understanding will be sustainable that they need in 21$^{st}$ Century.

# Chapter 24

# ICT as a Tool for Capacity Building of Learning-facilitators

✎ **Sapna Yadav**
*SCERT, Delhi*

## Preview at a Glance

The school is the place where intended education is imparted formally by the learning-facilitators. Learning-facilitators' community is the only agency that directly influences the learner and their learning process. Effective teaching learning process is the function of many variables which can be enumerated as school psychosocial learning environment, competencies' of learning-facilitators, instructional tools in the hands of learning-facilitators, technology with the learning-facilitators. In the contemporary global society, Information and Communication Technology (ICT) plays an important role. In the classroom situation ICT has enormous potential to make teaching learning process most interesting, interactive, illustrative and participatory. ICT facilitates development of user friendly learning material accessible to all irrespective of time and geographical distance. Online ICT blended learning directly address the 3E of education i.e. Enable, Engage and Empower. ICT also enhances outreach for qualitative education to all surmounting logistical difficulties. The study of online capacity building program and its impact on learning-facilitator's capability reviewed many problem faced by the learning-facilitators and academic enrichment of In-Service Learning-facilitators during their In-service Capacity building program which ultimately effect the classroom. For purposes of this study, OCBP is operationally defined as a format used in learning when learners do not need to be in bricks classrooms. The most desirable feature of the online capacity building programme is that the trainees can do the training at their 'own pace and own place'. The objective of this chapteris to help learning-facilitators on thorough understanding of Mathematics topic 'Mensuration' with a focus on improving their conceptual and pedagogical understanding through OCBP. To this end, 62 Learning-facilitators of Mathematics have been selected randomly. After data collection, 55 learning-facilitators were conducting the Online Capacity Building Programme completely and data were analysed. This work is designed by keeping in mind that learning-facilitators are very well versed about the content but sometimes a learning-facilitator face the problem in transacting the content.Major findings of the study were that theonline programme was helpful to improve their classroom transaction process. Multimedia'sand teaching strategies were easy tointegrate intoteaching. Pedagogical subject information connected withreallifeexampleswas relevant tomakeyourclassinteractiveandfun. Time given for completing the programme was enough. Findings also show that programme helped learning-facilitatorsin improvingconceptual understanding and how to deliver content. The programme was very easy to access on app through smart phone or tablet and through web also. The training experience on themobile was good. Theacademicteamforqueries was responsivetoanyqueriesor doubts that we had during theprogramme.

## Introduction

Capacity building of learning-facilitators is an essential part of a teaching learning process in an education setting. The school is the place where intended education is imparted formally by the learning-facilitators. Learning-facilitator's community is the only agency that can directly influence the learner and their learning process. Effective teaching learning process is the function of many variables which can be enumerated as school psychosocial learning environment, competencies' of learning-facilitators, instructional tools in the hands of learning-facilitators, technology with the learning-facilitators. All these variables do not exist in isolation particularly in a learning programme where everyone is influencing each other. It is also known that many of the learning-facilitators are well versed about the content of their subject but sometimes a learning-facilitator face the problem in transacting the content. A best classroom is that where each and every child learns and use the concept to solve the problem which one taught by learning-facilitator, and it is done by only that when a learning-facilitator taught by using multiple ways to teach the concepts as a class comprises of fast pace and slow pace learners.

With the focus on quality improvement in school education with latest content, transaction methodology and relevant pedagogical practices for creating effective learning environment in class rooms this programme was visualised. In the contemporary global society, Information and Communication Technology (ICT) plays an important role. In the classroom situation ICT has enormous potential to make teaching learning process most interesting, interactive, illustrative and participatory. ICT facilitates development of user friendly learning material accessible to all irrespective of age, geographical distance etc. Mobile learning, online and blended learning directly address the 3E of Education i.e. Enable, Engage and Empower. ICT also enhances outreach for qualitative Education to all surmounting logistical difficulties. The real strength of Educational Technology lies in its ability to unlock learners learning through enhanced engagement, personalised education and equal access to all. Online

# ICT as a Tool for Capacity Building of Learning-facilitators

Capacity Building Programme is an initiative of the SCERT, Delhi to provide specific topic based support to its learning-facilitators and build their capacity. The online capacity building programme enhances the sharing between the learning-facilitator and learning-facilitator; learning-facilitator and learning-facilitator educator. This programme is available 24x7 to the learning-facilitators and they can do the training at their own place, at their own pace without disturbing their routine work. This online platform also provides the learning-facilitator community to connect their peers online for help raise their concerns and get solutions from within the community. There are many components uses in the capacity building program of learning-facilitators. There is so much content available on the Internet with easy access focusing the learners (e.g. Text, images videos, infographics etc.). But there is very limited content is available for the Learning-facilitators perspectives. So, while designing the online capacity building program for learning-facilitators, our focus was purely on learning-facilitators that how can us support learning-facilitators pedagogically for their classroom to increase their teaching-learning process.

## Objectives

To support learning-facilitators in developing a thorough understanding of Mensuration with a focus on improving their conceptual and pedagogical understanding.

- To provide the history and connections of every topic with real life examples
- To support learning-facilitators for their classroom with enough teaching as well as evaluation methods/ ideas/ resources to make teaching-learning process interesting.
- To proliferate a technology-enabled teaching-learning process.
- To seek feedback from the learning-facilitators undergoing the OCBP to confirm that Online Mechanisms will be an effective tool to conduct future trainings for all subjects across all grades.

## Methodology

Classroom management is very necessary step of teaching learning process for a learning-facilitator, so to keep in mind the same and to provide them with enough teaching as well as evaluation methods/ideas/resources, the content forthe online capacity building program were developed by the learning-facilitators of Directorate of Education.

The OCBP has drawn inputs from various resources from the many excellent Online Educational Resources like NROER, Khan Academy etc. which are available. All the resources have been aligned to the curriculum followed in Delhi Govt. Schools i.e. NCERT based curriculum.

The resources used in OCBP were curated from the Open Educational Resources in the form of videos, images, info graphics, worksheets and activities. These were selected by a group of experienced TGTs and subject matter experts.

Following are the components of the online capacity building program which are divided into 5 Modules and each module focused on different academic aspects:

**Module 0** - Introduction To Training
Contains: Aim, History, Real Life Examples, Time distribution, and Outcome for Learning-facilitators

**Module 1** - Recapitulating Formulae and Definitions
- To provide all definitions and formulae related to the topic.

**Module 2** - Teaching Strategies
- This module has 'Connections' and 'Teaching Methods' for each concept.
- Provides learning-facilitators with real life connections for each of the topics, so that learning-facilitatorstrengthen their concept from around the surrounding and/or experiences.
- Provides topic mapped and grade appropriate teaching methods which are interesting as well as innovative.

**Module 3** - Common Misconceptions
- The objective is to address the misconceptions with the help of videos and some tips from fellow learning-facilitators!
- Talks about both, assumptions that learning-facilitators make about their learners and, conceptual misconceptions/ mistakes that learners have/ make.

**Module 4** - Evaluation Strategies
- Provides all resources related to CCE to facilitate classroom evaluation.

    A **'Take a Test'** feature existed with every module, wherever applicable.

## How to access Online Capacity Building Programme

This capacity building programme can be accessed from Smartphone through mobile application called 'chalk lit' and from the website www.chalklit.in.

Steps to Install App on your Phone to initiate online capacity building programme:

1. Go to Play store > Type Chalk Lit > Download and Install.
2. Enter the same Mobile number as you gave in the Google form.
3. Device will receive a SMS with an OTP (enter the OTP if not entered by the app automatically).
4. Provide Your Name, Email-Id, School Name, Gender and click on Update.

## How to start Capacity Building Programme

1. Click the Hamburger (three lines) on the top left, to see the Menu (shows the menu after clicking on Hamburger).

# ICT as a Tool for Capacity Building of Learning-facilitators

2. Click on Trainings
3. You will see a card showing the training (titled 'Mensuration')
4. Click on the training card to see 5 modules of the training
5. A module contains different posts. The number of posts in a module and suggested time for each module is given on the module card
6. Expand the module by clicking on it, to see the posts in that module
7. Click on a post to read it
8. Ask a Question: On every post you can ask a question, by simply keying in your query. Just like you add a comment on a face book post
9. A green tick in front of a post means you have read it. An orange tick on the post means you have yet not seen the complete video in the post
10. 10. Take a Test: At the end of the module there is a take a test to help you know if you have understood the module completely. You can answer a test only once, please do it carefully.There is a submit button at the end of the test to submit your test.

## Literature Review

Studies on learning-facilitator self-efficacy have largely been conceptualized within Bandura's (1994; 2002) notion of self-efficacy. Learning-facilitator self-efficacy has been defined as the extent to which a learning-facilitator is confident enough to his or her ability to promote learners' learning (Bandura, 1994). According to Bandura, human behaviour is motivated by the interaction of two kinds of expectations: Self efficacy and outcome expectancy; the former referring to peoples' judgments of their capability to undertake and execute successfully a specific task in a specific context, and the latter including judgments about the likely consequences that this performance would bring about.

The advent of the World-Wide Web (WWW) in 1991 was a powerful catalyst for moving distance education forward, and was a milestone in the rapid expansion and growth of online teaching and learning. Maloney-Krichmar and Abras (2003) stated that www'facilitated the wide-spread use of web sites and the development of online community groups supported by web pages and various forms of communications software'. Since then, colleges and universities both in the United States and around the world have offered not only just online courses but entire degree programs online as well (Wallace, 2003).

Throughout this study, the primary focus was to discuss how theories, practices and assessments apply to the online learning environment. It started with a basic overview of online education as studied and perceived by Garrison et al. (2000), which served as the theoretical framework for this study. We then examined how presented module has applied to various aspects of online course design and development. We first examined the online environment over time, its evolvement, and the technologic impacts on online capacity building program. In online teaching, we focused our attention on the relationships between cognitive and teaching presences to determine

the best and most desirable practices and strategies for online pedagogy. Within the realm of online learning, we directed our attention on the creation of an online learning community by means of promoting social presence, interactions, and collaboration between the instructor and learners and among learners.

## Findings/Results

At the end of OCBP an online feedback form was shared to be filled by participants. The questions asked to the learning-facilitators and their responses are given below.

| Quick glance at a few interesting things: | |
| --- | --- |
| Total Number of comments in 16 days | 476 (413 via mobile, 63 via web) |
| Maximum opinion shared by | NiranjanGoswami: 44 comments! |
| Total number of downloads of the 16 downloadable resources | 116 |
| Most talked about POST | 1.3 - Recalling 2D Shapes: 31 comments! |

A design flaws in the study may explain the findings:

1. Distribution of learning-facilitators based on the percentage completion of training by them
   - 89% of the learning-facilitators completed the training to a 100% completion mark,
   - about 5% learning-facilitators did not complete the training (between 42% to 91% completion marks) and
   - 6% did not start the training.
2. Understanding the Medium used by learning-facilitators, Mobile Vs Web.
   - Web Activity vs Phone Activity
   - 88% used phone only
   - 11% used Web only
   - 1% web and phone both

Finding shows that majority users (88%) prefer using only the mobile platform while only a small fraction uses both (11%), and the web-only users are negligible.

3. Distribution of Tests taken by Learning-facilitators and their scores

| | |
| --- | --- |
| 0% to 20% | 16% |
| 20% to 40% | 5% |
| 40% to 60% | 13% |
| 60% to 80% | 43% |
| 80% to 100% | 24% |

# ICT as a Tool for Capacity Building of Learning-facilitators

Feedbacks about the content

1. Overall, was the information covered in this training useful? Please mention what was observed useful in the training.
   - 94.8%: Very Useful
   - 5.2%: Somewhat Useful

When asked what was observed useful in the training, the learning-facilitators shared that:

- The history of Mensuration, learning objectives of the modules, derivation of formulae and videos helped them to enhance their knowledge and enabled them to learn new techniques of teaching.
- They also shared that the training saved time and was very convenient as they could do it while travelling,
- Learning-facilitators also acknowledged that innovative and interesting solutions to doubts were provided within 24 hours.
- A few learning-facilitators reported video loading issue due to low data connectivity.

Select which tools and strategies covered in the training you could/expect to integrate into your teaching

| Particulars | % of learning-facilitators who choose the particulars to integrate into teaching |
|---|---|
| Activities | 44% |
| Teaching Techniques | 38% |
| Videos | 50% |
| Images | 33% |
| Worksheets | 35% |

**Rate the subject information covered.**

| | |
|---|---|
| Extremely Helpful | 53.4% |
| Very Helpful | 43.1% |
| Somewhat Helpful | 3.4 % |

**Rate the real life examples, teaching techniques, and other materials given in the training for developing your concepts**

| | |
|---|---|
| Extremely Helpful | 51.7% |
| Very Helpful | 37.9% |
| Somewhat Helpful | 10.4 % |

Rate the availability of relevant materials to make your class interactive and fun.

| | |
|---|---|
| Extremely Helpful | 62.1% |
| Very Helpful | 29.3% |
| Somewhat Helpful | 8.6 % |

Rate the online course in terms of ease of reading and understanding

| | |
|---|---|
| Extremely Easy | 55.5% |
| Very Easy | 31.0% |
| Somewhat Easy | 7.5 % |
| Not at all Easy | 6% |

Rate the online course in terms of layout of training material.

| | |
|---|---|
| Excellent | 46.6% |
| Above Average | 41.4% |
| Acceptable | 8.0% |
| Needs Improvement | 4.0% |

Was the time given for completing the training enough?

| | |
|---|---|
| Yes | 91.4% |
| No | 8.6% |

Did the training help you improve your conceptual understanding? Why did the training help/did not help in improving your conceptual understanding?

| | |
|---|---|
| Yes | 93.1% |
| May be | 5.2% |
| No | 1.7% |

Among the learning-facilitators who shared their detailed feedback as to how training improved their conceptual understanding:

- More than 50% of learning-facilitators appreciated the content explained through videos, images and worksheets.
- Almost 25% learning-facilitators shared that the topic coverage in the training were quite detailed and it helped them revise their concepts.
- Almost 15% of the learning-facilitators acknowledged that training has enabled them to brief learners and make classroom live.
- One of the learning-facilitators has also suggested that there should be more peer level interaction.

## User Feedback

Technical - App

Features Liked

# ICT as a Tool for Capacity Building of Learning-facilitators

Doubts were heard and cleared, which was very helpful for many.

A few learning-facilitators used technology enabled teaching methods for the first time and want to continue with this. They observed this training and access to resources as very comprehensive and systematic.

Rabindra Nath go this learners to down load the app and use.

Did not work well

Jittery video viewing experience due to slow data connectivity

Off line 'Takea Test': Few learning-facilitators wanted to take the test while not being on mobile or Internet (data or Wi-Fi), whereas 'Takea Test' is an online(while connected to internet) feature.

## Suggestions

Learning-facilitators and school sare provided with Wi-Fi/ internet connectivity.

School sare provided with projectors or equivalent infrastructure to enable effectives haring of app content with learners, if learning-facilitators want to do so (particularly video sor images).

Content - Mensuration

Features Liked:

Appreciated most of the videos, and the total number of times videos are seen stands at 3639.

Some of the reasons shared by learning-facilitators are:-

Helped learning-facilitators to improve their concept at a basic level.

Could be used in classroom directly.

Some of the ideas were taken up by learning-facilitators and given as home work (like, making cone out of papers as shown in videos).

Helped in revising the concepts in details.

Covered every topic and concept from book, but took less time to cover the same since video swere comprehensive and interesting.

Real life examples were observed very nice and useful as that facilitated learning-facilitators to think of more examples and come up with new ones.

History of Mensuration was liked quite much.

Derivations of the formula ewere most talked about. Learning-facilitators observed it very useful because

Their own concepts go trevised/some learntas well

Could use that as posters for their learners as well

Could have been better:

Videos

    Absence of Hindi videos.

    Take a test

Need a more effective question nairetodetermine efficacy of learning from the training.

Learning-facilitators were participative and have provided many suggestions to add which is available agains teach of the posts in the training. This will help the team in improving content for the next round.

*Some User Stories*

*Learning-facilitator - Chirag Kumar*
*School - GBSS Azadpur Village*
*Grades - VI to X*
*Mentor -Jaspal Kaur*

Chirag teaches in the school which runs in the evening shift. When asked how he is planning to use the videos that he has liked so much he shared: 'I have downloaded all the videos from YouTube and put it in folder and planning to show it in classroom using projector'.

*Learning-facilitator - Indresh Kumar*

*School - GBSS Azadpur Village*

*Grades - VI to X*

*Mentor -Jaspal Kaur*

He is good at acknowledging his own learning. He shared over the telephonic conversation:

    Chalk Lit Support: How do you think this training has helped you sir?

    Indresh Ji: In the post showing how 3D shapes change from 2D shapes (Post 1.9 Conceptual Clarity-Area, Perimeter and Volume), even my own knowledge has improved, where it says that area has been related to volume.

    ChalkLit Support: Since you are teaching now, is it helping in your classroom preparation? Indresh Ji: Yes, I have shown it to all my learners as well and 30% understood. He has made a WhatsApp group with learners and wants his learners to also use the app since almost 80% of his learners have smartphones.

*Learning-facilitator - SashiGoel*

*School - GGSS Azadpur Village*

*Grades - VI to X*
*Mentor -Jaspal Kaur*

This training go the rquite excited ands he wants to use mobile mini projector (which was being used by team Chal k Lit during demonstration) in her classroom to ensure that these interesting resources reach her classroom.

*Learning-facilitator - Mamta Yadav*

*School - SKV, E Block, Nand Nagri*

*Grades - VII, IX, X*

*Mentor - Neha Sharma*

She shared that there all life examples have enabled her to make it more interesting in introducing topics to her class and is a keen learner. She appreciated the systematic way in which resources are provided in the training and wants to continue to optimize the technology enabled resources in her classrooms.

*Learning-facilitator - Manisha Arya*

*School - GSKV, E Block, Nand Nagri*

*Grades - VI to VIII*

*Mentor - Neha Sharma*

She has been a part of Digital Equalizer and has used technological tools in her classrooms before. She prompt lissy shared that her knowledge increased especially after reading derivation of all formulae and was very appreciative of the history of Mensuration, both of which she said she came to know for the first time and hence was very excitedtos hare with her class as well.

*Learning-facilitator - Kapil Bandhu*

*School - Govt. Boys Senior Secondary School Grades - VI*

*Mentor -Shalini Bahri*

Although he started with the problem of lack of time at his end but he shared the has liked all the videos,especially comparison of cone,cylinder(Post2.13-ConnectionsforCone,2.14-Teaching Methods) because it could be conducted practically in the classrooms. He was more pleased for being able to use the videos with his daughter who is in 7th standard, and said that those videos have helped her to clear her concepts.

*Learning-facilitator - Rabindranath Jha*

*School - P.C.R Sarvodaya Bal Vidyalaya Grades - VI to X*

*Mentor -Rajendra Goyal*

He shared that he has got his learners from 8th and 9th standard download Chalk Lit. He en-quired how long would it take for the team to start with all the other subjects so that his learners can use it too.

*Learning-facilitator - Sadan and Yadav School - PCRSBV*

*Grades - VI to X*

*Mentor -Rajendra Goyal*

After an interaction with learners and Sadan and learning-facilitator Mr. Rajendra could understand that not only did the training helped to enliven his classroom but also it has helped Sadan and to improve his concepts, with which he struggles most often.

*Learning-facilitator - Deependra Singh, School- RSBV*

*Grades - VI to VIII*

*Mentor -Rajendra Goyal*

Mentor Rajendra Goyal also shared that Deependra learning-facilitator's school caters to children who are from the resettlement area of Trilokpuri and are not very easy to deal with. On one of his observations he observed that classrooms had chart papers which are made using posters on derivations from Chalk Lit. Deependra also shared that it was for the first time that solid objects have been used in the classroom to introduce concept sand learners loved it.

## Conclusion

The review of its history clearly shows online education has developed rapidly, fuelled by Internet connectivity, advanced technology, and a massive market. It has evolved from 19th century correspondence programs to the 21st century's vibrant and well-designed institutional online contributions.

We can expect that online capacity building program will continue to increase its presence and influence learning-facilitator efficacy through an energetic process of reshaping, refining, and restructuring of content and pedagogy. It is unlikely, however, to replace traditional in-service training but merely to be an alternative. But, owing to its flexibility, accessibility and affordability, online capacity building program is gaining in popularity, especially for those learning-facilitators who are otherwise unable to attend capacity building program because of physical distance, schedule conflicts, and unaffordable costs.

Throughout this study, the primary focus was to discuss how content, pedagogy and assessments apply to the online capacity building program. The focus is also on to improve the transaction methodology of learning-facilitators for their classroom teaching. In online teaching, we focused our attention on the relationships between cognitive and teaching presences to determine the best and most desirable practices and strategies for online / offline pedagogy. Within the sphere of online capacity building program, we directed our attention on the content, pedagogical understanding and overall attention to the online capacity building program.

# Chapter 25

# ICT Enabled Learning: Digitalizing Homework

✍ **Sourabh Garg**
*University of Delhi and Jamia MillialsIamia, Delhi*

## Preview at a Glance

Learning after school' popularly known as 'homework' is as much as important as learning within the school. It should happen as unconsciously as possible because of the developed hatred for homework among learners. Because of the developed aggressions of learners toward word 'homework', the system of learning after school should be moulded in a frame without the word 'homework' and even essence of homework. In current Indian education scenario much emphasis is given upon the homework. As the syllabus is much more than the time period of the classes, the much work is given in the form of homework. The learners do not find it interesting or motivating at all. The traditional way of homework is not very much appreciated by the learners. They use to dodge it as much possible, they find it extra burden for them. And when we talk about Math the hatred amplifies to higher limits. Learners find Mathematics to be more terrific in form of homework. Researchers tried to dig down the roots of 'hatred towards homework' and reasons for negative attitude of learners' towards homework. What else tasks than homework, schools have been practicing is been listed out. And how those different techniques are helpful? ICT enabled project based learning is practiced in schools to generate learners' interest in the subject and to provide learners exposure to more real-life experiences rather than only theoretical knowledge. The approach of Project based learning (PBL) for the learning after school may provide the probable solution to the homework problems that whole Indian education system is facing. PBL can help learners by putting them in realistic, problem-solving environments that serve to make associations between learnings in the classroom and genuine encounters. And this approach of ICT enabled PBL is way more effective when it is carried out through the means of ICT. This research provides a probable solution for the problems related with mathematics homework i.e. project based learning. This research is an empirical study done on 134 grade 7 learners from two different schools of Delhi. Learning after school modules (The Magical Adventures) had been developed in the research as the intervention tool and probable solution that had been carried out on learners and then effect on learning and other homework related issues was examined.

## Introduction

Learning after school is popularly known as 'homework'. Homework is typically defined as 'any tasks assigned to learners by school learning-facilitators that are meant to be carried out during non-school hours' (Cooper, 1989). According to a survey conducted by the University of Phoenix, College of Education, 98% of learning-facilitators believe that homework does improve academic performance. Most of the learning-facilitators believe that homework helps them evaluate their learner's level of their topic's understanding, it improves problem solving skills, teaches time management, and it also helps learners to apply the knowledge to the real life situations and new circumstances.

Learning after school is as much as important as learning within the school. It should happen as unconsciously as possible because of the developed hatred for homework among learners. Because of the developed aggressions of learners toward word 'homework', the system of learning after school should be moulded in a frame without the word 'homework' and even essence of homework. In current Indian education scenario much emphasis is given upon the homework. As the syllabus is much more than the time period of the classes, the much work is given in the form of homework. The learners do not find it interesting or motivating at all. The traditional way of homework is not very much appreciated by the learners. They use to dodge it as much possible, they find it extra burden for them. And when we talk about Mathematics the hatred amplifies to higher limits. The procedure of homework needs some serious transformation.

The current system of Mathematics homework is analysed in this research. The 'demotivating and unpleasant things' about homework is the hot topic of the research. Researcher tried to dig down the roots of 'hatred towards homework'. What else tasks than homework, schools have been practicing is been listed out. And how those different techniques are helpful?

Project based learning is practiced in schools to generate learners' interest in the subject and to provide learners exposure to more real-life experiences rather than only theoretical knowledge. ICT Enabled PBL has emerged as a comprehensive approach to classroom teaching and learning that is designed to engage learners in investigation of authentic problems (Blumenfeld *et al.*, 1991; McGrath, 2004; MaKinster *et al.*, 2001). Findings about it show that project learning fosters a cognitive learning progress, networked thinking, social abilities and action competences (Bieberbach, 2000; Krajcik and Blumenfeld, 2006). A very few schools are already practicing ICT

# ICT Enabled Learning: Digitalizing Homework

Enabled PBL. The approach of Project based learning for learning after school may provide the probable solution to the homework problems that whole Indian education system is facing. The ICT Enabled PBL can help learners by putting them in realistic, problem-solving environments that serve to make associations between learnings in the classroom and genuine encounters.

This research provides a probable solution for the problems related with homework i.e. project based learning. This research is an empirical study done on 134 grade 7 learners from two different schools of Delhi. Learning after school modules had been developed in the research as the intervention tool and probable solution that had been carried out on learners and then effect on learning and other homework related issues was examined.

## Objectives

- To know the different current mathematics homework practices
- To know the negative impacts of homework and to know why learners use to skip and run away from homework
- To know the impact of ICT enabled PBL based learning after school modules on the Mathematics achievement, interest generation, self-motivation level, amusement level, enjoying level and burden level on $7^{th}$ grade learners of Government Girls Senior Secondary School (GGSSS) No. 2.
- To know the impact of ICT enabled PBL based learning after school modules on the Mathematics achievement, interest generation, self-motivation level, amusement level, enjoying level and burden level on $7^{th}$ grade learners of KulachiHansraj Model School (KHMS)?

## Methodology

The purpose of the study was to examine and analyse the current practices of 'learning after school' and then examine the impact of ICT Enabled PBL based learning after school modules on the Mathematics achievement, interest generation, self-motivation level, amusement level, enjoying level and burden level on 61 grade $7^{th}$ learners from two different schools.

The study utilized an exploratory research design. It was descriptive and experimental research in nature. As there were no standardized tools were available for such kind of research. The researcher developed his own tools as per the requirements. It was a Quantitative research but Qualitative analysis was also done to support the research. The research was carried on two groups of learners, one was in controlled environment on which no intervention was made and the other was experimental group, which was exposed to intervention. Then their achievement's comparison was made.

In this research Independent variable was ICT Enabled PBL based learning after school module. And the dependent variables were achievement, interest level, engagement level, motivational level, burden level.

The subjects for the study were from two schools of New Delhi as of 2017-2018 academic year. First school was a government school GGSSS and the other was private school KHMS. The Experimental group consisted of a non-probability sample of 66 grade 7th learners, 21 from GGSSS and 45 from KHMS that incorporated the after learning modules as part of the curriculum. The comparison group consisted of 69 grade 7th learners, 20 from GGSSS and 48 from KHMS where learning after school modules was not used as part of the curriculum.

**Learner sample**

Table 1: Sample of the research

| School | Controlled Group participant numbers | Experimental Group participant numbers |
|---|---|---|
| GGSSS | 20 | 21 |
| KHMS | 48 | 45 |

## Instrumentation

Detailed interviews were conducted to administer on learning-facilitators to identify the current practices of learning after school, alternate practices and the particularly negative attitude of the learners towards homework with extensive interview schedule.

Based on the learning-facilitators' suggestions and analysing the learning-facilitators' feedback on current practices and factors generating negative attitude of learners towards mathematics an intervention tool was prepared based on ICT Enabled PBL and story themed in collaboration with NCERT textbooks. The modules made were completely aligned with NCERT curriculum. Conscious efforts were made to incorporate the same questions in the module. Imaginative, creative plot was created to weave in those questions in the plot.

The module was designed on theme of a Magician losing his powers because learners find these types of thing were fascinating and interesting. The module was designed as engaging as possible. And it was considered that learners must not feel that they were doing homework. Learners must do unconsciously by reading the module were the prime objective of the module. The module was developed on the online software 'storyboardthat.com'.

The time for homework was also considered during the development of the module.

The learning module is designed for homework purpose in which NCERT questions are portrayed with some modifications and inculcating them in the story of the module.

## This module is for

- generating interest in the topic
- enhancing engagement in learning
- revision

# ICT Enabled Learning: Digitalizing Homework

- recapitulation
- concepts clarity
- strengthen learning
- visualizing mathematics in real world

The module contains Chapter 1 'Integers' and Chapter 2 'Fractions and Decimals' (exercises 1.4 and 2.1 in particular), NCERT Mathematics book grade 7th. Theme line of the story is about a Magician and his disciples looking for his magical tools. They come across various obstacles in the journey, and each obstacle is based on the NCERT book problems. Learners have to help magician by solving the problems for them. The mode of the communication of the module was bilingual. English and Hindi were the languages used to convey the information in the module. Some of the features of the module are creativity, curiosity to learn, imagination, and problem solving attitude.

A whole plot and situation was constructed for an inculcating a simple question in the module. Learning-facilitators were prior asked which question they wanted to give in the homework and specifically those questions were targeted in the module.

## For example

Q. The temperature at 12 noon was 10°C above zero. If it decreases at the rate of 2°C per hour until midnight

    a    At what time would the temperature be 8°C below zero?

    b    What would be the temperature at mid-night?

is the question from NCERT's grade 7th Mathematics text book chapter 1st and exercise 1.4. To portray this question in the module whole situation related with question was framed and the questions were made like the genuine real life situations not some exercise related question.

Here are some excerpts from the 'The Magical Adventures'- the learning after school module in which the given question is inculcated as the obstacle in the journey of Magician and his disciples.

After the questions asked there were also extensions of the questions which were generated by the researcher. For example:

These were the two extensions of the previous question. These extensions were not from the NCERT.

The process of the intervention was 4 day long. Participants were exposed to the module for 4 days. The execution of the intervention was carried out with their respective subject learning-facilitators. The learning-facilitators carrying out the execution in their classes were instructed with the following points:

- Learners must not to be told that they have to do the homework or fill the given modules.

- They should only be instructed to read the story and help Magician.
- They must not be forced to read it.
- They should be set free to read whenever, wherever they want to.

There must not be any changes in any other teaching learning process as the project is part of research work (transforming learner's engagement in learning after school) for which researcher has to keep other factors constant.

Post-test was made after discussion with the concerned learning-facilitators about which questions they wanted to give in the test. As all other variables than homework has to be keep constant, therefore no innovative or different test was made. The traditional class test was made with consulting the learning-facilitator of the sample learners. The test for both the schools was of 10 marks and of 20 mins duration consisting of 6 questions.

Feedback form was made to gather the learners' responses and opinions on the 'The Magical Adventures'- learning after school modules on the following parameters while reading the module:
- Level of enjoyment
- Level of burden
- Feeling of self-motivation
- Revision of concepts
- Any difficulty faced
- Most liked part

Feedback interviews were also conducted on learning-facilitators to know their opinion on the module.

## Data Collection

### *Quantitative Data:*

The data were obtained from the post-test conducted on both the groups of both the schools. The data includes the scores of the participants in the test according to grade, gender, socio-economic conditions, academic achievements etc.

Data of the feedback were obtained from the feedback form that learners filled.

## Qualitative Data:

The data were obtained in the form of the interviews conducted on learning-facilitators and principal for the current and alternate homework practices, negative attitude of learners towards homework and the feedback for the 'The Magical Adventures'- Module for learning after school.

## Results and Discussions

The purpose of the study was to examine the current and alternate practices in the homework. By the interactions with the learning-facilitators, researcher found out the following practices:

# ICT Enabled Learning: Digitalizing Homework

## *In GGSSS:*

Traditional type homework: the learning-facilitators told the major form of the homework given to learners was in traditional form. The learners were told to do certain homework and they had to do it in their respective notebooks.

Assignment based homework: there were assignment files for each learner, in which each learner had to attach her assignment monthly. Those assignments usually consisted of the same questions from the textbook; they have to write and solve those questions on the coloured papers and had to decorate them creatively.

## *In KHMS:*

KHMS was furnished with activities and projects. The school also had its Mathematics lab. The learning-facilitator herself was very enthusiastic about revolutionizing the meaning of Mathematics Education around learners. There were different projects and activities which were practiced in the schools. Few of the homework practices are listed below:

Traditional style: Majority of the Mathematics learning-facilitators of the school were practicing traditional style of homework.

Flipped Classroom: 'Flipped Learning is a pedagogical approach in which direct instruction moves from the group learning space to the individual learning space, and the resulting group space is transformed into a dynamic, interactive learning environment where the educator guides learners as they apply concepts and engage creatively in the subject matter'. Bishop and Verleger (2013) defined flipped classroom as 'an educational technique that consists of two parts: interacting group learning activities inside the classroom and direct computer based individual instruction outside the classroom' that must include videos.

One of the learning-facilitator used flipped classroom as the alternate practice, in which learners have to watch video lectures prepared by the learning-facilitator as homework, and next day in the class activities and doubt sessions on the topic was conducted. The learning-facilitator could interact with her learners by this method more efficiently. Learners also used to enjoy the activities and projects that had been carried out in classroom.

Project based: Learners were given different projects but that projects were given mostly in vacations. For example: the summer vacation project grade 10th learner was to gather different data from the newspaper and then apply the statistics they had learnt so far.

Online Work: Learners were given different type of online work in homework

Reasons of developed negative attitude of learners towards homework:

By the interviews with learning-facilitators and interactions with some learners, the researcher listed out the problems with the homework, or the reasons of negative attitude of learners towards homework:

- Learners' find it boring: The traditional style of homework, learners find it not at all interesting
- Less time with family, friends and for co-curricular activities
- Homework does not motivate to do well in class
- Lack of connections to real life
- No grading
- Causes stress
- It is not fun
- Not motivating
- Not engaging
- Extra burden

The impact of ICT Enabled PBL based learning after school modules on the Mathematics achievement, interest generation, self-motivation level, amusement level, enjoying level and burden level on 7th grade learners of GGSSS No. 2:

The score of the post test of the controlled group and experimental group were analysed by the mean, standard deviation, median, significance of standard error of mean and t-test.

As from the mean of controlled group was 9.74 with standard deviation of 4.70 and median of the data lies on 9.63, hence mean and median both are approximately equal therefore we can say this data is normally distributed. The mean of experimental group was 12.76 with standard deviation of 4.62 and median of the data lies on 12.75, therefore we can say that this data is also normally distributed.

There was a notable large difference in the means of controlled group and the experimental group. Then it was found out whether this difference was significant or not by the t-test.

**Table 2: Critical Ratio of the Data of the Schools**

| School | Differences of Mean | Standard Error of difference of Mean | Critical Ratio |
|---|---|---|---|
| GGSSS | 3.02 | 1.47 | 2.05 |
| KHMS | 1.18 | 0.438 | 2.69 |

On interpreting significance of the difference of the means, from table 2 Critical Ratio for the data was 2.05 which is more than 1.96, hence the differences between means was significant at 95% confidence because more than 95% lied in confidence interval. As the sample is less than 30, therefore researcher also performed t-test, from table 9, the 95% confidence level the significance came out to be 0.025, which was acceptable, so the researcher rejected Null Hypothesis and accepted alternate hypothesis.

# ICT Enabled Learning: Digitalizing Homework

Table 3: Significance of difference between Means of GGSSS data (Paired Sample Test)

| | Paired Differences | | | | | T | Degree of Freedom | Significance (2-tailed) |
|---|---|---|---|---|---|---|---|---|
| | Mean difference | Standard Deviation | Std. Error of Mean | 95% Confidence Interval of the Difference | | | | |
| | | | | Lower | Upper | | | |
| Controlled Group- Experimental Group | 3.02 | 5.70 | 1.24 | 4.27 | 5.62 | 2.429 | 20 | 0.25 |

On interpreting significance of the difference of the means, from table 2 Critical Ratio for the data was 2.05 which is more than 1.96, hence the differences between means was significant at 95% confidence because more than 95% lied in confidence interval. As the sample is less than 30, therefore researcher also performed t-test, from table 9, the 95% confidence level the significance came out to be 0.025, which was acceptable, so the researcher rejected Null Hypothesis and accepted alternate hypothesis.

The impact of ICT Enabled PBL based learning after school modules on the Mathematics achievement, interest generation, self-motivation level, amusement level, enjoying level and burden level on 7th grade learners of KHMS:

The score of the post test of the controlled group and experimental group were analysed by the mean, standard deviation, median, significance of standard error of mean and t-test.

As the mean of controlled group was 5.78 with standard deviation of 2.39 and median of the data lies on 5.77, hence mean and median both are approximately equal therefore we can say this data is normally distributed. The mean of experimental group was 6.96 with standard deviation of 1.92 and median of the data lies on 7, therefore we can say that this data is also normally distributed.

Table 4: Significance of difference between Means of KHMS data (Paired Sample Test)

| | Paired Differences | | | | | T | Degree of freedom | Significance (two tailed) |
|---|---|---|---|---|---|---|---|---|
| | Mean difference | Standard Deviation | Std. error of mean | 95% confidence interval of the difference | | | | |
| | | | | Lower | Upper | | | |
| Controlled Group- Experimental Group | 1.17 | 3.05 | .44 | 00 | 2.36 | 2.68 | 47 | 0.01 |

There was a notable large difference in the means of controlled group and the experimental group. Then it was found out whether this difference was significant or not and results were supported by the t-test.

On interpreting significance of the difference of the means, Critical Ratio for the data was 2.69 which is more than 2.58, hence the differences between means was significant at 98% confidence because more than 95% lied in confidence interval. Researcher also performed t-test to support his findings. From table 4, the 99% confidence level the significance came out to be 0.01, which was acceptable, so the researcher rejected null hypothesis and accepted alternate hypothesis.

**Feedback wof the Modules**

Learners and learning-facilitators both liked 'the Magical adventures'-learning after school modules very much. They all appreciated the efforts. The feedback was taken from learners and analysed. The learners were told to rate some questions. Thirty-five learners from KHMS filled the feedback form. Maximum learners enjoyed the modules, believed it helped them revising concepts, felt no burden, felt motivated towards solving problems and supported to do mathematics in such forms of work.

## Conclusion

The following conclusions can be drawn from the research:

- There are not any effective and different practices for homework in schools
- The homework had built a kind of stereotype that it would be boring and time waste among learners
- Learners are not motivated towards homework and feel burdened by homework
- The learning after school modules like 'The Magical Adventures' could be very helpful
    - To generate learners' interest in homework
    - To generate feeling of self-motivation towards homework among learners
    - To make them feel less burdened by homework
    - To make them relate learning to the real environment

Chapter

# ICT in Learning Processes in Higher Education: Attitude of Learners

✎ **SusmitaMondal**

*Visva-Bharati, Santiniketan, West Bengal*

## Preview at a Glance

We are living in a constantly evolving digital world. ICT has an impact on nearly every aspect of our lives - from working to socialising, learning to playing. The digital age has transformed the way young people communicate, network, seek help, access information and learn. We must recognise that young people are now an online population and access is through a variety of means such as computers, TV and mobile phones. As technology becomes more and more embedded in our culture, we must provide our learners with relevant and contemporary experiences that allow them to successfully engage with technology and prepare them for life after school. It is widely recognised that learners are motivated and purposefully engaged in the learning process when concepts and skills are underpinned with technology and sound pedagogy. ICT have impacted on educational practice in education to date in quite small ways but that the impact will grow considerably in years to come and that ICT will become a strong agent for change among many educational practices. Extrapolating current activities and practices, the continued use and development of ICTs within education will have a strong impact on: What is learned; how it is learned; when and where learning takes place; who is learning and who is teaching. This chapter has sought to explore the attitude of learners towards ICT in learning processes in higher education. To serve this purpose a study was conducted on 40 learners pursuing higher education at Visva-Bharati. The main objective of the study was to find out how far the use of Information and Communication Technology is helpful for the learners in their learning processes. The results indicated that most of the learners were on the view that ICT can be one of the promising pedagogical technologies to be employed in the higher education system as it helps in reducing educational boundaries of ideas, distance, time and ICTcan become the vehicle for the journey on the path of excellence.

## Introduction

In recent years, several studies and reports have highlighted the opportunities and the potential benefits of Information and communication technology (ICT) for improving the quality of education. We are living in a constantly evolving digital world. Information and communication technology (ICT) influenced our daily lives including our professional live and social live. In this digital age people differently share their information, communicate with other people differently, and also learn differently. Now the young generation are very much technology oriented and they access the technology by the help of computers, internet, e-learning etc. As technology becomes more and more embedded in our life, in educational field learners are also influenced by the technology a lot. Learning-facilitators must provide them appropriate technological tools so they can use it successfully in the learning process and apply it in their professional life in future. Information and communication technology (ICT) helps the learner to motivate easily and can engage in the learning process and they can construct knowledge, skills by using technology.

Information and communication technology (ICT) have impacted on educational practice in education to date in quite small ways but that the impact will grow considerably in years to come and that Information and communication technology (ICT) will become a strong agent for change among many educational practices. Extrapolating current activities and practices, the continued use and development of Information and communication technology (ICT) within education will have a strong impact on: What is learned; how it is learned; when and where learning takes place; who is learning and who is teaching.

Information and communication technology (ICT) are helps to reshape the thoughts of the people and enhancing the changes in the society. Information and communication technology (ICT) tools and techniques have vitally changed the communication process between the people. Because of the Information and communication technology (ICT) a huge transformation occurred in the education field. The role of learning-facilitator and learner also changes nowadays because of Information and communication technology (ICT). The learning process also changes, knowledge is not acquired now rather knowledge is constructed by the learner, and learning-facilitator is the facilitator in this process. In the learning process Information and communication technology (ICT) influenced in a positive way. There are many pedagogical factors which help to adopt e-learning in the teaching learning process. At present time Learners use information and communication technology more and more in education.

Information and communication technology (ICT) helps to improve the quality of learning by facilitating access to resources and services as well as remote exchange and collaboration. An information and communication technology (ICT) has had a major impact in the higher education. An information and communication technology (ICT) is not only the main support of the Information Era, but also an important facilitator for the educational reforms that change the learners into productive knowledge workers. In higher education, application of Information and communication technology (ICT) in form of e-learning is already changing teaching and learning processes. There are many factors that help to implement e-learning. These are greater information access, greater communication via electronic facilities, synchronous learning, flexible in time and place, increased cooperation and collaboration, cost effectiveness and pedagogical improvement through simulations, virtual experiences, and graphic representations. The attitude of Information and communication technology (ICT) on the learning process has a positive impact on learner motivation, self-learning, self-esteem, Information and communication technology (ICT) skills, collaborative skills, subject knowledge, information handling skills, meta-cognitive skills, etc. At present time Learners use information and communication technology more and more in the higher education.

## Review of Related Literature

Boateng *et al.* (2016) studied on 'Videos in learning in higher education: assessing perceptions and attitudes of learners at the University of Ghana'. This objective of the study was to assess the perceptions and attitudes of learners at the University of Ghana towards the use of videos as a medium for teaching and learning. Qualitative data was collected using semi structured interviews. The sample size was 20 learners from University of Ghana. The data was analysed by using content analysis method. The finding of the study was learners believed videos help in their learning activities. Although, learning outcomes of learners and instructors should be depend on the manner in which way videos are used.

Makewa *et al.* (2014) worked on 'ICT-Integration in Higher Education and LearnerBehavioural Change: Observations at University of Arusha, Tanzania'. At present time a paradigm shift occurred in the educational field, now education is learner centric not learning-facilitator centric by the influence of digital technology. So Information and communication technology (ICT) incorporation is important in teaching learning process. Learning-facilitator can use different technology in their teaching learning process and make it more interesting and fruitful and passes the information to the learners more easily. The objective of the study was evaluating ICT-Based Education and Learners Behavioural Change at University of Arusha, Tanzania. Data collection was held by Questionnaire and Cronbach alfa of above 0.887 was established to signify that questionnaire items were highly reliable. The data was analysed by T-test, ANOVA and Pearson product correlation coefficient. The null hypothesis was tested by the help of SPSS. The findings of the study was educators of University of Arusha were capable in the use of different technology programs like PowerPoint, Excel, Microsoft Word, online search procedures and internet programs and believe that Information and communication technology (ICT) integration propels learnercentred approaches and increases the rate of learning. Educators, however, indicated lack of skills in online marking and data management procedures and limited integration of Information and communication technology (ICT) resources in teaching learning transaction. Finally, the study established a positive and strong relationship between competence and application of Information and communication technology (ICT) in teaching-learning transaction. This implies that the higher the competence, the likelihood of educators to integrate Information and communication technology (ICT) in teaching-learning transaction. SSSSSSSsssfhrhr

Saunders and Pincas (2014) in their study on 'Learner Attitudes Towards Information and Communication Technologies in Teaching and Learning in the UK' opined that government funded initiatives to attain digital or e-literacy on college campuses were lacking because of least initiatives from both learners and staff. They were reported a survey on 1400 learners of University of Westminster in London. They analysed the learner responses on Information and communication technology (ICT) in assisting them to achieve their studies. The result leads to; learning-facilitators should effort to learner views in using Information and communication technology (ICT) for teaching and learning.

Kaur(2012) investigated on 'Attitude of learners towards use of Information and communication technology (ICT) in Higher Education'. Information and communication technology (ICT) mean integration of different technological tools like telecommunication, computer, software etc. and used to communicate by construct, store, circulate, collection of the information. The use of information communication technology in various modes like: print medium, radio, telephone, mobile, television, overhead and LCD projector, computer, internet, web services, web portals, e-portfolios, face book as a class room tool, modules, multimedia, space technology, software, on line journals, on-line learning, CCTV, e-learning, e-books, teleconferencing and other computer assisted technologies play a very important role in education for modernizing its input process to get the output in the form of quality oriented teaching. So the use of Information and communication technology (ICT) is essential need of society to cope with inevitable socio – economic changes and to enable more learner-centric 'constructivist' learning models. It has become the driving force of change in the new world.

Mahmood *et al.* (2011) conducted a study on 'Effects of use of ICT: learners' perception at higher education level'. The aim of the study was to investigate the perceptions of male and female learners on the use of Information and communication technology (ICT). The research study was descriptive in nature. The sample of the study was the male and female learners of the public sector universities. The purposive sampling technique was used to gather data from the faculty of social sciences of two public sector universities. Data were collected by administering a questionnaire that based on Likert - five point scales. The data were tabulated, analysed and interpreted. The Chi Square and Mean score were applied to analyse the data. Result of the study depicted that the Role of Information and communication technology (ICT) is very important to improve learning. It also observed that ICT is an agent of change; it enhances the teaching learning process.Top of Form

Sharma, Gandhar, Sharma and Seema (2011) studied on 'Role of ICT in the Process of Teaching and Learning' and attempted to examine the role of Information and communication technology (ICT) on learning through various tools such as

# ICT in Learning Processes in Higher Education: Attitude of Learners

computer, web-based learning, TV, audio-videotape etc. And because of this the teaching learning process has become more useful. This type of technology has become very powerful media for the learner and the learning-facilitators and it reaches the unreachable. The finding of the study was emerging learning Technology (ELT) of Integrated Learning Modules, pod cast, Wikis, Browsers, e-learning have started making rapid developments in teaching learning processes.

Sangra and Gonzalez-Sanmamed(2010) studied on 'The role of information and communication technologies in improving teaching and learning processes in primary and secondary schools'. The objective of the study is to analyse the role of Information and communication technology (ICT) on teaching learning processes and to Survey the learning-facilitators' perceptions of Information and communication technology (ICT) on teaching learning processes. Case-study was used by the researcher in methodology. From a previous exploratory research, four different types of schools were determined. The findings of the study was, Information and communication technology (ICT) favours teaching learning processes and by the using of different innovative technological tools, changing teaching models, learning-facilitator's role; schools also progress a lot.

Youssef and Dahmani (2008) studied on 'The Impact of ICT on Learner Performance in Higher Education: Direct Effects, Indirect Effects and Organisational Change'. The objective of the study was to examine the relationship between the use of Information and communication technology (ICT) and learner performance in higher education. The findings of the chapter were firstly differences observed in learners' performance are more related to the role of Information and communication technology (ICT). The second finding was advocates that uses of Information and communication technology (ICT) differ from one institution to another.

## Need of the Study

Studies by Boateng *et al.* (2016), Makewa *et al.* (2014), Saunders and Pincas(2014), Kaur (2012), Mahmood *et al.* (2011), Sharma, Gandhar, Sharma and Seema (2011), Sangra and Gonzalez-Sanmamed (2010), Youssef and Dahmani(2008) depicted that the learners have high positive attitude towards information and communication technology (ICT). Review of earlier research studies on the attitude of learners towards Information and communication technology (ICT) in learning processes in higher education and contribution of different factors responsible for their status improvement is essential to formulate an appropriate perspective for any further study. It is of vital significance in any study in order to collect up-to-date information about what has been thought and done in that particular area. Several studies, on attitude of learners towards Information and communication technology (ICT) as well as in learning processes have been confined to one or two aspects and only to some regions of a State or a Country. As no study is held on the attitude of learners towards Information and communication technology (ICT) in learning processes in higher education at Visva-Bharati, in this chapter, an attempt has been made on attitude of learners towards Information and communication technology (ICT) in learning processes in higher education at Visva-Bharati.

From the review of several related research literature presented in the forgoing section, it can be concluded that different studies has been conducted on attitude of learners towards Information and communication technology (ICT). But not even a single study has yet been conducted on attitude of learners towards Information and communication technology (ICT) in learning processes in higher education at Visva-Bharati.

All the possibly available studies were reviewed and it has been observed that there are many researches, which are conducted especially on attitude of learners towards Information and communication technology (ICT). In this context the study conducted by Kaur (2012) forms the best line of direction so far as the components of the topic are concerned.

Irrespective of her best effort the researcher failed to identify even a single study in the area which was focused over attitude of learners towards Information and communication technology (ICT) in learning processes in higher education at Visva-Bharati which establishes the rationale of initiating the study of present kind, where a significant knowledge gap exists in this area.

Irrespective of her best effort, keeping in view the spelt rationale, the researcher wants to conduct the study titled: The attitude of learners towards Information and communication technology (ICT) in learning processes in higher education.

## Objectives of the Study
1. To study the attitude of male and female learners towards use of Information and communication technology (ICT) in higher education at Visva-Bharati.
2. To study the attitude of science and social-science learners towards use of Information and communication technology (ICT) in higher education at Visva-Bharati.

## Hypothesis of the Study
1. There is no significant difference between the attitude of male and female learners towards use of Information and communication technology (ICT) in higher education at Visva-Bharati.
2. There is no significant difference between the attitude of science and social-science learners towards use of Information and communication technology (ICT) in higher education at Visva-Bharati.

## Delimitations of the Study
1. The present study is delimited to the Visva-Bharati.
2. The present study is delimited higher education learners of Visva-Bharati.

## Methodology and Design of Study
The study was quantitative in nature. Survey method had been used to collect data from the respondents using a questionnaire. A cluster sampling of 40 learners comprising 20 males and 20 female, social science and science learners was selected from Visva-Bharati, West Bengal. The main statistical technique used for the data analysis was

t-test for knowing the significance between the means of different comparative groups. The data was analysed with the help of computer by using SPSS to get accurate results and also to save time.

## Procedure of Data Collection

The data was collected by self-made questionnaire to the 40 social science and science learners and male and female learners.

## Procedure of Data Analysis

The study was analysed by quantitative method. The main statistical technique used for the data analysis was t-test for knowing the significance between the means of different comparative groups. The data was analysed with the help of computer by using SPSS to get accurate results and also to save time.

There is no significant difference between the attitude of male and female learners towards use of Information and communication technology (ICT) in higher education at Visva-Bharati

|  | N | Mean | Standard Deviation | t-value |
|---|---|---|---|---|
| Male learners | 20 | 38.950 | 5.306 | 0.416 |
| female Learners | 20 | 39.550 | 4.084 |  |

The study has obtained that there is no significant difference between the attitude of male and female learners towards use of Information and communication technology (ICT) in higher education at Visva-Bharati as the t value was 0.416 (> .05).

There is no significant difference between the attitude of science and social-science learners towards use of Information and communication technology (ICT) in higher education at Visva-Bharati.

|  | N | Mean | Standard Deviation | t- value |
|---|---|---|---|---|
| Science learners | 20 | 40.15 | 4.14 | 1.03 |
| Social-science learners | 20 | 38.35 | 5.11 |  |

The study has obtained that there is no significant difference between the attitude of science and social-science learners towards use of Information and communication technology (ICT) in higher education at Visva-Bharati as the t-value was 1.03 (> .05).

## Findings and Discussion

The study has obtained that there is no significant difference between the attitude of male and female learners towards use of Information and communication technology (ICT) in higher education at Visva-Bharati as the t value was 0.416 (> .05). It may be observed that the mean score of female learners is higher than male learners. But the t-value for difference in mean scores of science learners and social-science learners is 0.416, so, the hypothesis 'There is no significant difference between the attitude of male and female learners towards use of Information and communication technology (ICT) in higher education at Visva-Bharati' is accepted. It shows that male and female learners show positive attitude towards the use of Information and communication technology (ICT) in higher education at Visva-Bharati.

The study has obtained that there is no significant difference between the attitude of science and social-science learners towards use of Information and communication technology (ICT) in higher education at Visva-Bharati as the t value was $1.03$ ($> .05$). It may be observed that the mean score of science learners is higher than social-science learners. But the t-value for difference in mean scores of science learners and social-science learners is 1.03, so, the hypothesis 'There is no significant difference between the attitude of science and social-science learners towards use of Information and communication technology (ICT) in higher education at Visva-Bharati' is accepted. It shows that learners of both streams show positive attitude towards the use of Information and communication technology (ICT) in higher education at Visva-Bharati.

Hence it supports the study of Satwant Kaur (2012) who observed that there is no significant difference between the attitude of science and social-science learners towards use of Information and communication technology (ICT) in higher education.

## Conclusion

This chapter examined learners' attitudes towards the use of Information and communication technology (ICT) in higher education at Visva-Bharati. It depicted that the role of Information and communication technology (ICT) is very important to improve learning. From the result we can observed that both male and female learners agreed that Information and communication technology (ICT) is an agent of change; it provides high quality multimedia products which are helpful in learning. We can conclude that in the University every Department should have Computer laboratory to impart knowledge in more effective manner. Science and Social Science learners should have equal opportunity of using Internet in the computer laboratory. Male and female Learners should have the facility to access the computer in the department. They should also have the facility to access Internet easily by the help of Wi-Fi in the University campus. The awareness about the effects of excessive use of Computers, internet should be there also. Overall we observed that by using Information and communication technology (ICT), Learners are acquiring easily more skills, competencies, collaboration, team building, project management etc.

Chapter 27

# Potential of Radio Jamia for Functioning of Schools: An Exploration

✎ **Syedah Fawzia Nadeem**
*Jamia Millia Islamia, Delhi*

## Preview at a Glance

We are living in a world where ICT is making progress in leaps and bounds. Each day brings forth new innovations which imperceptibly make a lasting impact on the way we live our day to day experiences. However Radio has not yet lost its relevance in the lives of people. In fact it too has evolved and now more than ever it fulfils its role to inform, educate and entertain. With ever expanding internet networks, radio too has the potential to have an international audience. At the same time, at the micro level, radio has been harnessed as a tool by the community for its own limited networking, problem solving and general development. Radio has comparative advantage over other media as it is both cheap and easy to handle. Thus community radio came into existence. JamiaMilliaIslamia also has its community radio, called Radio Jamia which caters to the community living in the vicinity of the University. Potential of Radio Jamia has been explored for the present study because learners and their families who have been considered for this study belong to lower strata and usually enrol in Government managed schools. Findings of the study indicate that all the stakeholders were not aware of Radio Jamia, even though most of them did tune in to FM radio. Moreover learning-facilitators and other school functionaries were very excited at the idea of having live (or even recorded) interaction through radio.

## Introduction

In this era of growing inclination towards market-driven consumerist and commercial ideals, the role of community media is imperative. An essential component of this community media is community radio (CR). Sen (2011) says '… in terms of reach and access, India's print and broadcast media is strong: approximately 60 percent of the urban and 25 percent of rural Indians read print media on a regular basis and 96 percent of the country is reached by radio.'

For decades, radio has been one of the most appealing tools for participatory communication and development in the world (Noronha, 2003). He further elaborates that radio has several comparative advantages over the other media as a tool for social change, such as

- It is cost-efficient, for those who run the station and the audiences.
- It is ideal for the huge illiterate population that still remains marginalized, especially in the rural areas.
- Its language and content can be tailored to suit local needs. Hence, made relevant to local traditions and culture.
- After the initial investment, sustainability of the project is feasible, and one can depend on community participation. Radio has a strong advantage in terms of outreach and geographic coverage as well.
- The convergence of radio and the Internet is providing new strength to community and is seen to have enormously increased networking opportunities.

In layman terms, Community radio can be understood as a radio service that serves either geographical community or communes and may not be run by that community. An essential feature of all community media is that it is completely free of market influences / pressures and thus is a not-for-profit enterprise.

In the Community Radio Handbook published by the UNESCO in 2001, Fraser and Estrade argued that community broadcasting gives a voice to the voiceless, enabling local communities get attention to their concerns so that their rights are respected.

In this way, it provides a platform to the local people to share their experiences, concerns (sometime) solutions and thus become active participants and contributors in their societies. It also helps broaden their perspectives. In many parts of the world CR acts as a vehicle for community and voluntary sector, civil society and NGOs and citizens to work in partnership for community development.

In retrospect we find 1995 as a landmark year when Supreme Court, presided over by Justice PB Sawant, made a historic ruling which, in essence, stated that airwaves are public property and must be used for the public good. It did add that because airwaves are limited, they should be used with reasonable restrictions. The ruling also asserted that the right to receive and impart information is enshrined in Article 19 of the Universal Declaration of Human Rights which describes the fundamental right to freedom of speech and expression.

The 1995 ruling also serves as the foundation stone for community radio as we see and know, today. Immediately after the Supreme Court judgment, civil society groups formulated the Bangalore Declaration, articulating the need for a third tier of broadcasting, i.e. community radio. This was followed up by the Pastapur Declaration in 2000 which re-articulated the need for community radio and also asserted that it ought to be non-profit making, localized and community owned.

Between 1999 and 2001, several initiatives were launched in Karnataka (NammaDhwani), Andhra Pradesh (Sangam Radio), Jharkhand (ChalaHoGaon Mein) and Gujarat (Radio Ujjas), which used cable radio or bought time on AIR to broadcast local content. These efforts were an outcome of the Bangalore and Pastapaur Declarations.

In 2004, the UPA Government declared a community radio policy that defined 'communities' rather narrowly to include only educational institutions. The exclusion of grassroots communities somewhat defeated the purpose of the legislation.

It was only in November 2006, eleven and a half years after the Supreme Court judgment that the dream for community radio in India was realized. The new policy allowed agricultural universities, educational institutions and civil society institutions to apply for a community radio broadcasting license under the FM band 88–108 MHzseveral hundred community members all over the country had untiringly worked towards this achievement. The formulation of India's community radio policy gave power to those who were fighting for the freedom of speech and expression for this medium.

## Meaning and Role of Community Radio (CR)

Community Radio is a unique concept, a collaborative medium that blurs the lines between a broadcaster and listener. The CR movement challenges media ownership, and insists that ownership lies with the larger community. Community participation thus becomes central to the programming of community radio.

When other media such as Television and print, get dictated by management and ownership in deciding content, determining ideology, participation, and the function, community radio gets driven by the needs and demands of the community where the station operates from.

Author, entrepreneur and firm believer in the power of Radio, Louie Tabing from Radio Tambuli, Philippines, defines a community radio station (CRS) as 'one that is operated in the community, for the community, about the community and by the community.' According to Tabing (2009), 'the community can be territorial or geographical- a township, village, district or island and can also be a group of people with common interests, who are not necessarily living in one defined territory'.

Federacion Argentina de Radios Comunitarias (FARCO, Argentina) describes CRS as 'entities which see communication as a universal right and which are run by community-service-oriented radio practitioners. Such radio stations develop pluralistic and participatory communication, and exercise the right to communication and to information by challenging the traditional division between broadcasters on the one hand and listeners or consumers on the other.'

Radio gives audience the advantage of 'tuning in' to its programs without their daily activities being held up. 'Radio is an inexpensive medium, with comparatively simple technology, and more suitable for illiterate and peasant communities and societies characterized by oral and folk traditions' (Pavaral, 2003).

AMARC, the World Association of Community Radio Broadcasters, is an international non-governmental organization for the promotion, support and development of community radio worldwide. The international headquarters is located in Montreal, Canada ever since the founding Assembly was held there in 1983.

In 1995 members of the AMARC described CR as follows:

'CR can be rural radio, cooperative radio, participatory radio, free radio, alternative, popular, educational radio. If the radio stations, networks and production groups that make up the World Association of CR Broadcasters refer to themselves by a variety of names, then their practices and profiles are even more varied. Some are musical, some militant and some mix music and militancy. They are located in isolated rural villages and in the heart of the largest cities in the world. Their signals may reach only a kilometre, cover a whole country or be carried via short waves to other parts of the world.

Some stations are owned by not-for-profit groups, NGOs or by cooperatives whose members are the listeners themselves. Others are owned by learners, universities, municipalities, churches or trade unions. There are stations financed by donations from listeners, by international development agencies, by advertising and by governments.'

The 7th World Congress of AMARC held in Milan from 23rd–29th August, 1998 stressed on just and equitable access to and participation in communications media for strengthening the rights of indigenous people, minorities, migrants and refugees. It also focused on educating and training, to enable people to develop their own media and communication skills.

The Indian CR policy lists following main eligibility criteria in order to apply for an FM license:

- The CR must be run by non-profit organizations or civil society institutions, KrishiVigyanKendras (agricultural centres or institutions) and educational institutions.
- The policy mentions that CR programs should be of immediate relevance to the community and should emphasize development, agriculture, health, education, environment, social welfare, community development and culture.
- The programs should reflect the special needs and interests of the community.

Critically, the Indian policy also mentions that CR should 'have an ownership and management structure that is reflective of the community it seeks to serve'.

In the present context Radio Jamia was established in AJK MCRC of the JamiaMilliaIslamia. As part of its social commitment to the area in which the University is located, AJK MCRC, runs a community radio station on 90.4 FM. Addressing itself to the residents of the Jamia area, RadioJamia broadcasts programmes that serve to educate and enrich its listeners through addressing a wide range of socio-culture issues. The programmes are produced by the learners and faculty of the Centre in collaboration with diversity of groups and organizations in Delhi). It caters to the community living in and around the Jamia campus with programmes focusing on health and social awareness.

Nadeem and Saeed (2012) had described the conditions of Government managed schools located in the vicinity of JamiaMilliaIslamia. They concluded that issues related to discipline, cleanliness, attendance, motivation etc. need to be resolved in order to improve overall school functioning. They concluded that Radio Jamia can play a proactive role in mobilizing the local community to improve functioning. There are approximately 34 MCD/NDMC run schools in the vicinity.

The present investigator came across studies which highlighted the role of community radio in setting in motion community involvement and thereby like the ACER report of Australia show that involving the community result in improving school functioning. However, the present investigator did not come across any study whereby the community radio had been used to bring about improvement in school functioning and school-community relationship.

In order to assess the potential of Community radio, the present study aimed to explore the potential of Radio Jamia to improve school functioning. It was proposed to examine the perceptions of the key stakeholders (i.e. school functionaries and parents) in this regard.

## Objectives

1. To study the situation in schools with regard to the following
   - Discipline
   - School result
   - Infrastructure
   - School environment

2. To examine the experience, views and perceptions of Principals and learning-facilitators with regard to the following
   - Learner discipline
   - Parent involvement
   - Resources (Material and Human)
   - Support and monitoring
   - Learning-facilitator morale

3. To study parents' and learning-facilitators' experiences (if any), views and perceptions regarding role of Radio Jamia in improving school functioning.

4. To develop a plan of intervention using Radio Jamia to improve school functioning.

## Sample

Investigator chose 4 schools in the Vicinity of Jamia Millia Islamia.

Table 1: Sample of the Study

| District | Zone | School Name | Learning-facilitators | Learners | Parents* |
|---|---|---|---|---|---|
| South | 25 | Noor Nagar- SKV | 10 | 27 | 20 |
| South | 25 | Noor Nagar- SKV | 7 | 32 | 18 |
| South | 25 | Joga Bai – GGSSS | 9 | 34 | 21 |
| South | 25 | Joga Bai – GBSSS | 12 | 31 | 13 |

*parents were usually those who came to school for various reasons. They were all one parent with whom the author interacted.

## Tools and Techniques

Focus group discussions (with parents and learners)
Interview (with principals and learning-facilitators)
Observation schedule

## Methodology

Data was collected from the schools mentioned in table 1. Since the schools were in the vicinity of the Jamia, they had been part of the Faculty's school experience programme organized as a mandatory input in all learning-facilitator education programmes offered by the Department of Learning-facilitator Training and NFE (IASE) and thus the researcher has personal access to all the principals and most of the staff.

Information was gathered by visiting schools frequently. Initial visits helped the researcher in making the principal and learning-facilitators comfortable. Once the entry in the school became smooth, the researcher interacted with learners. In the beginning, a group of highly motivated learners was provided to the researcher. Later she interacted with random learners in the corridors to get and honest feedback and review. Learners were also observed in the class room teaching – learning situations.

Researcher spoke to learning-facilitators in their staff rooms. At times a discussion happened in a group. One on one interaction with learning-facilitators was more fruitful in terms of fetching figures and accuracy of answers.

Researcher spoke to learners, teaching staff, parents and principals. Observation was used to note down the observation on the field. The data thus collected was qualitatively analysed.

## Findings

The findings of the study have been formulated on the basis of the objectives and research questions that have been the focus of this study.

The findings of the study are explained as follows:

Situations in Schools

The research sought to examine the situations prevalent in the schools selected as sample with reference to Discipline, School result, Infrastructure and School environment.

Investigator observed that Learners were unhappy with school maintenance. The basic amenities of clean drinking water and clean toilets were observed lacking in schools. Hygienic surroundings, basic infrastructure like furniture (in good condition), working libraries and science labs would go a long way in creating conducive environment for learning.

Other improvements pertaining to infrastructure, that learners especially demanded, were;

- Transport Facility
- Stationary Shop
- School Canteen

On probing matters related to discipline, it came to light that school authorities faced the problems of truancy and drug addiction among learners. Learners did not show respect towards the system or faith in learning-facilitators.

## Experience of School Functionaries

The experiences, views and perceptions of Principals and learning-facilitators with regard to Learner discipline, Parental involvement, Resources (Material and Human), Support and monitoring and Learning-facilitator morale was analysed so as to understand how Radio Jamia could be harnessed to address their concerns and thus improve schooling experience.

Learning-facilitators and school staff expressed their concerns regarding school discipline, result and administration. Following were their views.

Since corporal punishment is banned in schools, learning-facilitators were of view that the learners could not be reprimanded; this problem was reported more in boys' school. The other disturbing side was that few learning-facilitators remained unaffected by the problem of indiscipline. As sensed by the researcher during school visits, fear of retaliation by learners made the learning-facilitators refrained from reporting the problem. Learning-facilitators confided in investigator that many boys indulged in drug abuse and porn addiction. They would steal metal ware like fans; rods door handles etc. in order to buy drugs. The learning-facilitators further said that this was done in connivance with the sweepers and guards of the schools.

Learning-facilitators also carried a perception that learners came from dysfunctional families, or the poor strata, where abusive language and untamed behaviour was norm.

Learner Learning-facilitator ratio was also a point of concern. In some classes one learning-facilitator was responsible for 50-70 learners, sometimes even more. Due to which, individual attention was difficult to give to learners and also posed problems in the teaching-learning as well as class management.

A common complaint by learning-facilitators was against the Non Detention Policy. It was explained to the researcher that learners pass exams till class VIII (under the purview of the policy) but their real mettle is tested when they appear in class IX exams. Thus, the result shows lesser learners passing higher level exams and getting promoted to senior classes. Most learners being first generation learners with no atmosphere of learning at home, this problem was reported commonly.

When it came to parent - learning-facilitator interaction, Researcher examined two different views

- Learning-facilitators believe that parents wash their hands off once they admit their child in school.
- Parents opined that learning-facilitators pass the blame to them if their child fails.

Learning-facilitators also expressed their concern about how school management committees functioned. More commitment from parents' side was expected by learning-facilitators.

When investigator examined the motivation level and morale of learning-facilitators, she noted down their challenges. These challenges included: workload/overload and administrative duties that meddle with their teaching part, duties related to distribution of Mid-day meal and scholarships, Election duties, data collection during census and Aadhar Card initiative were some of the n on academic jobs where learning-facilitators were engaged in. involvement in these tasks during school hours disrupted the classes as well as brought down the quality of teaching.

Learning-facilitators also spoke about the vacancies that needed to be filled. Guest learning-facilitators get paid on day basis and remuneration was low as compared to that of permanent learning-facilitators. This was another factor which strongly affected the motivation and morale of a learning-facilitator, especially the guest and contractual staff.

Learning-facilitators also shared that when in class, learners did not respect them. The investigator observed that with time learning-facilitators developed an attitude that said, 'InhePadhaneKa Koi FaaydaNahi, Ye kuchnahikarenge' (No point teaching them….. they will do nothing).

## School and Radio Jamia

The main purpose of the research was to study parents' and learning-facilitators' experiences (if any), views and perceptions regarding role of Radio Jamia in improving school functioning.

It was fond that Parents did not listen to Radio Jamia. Learners were aware of the FM station; on being asked, what they liked to hear on Radio, they all said 'File songs'.

Learning-facilitators on the other hand, were very positive about the constructive role that Radio Jamia could play. They suggested that Radio could run tutorial on various subjects like Mathematics and language, update on various CBSE and other government circulars make learning-facilitators and learners voice their problems, concerns and even possible solution.

Some learning-facilitators also believed that Radio programs could also speak about deteriorating moral values. They desired radio programs that could help in still values in children.

## Suggestions

An important advantage of radio is even though it plays in the background, it has the power to engage people. A radio host sitting in a closed studio, talks to thousands of listeners in one go. Live interaction gives Radio, the strength to mobilize community. With the use of telephone, SMS and email, response time has come down to few seconds. Listeners can raise their concerns, report a problem and give an opinion. While they talk, their message is conveyed to concerned authorities. Therefore, a plan of intervention through Community radio can help make the school functioning and environment better, by bringing the concerns to the fore.

Radio programs can be designed with a view to improve school functioning. These programs must involve parents, learners and learning-facilitators, who report the real scenario, suggest feasible solutions and voice their concerns and requirements to the concerned authorities. Involvement of learning-facilitators, parents and learners is crucial as it not only empowers them but also entrust them with a responsibility to bring about a change.

**Following programs to improve school functioning, can be devised:**

**Learner Hour:** A call-in show where learners call and express their ideas about how the school should function or they simple voice out their opinions on the specific theme/topic taken on the show.

**Teach the Learning-facilitator:** A weekly show about teaching methods and ways to make learning fun. An expert in the studio can talk to learning-facilitator over phone and guide them.

**Complaint Box:** A five minute weekly capsule where radio host reads one or two complaints about the infrastructure / school functioning and administration and connects to the person answerable.

**Guest:** A celebrity interview that can inspire learners Show should have some film songs broadcasted to increase mass appeal.

**Coverage of school events on Radio:** This will give school benefits in terms of popularity in the area and sense of belonging for learners as well as community.

Inter school creativity contests/competition on Radio: When the winner / team of an event appear on radio, it inspires and motivates other learners as well.

## Conclusion

Radio, as a mass medium can be harnessed to bring the issue of the marginalized groups or weaker sections of the society to the fore as well as give power to communities. Using community radio for betterment of education system through interventions in school functioning can go long way for development of our society.

# Chapter 28

# ICT and Administration in Education

✑ **Tanuj Sharma**
*PCGE, Jaipur, Rajasthan*

## Preview at a Glance

In the current chapter, an effort has been made to discuss about the concept of the ICT and educational administration in order to understand the relationship between ICT and educational administration. This helps to know how much useful the ICT is for us. And the relation between these two terms will help to move ahead with the research. ICT is short form of information and communication technology. ICT plays an important role in educational administration as well as every aspect of life. Educational administration is a system which runs an educational institute. It includes all the institutional works other than teaching. In the 21st century ICT has entered in the educational administration too. It affects educational administration to the great extent. Change in attitude of Administrators due to ICT is the main objective of this new venture. Usefulness of ICT for educational administrators, their perspective towards future changes in ICT for educational administration, why are they frustrated with present system etc. are the questions that have been tried to find out in this research chapter. Because of ICT the attitude of administrators became positive. They started to work with more efficiency and skill. This has brought a significant change in education system as the whole education system is operated by administration. India, along with the world, is also discussed in this chapterin order to make us able to analyse ourselves and to reflect upon our past. The future possibilities of ICT for educational administration are cleared in this chapter with the perspective of administrators.

## ICT: Its Meaning and Concept

ICT stands for information and communication technologies. It is an initiation for learners, businessmen and administration, too, to shape their career opportunities. It considers all usage of digital technology that already exists to help individuals, business and organizations which uses information

## ICT for Education: *A Few Concepts and Researches*

The concept of ICT can be understood in the following manner:
There are two options of what the acronym ICT could stand for:
- Information and Communication Technology
- Information, Communication and Technology

|  | Information | Communication | Information Technology | Communication Technology |
|---|---|---|---|---|
| Information and Communication Technology |  |  | Wrong | Wrong |
| Information, Communication and Technology | Wrong | Wrong | Wrong | Wrong |

## Option-1

Most of us know in this way that ICT is a short form for 'Information and Communication Technology' option 1 above. Let's unpack the terms; these are information technology and communication technology. 'Information' or 'Communication' has to go with technology. These terms cannot exist independently. We can shorten IT and CT to just Technology.

## Option-2

Secondly, we can define ICT that it can be information, communication and technology. Each aspect of acronym can stand for its own. So it includes information and communication. It also includes technology.

Another way of looking at it is that ICT stands for:

1. Information - (or data) in text or electronic format
2. Communication- in person or electronically, in written or voice format, telecommunications or broadcasting
3. Information Technology- include software, hardware and electronics
4. Communication Technology- include software, hardware and protocols (http://michalsons.com)

## Educational administration: Its meaning and concept

According to the Concise Dictionary of Education (1982), 'educational administration' includes management, organization and supervision of an educational institution. Usually includes all institutional functions other than teaching. To understand educational administration, first of all we should introduce administration as we have already defined the term 'educational'. Administration is a process of systematically arranging and coordinating the human and material resources available to any organization for the main purpose of achieving stipulated goals of that organization. When applied to the education system, the process is referred to as educational administration. Educational administration is the process bringing men and materials together for effective and functional teaching and learning in the school or college. The focus of educational administration is the enhancement of teaching and learning. We can define educational administration as a process through which the administrators related to education arrange and to co-ordinate the resources available to education, for the purpose of achieving the goals of education system. Now, our motto is to understand relation between ICT and educational administration in order to understand ICT for educational administration. Initial days of educational administrations and middle age of educational administration were fully dependent on textual work .All the records have to put in manual ways. There was fear of losing records and maintaining them was also a challenge along with making hard-copy, self–copy and creating relevantrecords of the concerned documents. Besides, records of employees had to be maintained.

After having troublesome to find out data about that employee was also too difficult as that was in files and to find out concerned data was too hard. It consumes a giant part of official time. So to concentrate on other productive work was about impossible. Besides this, managinglearners' records was also a problem. To prepare their result after exam by pen and paperwas too boring after a limit. At that time, there was lack of staff, so learning-facilitators had to do official work too and as it consumed a lot of time to inform government officials. Because of this, their prime work teaching was avoided. And this affected learners' performance and ultimately learning-facilitator was blamed for this. High rank officers had looked towards their subordinates. And they further looked towards learning-facilitators. What answer could be given by the learning-facilitator, as he was the product of this system only.

Administrations system: To keep records of yearly school or college buildings' maintain was too challenging as well as learners' records. Planning of institutional functions (extra-curricular activities) consume a lot of time. Plan to class room teaching functions also have to think more and more to make that effective and learnable. Finding places availability of resources for institutional management was hard. First have to find related representative and their market value. Then to select and to collect fees of learners and have up to date records of deposited or not-deposited cash was also a systematic problem. To keep a sharp and constant watch on learners' activities and find out naughty learners who disturbs class. Attendance problems of learning-facilitators and learners were also unreliable. To evaluate learning-facilitators' performance was also critical. To inform learners about any information, have to inform in classroom and by notice. Some of learners were advantage as because of bunking class

They were unable to know about problems. Thus, it can be said that because of these problems learning-facilitators and learners were not able to solve their problems. Performance,accuracy, working-load,dullness,hard-working, repetition,calculations, not to keep up to date actual data collecting was really a troublesome.

Objective of the study: Above problems and quest for finding their solutions made ICT to enter in educational administration. And this turned into today's up to date educational administration i.e. present form of educational administration from traditional form of educational administration.

## Objectives of the Study

After this research we wereable to know:

- What changes ICT brought in attitude of administrators towards work
- How it made educational administration to reach its goals of providing overall education
- What possibilities can be in future from the perspective of administrators

**Research Methodology:** To find above objectives primary sources and secondary sources were used. Definitions of the terms for the study were taken from secondary sources as well as primary sources. And research about above objectives was fully based on primary sources.

**Used sources are detailed as following:**

**Primary Sources:** Written interview of administrators and oral interview of HOD, who seeks administrative tasks, and Administration Officer, Management, ICT Experts of colleges. The researcher also tried to collect information from other colleges, but could not succeed as they were not interesting.

**Secondary Sources:** Sites related to ICT and educational administrations. Widely used, secondary sources are in bibliographical section.

**Research about ICT for educational administration:** Firstly, created a questionnaire based upon the objectives. Then it was tried to find answers of objectives by the questionnaire. And primary and secondary sources helped much to find out the objectives.

In this research, efforts were made to find following things in educational administration:

- Ways of working in initial days without ICT
- Attitude towards work before use of ICT
- Changes due to ICT
- Attitude towards work after entry of ICT
- Facilities by ICT
- Usefulness of ICT in perspective of administrators
- Their views about Indian level ICT with the Global level
- Changes that they want to see in future in reference of their work

Research includes mostly working administrators' views. They had a good experience while working in educational administration with ICT and without ICT. To understand research easily, the researcher categorized different questions and ultimately obtained the results with summing up above 8 questions. And after analysing these questions, answers of oral questions for interviews were found. The discussions of the questions and responses shared by the interviewees are presented here:

- Ways of working in initial days by the research it emerged that administrators were bored and tired with traditional system. The ways have been discussed in the phrase of ICT and educational administrations with their backwards.

- Attitude towards work before use of ICT In the study, attitude towards work before use of ICT is made.

The result of the study is very negative. It can be divided into following two perspectives:

**Positive:** Null

## Negative
- According to the survey administrators stressed that they had problem to find accurate and actual data.
- According to the administrators their performance was also dull.
- They have much working load and always stressed about work.
- Administrators who loved their work although feel joy but due to workload there was dullness in environment.
- Repetition of work made so much frustration.
- Calculations take much time.
- They were not up to date.
- Whole time chapter work.

Thus, above results shows laziness in working environment. That directly affected performance. And this is the reason why learning-facilitators were blamed and objectives are affected.

That system did not make educational administration so useful and powerful that why objectives of a learning-facilitator can't be fulfilled. Educational administration had a weak backbone.

Changes in attitude towards working due to ICT: The study is mainly started from here. As this is the entering of ICT in educational administration. What changes administrators feel due to entering of ICT? These questions Consists negative and positive changes but changes were felt more positive than negative. This shows that ICT made effective changes in educational administration. How it made working of educational administration easy will find out by the positive views and by the negative views will find out problems in starting days of ICT.

Thus, on the basis of above study it can be seen that after the entry of ICT turned educational administration in its easy ways. It took grand changes. Because of ICT the behaviour towards work changed. They started to see administrative work with positivity. Although, unemployment increased .But in overall the work made easy and authentic. Problems faced by administrators reduced in a good ratio. This inspired the objectives of the education.

## Changes due to ICT

This question is also related to the last one. But this will focuses on changes utmost .This will help to go next question as we will Able to find backwards and onwards of the

## ICT for Education: *A Few Concepts and Researches*

ICT in educational administration this analysis will inform us to about the uses of ICT in Administration. How it solved traditional problems in educational administration. The behaviour change due to it has discussed in last question. Besides, possibilities of future will be well discussed with help of these in the question 6.

### The Study on the questions is presented below:

| Positive | Negative |
|---|---|
| According to librarians Due to ICT 5 rules of ICT Were able reach | In staring it looks that it destroys independence of officials |
| Administrators said that they are able to do their Work with diversity of methods | Enhanced unemployed too |
| They made themselves instant for their Work | |
| More interested increased in administrative work | |
| Administrators and their work became punctual | |
| Work of days and hours can be completed in minute's and/seconds | |
| Because of having more information has very low workload | |
| To librarians to issuing books long term referenced service converted Into short term | |
| It made searching easy and reduced hard work | |
| Management came in easy path | |
| Resembles that the world and the work is in Fist | |

### The changes are following due to ICT:

| Positive | Negative |
|---|---|
| Regular update about information | Problem in learning |
| Connection increased with other administrators | Still have to do manual work too |
| Things easy going | |
| Self-dependency growth | |
| No need have experienced to learn as all instructions are available on internet as you tube and google | |
| Apps made for administration helped too much as software to library, fees depositing, to make plan, to keep records made easy | |
| To keep constant watch on learners is easy | |
| After ICT lose fear of losing data. | |
| Activeness increased | |
| Easy to supervise | |
| Can't hide wrong information by employee | |
| Time to time delivery | |

# ICT and Administration in Education

By the above discussion it is apparent, due to ICT there are a lavish change in working methods.As we discussed in the starting of the question that this will lead us to the next questions, by abbreviating Q.3 and Q.4. We find changes and change in attitude due to ICT. And after analysing factors weakness of ICT in educational administration leads to reformation in ICT for educational administration. And strong factors of ICT for educational administration in India leads to comparison of Indian level ICT with the world level ICT.

## Usefulness of ICT

Apparently, positive changes due to ICT in educational administration are the usefulness of ICT. ICT made work dynamic and rapid. Quality improvement and vulnerability increased level of Indian level ICT in comparison to the world.

Positivity and negativity of ICT for administrative works will be find out here .Thus answer of this questions will carry on other curiosity and future aspect of ICT in attitude of India.

| Negative | Positive |
|---|---|
| We are very behind in use of ICT for educational administration. Although, in some factors we are very good but overall and whole use of ICT for educational administration we are very weak and unknown. | Although ICT is very weak in India but it serves with good things also, what are they will be described in conclusion? |
| Indian educational administration services are not fully digitalize, everything is not available online about educational administration | |
| We have not proper availability of resources and nor have developers for making work easy for administrators as all thinkers of us are in foreign countries. | |
| We have too much work to do. | |

As we have discussed about the negativity and positivity of the ICT for global level along with the Indian level. It is clear that we are seeking more possibilities for educational administration so that we will be able to fulfil more objectives of education as every objective of education is related to educational administration and fulfilment of these dependsupon educational administration.As all the functions of overall development of a child through education depends on good arranging and administrations and this will help to drag our country's education system to the top of all the countries. We will be able to gain our pre-prestige. This is related to Indian development, as education is the basic pillar of any country. And this depends on educational administration which is the backbone of development. And coming to the next set of questions i.e. what are possibilities of ICT in India and what scene will be seen with the help of ICT for educational administration in future will be clear from the further discussion.

The following changes were wished by educational administration related to ICT:

- Administrators wanted to create an environment of positive attitude towards ICT.
- Administrators wanted to connect to people of administration with each other, so that they could make it easy to learn ICT and it could be possible by the ICT itself only.
- As librarians wants to available more and more books for learners with free of cost.
- Librarians wished to provide fully ICT-based and more sitting-at-home reading services with comfort.
- Talking with educational administrators depicted their sadness for not having global resources.
- Administrators shared that if they have facilities then they do not have good connectivity and speed of internet.
- According to the administrators, ICT should not be centralized for educational administration. It should be decentralized so that its operation will be helpful.

Thus, we have seen that administrators in India are seeking for more possibilities for India. They wanted to use of ICT in every region so that they can elaborate their knowledge and can make more and more people's distribution for a grand changing by ICT. That will lead to objectives told in last questions and last phrase.

I tried for the answer of the above questions and reached to optimistic answer with the help of primary and secondary sources. Now, I will reach on the conclusion of the Study. That will help us in identifying answers to all seven questions.

## Conclusion of the Study

Before beginning the research, three major goals were planned. These were to evaluate changes due to ICT in educational administration, collecting possibilities of ICT for educational administration and exploring attitude of administrators towards ICT. In this research, the major focus was on these three areas and the aim was to reach up to the right answers to the queries. Startedwith the first question, the entire study itself was about the evaluation of changes made due to ICT in the educational administration. Mostly other questions of the tools were the product of this objective only and the questions were about the changes in working methods and changes in attitude towards work. Possibilities of ICT for educational administration were discussed. Attitude of administrators can be easily understood by this study. And though we are in the modern era, but yet technology is being played with and in developed countries the administrators play with the technology that's why we are far behind in field of good administration than that of the expected.

# Chapter 29

# Geogebra as an ICT Tool for Learning of Mathematics

*Tarun Aggarwal*
*University of Delhi and Jamia Millia Islamia, Delhi*

## Preview at a Glance

Due to rapid growth in field of technology for learning software and use in pedagogy of learning there has been an immediate need for integrating technology with current learning practices, also crucial subject like mathematics which has various oddity and complexity from learners perspective can become more easy to relate and understand by combining the current technology with it, there multiple of online free open source software available but still the effectiveness of the software's is still a dilemma. This study talks about the use of one such software for teaching and learning mathematics to and for learners, this software is Geogebra. Here in this study Geogebra is used as an ICT tool to integrate mathematical concepts like coordinate geometry and circles among the 32 learners of 9$^{th}$ grade and checking their responses for measuring their understanding towards the said concepts, also further enabling them to design and create their own applets. To check the response and effectiveness of the study pre and post test was conducted for both the topics of coordinate geometry and circle on sample of 32 learners and it was seen through statistical analysis that there is significant increase in learners' aptitude of problem solving, mathematical thinking and that the result concluded has 95% level of significance.

## Introduction

### Mathematics, Technology and Geogebra

At present across the world in many places there seems to be a gap between knowledge and skills among the learner required to work in communities. As result of which schools today face constantly increasing demands in their attempt to assure that learners are proficiently equipped to enter the main workforce and to navigate in a complex world. Many researches indicate that computer technology can support and helps in learning. Not only that but it also helps in increasing and creating high order thinking skills among the learners. Technology has become a very reliable and effective tool to impart knowledge and spread of it. Multiple of tools have been created and are used in field of mathematics as well for e.g. Geogebra, Mathematica, Maxima, Geometers Sketchpad, and Mat Lab. A lot of studies have been done to see the effect of Geogebra on learning abilities of learners and it has developed into a tool for learning-facilitator for creating useful, evaluative and effective for creating and designing instructional lesson plans (Nazihatulhasanahand Nurbiha, 2015).

Geogebra was designed by Markus Hohenwater as an open □ source dynamic mathematics software that incorporates geometry, algebra and calculus into a single, open □ source, user □ friendly package (Hohenwarter, Jarvis and Lavicza, 2009). Geogebra is free software designed for algebra, geometry, and calculus. Points, lines, vectors, algebraic functions, conic- section 2 dimensional as well as 3 dimensional, function and calculus theorem can be graphically viewed and dynamically modified. Not only that but it is also possible to find integrals and derivatives of any function and to find out its, differentiability and singularity. The Geogebra is available online at www. Geogebra.org. It also brings the opportunity for both learners and facilitators to develop and create their own applets ranging from dynamics to web pages. The free accessibility and easy to use interface of software in many languages makes it easy and compressive also widely use across globe, also in many countries like Malaysia has even accepted the use of Geogebra in their curriculum for 8th graders and above.

In the modern world situation are forever changing and we expect learner to perform in all departments of academics, we require a more elaborate and efficient experimental system and structure for imparting education among learners. Among the various subjects offered one that is most crucial and useful is mathematics. Mathematics to most appears to be complex and tedious subject. The perception of learner towards the subject as boring subject is the cause of lack of interest of learners towards subject. This makes a great challenge for the learning-facilitators and educators, especially in the grade of primary and intermediate levels of schooling where the concept building is in its initial stages and misconceptions can be easily rooted among learners. In country like India mathematics is a compulsory subject for learner till 10th grade and our government is entitled to provide high quality mathematics education among the learners. Various attempts are made to ensure quality education and also according to NCF 2005, the government has worked in favour of providing hands on learning among learners by introducing mathematics labs in schools across the country. Mathematics to most appears to be complex and tedious subject. The perception of learner towards the subject as boring subject is the cause of lack of interest of learners towards subject. This makes a great challenge for the learning-facilitators and educators, especially in the grade of primary and intermediate levels of schooling where the concept building is in its initial stages and misconceptions can be easily rooted among learners.

## Statement of the Problem

Geometry is a branch of mathematics dealing with shapes and figures and conduction of statement of defined results and proofs associated with them also part of geometry dealing with coordinates and equation of conic section is coordinate geometry. Learners first encounters with geometry in early stage of classes most probably in primary grade and continues to develop their concepts of figures and shapes, understanding their properties and drawing conclusions in form of theorems and their proofs in grade $9^{th}$ they are introduced to concept of higher geometry that is coordinates geometry where they are told to locate and find points with regards to some given plane mainly termed as x-y plane or in simpler term called as coordinate plane. Here learner are first introduced to concept of algebra and geometry combined together in form of equations of line and representation of points in form of numeric, the complexity and oddity of understanding the concepts always lead to children being strayed from the root concepts of coordinate geometry. So in order to develop the foundation among learners this was conducted where topic of coordinate geometry and circle was chosen and was tested using teaching learners by Geogebra and see the impact of learner learning was increased or not as compared to the traditional method of teaching. Not only that but main purpose of study was to mainly make learners able to understand how they can develop their own Geogebra applets using the Geogebra software and become active learners and able to fill the gaps between their concept understanding.

## Objective of Study

- To exploreGeogebra as a tool for developing visual models, helping in able to understand the concepts of coordinate geometry and circle also integrating and associating it in their curriculum.
- To let learner explore and learn how to create their own applets use Geogebra
- To use applets as medium to increase hand on and self-exploration learning among learners
- To conduct pre-test and post-test experimental research design to see the effectiveness of Geogebra as a teaching tool for circles and coordinate geometry in grade IX.

## Significance of the Study

Findings from the study can be served to inform learning-facilitators about the learners' understanding and learning processes, especially for those related to using the Geogebra software for teaching mathematics. The findings also highlights the steps involved as well as the problems and issues a learning-facilitator will need to face when applying Geogebra software as a means to study. The different interaction and relationship between technology, learners and learning-facilitator affects the result and outcome of learning practices. Based on, how learners co-relate and interact with their age group, also with experienced and knowledgeable adults they can advance their thinking and reasoning process which can works as a guide for the educators on how to efficiently use the Geogebra software. Also not only this in addition to that, the study provides and gives a detailed knowledge and information on how learners of different abilities co-interact among themselves to perform or carry out assigned tasks. Such information's are very crucial and important in future planning of lessons for larger groups and where learners are of different and varied abilities. The study also reveals how the use of technology integration mushrooms the teaching and learning of circles and coordinate geometry in grade 9$^{th}$ particularly, help to redefine the role of the learning-facilitator such that concepts such as guides and vacillators become more prominent.

## Research Questions

- Will there be any increase in mathematical abilities of learners after learning throughGeogebra.
- By introducing new style of pedagogy will learnersable to accept and adjust according to them

## Delimitations of Study

There is large number of schools in Delhi but due to time constraint and only one was selected accordance to convenience of reach also from range of topic offered in mathematics text book at 9$^{th}$ grade only two were taken because of convenience of data collection due to time bound.

## Research Design

### Introduction

Research deign is an outline which in detail talks about how an investigation has taken place. A typical design include the way some population is chosen and how sample taken out of it, procedure of collection of data and instruments used in the complete process, the way tools and instrument are put to actual use.

Research design is like a blue print for conducting a research or study and ensuring of control of factors which may interfere in validity of the findings. It is also a plan which describes on how data is collected i.e. when where and how to be analysed.

This study talks about collection of data and using Geogebra applets as an effective means in learning process.

## Nature of Study

This study is a Pre-experimental design without any control group; the experiment was conducted on 32 learners of 9$^{th}$ grade. The pre-test and post test was conducted on learners for 2 topics of mathematics chapter talked in NCERT textbook. Here topics taken were circles and coordinate geometry.

### Methodology

In this study there was one group of 32 learners of 9$^{th}$ grade and pre-test and post-test for 2 topics of geometry (here coordinate and circle) were taken. The study was conducted for 2 weeks and learners were originally taught through traditional method and then intervention was done the scores of pre-test and post-test determines the significance of this study.

## Sampling and Hypothesis

Population: all the school of Delhi

Here the population was taken as all the private school were availability of ICT tool was ensured.

Sample: learners of S.D. public School

Here in this study 32 learners of 9$^{th}$ grade of S.D. public School were taken accordance to convince of data collection.

In this study we have taken null hypothesis

$H_o$ = There is no significance difference between the learning aptitude among learners even after using Geogebra.

As contour to that the Alternative hypothesis is defined as

$H_a$ = There is a significance increase in learners learning after use of Geogebra

## Tools for Data Collection

In this study data was collected using pre and post-test design. The data is obtained from 32 learners of 9$^{th}$ grade learners of public school. Obtaining data from multiple sources validated the credibility of data.

## Procedure

This study was conducted in 4 phases and each phase talks about how study proceeded.

- In the first phase the learners were taught the concepts of circles and coordinate geometry for three -three days each using traditional method.
- In phase 2 pre-test was conducted for both circles and coordinate geometry and scores were evaluated for further testing
- In phase 3 interventions was done and learners were taught topics using Geogebra and was used as medium to let learner use that as source for developing their own applets.
- In phase 4 post –test was conducted for both the topics and scores were evaluated and compared to check the significance of the study.

## Procedure of Data Collection

The data collected was first analysed on basis of 2 test pre and post-test for both circles and coordinate geometry and with aid of software's like Ms-excel and SPSS the data was checked and result of various expects was concluded out. The analyses include plotting of graphs and descriptive analyses of two tests conducted and finding out the significance of the study the detailed listing is present in data analyses section.

## Data Analysis

Item Wise Analysis of Pre and Post-Test of Coordinate Geometry

Pre-test and post-test were made in accordance to learner understanding before and after use of Geogebra as a medium of teaching. The scores generated by test are listed as given below in table 3.

**Table 1: Descriptive statistics of test**

|  | Pre-test 1 | Post-test 1 |
|---|---|---|
| Number of learners | 32 | 32 |
| Mean | 7.219 | 17.781 |
| Std. Error of Mean | .2830 | .4789 |
| Median | 7.000 | 19.000 |
| Mode | 6.0 | 20.0 |
| Std. Deviation | 1.6011 | 2.7088 |
| Variance | 2.564 | 7.338 |
| Skewness | .423 | -.698 |
| Std. Error of Skewness | .414 | .414 |
| Range | 5.0 | 10.0 |
| Minimum | 5.0 | 11.0 |
| Maximum | 10.0 | 21.0 |

The above table shows the descriptive statistics of the two tests and comparison between their means and central tendencies from the above table we see that there is an increase in mean scores from pre-test (7.291) to post-test (17.781) implying there is an increase in scores of learners after intervention is done.

As we have seen that there is positive increase in learners learning the pre and post-test results were again compared to check the significance of the study at significance level of 95% and from the figure we can see that the p value of our comes out to be 0.00 which is ($p<0.05$) for t value of -23.414 so we can say that our null hypothesis is rejected and that there is a significance in learners learning and problem solving after the use of Geogebra.

**Table 2: t test table**

**Paired Samples Test**

| | Paired Differences | | | | | t | df | Sig. (2-tailed) |
|---|---|---|---|---|---|---|---|---|
| | Mean | Std. Dev. | Std. Error Mean | 95% Confidence Interval of the Difference | | | | |
| | | | | Lower | Upper | | | |
| Pre-test & Post-test Pair | -10.5625 | 2.5519 | 0.4511 | -11.4826 | -9.6424 | -23.414 | 31 | 0.00 |

## Item Wise Analysis of Pre and Post-Test of Circles

Pre-test and post-test were made in accordance to learner understanding before and after use of Geogebra as a medium of teaching. The scores generated by test are listed as given below.

### Table 3: Descriptive Statistics

|  | Pre-test | Post-test |
|---|---|---|
| Number of learners | 32 | 32 |
| Mean | 5.28 | 10.25 |
| Std. Error of Mean | .328 | .496 |
| Median | 6.00 | 11.00 |
| Mode | 6 | 12 |
| Std. Deviation | 1.853 | 2.806 |
| Variance | 3.434 | 7.871 |
| Skewness | -.441 | -1.180 |
| Std. Error of Skewness | .414 | .414 |
| Range | 7 | 11 |
| Minimum | 1 | 3 |
| Maximum | 8 | 14 |
| Sum | 169 | 328 |

The above table shows the descriptive statistics of the two tests and comparison between their means and central tendencies from the above table we see that there is an increase in mean scores from pre-test (5.28) to post-test (10.25) implying there is an increase in scores of learners after intervention is done.

As we have seen that there is positive increase in learners learning the pre and post-test results were again compared to check the significance of the study at significance level of 95% and from the figure we can see that the p value of our comes out to be 0.00 which is ($p<0.05$) for t value of -10.931 so we can say that our null hypothesis is rejected and that there is a significance in learners learning and problem solving after the use of Geogebra.

### Table 4: t test for circles

**Paired Samples Test**

**Paired Differences**

|  | Mean | Std. Dev. | Std. Error Mean | 95% Confidence Interval of the Difference | | t | df | Sig. (2-tailed) |
|---|---|---|---|---|---|---|---|---|
|  |  |  |  | Lower | Upper |  |  |  |
| Pre-test & Post-test Pair | -4.969 | 2.571 | 0.455 | -5.896 | -4.042 | -10.931 | 31 | 0.00 |

**Findings, Conclusions and Suggestions**

*Findings of the Study*

The study used Geogebra applets as means to test performance and significance of using Geogebra as a tool in classroom teaching its effectiveness and efficiency and based on data collected using pre and post-test we say that study has following outcomes:

1. Learners performance in able to solve questions appears to be have increased according to results analysed.
2. Learners at initial stage had some trouble in getting along with user interface but later on with correct guidance they were able to adapt to the technology and were able to perform well.
3. Teaching along with traditional use and ICT was seen to be in growing trends among schools and majority of learning-facilitators are slowly shifting in integrating technology in day to day classrooms e.g. of smart board is evident to claim the said remark .
4. In class room practice it was observed that learners were open to use technology as medium of study and were eager in few cases on learning the proper and efficient use of technology.
5. Learners do faced the trouble of getting familiar with Geogebra but in later stage were able to use efficiently the tools with some guidance and help from learning-facilitator as well as from peers.
6. Learning mathematics through visualisation has an impacting result among learners so we can say that learning through Geogebra is effective and productive.
7. Use Geogebra has proven to increase the learning and thinking process among learners and is verified by multiple of research, few of who are listed in chapter 3
8. From this study we can say that introducing ICT tools as medium of teaching is productive and useful to train individuals with skill based learning aptitude.
9. There was development in learners' way of understanding when tools were properly used witch predesigned lesson plan.

# Conclusion

The conclusion of this research study is based on the data analysed and findings of the study which indicate to the significance and effectiveness of the use of Geogebra as an ICT tool in teaching mathematics and letting learners develop their own applets with the aid of software helping to in cooperate Geogebra as a tool in mathematics curriculum.

In this study Geogebra has given a fruitful impact on learning and thinking process of learners especially in topic related to circles and coordinate geometry. This brought a positive impact in learners understanding towards the topic and actually visualising the concepts of somewhat tedious and hard to understand topics making the learner is an active learner in class rather than being a passive learner.

It also brings a chance for learners and learning-facilitators to co-interact and co-relate in learning of concepts using exploration and visualisation. It deepens the bond of interaction among the peers also enabling them to critically think and cooperate in groups to increase the collaborative learning. Also creating an environment where one is self-learner and able think rationally and finding the solution to the problems given or assigned to him.

On in all it is reliable to say that Geogebra is an effective tool in teaching and learning process and learning-facilitators should be encouraged on using Geogebra as a means for classroom teaching of mathematics by creating group exercises and letting learners learn through a virtual platform.

## Suggestions

1. The research could be carried out at large scale to validate the findings.
2. The same type of research could be conducted on different types of topic and whether it is effective to teach through Geogebra or not.
3. The research could be conducted at various grade levels to see how effective it is to use Geogebra in mathematics curriculum, whether it should be adopted as part of curriculum or not.

Researches involving special worksheet for learners who are dyslexia or dyscalculia can be conducted through Geogebra.

## Summary

In present scenario it is seen that learning through computer technology and self-learning has become a major source of gaining knowledge. It has become necessary for school to integrate ICT tools as medium of learning and teaching although it has seen has govt. has taken steps in this field by introducing smart classes to classroom but there is still some lag which needs to be overcome. Teaching mathematics through ICT is also a tedious task assigned to learning-facilitators that lacks efficient skills in handling it. Geogebra is one such tool which can make it easy to use. In this study a more emphasis was given on Geogebra as ICT tool for teaching mathematics as it is seen that use of such software enhances the learning skill of learners. The study was conducted in Delhi on 32 9th graders of a public school as a sample, for this study a well-designed model was graphed indicating the stages at which study will take place and how to proceed along it as shown in table 1

The different phases of study included conduction of pre and post-test for the purpose of data collection to be analysed and also formation of hypothesis take place in which null hypothesis was that there is no significance between learning outcomes after using Geogebra and the alternate hypothesis was that there was a significant increase in learners learning ability by using Geogebra a medium of teaching mathematics to 9th graders. The data of 32 learners was collected for two different topics of circle and coordinate geometry, each one having one pre and one post-test and with help of software SPSS data was analysed and listed.

It was shown with the help of statistics that there was an increase in mean scores of learners after intervention through Geogebra has taken place also there were number of learners who have scored better than before and also from the histograms it was evident that there was as shift in average mean scores of learners towards higher value. The significance value or say p value came out to be p= 0.00 < 0.05 ensuring data was significant for 95% confidence interval. Indicating that the study was significant and that learner achieve when guided through process of learning through visual means.

Chapter

# Self-Esteem and Attitude in Using ICT for Language Teaching

✎ **Vandana Chaudhary**
*SCERT, Delhi*

## Preview at a Glance

Self Esteem is perception about self which is an important aspect of personality and attitude. As it leads to confidence and feeling of satisfaction in self which further impacts our acts and attitudes towards other things. Positive Self Esteem brings happiness and contentment which is very important for a learning-facilitator to connect to his/her learners. Education is not merely imparting theoretical or technical knowledge but all round development of a child which includes social and emotional aspects also. As we know that education is dynamic and the methodologies and practices also keeps on evolving and changing, use of ICT also brought a revolution in the field of education. Teaching language through ICT has opened new scopes and areas of learning for learners. In any language main four skills are L, S, R, W means listening, Speaking, Reading and Writing. Now the question arises how we can develop these skills among learners by using ICT. ICT is a magic in the hands of a language learning-facilitator to enhance the basic skills of language. This chapter tries to find out the correlation between the self Esteem and the attitude of learning-facilitators towards use of ICT for language learning. The sample chosen was language Learning-facilitators from MCD and DOE schools of Delhi. There were two scales used as tools- Rosenberg Self Esteem Scale and other one is self-made scaleAttitude Scale towards using ICT for language learning. The data was collected on WhatsApp. Both the scales were sent to total 22 Language learning-facilitators of MCD and DOE schools out of which only 15 responded back on WhatsApp and the responses were then analysed and scoring was done. Analysis was done quantitatively and qualitatively both. The correlation coefficient was calculated. A positive correlation between the two proved that both impacts each other to a greater extent which shows that the highly selfesteemedlearning-facilitators also possess positive attitude towards using ICT for teaching language.

## Introduction

In every sphere of life, human development is the result of advancement in education. Hence in turn education itself becomes more enriched with the development of user friendly technology imparting education becomes more planned, systematic and monitored than before and even in the situations education is formally provided in our schools and colleges. The learning-facilitator who is having good self-confidence and is expert in his/her subject area is always considered to havee ggood lesson/skill delivery skills in one's teaching subject and believes to be good in delivery of the content in an effective and successful way. As we know traditional teaching is now considered as the discarded one and new methods and approaches are taking place to make education more powerful and interesting. In addition to that capacity building of learning-facilitators in their academic field as well as in life skills is given due importance now a days. Personality aspects of learning-facilitator also considered as the bench marks of learning-facilitators' rate of success in their careers. Self-esteem is one of the important aspects of a learning-facilitators' personality which can directly affect the skills of a learning-facilitator inside as well as outside the class. Self Esteem refers to the one's own perception about self. Everyone has some perception about oneself. And for learning-facilitators the self Esteem would definitely impact the teaching learning processes of classroom as self-perception reflects thinking pattern, confidence and dealing of situations of teaching and learning in the classroom. Positive Self Esteem brings happiness and contentment which is very important for a learning-facilitator to connect to his/her learners. Whereas if a learning-facilitator has negative self-esteem, then he/she would be indifferent to the needs of learners and always tries to make excuses on the part of children. He/ She may also show signs of pessimism as well. Self Esteem forms the part of our personality. And learning-facilitators are ideals to their learners. They are considered as role models for the learners/learners. Education is not merely imparting theoretical or technical knowledge but all round development of a child which includes social and emotional aspects also.

In teaching profession it is very important for a learning-facilitator to know about the new technologies etc. in the field of education as it is dynamic. But the preparedness of learning-facilitators is equally important for effectiveness. Hence the attitude of learning-facilitators towards using ICT for language teaching/learning should be such that they can contribute to positivity and creating more learning environment. Moreover ICT embedded learning in case of language is challenging and exciting at the same time. It is challenging from the point of view, that the learning-facilitators should have the knowledge of managing ICT devices well as well as make the optimum use of it for teaching various skills. Planning part should also be strong along with the implementation part. So before actual handling and implementation the attitude of using it can make a difference. For example if someone thinks that I can't attach the projector to the computer, I may dysfunction it. Then that negative attitude always stops him to use projector on his own. ICT using is a skill and skill can be learnt

# Self-Esteem and Attitude in Using ICT for Language Teaching

at any age but the person should have the motivation and self-awareness regarding it is must. Hence a learning-facilitator should always be ready to learn and make optimum use of his/her learning's in the classroom with the learners and should note down its impact so that benefits can be maximised by minimising the loop areas.

English is considered as the second language in our schools. And many learners do not have its exposure at their homes due to presence and use of various regional languages and their dialects at home. So even in normal scenario, a language learning-facilitator specifically English language learning-facilitator struggles a lot with the learners. For that purpose it is mandatory to develop interest and love for this second language among the learners. Teaching language through ICT has opened new scopes and areas of learning for learners. In any language main four skills are LSRW means listening, Speaking, Reading and Writing. Now the question arises how we can develop these skills among learners by using ICT. ICT is a magic in the hands of a language learning-facilitator to enhance the basic skills of language. Primarily listening and speaking skills are necessary to cater in earlier stages of child. That even too with concrete examples and ICT is a way of providing such concreteness to many abstract things and also helpful in seeking and catching the attention of learners in primary classes which are the base of further learning. For listening audios, videos, CDs and language labs provide a great exposure to the learners. Mobile phone recorder is a very good and cheap option for the purpose as they can be easily available and within reach. Smart boards are also used in the schools. For enhancing listening and speaking skills, language learning-facilitator can play and audio or video and after pausing it, she can further ask questions based on audio/video shown. But learning-facilitator should keep in mind that the audio/video shown should be strictly according to interest and level of learners and cater inclusiveness of the classroom. Apart from that it should also be kept in mind that they should be for short duration as learners don't have capacity of sitting at a stretch for more than 10 min., without live interaction with learning-facilitator. A learning-facilitator's attitude towards adopting and adapting this kind of teaching learning is a matter of concern. Because a highly positive learning-facilitator can correctly and effectively use this miracle in her class and achieve optimal success. This kind of exposure is very important for our learners to become extrovert, interactive and proceeds towards learning.

When we consider the part of reading means reading skill again ICT is very helpful, for example movies of learners' interest can be shown but in mute manner and then they have to give audio to the written text which are written on the screen with each scene. Similarly English songs can be taken, cartoons can be shown. In writing skill, it can be improved by showing them the video and asking them to write what they've seen and there can be many other ways too. Hence we can say that a language learning-facilitator can use it in a very innovative and productive way.

Besides all these four skills, there are other sub skills too which can also be enhanced by using ICT in language learning like prediction, inference, skimming, scanning etc. Along with them confidence, managerial, planning skills etc. are also enhanced side by side. And the learning-facilitator and learner become more interactive and communicative. Hence the environment of teaching learning becomes natural and productive which is capable of yielding the learning outcomes in a natural and holistic way.

The learning-facilitator who is very confident in taking language classes and attitude of such learning-facilitators using ICT for language teaching can impact the teaching or are these two factors impact each other ? These are matters to explore out yet.

## Need of the Study

As teaching is now strengthened by collaborating/blending with use of ICT. Through ICT even abstract and complex concepts can be delivered easily by showing them with ICT use and can easily grasp the attention and interest of learners as well but from learning-facilitators' point of you, in the present scenario, it becomes very important to find out whether the learning-facilitators self-esteem and their attitude towards using ICT for teaching language has any correlation or not?

These two variables- Self Esteem and attitude towards using ICT for teaching language are very important to be studied side by side in order to see their correlation and finding out whether they are dependable or not.

Moreover, it is important to know about the attitude of learning-facilitators towards the new technologies so that we can understand their problems and inhibitions. After knowing the correlation between self-esteem and attitude towards use of ICT for teaching language can provide them the capacity building programmes for providing correct information, knowledge and understanding required to change their attitude towards positivity and also towards boosting their self Esteem. This research study also provides an insight to education planners, administrators and learning-facilitator educator to design such in-service and pre-service programme which can build their capacity to be a professionally effective learning-facilitator.

## Objectives

Following are the objectives of the study:

1. To find out the self Esteem of learning-facilitators teaching Language
2. To find out the attitude of Language learning-facilitators towards use of ICT for language teaching
3. To find out the correlation between the self Esteem and attitude of learning-facilitators towards using ICT for teaching language

## Hypothesis

Following is the hypothesis of the study:

1. There exists a positive correlation between the self Esteem and attitude of learning-facilitators towards using ICT for teaching language

## Methodology

First of all for carry out the research, population was thought of. Population taken for the studies are learning-facilitators from MCD and primary schools and then sampling was done. Purposive sampling was done to carry out the research. After that statistical methods were applied and results were analysed qualitatively and quantitatively. On the basis of which findings and further suggestions were given.

## Sample

As the research is meant for learning-facilitators, so the sample was selected from DOE and MCD schools that is, language learning-facilitators of MCD schools and DOE schools. Two scales one is Rosenberg Self Esteem Scale (it was developed by Rosenberg in 1965 which measures global self-worth) and other scale used in the study is a self-made scale which is Attitude Scale towards using ICT for language learning, were used. The earlier one is having 10 statements consisting of both positive and negative. The later one is having 12 statements both positive and negative. Then analyses were done quantitatively as well as qualitatively.

## Tool

Psychological standardised tool 'Rosenberg Self Esteem Scale' was used to measure the self Esteem of learning-facilitators consisting of 10 statements having both negative and positive statements about self. It reveals the perception about self. It is a standardised test. It is a 4 point Likert scale ranging from Strongly Agreed to strongly disagree. Other one is self-made scale on 'Attitude Scale towards using ICT for language learning'. It is consisting of 12 statements in total. The statements given in the scale depicts the attitude of learning-facilitators about ICT using for language learning. It is also a 3 point Likert scale ranging from Agreed to disagree.

## Data Collection Procedure

For data collection the simplest ICT mode was used that is social media via WhatsApp messenger. The scales (both Self Esteem and Attitude scales) were posted to 25 Language learning-facilitators (MCD and DOE) on WhatsApp. Out of those 25, only 15 learning-facilitators responded back. The responses received were 8 from MCD and rest 7 were from DOE schools. The responses were saved for further analyses. After the collection of data their feedback was taken whether they were comfortable in answering on WhatsApp or not and most of them were responded positively.

## Data Analysis

The data collected by above mentioned process was analysed quantitatively and qualitatively.

The Scale 1 is Self Esteem Scale and Scale 2 is Attitude Scale towards using ICT for language learning. In Scale1 maximum score can be 40 and minimum 10 while in Scale 2 maximum score can be 24 and minimum 0. A table was composed containing the scores obtained in both the scales. Then total of each scale was done to find out the correlation coefficient. The following table is showing the scores attained by the learning-facilitators in two scales. In the table as under first column depicts the learning-facilitators participated in the research, second column contains score of scale 1 which is Self-esteem scale and represents the respective learning-facilitator score in column one. Thirds column is containing scores of the learning-facilitators in column one and the score scale of their attitude towards using ICT for English teaching and is score scale 2.

**Table 1:**

| Learning-facilitator | Score Scale 1 | Score Scale 2 |
|---|---|---|
| T1 | 30 | 22 |
| T2 | 38 | 24 |
| T3 | 18 | 15 |
| T4 | 15 | 10 |
| T5 | 32 | 22 |
| T6 | 19 | 10 |
| T7 | 18 | 13 |
| T8 | 34 | 23 |
| T9 | 35 | 22 |
| T10 | 17 | 15 |
| T11 | 30 | 23 |
| T12 | 15 | 15 |
| T13 | 19 | 18 |
| T14 | 32 | 22 |
| T15 | 34 | 23 |

The above table is having data of 15 learning-facilitators of MCD schools and DOE schools.

Coefficient of correlation = 0.91

The correlation was obtained by applying the formula and the answer was 0.91 which is on a very high side.

The correlation coefficient clearly establishes the hypothesis that there exists a positive correlation between the self Esteem and attitude of learning-facilitators towards using ICT for teaching language. The correlation value of both the scales is .91 is very high on positive side and reflect that the learning-facilitators who are having high positive self-esteem are also have positive attitude towards using ICT in the classroom teaching learning processes.

From the above table it is also clear that the learning-facilitators T1, T2, T5, T8, T9, T11, T14, and T15 are having high self Esteem which correspondingly shows their attitude towards using ICT for language teaching/learning, which is also on high side that is positive side. From which we can conclude that they are comfortable in using ICT for teaching learning purpose. Whereas T3, T4, T6, T7, T10, T12, T13 are having average or lower self Esteem which correspondingly shows their attitude towards using ICT for language teaching/learning, which is also average or negative which shows that these learning-facilitators are not so much comfortable in using ICT the reasons may be different like some might not have ICT knowledge and advancement, Some may think it as time consuming task etc.

## Findings

After analysis of the data received, it was obtained that

- Some of the learning-facilitators are having high Self Esteem while some are having average.
- The attitude of learning-facilitators towards Using ICT for language teaching is positive in most cases but in the rest of the cases the attitude is neither negative nor positive.
- Self Esteem and attitude of learning-facilitators towards using ICT for language learning is positively Correlated
- It shows that a learning-facilitator having high self Esteem has positive attitude towards using ICT for language teaching/learning.
- Learning-facilitators having low self Esteem also show negative attitude towards using ICT for language teaching/learning.

## Further Suggestions

This study can be very useful for further consolidation of the relationship between self-esteem and attitude towards use of ICT across different subjects and on different samples. This can be very useful for education practitioners and stakeholders in designing the prospective and holistic learning-facilitator training programmes for learning-facilitators. It is equally important for learning-facilitator himself/herself to improve in the required area. This idea of finding the correlation between psychological aspects and different aspects of teaching learning process can provide insights in evolving futuristic capacity building programmes for twenty first century learning-facilitator and skills required. It can also provide insight for need assessment and providing onsite and offsite support to learning-facilitators and enhancing their knowledge, understanding and capabilities of teaching language in primary classes. Many opportunities should be provided to them where they can improve their self-esteem. Even Psychologists should be appointed at work place to assess learning-facilitators'self-esteem and to improve it. Apart from that Technical supporter should be appointed not only to facilitate them but to get them trained in handling and using ICT and also for providing them updating knowledge about latest tools and techniques available in ICT. It is also suggested that while recruiting learning-facilitators their self-esteem should be checked along with their attitude towards adopting new techniques and experimentation in the field of education which is dynamic and ever changing.

## Conclusion

If we want our education system strong and productive, new methods and technologies should be tried out and experimented out and their results and impact should be taken into account for further researches. It is also clear that a learning-facilitator having confidence and knowledge can create miracle in the classroom i.e. a high Self Esteemed learning-facilitator is always innovative and experimental to create magic in the class. Now ICT is the boon for education so positive attitude of such learning-facilitators towards using ICT for language teaching/learning can bring more positive results in creating language learning environment in the school as well as in classroom. According to NCF and in light of present learning outcomes teaching should be enjoyable and meaningful. And use of ICT by learning-facilitators should be mandatory at least for thrice a week in order for maximum output and learning of learners that too without thinking as burden by the learning-facilitator. As anything imposed loses its charm and real worth so for that learning-facilitator should themselves be ready forehand. The learning-facilitators who are having negative self-esteem or an average Self Esteem are expected to bring average result/learning as they themselves are less motivated. Self Esteem leads to self-motivation and creativity too. So a sincere learning-facilitator needs to have self-motivation to be ready for experimentation. As some learning-facilitators responded in the scale 2, that using ICT sometimes creates chaos and lack of discipline in the class but this too because of lack of training in how to use ICT in language teaching. Govt. or training institute needs to analyse the need assessment in this area and hence should provide the required in service or pre service training in this area. And after that follow up programmes should be scheduled to assess the success and further gaps. In order to keeping in pace with the modern world and updating oneself as well as teaching learners with modern technology learning-facilitators must be confident and positive in thinking about and using new upcoming and modern technologies. As language can't be taught by cramming methods in fact maximum opportunities of listening can be provided by the use of ICT in the school situations that we presently have. So learning-facilitators must be trained to imagine and plan one step ahead of the learners and their learning interests and needs.

Chapter

31

# ICT Intervention in Schools of Madhya Pradesh

✎ **Vandana Khare**

*Government Higher Secondary School, Sihora, MP*

## Preview at a Glance

The government of Madhya Pradesh initiated a computer enabled education program to school children in the year 2000. The program uses computer as a teaching learning tool at the elementary education level. The objective of this study was to measure an impact and do a comparative analysis of ICT interventions in improving the quality of school education in private and government schools in Madhya Pradesh. A comprehensive survey was done with the designed questionnaire constructed by the opinion of experts. Total 40 (20+20) faculty members from the randomly selected government and private schools were asked to participate in the survey. The schools were selected based on the availability of ICT facilities for integrating technology in the teaching learning process. MS Excel was used for data analysis. The small interviews were followed with the process of filling responses for closed ended questions designed basically. Findings from the present study bring the extent of actual use of ICT in teaching learning process by in- service learning-facilitators at school with the requisite facilities. The study will help Government in improving teaching learning programs with ICT. The research is original. Keeping the observers' status in mind the questionnaire was designed both in Hindi and English language. Most of the data was personally collected by the researcher; some responses were collected on e-mail.

## Introduction

With the enforcement of the 2009 Right of Children to Free and Compulsory Education Act, the Indian government aspires to emerge as the information and communication technology leader among the knowledge-based societies. This has made education of children as a primary concern. Part of India's rights to education commitment includes the vision of preparing Indian children with 21st century skills, such as learning to operate a computer. Information and communication technology (ICT), and free and compulsory elementary schooling for all Indian children between 6 and 14 years old have become one of the biggest commitments of our country. While India's policymakers often expect ICT to usher in promising education changes, there is a limited understanding of how that technology is used and negotiated at the beginning level of Indian schooling: the elementary school classroom (Byker, 2014). Present study compares the impact of ICT intervention in public and private schools in a small region Bundelkhand at Madhya Pradesh (India) and recommends strategies to improve the same.

## Literature Review

The United Nations Development Programme (UNDP) has defined Information and Communication Technologies as 'ICTs are basically information-handling tools - a varied set of goods, applications and services that are used to produce, store, process, distribute and exchange information. They include the old ICTs of radio, television and telephone, and the new ICTs of computers, satellite and wireless technology and the Internet. These different tools are now able to work together, and combine to form our networked world, a massive infrastructure of inter-connected telephone services, standardized computing hardware, the internet, radio and television, which reaches into every corner of the globe'.

No particular research has been published to prove that learner achievement is superior when ICT is imbibed in the day to day education space, either in the developed or in developing countries. However, there is a general consensus among practitioners and academicians that integration of ICTs in education has an overall positive impact on the learning environment (Budhedeo, 2016). In India, various ICTs have been employed over the years to promote primary and secondary education in schools. However, there have been enormous geographic and demographic disparities in their use. Some states and regions in the country currently have an enabling environment in place that allows for a greater use of ICT for education, whereas others lack such an environment (Budhedeo, 2016).

A debate webinar hosted by World Bank in 2010 initiated a discussion on the harsh ground realities existing in India. It talked about a dozen of computers received by small Indian village elementary school by a corporate sponsor. A year later when a representative of the sponsor came to visit the school he saw the computers still lying neatly in the boxes. Inquiring into the matter, he was told that the village has no electricity. It focused upon real existing issues which are creating hurdles in successful implementation of ICT in Indian schools. While the intention of Indian government to match its industrial strength (ICT) with human capital potential the illuminating and instructive lens that research offers remains obscure. Detailed study done by Byker identified three significant barriers to elementary school ICT program in India: Lack of resources, lack of learning-facilitators' preparation and lack of local understanding (Byker, 2014).

There are almost two million elementary schools spread across 35 Indian states and union territories (MHRD, 2010). Providing education to all children has always been one of the biggest challenges of the Government of India. Out of various initiatives take by the government, in 2000, the Indian legislature instituted a national campaign called the Universalization of Elementary Education (UEE) campaign, also known as Sarva Shiksha Abhiyan, to increase enrolment and retention of India's elementary school children. Manny researchers have considered ICT as a multi-billion industry that may contribute in the India's high growth economy(Balakrishnan, 2004; Bhagwati, 2004; Bhasin, 2010).

Importance of ICT in schools has been asserted by many researchers in past (Al-Ansari, 2006; Manduku, 2012; Sarkar, 2012). The National Policy on Information and Communication Technology (ICT) in School Education 'aims at preparing youth to participate creatively in the establishment, sustenance and growth of a knowledge society leading to all round socio-economic development of the nation and global competitiveness. It is felt that ICT will play a vital role in connecting the rural economy to the outside world for exchange of information, a basic necessity for economic development. Effective use of ICT will help in uplifting rural communities closer to global economic systems.

In India, a report suggests small increase in the availability of computers in the rural schools visited. Computer availability has increased from 15.8 percent in 2010 to 19.6 percent in 2014. Several states stand out in this regard. In Gujarat, 81.3 percent of schools visited had computers; Kerala witnessed a record of 89.8 percent schools with computer facilities; Maharashtra with 46.3 percent computer-enabled schools and 62.4 percent schools in Tamil Nadu (ASER, 2014).

## ICT in Madhya Pradesh

Realising that within the next several years, nearly all jobs will require Information Communication Technology (ICT) related skills, the state is in the continuous process of exploring strategies for improving learning. Providing meaningful access of technology to all children stepping into 21$^{st}$ century has become an essential element in the area of education. The state initiated a computer based education program in the year 2000 called 'Headstart'. The program used computers as a teaching learning tool in schools. The program was initially operational in 648 JSKs, it was expanded to 2070 more JSKs in 2003, 494 JSKs in 2005-06. Present study was conducted in the Bundelkhand region of Madhya Pradesh.

## Methodology

The chapter focused on the phenomenon of ICT use at Bundelkhand region in Madhya Pradesh (India). The researcher did a comparative study on the use of ICT in the private and government schools. Total 40 learning-facilitators, 20 from government schools and 20 from private schools were approached. Mixed methods (Creswell, 2011; Leech, 2009) were used to collect, analyse, and integrate the results to gain a richer picture and fuller understanding of the situation studied. Questionnaires, interviews, and document analyses were the methods used. Participants were selected according to purposive sampling (Creswell, 2013), meaning that the target group was all educators who were working in the schools that have ICT infrastructure in place. Assuring that their identity will be kept anonymous, unbiased opinions were sought. Many responses were collected personally while some were procured through e-mail. The small interviews were followed with the process of filling responses for closed ended questions.

Inspired by the findings of Erik Jon Byker in his study of ICT in India's elementary school used three-step interpretive approach, and constant-comparative method the questions asked focused on three significant components instrumental in the successful implementation of the ICT. They were related to infrastructure, learning-facilitator's preparedness and acceptability of ICT among learning-facilitator's fraternity, schools, parents and learners (Byker, 2014). Quantitative strands were used to do a comparative analysis of the use of ICT in private and government schools and qualitative strand was used to gain a deeper understanding of the issue.

## Findings

Responses from Government schools

Out of 20 government schools selected across Bundelkh and region 45% reported that the infrastructure provided by the government is not at all used by the learning-facilitators in the classroom teaching. 20% claimed that they have projectors but are occasionally used. 5% schools have internet access on school campus and 10% responses claimed that they are provided mobile devices for teaching purpose.

When asked what percentage of this infrastructure is in full use for the previous year 45% responded that it is not at all operational. Rest half of the respondents claimed that though it is used the percentage is not more than 50%.

None of the schools has their own homepage or websites. Though 100% learning-facilitators have their own e-mail ids, none of the learners has one. Only 5% of learning-facilitators and learners claimed that they can access their e-mails out of the school campus also. Parents do not have any access to school information as none of the school has homepage.

When asked in the past two school years (2014-16), have they undertaken any professional development program? 55% of the respondents claimed that they have not attended any professional development program. 45%, who responded in yes, informed that the training was introductory courses on internet use and general applications (basic word- processing, spreadsheets, presentations, databases etc.)

While trying to understand the barriers almost all the respondents felt that learning-facilitators as well as parents are in favour of using ICT in schools but highlighted certain barriers. They informed insufficient number of computers, and insufficient number of Internet- connected computers as the biggest issue.65% claimed that they do not have interactive white boards, 40% of the learning-facilitators felt that lack of training is also a big barrier that stops them from implementing ICT in schools. 20% claimed language as another big barrier as all material is available in English only.

**Responses from Private schools**

Contrary to the government schools, out of 20 private schools selected across Bundelkhand region 100% reported that the schools have good infrastructure related to ICT. Each school has desktops with and without internet connection, projectors and white interactive boards. All learning-facilitators were observed to be trained to use them in the classroom teaching. Respondents informed that approximately 70% of this equipment (computers, interactive white boards, laptops, data projectors) is fully operational and are used in day to day teaching.

70% of the private schools claimed to have their own homepage or websites and 100% learning-facilitators as well as learners have their own e-mail ids. Similarly 100% learners, parents and learning-facilitators have access to their e-mails out of the school campus also.

When asked in the past two school years (2014-16), have they undertaken any professional development program? 100% of the respondents claimed that they have attended professional development program. These trainings were from time to time in the following areas:

- Introductory courses on internet use and general applications (basic word-processing, spreadsheets, presentations, databases etc.)
- Advanced courses on applications (advanced word-processing, complex relational databases, Virtual Learning Environment etc.)
- Advanced courses on internet use (creating websites/home page, video conferencing etc.)
- Equipment-specific training (interactive white board, laptop etc.)
- Courses on the pedagogical use of ICT in teaching and learning
- Subject-specific training on learning applications (tutorials, simulations etc.)
- Course on multimedia (using digital video, audio equipment etc.)
- Participation in peer learning communities or group work with other learning-facilitators about the use of ICT for learning and teaching
- Other professional development opportunities related to ICT

However the respondents pointed out certain areas where school capacity to provide ICT teaching and learning is affected by a shortage or inadequacy in the following areas:

- Insufficient number of computers
- Insufficient number of Internet- connected computers
- Insufficient number of interactive whiteboards
- Insufficient technical support for learning-facilitators
- Lack of adequate content/material for teaching
- Using ICT in teaching and learning not being a goal in our school

## Discussion

Clear distinction is visible while comparing the impact of ICT intervention in government vs private schools. Based on the three parameters we tried comparing following factors:

Table 1: Use of ICT in Government and Private Schools in Bundelkhand Region (M.P.)

| Criterion | Govt. Schools | Private Schools |
|---|---|---|
| Infrastructure | 45% | 100% |
| Internet access | 5% | 95% |
| Projectors | 20% | 100% |
| Homepage/website | 0% | 100% |
| e-mail ids Learning-facilitators | 100% | 100% |
| Email ids Learners | 0% | 100% |
| Access from outside | 5% | 100% |
| Learning-facilitator's preparedness | 45% | 100% |
| Acceptability | 100% | 100% |

While we see that the willingness to adopt ICT in classroom teaching from learning-facilitators, learners and parents is 100% in both government and private schools, there is a huge gap between the interventions done by the two. Not surprisingly, there are various barriers that are stopping the smooth implementation of ICT in government schools. First two factors i.e. infrastructure and learning-facilitator's preparedness are strongly interrelated. Despite good infrastructure if the learning-facilitators are not given proper training, they may not be in a position to operate and implement the resources in the classroom. Similarly irrespective of excellent training, if the basic infrastructure like smart white board, electricity and internet are not available, the implementation will be a big problem.

In the personal interviews conducted with some respondents, it was revealed that many learning-facilitators hold wrong perception about the use of ICT. They feel that ICT is largely a process of acquiring computer literacy skills and it is commonly taught as a separate class rather than being integrated into the subject matter. While some learning-facilitators believed that children will benefit the most only when curriculum is integrated with ICT, most learning-facilitators interviewed felt that implementation of ICT will add extra work on learning-facilitators.

These results shed light on the juxtaposition of policy and practice and can have implications for how the two areas can better be equipped to meet the challenges of successful implementation of ICT in India.

### A Few Suggestions and Conclusion

ICT in schools is a very positive initiative taken by government of India. Irrespective of its good intentions, the interventions in most of the government schools are discouraging. There is a serious need of structuring the existing policy in such a way that all the significant elements related to ICT are strongly and positively correlated. Few initiatives could be:

Intensive compulsory training to the learning-facilitators on how to use ICT in classrooms.

Workshops can be conducted in creating awareness on the significance of ICT.

The management and the higher authority should encourage and support the schools to develop language laboratory and use it for the teaching of languages.

The management should motivate learning-facilitators to use ICT for the teaching-learning process by providing them incentives and framing the policies at the institute.

Number of learning-facilitators attending workshops and seminars on the use of ICT in the teaching-learning processes should be increased.

ICT has huge potential to change the traditional concept of learning process and develop new processes based on digital technology. It can definitely create information-rich society. It is essential to redefine the role and responsibility of learning-facilitators to meet the challenges of ICT in 21st century so that they do not look at it as a threat but as opportunity.

Chapter

32

# ICT in Teaching Learning of Chemistry at School

✎ ZebaTabassum

*Jamia Millia Islamia, New Delhi*

## Preview at a Glance

The present study focuses on the impact of learning-facilitators using traditional method and ICT tools on the attitude of the learners towards the subject chemistry and towards the use of ICT tools in teaching learning of Chemistry. Sample for the present study comprised of learners of 4 sections of class XII Science enrolled in Jamia Senior Secondary School and Syed Abid Hussain Senior Secondary School. Total sample of 103 learners were selected from the four sections of class XII science of Jamia Senior Secondary School and Syed Abid Hussain Senior Secondary School. As random assignment of subjects to control and Experimental Groups has not been applied, the present study is Quasi Experimental in nature. Of the many quasi experimental designs, Pre-test-Post-test non-equivalent Groups Design was employed for the present study. The following tools were used for attaining the objectives of the study: Attitude Scales: a) Five point Likert scale for measuring Impact of ICT tools on the attitude of learners towards chemistry (ATCS) and b) Five point Likert scale for measuring impact of ICT tools on the attitude of learner towards the use of ICT tools in teaching learning of chemistry (ATIS). In accordance with the objectives of the study, the obtained data was analysed using specific statistical techniques, which include computation of mean, S.D, t-test, ANCOVA (analysis of covariance).

## Introduction

The rapid advances recently made in ICT, particularly in the Internet, have very important implications for us. As we begin the 21$^{st}$ century, it is almost impossible to imagine what ICT will be like by the end of the century. We can already start to see how these advances are changing our ideas about traditional education, distance education, just in time learning and the importance of life- long learning. Advances in ICT will mean an enormous increase in the amount of information available to our learners as they study their courses and as they move into the workplace, but this must not be the limit of our expectations. If we wish to provide our learners with a quality education, we must consider more than mere transmission of information and facts. We must take account of what the educational research tells us about learning, namely learners learn best by building on pre–existing knowledge; active learning with understanding and adopting a metacognitive approach. It is generally accepted that new knowledge must be constructed from existing knowledge, that learners are given opportunities to study topics in depth rather than superficially, that they are assisted to take more control of their learning and they engage in the internal dialogue as they monitor and evaluate their own understanding and learning (metacognition).

**Tell me and I forget, Show me and I remember, Involve me and I understand**

Potential role of ICT may play in revitalizing Science education to meet growing aspiration of today's World. ICT as a powerful tool can be employed flexibly to support new pedagogic approach, one that moves away from knowledge delivery to involving pupils more actively in engaging with science ideas and developing skills and hence enhance learner's understanding.

Education embraces almost all activities of life. Education system is dynamic and vibrant. Education enriches a society with the help of dynamic teaching activity. It unfolds a world of knowledge and information to the learner. A good learning-facilitator can communicate the divine spark of learning in a barn. In the modern society the influence of learning-facilitators is much wider than their immediate impact on their pupils: through their work and example. They not only help raise cultural and moral standards, but contribute to economic betterment of society. What do our learners really need to learn and what skills will they actually need when they move into the workplace. In 1996, UNSCO appointed the international commission for Education under the leadership of Jacques Delor. This commission came to be known as Delor'sCommission. One of the members of this commission was Karan Singh. The commission believed that education must be organized around four fundamental types of learning, which through a person's life will in a way be the pillars of knowledge. These four pillars emphasized by Delor's Commission are:

- Learning to know:That is acquiring the instrument of understanding
- Learning to do: So as to be able to act creatively on one's environment
- Learning to live together:So as to participate and co-operate with other people in all human activities
- Learning to be:To develop one's personality and be able to act with greater autonomy, judgment and personal responsibility
- Formal education system tend to emphasis the acquisition of knowledge to the determent of other types of learning, but it is vital now to conceive education in a more encompassing fashion

# ICT Mediated Pre-Service Learning-Facilitator Training

In recent years, we have seen a growing emphasis in many universities on their learner's acquisition of 'generic skills' or attainment of certain 'graduate attributes'. This is partly of employers, who express a need for graduates with well-developed skills such as: effective communication both orally and in writing, ICT skills, team work, problem solving etc.

Attributes of social responsibility, a global perspectives and a desire to undertake lifelong learning are similarly valued.

Concept of ICT: For the purpose of this study, Information and Communication Technologies are defined as all digital devices, tools, content and resources, which can be deployed for realizing the goals of teaching- learning as well as management of the educational system. ICT tools in the present study may be understood as the application of digital equipment to all aspects of teaching and learning. Thus the components of ICT would be video tapes, audio tapes, CDs, DVDs, television broadcast, video cassettes; computer based learning materials, teleconferencing, video conferencing, internet, web conferencing etc. ICT tools used in the present study are:-Internet, Power point Presentations, MS word, MS Paint, CD ROM. The potential role of ICT in science education is multifaceted and evolutionary. This can be realized from the opportunities provided by various ICT tools to provide a huge range of resources that are of high quality and relevant to science learning. There is a considerable research audience that learners are more highly motivated when their learning is supported by ICT and ICT also provides opportunities for learning-facilitators to be creative in their teaching. It is established through various researches that ICT increase the efficiency of the subject to be taught. In the present study, the impact of ICT tools on the attitude towards Chemistry and attitude towards the use of ICT tools in teaching learning process of the learners is studied.

The face of the classrooms is changing; the learning-facilitators should prepare to keep up with the technology utility in classroom. ICT is not only an essential tool for learning-facilitators in their day to day work, but it also offers them opportunities for their own professional development. In conventional teaching, the most of the time is consumed for input output and less time left for process. But, in teaching with the ICT the input and output time is reduced and process time increased. When the process time is increased, the time of learner's activities, discussion, correlation with other subjects, brainstorming, learning etc. will increase. When we do teaching with the help of ICT, we give more time to process phase, which is more important in a period of 45 minutes or one hour.

## Classroom Teaching Time

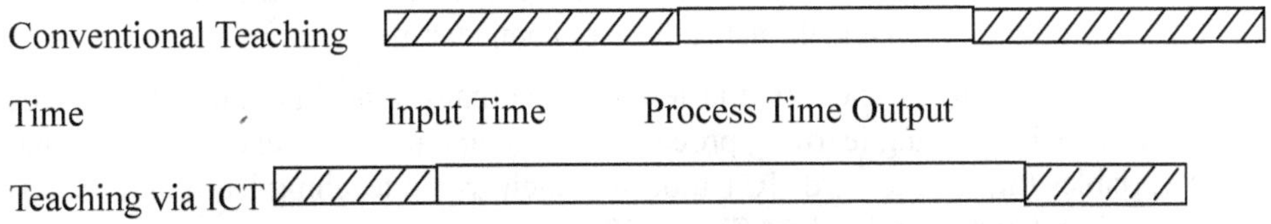

Conventional Teaching ▨▨▨▨▨▨▨▨▨▨▨▨▨▨▨

Time , Input Time    Process Time Output

Teaching via ICT ▨▨▨▨▨▨▨▨▨▨▨▨▨▨▨

**Figure 1: Time taken in Conventional Teaching and Teaching via ICT**

## Form of ICT in the Classroom

ICT can take in many forms in classrooms. We can use ICT as a core or complementary means to the teaching process. ICT in classrooms can be used in four forms, using the following framework:

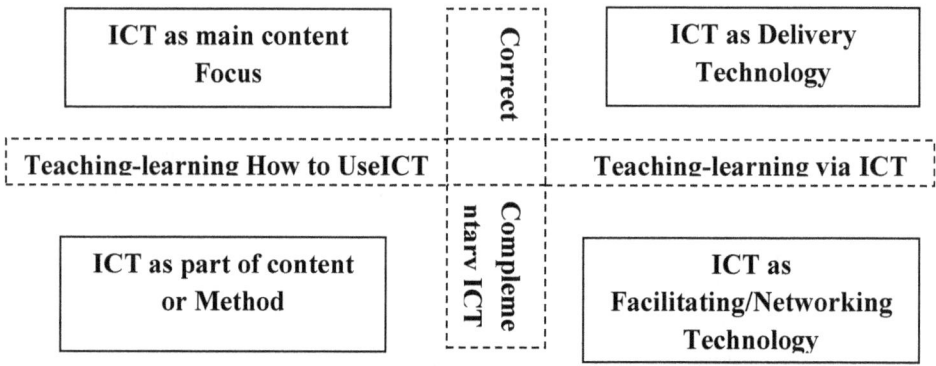

Figure 2: Forms of ICT in Classrooms

## Attitude

In the present study, the Central attribute of the attitude concept is evaluative quality. The attitude towards anything is expressed as like or dislike of the thing. The Central attribute of the attitude is very broadly used in discussing issues in science education and is more often used in various contexts. There is a great agreement among science theorists and practitioners on the importance of learner's attitudes toward chemistry lessons in school (Geban *et al.*, 2011; Collins *et al.*, 2003; Coll, 2002). Learner's attitude toward the learning of chemistry is seen as one of the factors influencing their academic achievement. The development of learner's positive attitude toward chemistry as a school subject is an important issue.

It is worth mentioning that learner's positive attitude to chemistry is necessary because researches on the relationship between attitudes and academic achievement discovered that these variables were closely related to each other.

The researches indicated that learning-facilitators and learner attitude levels towards the use of ICT had a direct relation with the use of ICT for educational purposes. In other words, the correlation findings revealed that there was significant positive correlation between learning-facilitators and learner's level of ICT use and their attitudes level (Lai Mei and Fook, 2010). A similar finding was reported by Albiri (2004) and Isleem (2012). Results of their research indicate that there is a significant relationship between user's attitude towards computers and the actual level of computer use.

The development of learners and learning-facilitator's positive attitude towards the use of ICT in teaching learning process is important and researches indicated that these variables (attitude towards ICT tools and their use in teaching learning process) were closely related to each other (Shehu, 2012).

# ICT Mediated Pre-Service Learning-Facilitator Training

In the present study impact of teaching with ICT tools on the attitude towards Chemistry and attitude towards the use of ICT tools in teaching learning of Chemistry is studied.

## Attitude towards Chemistry

Attitude towards subject chemistry is the evaluative beliefs of the learners regarding chemistry theory, structures of molecules, laboratory work, assignments, projects etc. Attitude towards chemistry is expressed as learners likes and dislikes to the above aspects.

### Attitude towards the use of ICT tools in teaching learning of Chemistry

The attitude towards the use of ICT tools in teaching learning of chemistry is defined as ICT tools related learner's disposition based upon their liking, thinking and feeling about the use of ICT tools in teaching learning process.

## Objectives of the Study

The study was planned with the following major objectives:

1. To study the impact of teaching with traditional method on the attitude of thelearners towards the subject chemistry.
2. To study the impact of teaching with ICT tools on the attitude of the learners towards the subject chemistry.
3. To compare the impact of teaching with traditional method and teaching with ICT tools on the attitude of the learners towards the subject chemistry.
4. To study the impact of teaching with ICT tools on the attitude of the learners towards the use of ICT tools in teaching learning of Chemistry.

## Methods and Procedure

An experiment involves the comparison of the effects of a particular treatment with that of a different treatment or of no treatment. In a simple conventional experiment, reference is usually made to an Experimental Group and to a Control Group. In the present study, there are two Control Groups and two Experimental Groups. As random assignment of subjects to control and Experimental Groups has not been applied, the present study is Quasi Experimental in nature. Of the many quasi experimental designs, Pre-test-Post-test non-equivalent Groups Design was employed for the present study.

## Results and Discussion

1. Impact of teaching with Traditional Method on the attitude of the learners towards the subject Chemistry

It may be concluded that Traditional Method has moderately positive impact on the attitude of the learners towards subject Chemistry. Although before and after the treatment i.e. in both pre-test and post-test phases the Control Groups have shown moderately positive attitude towards subject Chemistry but use of Traditional Method in teaching learning of Chemistry has not resulted in improving the attitude of the learners towards subject Chemistry. When mean attitude scores obtained on ATCS in the pre-test phase and post-test phase compared using t-test. Therefore, Traditional Method must be used along with suitable teaching aid which may help in improving the teaching learning process and increasing the comprehensibility of the subject Chemistry.

Traditional talk and chalk method, which is most practiced approach of instruction in majority of schools, is most familiar for the learners and convenient for the learning-facilitators to follow. Learners are well versed with expectations to memorize the facts and produce the same in examination. It may be interpreted that Traditional Method has positive impact on the attitude of the learners towards subject Chemistry, if used in accordance with the need of the learners and the content to be taught.

2. Impact of teaching with ICT tools on the attitude of the learners towards the subject Chemistry

The analysis revealed that use of ICT tools in teaching learning of chemistry in the treatment phase has resulted in observed difference in the mean attitude values of Experimental Group-I and Experimental Group-II in the pre-test and post-test phases.

It may be concluded that teaching with ICT tools has positive impact on the attitude of the learners towards subject Chemistry. Although before and after the treatment i.e. in both pre-test and post-test phases the Experimental Groups have shown moderately positive attitude towards subject Chemistry but use of ICT tools in teaching learning of Chemistry has resulted in improving the attitude of the learners towards subject Chemistry as the difference in mean attitude values obtained on ATCS in the pre-test and post-test phases was significant. Therefore, ICT tools must be incorporated in the teaching learning of Chemistry when and where required so as to make the subject more interesting and comprehensive which is today's need.

3. Comparison of the impact of teaching with traditional method and teaching with ICT tools on the attitude of the learners towards the subject Chemistry

It may be concluded that the difference in the impact of teaching with traditional method and teaching with ICT tools on the attitude of learners towards subject chemistry is not significant. It may therefore be inferred that there is no significant difference in the attitude of learners towards subject chemistry taught through traditional method and use of ICT tools and there are other factors, other than method of instruction, which have impact on the attitude of the learners towards any subject. A review of the major literature point out that learner' attitudes towards chemistry is influenced by many factors such as gender, learning-facilitators, curricula, motivation, cultural and other variables. The literature itself points to the crucial importance of gender and the quality of teaching. Given the importance of the latter we argue that there is a greater need for research to identify those aspects of science teaching that make school science engaging for pupils. In particular, a growing body of research on motivation offers important pointers to the kind of classroom environment and activities that might

# ICT Mediated Pre-Service Learning-Facilitator Training

raise pupils' interest in studying chemistry and a focus for future research, Further, the analysis has shown that the use of ICT tools in teaching learning of Chemistry has resulted in improving the attitude of the learners towards subject Chemistry as the difference in mean attitude values obtained on ATCS in the pre-test and post-test phases of Experimental groups was significant. Therefore, ICT tools must be incorporated in the teaching learning of Chemistry when and where required so as to make the subject more interesting and comprehensive which is today's need. Analysis shows that before and after the treatment i.e. in both pre-test and post-test phases the Control Groups have shown moderately positive attitude towards subject Chemistry but use of Traditional Method in teaching learning of Chemistry has not resulted in improving the attitude of the learners towards subject Chemistry. Therefore, Traditional Method must be used along with suitable teaching aid which may help in improving the teaching learning process and increasing the comprehensibility of the subject Chemistry.

4 Impact of teaching with ICT tools on the attitude of the learners towards the use of ICT tools in teaching learning of Chemistry

It was observed that use of ICT tools in teaching learning of chemistry in the treatment phase has resulted in changing the attitude of the learners from neutral to moderately positive towards the use of ICT tools in the teaching learning of chemistry. Learners are less attracted by structural and monotonous nature of traditional method as compared to use of ICT tools. Use of ICT tools in teaching learning of chemistry allures the learners through its text based effect and multisensory approach. It may thus be concluded that use of ICT tools had a moderately positive impact on the learner's attitude toward the use of ICT tools in teaching learning of chemistry. The analysis shows that use of ICT tools in teaching leaning of Chemistry in the treatment phase has resulted in changing the attitude of the learners from neutral to moderately positive towards the use of ICT tools in the teaching learning of chemistry.

## Implications of the Study

Learning-facilitators should be trained to use ICT in their pedagogy. This may be initiated with inculcation of ICT in learning-facilitator education, which already had started and should be done more rigorouly on a wider scale. Lack of time, unavailability of ICT resources and untrained learning-facilitators are some of the important reasons for the learning-facilitators not appreciating and using the ICT tools in the teaching learning process. Therefore, these constraints should be overcome through proper planning and initiatives on the part of higher authority. Learning-facilitator should pay attention to the teaching strategies using ICT tools to be used in the classroom for teaching a particular concept in Chemistry i.e. which ICT tools will be suitable for teaching a particular content. The y should be able to plan their teaching learning activities and learning materials. There should be programmes in the school itself for learning-facilitators by the Government agencies, private agencies and public-private agencies on effective integration of technology (ICT) in the teaching learning process. There must be some special provisions for learning-facilitators attending such programmes, so that percentage of school learning-facilitators attending these programmes is high.

Learning-facilitators should be trained to use ICT in their pedagogy. This may be initiated with inculcation of ICT in learning-facilitator education, which already had started and should be done more rigorously on a wider scale. For learning-facilitators already in schools, 'in-service' training should be given to get a grip to use of ICT tools. This task has been taken up already by Intel and other institutions. But more importantly and often less developed are measures to meet the need of learning-facilitators appropriate to their teaching subject. Also what is provided in name of training is 'one-time event' which ignores the aspect of practice and hands on experience with ICT Tools. Prelude is to develop a positive attitude among learning-facilitators regarding the affordances of ICT.

# Bibliography

Adams B.S., Cummins, M., Davis, A., Freeman, A., Hall Giesinger, C. and Ananthanarayanan, V. (2017). *NMC Horizon Report: 2017 Higher Education Edition*. Austin, Texas: The New Media Consortium.

Adesoji, F. and Fabunmi. (2012). Undergraduate students perception of the effectiveness of ICT use in improving teaching and learning in Ekiti University, Ado Ekiti, Nigeria. International J. of library and information science, VI (7), pp.121-130.

Aduwa-Ogiegbaen, S.E., and Iyamu, E.O.S. (2005). Using Information and Communication Technology in Secondary Schools in Nigeria: Problems and Prospects. Educational Technology and Society, 8 (1), 104-112.

Aggarwal, B.C. (2006) Communication technology for Rural Development. Indian J. of Communication Technology, 22(2), 1-9.

Aggarwal, J.C. (2003).Educational technology and management. New Delhi: Vinod Pustak Mandir.

Aggarwal, Y.P. (1998). The Science of Educational Research: A sourcebook. Kurukshetra: Nirmal Book Agency.

Aggarwal, Y.P. (2013). Statistical methods concepts application and computation. Kurukshetra: Nirmal Book Agency.

Ahmad, S. (2012). Teacher-trainees awareness regarding open educational resources. Global Research analysis, vol. 1. Retrieved from www.slideshare.net/ROER4D/researching-open-educational-resources-and-open-peda.

Al-Ansari, H. (2006). Internet Use by the Faculty Members of Kuwait University. The Electronic. 24(6), 791-803.

Albaugh, P. (1997). The role of skepticism in preparing teachers for the use of technology. Education for community: a town and gown discussion panel. Westerville, OH

Albuquerque, T. (2008). Do abandono a permanência no ensino superior [From drop out to permanence in higher education]. *Revista De Ciências Da Educação*, September 1, 19-28.

All India Educational Survey (1982). New Delhi: NCERT.

Allan, H.K.I. *et al.* (2003). ICT implementation and school leadership case studies of ICT integration in teaching and learning. J. of Educational Administration, 41(2), 158-170.

Allen, E. and Seaman, J. (2011). Going the distance: Online educator in the United States. (Survey). Newburyport, MA: Babson Survey Research Group.

Allen, I.E. and Seaman, J. (2007). Online nation: Five years of growth in online learning. Needham, MA: Sloan Consortium. Retrieved from http://sloanconsortium.org/publications/survey/pdf/online_nation.pdf.

AMARC (1981). Community Radio Handbook. Canada.

AMARC (1995). Waves for Freedom: Report on the Sixth World Conference of Community Radio Broadcasters, Sakar, Senegal, January 23-39.

Ampiah, J.G. (2018). Vice Chancellor Address: Matriculation of College of Distance Education Students for the 2017/2018 academic year. Retrieved from https://code.ucc.edu.gh/news/ucc-holds-matriculation-code-southern-zone

Ampiah, J.G. (2018). Vice Chancellor Address: Matriculation of Fresh Regular Students for the 2017/2018 academic year. Retrieved from https://ucc.edu.gh/news/ucc-matriculates-201718-fresh-students

Anastasia Kitsantas, J. C. (2011). Mathematics achievement: The role of homework and self-efficacy beliefs. Virginia: George Mason University.

Anderson, T. and Dron, J. (2011). Three generations of distance education pedagogy. *The International Review of Research in Open and Distributed Learning*, *12*(3), 80-97.

Anderson, T.D. and Kanuka, H.P. (2009). Ethical Conflicts in Research on Networked Education Contexts. In U. Demiray, and R. Sharma (Eds.), Ethical Practices and Implications in Distance Learning (pp. 108-124). Hershey, PA: IGI Global. doi:10.4018/978-1-59904-867-3.ch009.

Angrist, J. and Lavy, V. (2002). New evidence on classroom computers and pupil learning. The Economic J., 112: 735–765. doi:10.1111/1468-0297.00068.

Angule (2009). The Challenges to ICT in Many Schools. Retrieved from http://www.changemakers.com/groups/integration-ict-quality-education-sustainable-developme/discussion-7.

ASER. (2014). Annual Status of Education Report (Rural). . Retrieved from www.asercentre.org

Asiedu, N.K. (2017). Influence of social networking sites on students' academic and social lives: The Ghanaian perspective. Library Philosophy and Practice (e-J.), 1-22. Retrieved from http://digitalcommons.unl.edu/cgi/viewcontent.cgi?article=4384andcontext=libphilprac

Bailey, G. (1994). Supporting technology integration within a teacher education system. J. of Educational Computing Research, 31(4), 423-435.

Bairagi, A.K. (2011). Status and role of ICT in educational institution to build digital society in Bangladesh: Perspective of a divisional city, Khulna. International J. of Advances in Engineering and Technology, 1(4), 374-383.

Bakshi, A.K. (n.d.). ICT in Education: Need of the Hour, India Education Review. Retrieved from http://www.indiaeducationreview.com/article/ict-education-need-hour.

Balakrishnan, P. (2004). Measuring productivity in manufacturing sector. Retrieved from http://dspace.iimk.ac.in/bitstream/handle/2259/325/Productivity.pdf?sequence=1andisAllowed=y.

# Bibliography

Bandura, A. (1994). Self-efficacy. Encyclopedia of human behaviour, 4, 71-81.

Bandura, A. (2002). Social cognitive theory in cultural context. J. of Applied Psychology: An international Review, 51, 269-290

Banks, F. (Ed.) (1994). Teaching Technology. London: Routledge.

Banu, N., Kamal, A.R. and Banu, T (2010). ICT in higher education: A Study. Canadian J. on Data, Information and Knowledge Engineering, 1(1), 12.

Baran, B. (2010). Facebook as a formal instructional environment. British J. of Educational Technology, 41(6), 146-149.

Barr, R.B. and Tagg J. (1995). From teaching to learning: A new paradigm for undergraduate Education( Academic abstract). Change: The Magazine of Higher Learning, 27(6), 12-26. Retrieved from http://www.tandfonline.com/doi/abs/10.1080/00091383.1995.10544672?journalCode=vchn20.

Barreto, A.L. and Filgueiras, Carlos A.L. (2007). Origens da Universidade Brasileira [Origins of the Brazilian University]. *Química Nova*, 30(7), 1780-1790.

Baskin, C. and Williams, M. (2006). ICT integration in schools: Where are we now and what comes next? Australasian J. of Educational Technology and Society, 22(4), 455-473.

Bates, A.W. (1990). Third Generation Distance Education: The Challenge of New Technology. *Research in Distance Education, 3*(2): 10-15

Batsila, M., Tsihouridis, C and Vavougios, D. (2014). Entering the web 2 Edmodo world to support learning: Tracing teachers opinion after using it in their classes. IJET, 9(1), 53-60.

Baumeister, R.F., Campbell, J.D., Krueger, J.I. and Vohs, K.D. (2003). Does high self esteemcause better performance, interpersonal success, happiness, or healthier lifestyles? Psychological Science in the Public Interest, 4, 1-44.

Becker, H.J. and Riel, M.M. (2000) Teacher Professional Engagement and Constructivist-compatible Computer Use. Centre for Research on Information Technology and Organisations, University of California, Irvine. Retrieved from http://www.crito.uci.edu/tic/findings.html.

BECTA (2001). Computer Games in Educational Report. England: British Educational Communications and Technology Agency.

BECTA (2002). What is ICT? England: British Educational Communications and Technology Agency. Retrieved from http://schools.becta.org.uk/index.php?section=cuandcatcode=ss_cu_skl_02andrid=1701.

BECTA (2003) Primary schools: ICT and Standards. An analysis of national data from Ofsted and QCA. England: British Educational Communications and Technology Agency. Retrieved from http://www.becta.org.uk/research/research.cfm?section=1andid=538.

BECTA (2008). *How do boys and girls differ in their use of ICT?* UK: Becta Research Report.

Bell, S. (2010). Project based learning for 21$^{st}$ century: Skill for the future. The Clearing House, 83(5), 39-43.

Bembenutty, H. (2009). Self-regulation of homework completion. Psychology J., 6, 138-153.

Bennet, S. and Nancy, K. (2006). The Case Against Homework. New York: Crown Publishers.

Beresford, J. (2000). Student perspectives on school improvement. Paper presented at the British Educational Research Association Conference, Cardiff University, September 7-10. [Online] http://www.leeds.ac.uk/educol/documents/00001529.doc.

Best, J.W. and Kahn, J.V. (1999). Research in education. India: Prentice Hall.

Bevilaqua, C.B. (2005). Entre o previsível e o contingente: etnografia do processo de decisão sobre uma política de ação afirmativa [Between predictable and contingent: ethnography of the decision-making process on an affirmative action policy]. *Revista de Antropologia*, 48(1), 167-225.

Bhagwati, J. (2004). In defense of globalization. New York: Oxford University Press.

Bhasin, P. (2010, February). The world wants to follow the ICT-driven Indian economy. Retrieved from Retrieved from http://www.business-standard.com/india/news/the-world-wants-to-follow-ict-driven-indian-economy/385246/

Bhatnagar, A.B. and Bhatnagar, A. (2013). Teaching of Physical Education. Meerut: R. Lal. Book Depot.

Bhatnagar, S. and Anand, S. (1988). Education and communication technology: (Perspective, planning and implementation). New Delhi: Ess Ess Pub.

Bhatt, R. (2011). The Story So Far. Ground Realities: Community Radio in Indi, UNESCO.

Bhatt, R. (n.d.). Community Radio: An Introduction, Module -1, Certificate in Community Radio Technology. Commonwealth Educational Media Centre for Asia, New Delhi and Broadcast Engineering Consultants India Ltd. Noida, UP.

Biswas, P.C. (2002). Building ICT skills for Quality Teacher Education. University News, 40(50), 16-22.

Blackboard Learn (n.d.). Retrieved from https://bboard.uhk.cz/.

Blurton, C. (1999). New Directions of ICT-Use in Education. Retrieved from http://www.unesco.org/education/lwf/dl/edict.pdf.

Boateng, R. *et al.* (2016). Videos in learning in higher education : assessing perceptions and attitudes of students at the University of Ghana. Smart Learning Environments. 3(8).

Bowers, C.A. (2000). Let them eat data. How computers affect education, cultural diversity, and the prospects of ecological sustainability. Athens: The University of Georgia Press.

Boyn, D.M. and Ellison, N.B. (2007). Social networking sites: Definition, history and scholarship. J. of Computer-Mediated Communication, 13(1), 210-230. Retrieved from http://onlinelibrary.wiley.com/doi/10.1111/j.1083-6101.2007.00393.x/full

Bozkurt, A., Honeychurch, S., Caines, A., Bali, M., Koutropoulos, A. and Cormier, D. (2016). Community Tracking in a Cmooc and Nomadic Learner Behavior Identification on a Connectivist Rhizomatic Learning Network. Turkish Online J. of Distance Education. doi:10.17718/tojde.09231. Retrieved from https://www.researchgate.net/publication/308791822.

Bradley, G. and Russell, G. (1997). Computer experience, school support and computer anxieties. Educational Psychology, 17(3), 267-284.

Brazilian Government [Brazil] (2007). Decreto N. 6096 [Decree No. 6096]. *Diário Oficial da União*, April 25.

# Bibliography

Brock, C.H., Lapp, D., Flood, J., Fisher, D. and Han, K.T. (2007). Does homework matter? An investigation of teacher perceptions about homework practices for children from non-dominant backgrounds. Urban Education, 42, 349-372.

Brown, J.S., Collins, A. and Duguid, P. (1989). Situated cognition and the culture of learning. Educational Researcher, 18, 32-42.

Bryan, T. and Sullivan-Burstein, K. (1997). Homework how-tos. Teaching Exceptional Children, 29(6), 32-37.

Buch, M.B. (1997). 5th Survey of Educational Research 1988-1992. New Delhi: NCERT.

Budhedeo, S.H. (2016) Issues and challenges in bringing ICT enabled education to rural India. IJSRE, 4(1), 4759-4766.

Bush, M. and Mott, J. (2009). The transformation of learning with technology. Educational Technology, 49(1), 3–20.

Butler, D. *et al*. (2013). A Consultative Paper Building towards a Learning Society: A National Digital Strategy for Schools. Retrieved September, 2015, from http://www.education.ie/en/Schools- Colleges/Information/Information-Communications-Technology-ICT-in-Schools/Digital-Strategy-for-Schools/Building-Towards-a-Learning-Society-A-National-Digital-Strategy-for-Schools- Consultative-Paper.pdf.

Byker, E.J. (2014). ICT in Indias elementary schools: The vision and realities. The International Education J.: Comparative Perspectives, 13(2).

Caligaris, M.G., Schivo, M.E. and Romiti M.R. (2015). Calculus and GeoGebra, an interesting partnership. Procedia - Social and Behavioral Sciences, 174, 1183 – 1188.

Capan, S.A. (2012). Teacher Attitudes towards Computer Use in EFL Classrooms. Frontiers of Language and Teaching, 3, 248-254.

Caroline, S. (2009). Administers Role in Technology Integration. Education World 2009. Retrieved on November 20, 2017 at: http://www.educationworld.com/a-

Carr, A., **McKenzie, K. and Copeland**, C. (2012). ICT in education is important! Naace University of Nottingham Innovation Park, Nottingham, NG7 2TU, 1060683. Retrieved from http://www.naace.co.uk/1068.

Cech, P. and Klimova, B. (2003). e a souteze e- learning 2003. Kurz Teaching written business English (TWBE). In Sedlack (ed.), Sbornik prispevkuze ze seminar as a soutezes e-learning 2003. Hradec Kralove: Gaudeamus, 23-26.

CEMCA (n.d.). Innovations in Community Radio with special reference to India New Delhi: Commonwealth Educational Media Centre for Asia.

Cesar, S. (2016). Novos rumos da Educacao. Retrieved from http://www.abed.org.br/site/pt/midiateca/textos_ead/1390/2016/08/novos_rumos_da_educacao.

Chand, R. (2015). 1st Half of 1st Year Monitoring Report of Himachal Pradesh University, Shimla. Submitted in Department of Education, Himachal Pradesh University, Shimla. Retrieved from http://ictschools.gov.in/sites/default/files/pdf/ICT_Report_of_Himachal_Pradesh.pdf.

Chao, J., Chiu, J.L., DeJaegher, C.J. and Pan, E.A. (2016). Sensor-augmented virtual labs: Using physical interactions with science Simulations to promote understanding of gas behavior. J. of Science Education and Technology, 25(1), 16-33.

Chavan, K. (2009). Instructional System. Nashik: Insight Publications.

Chickering, A.W. and Gamson, Z. (1991). Applying the seven principles for good practice in undergraduate education. San Francisco: Jossey-Bass.

Chigona, A., Kayongo, P. and Kausa, M. (2010). An empirical survey on domestication of ICT in schools in disadvantaged communities in South Africa. International J. of education and development using information and communication technology, VI (2), pp. 21-32.

Chong, C, Wahab, M and HeongLe, C. (2016). Open educational resources. A Malaysian case study. Library Philosophy and practice e-J., retrieved from www.unescobkk.org/.../ user.../OutcomeDocument_RDTCRegionalSeminar2015.pdf.

Christen, A. (2009). Transforming the classroom for collaborative learning in the 21st century. Techniques: Connecting Education and Careers, 84(1), 28-31.

Chritensson, P. (2010). ICT definition. Retrieved from https://techterms.com/definition/ict

Chu, K. (2007). Using Scenario-based Learning for E-Learning in Vocational Education. In R. Sharma and S. Mishra (Eds.), Cases on Global E-Learning Practices: Successes and Pitfalls (pp. 232-246). Hershey, PA: IGI Global. doi:10.4018/978-1-59904-340-1.ch018.

Churchill, D. (2009). Educational applications of Web 2.0: using blogs to support teaching and learning. British J. of Educational Technology, 40(1), 179-183.

Ciarrochi, J., Heaven, P. C. L., and Fiona, D. (2007). The impact of hope, self-esteem, and attributional style on adolescents school grades and emotional well-being: A longitudinal study.

Collins English Dictionary. (2012a). Social. Retrieved from http://www.dictionary.com/browse/social

Collins English Dictionary. (2012b). Networking. Retrieved from http://www.dictionary.com/browse/networking

Collis, B. (2002). Information technologies for education and training. In Adelsberger, H., Collis, B and Pawlowski, J. (Eds.) Handbook on Technologies for Information and Training. Berlin: Springer Verlag.

Communication (2017). In Business Dictionary. Retrieved from: http://www.businessdictionary.com/definition/communication.html

Connie, W. and Janet, P. (1983). Computer Phobia: Causes and Cures. Action in Teacher Educatio, 5, 23-25.

Conole, G. (2012). Finding Relevant OER in Higher Education: A Personal Account. Retrieved from https://oerknowledgecloud.org/sites/oerknowledgecloud.org/.../pub_PS_OER_web.pdf

Conye, R. (1999). Technoromanticism: digital narrative, holism, and the romance of the real. Cambridge, MA: MIT Press.

Cooper, H., Jackson, K., Nye, B. and Lindsay, J.J. (2001). A model of homeworks influence on the performance of elementary school students. J. of Experimental Education, 69, 181–199.

Cooper, H., Lindsay, J.J., Nye, B. and Greathouse, S. (1998). Relationships among attitudes about homework, amount of homework assigned and completed, and student achievement. J. of Educational Psychology, 90, 70–83.

Coopersmith, S. (1967). The Antecedents of Self-esteem. San Francisco: Freeman WH.

Cormier, D. (2008). Rhizomatic Education: Community as Curriculum. Innovate. J. of Online Education, 4(5).

Coulon, A. (2008). A condição de estudante: A entrada na vida universitária [The student's condition: The entrance in university life. S Salvador, Bahia: EDUFBA, 276.

Cox, M., Preston, C. and Cox, C. (1999).What factors support or prevent teachers from using ICT in the primary classroom. University of Sussex, Brighton. Retrieved from http://www.leeds.ac.uk/educol/documents/00001304.htm.

Cox, M.J. and Marshall, G. (2007). Effects of ICT: Do we know what we should know? Education and information technologies, 12(2), 59-70.

Cox, M.J. (1997). The effects of information technology on students motivation, London, UK: Kings College, London. Final Report.

Crade, M. (2005). Knowledge societies in a nutshell: Information technologies for sustainable development. Ottaway, Canada: IRDC.

Cradler, J., McNabb, M.., Freeman, M. and Burchett, R. (2002). How Does Technology Influence Student Learning?, Learning and Leading with Technology, 29(8).

Creswell, J.W. (2011). Designing and conducting mixed methods research (2nd ed.). Thousand Oaks, CA: Sage.

Creswell, J.W. (2013). Qualitative inquiry and research design: Choosing among five approaches (3rd ed.). Los Angeles: CA: Sage.

Cuban, L. and Jandric, P. (2015). The dubious promise of educational technologies: Historical patterns and future challenges. E-Learning and Digital Media, 12(3–4), 425–439.

Cunha, L.A. (2007). A universidade reformada: o golpe de 1964 e a modernização do ensino superior [The Reformed University: the coup of 1964 and the modernization of higher education]. 2nd ed. São Paulo: UNESP.

Curriculum Framework for Quality Teacher Education by NCTE. [Online] Available at http://www.ncte india.org/pub/ curr/curr_0.htm

Cuttance, P. and Stokes, S. (2000). Monitoring progress towards the national goals for schooling: Information and communication technology (ICT) skills and knowledge. Report to the National Performance Monitoring Taskforce of the Ministerial Council on Education Employment, Training and Youth Affairs (MCEETYA). Retrieved from http://www.edfac.unimelb.edu.au/EPM/CAER/ICTJune2000.htm

Dash, M. (2007). Curricula and the Use of ICT in Education: Two Worlds Apart? British J. of Educational Technology, 38 (6), 962-976.

Davidson (1994). Removing Computer Phobia from the Writing Classroom. Retrieved from the ERIC database (ERIC.EJ 493145).

Davis (2007). A Web 2.0 education. Retrieved from http://www.education.ed.ac.uk/elearning/gallery/davis_web2education.html#%5B%5BStart%20Here%5D%5D.

Dawam, S.R., Ahmad, K.A., Jusoff, K., Tajuddian, T., Elias, S.J. and Mansor, S.W. (2009). The use of ICT in public and private institutions of higher learning, Malaysia. Computer and Information Science, 2 (4), 122–128.

DCSF (2008), Safer Children in a Digital World: The Report of the Byron Review, Department for Children, Schools and Families, London.

Deka, P.P. (2015). A study on impact social media on educational efforts in Guwahati city, Assam. International J. of Advanced Research in Educational Technology (IJARET), 2(3), 90-94.

Denning, T. (1997) IT and Pupil Motivation: A Collaborative Study of Staff and Pupil Attitudes and Experiences, Stafford, UK: Keele University.

Dennis (2009). Anxiety in e-learning: The effect of computer self-efficacy. Retrieved from the ERIC database (ERIC.EJ 85897).

Department of Education Science and Training (2003). Australias teachers: Australias future: Advancing innovation, science, technology and mathematics. Canberra: AGPS.

DePasquale, R., McNamara, E. and Murphy, K. (2003). Meaningful connections: Using technology in primary classrooms. Young Children on the Web, Retrieved from http://J..naeyc.org/btj/200311/techinprimaryclassrooms.pdf

DEP-SSA (2006). ICT Initiatives Quality Improvement in Elementary Education. New Delhi: DEP-SSA, IGNOU.

Dept. of School Education and Literacy, (2009). National Policy on Information and Communication Technology (ICT) in School Education (Draft), New Delhi: GOI, MHRD.

Derar, S. (2007). School Principles Attitude Towards The Use Of Technology: United Arab Emirates Technology Workshop, The Turkish Online J. Of Education Technology, 6, 1-5.

DfES (2004). A National Conversation about Personalised Learning, Nottingham: DfES Publications.

Diamantis, R. (1982). The concept and correlates of computer anxiety. Behaviour and Information Technology, 11, 99-108.

Digital trends (2016). The history of social networking. Retrieved from https://www.digitaltrends.com/features/the-history-of-social-networking/

Dignath, C., Buettner, G., Langfeldt, H. (2008). How can primary school students learn self-regulated learning strategies most effectively?: A meta-analysis on self-regulation training programs, Educational Research ReVew, Volume 3, Issue 2, 2008, Pages 101–129

Dillman, D.A., Smyth, J.D. and Christian, L.M. (2008). Internet, mail and mixed-mode survey: The tailored design method. 3rd ed. Hoboken, New Jersey: John Wiley and Sons, 512.

Dogan, M. (2010). The role of dynamic geometry software in the process of learning: GeoGebra example about triangles. Retrieved from http://www.time2010.uma.es/Proceedings/Papers/A026_Paper.pdf

Downes, S. (2005) E-learning 2.0. eLearn *Magazine*, October 2005.

DSME (n.d.). Ame o Ama Parivesha Text book for class V. Department of School and Mass Education, Odisha.

Dudeney, G. (2010). The Internet and the language classroom (Vol.X). Cambridge University Press.

# Bibliography

Elmo (2012). What is ICT in education? Retrieved from http://www.elmoglobal.com/en/html/ict/01.aspx

Englund, C., Olofsson, A.D. and Price, L. (2017). Teaching with technology in higher education: understanding conceptual change and development in practice. *Higher Education Research and Development*, 36(1), 73-87.

Ertmer, P.E.A. (1999) Examining teachers beliefs about the role of technology in the elementary classroom. J. of Research on Computing in Education, 32 (1), 54-72.

Estanque, E. and Nunes, J.A. (2003). Dilemas e desafios da universidade: recomposição social e expectativas dos estudantes da universidade de Coimbra [Dilemmas and challenges of the university: Social recomposition and expectations of students of the University of Coimbra]. *Revista Crítica de Ciências Sociais*, n. 66, 5-44.

Evan-Andris, M. (2014). Barrier to Computer Integration: Microinteraction Among Computer co-ordinators and classroom teachers in elementary schools. J. of Research on Computing in Education, 28(1), 29-45.

Evans-Andris, M. (1995) Barrier to Computer Integration: micro-interaction among

Fadde, P.J. and Phu, V. (2014). Blended Online Learning: Benefits, Challenges and Misconceptions. In P. Lowenthal, C. S. York, and J. C. Richardson (Eds.), Online Learning: Common Misconceptions, Benefits and Challenges (pp. 33 – 48). New York: Nova.

Fatima, S. (2013). Challenges of ICT in teaching learning process. International J. of engineering and science. II (12), 51-54.

Favero, M.D.L.D.A. (2006). A universidade no Brasil: das origens à reforma universitária de 1968 [The university in Brazil: from the origins to the university reform of 1968]. *Educar*, May 4, 17-36.

Federal University of Bahia [UFBA] (2007). Universidade Nova: Plano de expansão e reestruturação da arquitetura curricular na Universidade Federal da Bahia [Universidade Nova: Plan for the expansion and restructuring of curriculum at the Federal University of Bahia]. Retrieved from https://www.ufba.br/.

Federal University of Bahia [UFBA] (2016). UFBA in numbers: Retrospective. Retrieved from https://proplan.ufba.br/sites/proplan.ufba.br/files/UFBA%20in%20numbers%20Retrospective%20Special%2070%20Years_1.pdf

Federal University of Bahia [UFBA]. (2005). Políticas de inclusão social na UFBA: Programa de ações afirmativas [Policies of social inclusion in UFBA: Affirmative action program]. Retrieved from https://www.ufba.br/.

Ferguson, R., Faulkner, D., Whitelock, D. and Sheehy, K. (2015). Pre-teens' informal learning with ICT and web 2.0. *Technology, Pedagogy and Education*, 24(2), 247-265.

Fifth Survey of Educational Research, (1988-92), Trend Reports, Vol.1, NCERT, New Delhi.

Filho, A.N.D. (2007). Universidade Nova: Textos críticos e esperançosos [Universidade Nova Project: Critical and hopeful texts]. Salvador, Bahia: EDUFBA, 300.

Freitas S.D. and Yapp, C. (Eds.) (2005), Personalizing Learning in the 21st Century, Bloomsbury Publishing.

Frydrychova, K.B. (2011). Blended learning in the teaching of foreign languages. In I. Semradova *et al.*, Reflections on the exploitation of a virtual study environment. Hradec Kralove: Milos Vognar. Publishing House, 63-75.

Fu, J.S. (2013) ICT in Education: A Critical Literature Review and Its Implications. International J. of Education and Development using Information and Communication Technology (IJEDICT), 9(1), 112-125. Retrieved from ijedict.dec.uwi.edu/include/getdoc.php?id=5402

Furlong, J. and Davies, C. (2012). Young people, new technologies and learning at home: Taking context seriously. *Oxford Review of Education, 38*(1), 45-62.

Ganapathy, M and Peiwei.C.V. (2015). Teachers Perception of creating sharing and using OER in University: Sains Malaysia, International J. of e-education,vol.no-5. Retrievedfromwww.ijeeee.org/index.php?m=contentandc=indexanda=showandcatid=54andid

Ganguly, A.B. (1990). The microcomputer as demonstration tool for instruction in mathematics, J. for Research in Mathematics education.

Gardner, H. and Davis, K. (2013). The App Generation: How Today's Youth Navigate Identity, Intimacy, and Imagination in a Digital World. Yale University Press.

Garrison, D. and Anderson, T. (2003). E-Learning in the 21st century. London: Routledge Falmer. Cross Ref

Gay, L.R. (1992). Educational research Competencies for Analysis and Application, Macmillan publishing company, New York.

Gee, J.P. (2003). What video games have to teach us about learning and literacy.

Gee, J.P. (n.d.). Good Video Games and Good Learning.

George P.L. and Fraser, B.J. (1994). An evaluation of computer s◻ assisted learning in terms of achievement, attitudes and classroom environment, Evaluation and Research in Education, 8(3).

Gerard, B. and Spek, J.V.D. (2002). The Potentional for Community Radio in Afganistan: Report of a Fact Finding Mission. November 5, 2002. http://communica.org/afganistan/.

Ghavifekr, S. and Rosdy, W.A.W. (2015). Teaching and learning with technology: Effectiveness of ICT integration in schools. International J. of Research in Education and Science (IJRES), 1(2), 175-191.

Ghavifekr, S., Afshari, M., and Amla, S. (2012). Management strategies for E-Learning system as the core component of systemic change: A qualitative analysis. Life Science J., 9(3), 2190-2196.

Ghwanmeb and Sameh (2012). Utilizing ICT to enhance pedagogy within the educational system in Jordan. 2nd Annual international conference on education and E-learning.

Gibbons, S. (2007). The Academic Library and the Net Gen Student: Making the Connections, American Library Association, Chicago, IL.

Giles, J. (2017, January 5). What is ICT? What is the meaning and definition of ICT? [Web log post]. Retrieved from https://www.michalsons.com/blog/what-is-ict/2525

Girard, B. and Spek, J.V.D. (2002). The Potential for Community Radio in Afghanistan, November. Retrieved from communica.org/resources/.

Gomes, M.A.L. (2017). Museu Virtual do Teatro Sao Joao da Bahia, Atraves de uma Abordagem Socioconstrutivista. Tese: Doutorado, Universidade do Estado da Bahia.

Goodwyn, A., Adams A. and Clarke, S. (1997) The Great God of the Future: the views of current and future English teachers on the place of IT in literacy English. Education,

# Bibliography

31(2), 54-62.

Grabe, M. and Grabe, C. (2007). Integrating technology for meaningful learning (5th ed). Boston NY: Houghton Mifflin.

Graham, C.R. (2005). Blended learning systems: definition, current trends, and future definitions. In C.J. Bonk and C.R. Graham (Eds.), Handbook of blended learning: Global perspectives, local design. (pp. 3-21). San Francisco, CA: Pfeiffer Publishing.

Gray, L., Thomas, N. and Lewis, L. (2010). Educational Technology in U.S. Public Schools: Fall 2008 (NCES 2010-034) U.S. Department of Education, National Center for Education Statistics. Washington, DC: U.S. Government Printing Office.

Gray-Little, B., Williams, V.S.L. and Hancock, T.D. (1997). An item response theory analysis of the Rosenberg Self-Esteem Scale. Personality and Social Psychology Bulletin, 23, 443-451.

Grimus, M. (2000). ICT and multimedia in the primary school. Paper presented at the 16th conference on educational uses of information and communication technologies, beginning, China

Guerin, C. (2013). Rhizomatic research cultures, writing groups and academic researcher identities. International J. of Doctoral Studies, 8, 137-150. Retrieved from http://ijds.org/Volume8/IJDSv8p137-150Guerin0400.pdf.

Gupta, S.C. (1981). Fundamentals of statistics. Bombay: Himalayas Publishing House.

Guskey, T.R. (1988). Teacher efficacy, self-concept, and attitudes toward the implementation of instructional innovation. Teaching and Teacher Education, 4, 63-69.

Hamidi, F., Meshkat, M., Rezaee, M. and Jafari, M. (2011). Information technology in education. Procedia Computer Science, 3(2011), 369–373.

Hammer, O. (2001). Claiming knowledge: Strategies of epistemology from theosophy to the new age. Leiden: Brill.

Hammond, K. (2015). What is Artificial Intelligence? Blog entry, 10 April. Available at https://www.computerworld.com/article/2906336/emerging-technology/what-is-artificial-intelligence.html.

Hammond, M., Crosson, S., Fragkouli, E., Ingram, J., Johnston-Wilder, P., Johnston-Wilder, S., Kingston, Y., Pope, M., and Wray, D. (2008). Why do some student teachers make very good use of ICT? An exploratory case study. Coventry: University of Warwick.

Haneefa, M.K. and Sumitha E. (2011). Perception and use of social networking sites among university students Calicut University. DESIDOC J. of Library and Information Technology, 31(4), 295–301. doi:10.1108/LR-12-2012-0131

Hargreaves, D. (2004), Personalising Learning, London, Specialist School Trust.

Harinarayana, N.S. and Raju, N.V. (2010). Web 2.0 features in university library web sites. The Electronic Library, 28(1), 69–88. doi:10.1108/02640471011023388

Harris Cooper, J.C. (2006). Does Homework Improve Academic Achievement? A Synthesis of Research, 1987-2003. Review of Educational Research Spring, 1-62.

Harris, S. and Kington, A. (2013) Innovative classroom practice using ICT in England: The second information technology in education study, [Online], Available: HYPERLINK http://www.nfer.ac.uk/research/down_pub.asp.

Hartley, J. (2007). Teaching, learning and new technology: A review for teachers. British J. of Educational Technology, 38(1), 42-62.

Hasan *et al*. (2007). CIT reflections, Annual Magazine of the FTK-Centre for Information Technology, Jamia Millia Islamia, New Delhi, Vol. 1.

Hashim, J. (2015). Information communication technology (ICT) adoption among SME owners in Malaysia. International J. of Business and Information, 2(2).

Hatzipanagos, S. and Gregson, J. (2015). The Role of Open Access and Open Educational Resources: A Distance Learning Perspective: The Electronic J. of e-Learning, 13(2), 97-105. Retrieved from www.ejel.org/issue/download.html?idArticle=398.

HDF (2012). Mid-Term Assessment Survey of ICT Programme: Study by Human Development Foundation, March 2012, study supported by OPEPA.

Henderson, M. (1996). Helping your student get the most out of homework. Washington, DC: National Education Association.

Hew, K.F. and Cheungs, S.C. (2013). Use and production of OER: a pilot study of undergraduate students perception: International Conference on Educational Technologies, retrieved from www. files.eric.ed.gov/fulltext/ED557188.pdf.

Hew.K.F. and Brush T. (2007) Integrating technology into K-12 teaching and learning: current knowledge gaps and recommendations for future research. Education Tech Research Dev., 55, 223–252. doi:10.1007/s11423-006-9022-5.

Hill, P. (2012). Four Barriers that MOOCs must overcome to build a sustainable model. Retrieved from http://mfeldstein.com.

Hohenwarter, M. and Fuchs, K. (2004). Combination of dynamic geometry, algebra and calculus in the software system GeoGebra computer algebra system and Dynamic Geometry System in Mathematics Teaching Conference.

Hohenwarter, M., Jarvis, D. and Lavicza, Z. (2009). Linking Geometry, Algebra and Mathematics teachers: GeoGebra software and the establishment of the International GeoGebra Institute. The International J. for Technology in Mathematics Education, 16 (2), 83-86.

Horton, M. and Freire, P. (1990). We Make the Road by Walking. Philadelphia: Temple University Press.

Hsu, Y.C. and Ching, Y.H. (2012). Mobile microblogging: Using Twitter and mobile devices in an online course to promote learning in authentic contexts. *The International Review of Research in Open and Distance Learning, 13*(4), 211-227.

Hurt, L. (2013). Students Perceptions and Understanding of OER. Retrieved from www.sicklecellanaemia.org/.../Libor-Hurt Student-perceptions-of-OER

ICBSE (2013). ICT in Education in India, 2012-13. Retrieved from http://www.icbse.com/ict-education.

Idiegbeyan, J, Nkiko, K. and Osinulu, I. (2016). Awareness and perception of plagiarism of postgraduate students in selected Universities in Ogun State Nigeria., Library Philosophy and practice e-J.. Retrieved from digitalcommons.unl.edu/cgi/viewcontentc.

Iding, M., Crosby, M.E., and Spietel, T. (2002). Teachers and technology: Beliefs and practices. International J. of Instructional Media, 29(2), 153-171.

# Bibliography

Information (2017). In Oxford Dictionaries. Retrieved from https://en.oxforddictionaries.com/definition/information.

International Educational e-J., 3(2), Apr-May-June 2014.

International J. of Enhanced Research in Management and Computer Applications, 3(11), November-2014, 16-19.

International J. of Multidisciplinary Educational Research, Quality in Teacher Education: Integration and Duration, 6(3), March 2017.

International Telecommunication Union (2017). ICT Facts and Figures 2017 Report. Retrieved from https://www.itu.int/en/ITU-D/Statistics/Pages/facts/default.aspx

Investopedia. (n.d). Social networking. Retrieved from http://www.investopedia.com/terms/s/social-networking.asp

Investopedia. (n.d.). Networking. Retrieved from http://www.investopedia.com/terms/n/networking.asp

Iqbal, Z. (2016). Guide lines for In-service Training Programme Need- based Integration of ICT in Schools. J. of Indian Education, NCERT, Vol-XXXVI

ITU (2018). Internet of Things Global Standards Initiative. Accessed on 10 January 2018, available at https://www.itu.int/en/ITU-T/gsi/iot/Pages/default.aspx.

Iwu, A.O. and Ike, G.A. (2009). Information and Communication Technology and Programme Instruction for the Attainment of Educational Goals in Nigerias Secondary Schools. J. of the Nigeria Association for Educational media and Technology, 1.

Iyamu, O. and Sumuel (2016). Using ICT in secondary schools in Nigeria: Problems and prospects. Educational technology and society, VIII (1), 104-112.

Jair, S.J. (2017). Portaria Regulamenta Novo Marco Regulatorio da Educacao a Distancia Brasileira. Retrieved from http://www.abed.org.br/arquivos/Artigo_Portaria_Regulamenta_Novo_Marco_Regulatorio_EAD_SANTOS_JR.pdf.

Jhangiani, S.R. and Pitt, R. and Hendricks, C. (2016). Exploring faculty use of Open educational resources at British Columbia, BC campus Research Report., retrieved from https://open.bccampus.ca/2016/.../new-study-exploring-faculty-use-of-oer-at-bc-instit

Jhurreev, V. (2005). Technology integration in education in developing countries: Guidelines to policy makers. International Education J. [Electronic], 6(4), 467-483. Retrieved from http://ehlt.flinders.edu.au/education/iej/articles/v6n4/jhurree/paper.pdf.

John, H.J. (2016). Open educational resources and college textbook choices: a review of research on efficacy and perceptions, Education Technology Research Development, 64(4), 573-590. Retrieved from conference.oeconsortium.org/.../OER-and-college-textbook-choices-final-published-ET.

Johnson, L., Adams, S. and Cummins, M. (2012). Mobile apps. *The NMC horizon report: 2012 Higher education edition*. Austin, Texas: The New Media Consortium.

Johnson, L., Levine, A., Smith, R. and Stone, S. (2010). *The 2010 horizon report*. Austin, Texas: The New Media Consortium.

Jones, R.D. and Colvin, R. (1964). Abolish homework: Let supervised school work take its place. Clearing House, 39, 206–209.

Juhitha, A. *et al.* (2011). ICT in Teaching Learning. New Delhi: APH Publishing.

Kaka, S. (2008). The role of ICT in education sector. Inside Magazine, Vol. 2. Retrieved from http://www.verykaka.wordpress.com/2008/07/25/the-role-of-ict-in-education-sector/.

Kanvaria, V.K. (2009). Orienting Pre service Teachers to Develop Educational Multimedia Presentation: A retrospective approach. J. of Indian Education, XXXIV(4), Feb, 2009.

Kanvaria, V.K. (2013). Plagiarism and citing references: Core issues and APA style exemplar. Retrieved from http://static.lulu.com/shop/vinod-kumar-kanvaria/plagiarism-and-citing-references-core-issues-and-apa-style-exemplar-through-a-presentation-a-ready-reckoner/ebook/product-20980172.html.

Kanvaria, V.K. (2014). A comprehension on educational technology and ICT for education. New Delhi: GBO.

Kanvaria, V.K. (2015). ICT augmented elementary teaching and learning. *The Primary Teacher,* *XXXX*(2,3), 59-69.

Kanvaria, V.K. (2017). *A resource book on pedagogy of mathematics*. New Delhi: Scholar Publishing House.

Kanvaria, V.K. (Ed.) (2016). Perspectives and perceptions on academic writing and citations. New Delhi: VL Media Solution.

Kate, T. (2013). Elementary Teachers Computer Phobia and Self Efficacy In Taiwan, TOJET: The Turkish online J. of educational technology , 11(2), 100-108.

Kaur, S. (2012). Attitude of students towards use of ICT in Higher Education. IJCST, 3(4).

Keates, N. (2007). Schools Turn Down the Heat on Homework. The Wall Street J..

Kebritchi, M. (2008). Effects of computer games on mathematics achievement and class motivation: An experimental study.

Keegan, D.J. (1980). On defining distance education. *Distance education, 1*(1), 13-36.

Keengwe, J. (2007). Faculty integration of technology into instruction and students perceptions of computer technology to improve students learning. J. of information technology education, VI (1), 169-180.

Kelly, T. (2010). Survey of ICT for education in India and south Asia: How is ICT used in education in India and South Asia, and what have we learnt? infoDev Lead. Retrieved from http://www.infodev.org/en/Project.103.html.

Ketamo, K.K. (2013). Integrating games into the classroom: towards new teachership. CURVE.

Khan, A. (2015). MOOCs and Life Long Learning Education Proceedings of International Gandhi Jayanti Conference 2015 on Education as a Basic Right of Humankind, organised by Indialogue Foundation, JMI and Gandhi Smriti and Darshan Samiti, pp. 168-170.

Khan, A. (2017). MOOCs: The Road Ahead, paper presented in the National Conference on ICTs in School Education, RIE Ajmer, from 27-29 November 2017.

Khan, S.A. (n.d.). Role of Community Radio in Rural Development. Aligarh Muslim University. Retrieved from www.caluniv.ac.in/globaldia...june.../s%20u%20khan%20-amu.pdf.

Khandpur, N.K. (2007). ICT resources and their use by physics teachers at the senior secondary level: An exploratory study. M.Ed. Dissertation, JMI.

# Bibliography

Kickmeier-Rust, M.D. and Albert, D. (2010). *Micro-adaptivity: Protecting immersion in didactically adaptive digital educational games.* J. of Computer Assisted Instruction, 26, 95-105. doi:10.111/j.1365-2729.2009.00332.x

Komineas, T. and Tassopoulou, A. (2016). Use of OER in ASPETE: Students attitude, awareness and benefits. Olympiad technology plzen. Retrieved from/www.olympiadatechnoljy.zcu.cz dated17.10.2015

Koohang, A. (1989).Computer phobia: An empirical study, Retrieved from the ERIC database ( ERIC.EJ 306984).

Koomson, A.K. (2009). Widening access to quality higher education in developing countries through distance education – The success story of the University of Cape Coast, Ghana. Retrieved from https://www.ou.nl/Docs/Campagnes/ICDE2009/Papers/Final_Paper_313Koomson.pdf

Kozma, R. (2005). National policies that connect ICT- based education reform to economic and social development. Human Technology [Electronic], 5(4), 358-367.Retrieved from www.humantechnology.jyu.fi/current/abstract/kozma05.html.

Krajcik, J.S., and Blumenfeld, P.C. (2006). Project-Based Learning. In K. R. Sawyer (Ed.), The Cambridge Handbook of the Learning Sciences (pp. 317-333). Cambridge: Cambridge University Press.

Kralovec, E. and John, B. (2000). The End of Homework. Boston: Beacon Press.

Krishnaveni, R. and Meenakumari, J. (2010). Usage of ICT for Information Administration in Higher Education Institutions- A Study. International J. of Environmental Science and Development 1(3), 282-286. Retrieved from http://www.ijesd.org/pages/55-D461.pdf.

Kulik J. and Kulik, K. (1991). Effectiveness of computer based instruction: An update analysis. Computers in human behaviour, pp 75-94.

Kulkarni, M.V. (2016). *Benefits of ICT-based learning strategies for students.* Solapur: Laxmi Book Publication.

Kumar, S. (2012). Education System in India: Issues and Challenges. In I. Rihani (Ed.), Challenges for education in knowledge society (pp. 289-295). Twenty first century publications: Patiala.

Kumar, S. (2017). Mathyoga9211. India: Partridge India.

Kuppuswamy, S. and Shankar Narayan, P.B. (2010). The Impact of Social Networking Websites on the Education of Youth, In International J. of Virtual Communities and Social Networking, 2(1), 67-79.

Lai, F., Luo, R., Zhang, L., Huang, X. and Rozelle, S. ( 2011). Does Computer-Assisted Learning Improve Learning Outcomes? Evidence from a Randomized Experiment in Migrant Schools in Beijing, Working Paper 228 ofRural Education Action Project, Stanford University, May 2011.

Lane, A. (2012). Design and Development of OER: A Student Perspective. Commonwealth of Learning, pp. 141–153. Retrieved from/oro.open.ac.uk/33976/.

Lantz-Andersson, A., Linderoth, J. and Saljo, R. (2009). What's the problem? Meaning making and learning to do mathematical word problems in the context of digital tools. Instructional Science, 37(4), 325-343.

Larner, D. and, Timberlake, L. (1995) Teachers with limited computer knowledge: variables affecting use and hints to increase use. The Curry School of Education, University of Virginia.

Leech, N.L. (2009). A typology of mixed methods research designs. Quality and Quantity, 43, 265-275.

Lemke, C., Coughlin, E., Garcia, L., Reifsneider, D. and Baas, J. (2009). Leadership for Web 2.0 in education: Promise and reality. Culver City, CA. Retrieved from http://www.cosn.org/Portals/7/docs/Web%202.0/CoSN%20Report%20042809Final%20wcover.pdf.

Lenhart, A. (2009, April). Teens and Social Media: An Overview, 22. New York, New York: Pew Internet and American Life Project

Lim, C.P. (2007). Effective integration of ICT in Singapore school: pedagogical and policy implications. Educational Tech Research Dev, 55, 83-116.

Lima, L.C., Azevedo, M.L.N.D. and Catani, A.M. (2008). O processo de Bolonha, a avaliação da educação superior e algumas considerações sobre a Universidade Nova [The Bologna process, the evaluation of higher education and some considerations about the Universidade Nova]. *Avaliação: Revista da Avaliação da Educação Superior* (Campinas), 13(1), 7-36.

Liverpool, E.O. and Jacinta, A.O. (2013). Information and Communication technologies (ICT): A Panacea to Achieving Effective Goals in Institutional Administration. Middle east J. of Scientific Research, 18(9), 1380-1384. Retrieved from http://www.idosi.org/mejsr/mejsr18(9)13/22.pdf.

Lobo, D. (2006). ICT and skill based education in the scenario of teacher education. Quality concerns in teacher education CASE, faculty of education and psychology M.S.Univ. Baroda. 101-105.

Macedo, A.R.D., Trevisan, L.M.V., Trevisan, P. and Macedo, C.S.D. (2005). Educação superior no século XXI e a reforma universitária brasileira [Higher education in the 21st century and the Brazilian university reform]. *Ensaio: Avaliação de Políticas Públicas*. June 29, 127-48.

Maggie, Y. and Fry, F. (2004). A reserva de vagas para negros nas universidades brasileiras [The reserve of vacancies for blacks in Brazilian universities]. *Estudos Avançados*, January 15, 67-80.

Magni (2009) ICT usage in Higher education. International Technology and Education and Development Conference, Spain, March 9-11, 2009.

Magre, S. (2011). Computer phobia. Behavioural Research Methods: Instruments and computers, 19(2), 167-179.

Mahenge, M.P. and Sanga, C. (2016). ICT for e-learning in three higher education institutions in Tanzania. *Knowledge Management and E-Learning: An International Journal (KMandEL)*, 8(1), 200-212.

Mahmood, A. *et al*. (2011). Effects of use of ICT: Students' perception at higher education level. Elixir Social Studies. 38, 4218-4221.

Makewa L.N. *et al*. (2014). ICT-Integration in Higher Education and Student Behavioral Change: Observations at University of Arusha, Tanzania. American J. of Educational Research, 2(11A), 30-38.

# Bibliography

Mallik, U. (2001). Computers in Indian schools. J. of Indian Education, 27(3), 6-12.

Manduku, J.K. (2012). Adoption and Use of ICT in Enhancing Management of Public Secondary Schools.

Manternach-Wigans, L. *et al.* (1999) Technology integration in Iowa high schools: perceptions of teachers and students. College of Education, Iowa State University.

Marsh, L. (2010). The Meaning of Constructivism. Tradition and Discovery, 28(2), 23-34.

Mayfield, A. (2007). What is social Media? An e-book from iCrossing. Retrieved from http://www.icrossing.com/uk/sites/default/files_uk/insight_pdf_files/What%20is%20 Social%20Media_iCrossing_ebook.pdf.

McGinn, A. (2007). Senior High School Education in the 21st Century. The Educational Forum, 71(4), 331-344.

McGorry, S. (2002). Online, but on target? Internet-based MBA courses: A case study, The Internet and Higher Education, 5(2), 167-175.

McKerlich, R. and McGreal, R. (2013). Measuring Use and Creation of Open Educational Resources in Higher Education: the international review of research in open and distributed learning, vol 14. Retrieved from www.irrodl.org.

Mehra, V. (2011). A Comparison of Computer Anxiety among Indian and Iranian University Students, International J. on New Trends and Their Implications, 2(1), 36-46.

Merriam-Webster. (n.d.a). Social. Retrieved from https://www.merriam-webster.com/dictionary/social

Merriam-Webster. (n.d.b). Networking. Retrieved from https://www.merriam-webster.com/dictionary/networking

Mertens, D.M. (2010). Research and evaluation in education and psychology: Integrating diversity with quantitative, qualitative and mixed methods. Los Angeles: SAGE Publications Inc.

MHRD (2010). Annual Education Report 2009-2010. Indian Government, India. Retrieved from http://education.nic.in/AR/AR2009-10/AR2009-10.pdf.

MHRD (2011). Sarva Shiksha Abhiyan- Framework for Implementation. New Delhi: Department of School Education and Literacy, MHRD, GOI.

MHRD (2012). National Policy on Information and Communication Technology in School Education. New Delhi: Government of India. Retrieved from http://mhrd.gov.in/sites/upload_files/mhrd/files/upload_document/revised_policy%20document%20ofICT.pdf.

MIB (1966). Report of the Committee on Broadcasting and Information Media. New Delhi

Mishra, P. and Koehler, M.J. (2006). Technological pedagogical content knowledge: A framework for teacher knowledge. Teachers College Record, 108(6), 1017-1054.

Mitra, H. (2012). ICT in Indian Education. University News, 12(9), 35-42.

Mohanty, R.R. (2011, February 19). ICT advantages and disadvantages. [Web log post]. Retrieved from http://ict-adv-disadv.blogspot.in/

Mojavezi, A. and Tamiz, M.P. (2012). Theory and Practice in Language Studies, 2(3), 483-491. Finland: Academy Publisher. doi:10.4304/tpls.2.3.483-491.

MoLeNET (2010) Mobile Learning Myths. Available at http://web.archive.org/web/20101015234706/http://www.molenet.org.uk/mobilearinprac/myths.

MOOC (2015). Retrieved from https://en.wikipedia.org/wiki/Massive_open_online_course.

Moore, D., McGrath, P. and Thorpe, J. (2000). Computer-Aided Learning for People with Autism: A Framework for Research and Development, Innovations in Education and Training International, 37(3).

Moore, M. and Kearsley, G. (1996). Distance education: A system view. Belmont, California: Wadworth

Mumtaz, S. (2000) Factors affecting teachers use of information and communications technology: a review of the literature. J. of Information Technology for Teacher Education, 9 (3), 31-34.

Myers, R.J. (1993). Problem-Based Learning: A case study in integrating teachers, students, methods and hypermedia data bases. Unpublished doctoral dissertation, Virginia Polytechnic Institute and State University.

Nagpal, B. (2017). Perceiving e-learning in distance education through facilitators' eye. *Proceedings of the National Seminar on Distance and E-Learning in Global Context*, 87-92.

Naseema, C. and Alam, M.A. (2005). From blackboard to the web: Integrating technology and education. New Delhi: Kanishka Publishers.

Naslundh, C. (2001). Homo zappiens. Datorn i Utbildningen, 5, 14.

Nath, S. and Srivastava, S. (2015). Effectiveness of ICT on Students Achievement in Science. International J. of Innovative Research, 1(1), 7-14.

Natia, J. and Wassan (2015). Promoting teaching and learning in Ghanain basic schools through ICT. International J. of education and development using Information and Communication Technology, IX (2), pp. 113-125.

Nations, D. (2017). What is social networking? [Web log post]. Retrieved from https://www.lifewire.com/what-is-social-networking-3486513

Nayak, R., (2011). Role of ICT in Indian educational sector. Retrieved from http://www.financialexpress.com/news/role-of-ict-in-indian-educational-sector/794286.

Nazerenko L.A. (2015). Blended Learning vs Traditional Learning: What Works? (A Case Study Research) Procedia – Social and Behavioural Sciences, Volume 200, pp 77-82.

Nazihatulhasanah, A. and Nurbiha, A.S. (2015). The effects of GeoGebra on students achievement. Procedia - Social and Behavioral Sciences, 172, 208 – 214.

NCERT (1998). Information technology action plan. Retrieved from http://www.dsir.g6v.in/pubs/itt/itt9803/itap.htm

NCERT (2001). Curriculum Guide syllabus for information technology in schools NCERT. Retrieved from http://www.ncert.nic.in/html/itcurriculum.htm/webdoc.ubn.kun.nl/anon/i/impaofina.pdf.

NCERT (2005). National Curriculum Framework 2005. New Delhi: National Council of Educational Research and Training. Retrieved from http://www.ncert.nic.in/html/pdf/schoolcurriculum/framework05

NCERT (2017). Learning outcomes at elementary stage. New Delhi: NCERT.

# Bibliography

NCTM. (2000). Principles and Standards for School Mathematics. Reston, VA: National Council of Teachers of Mathematics.

Neurath and Mathur (1959). An Indian Experimental in Farm Radio ForumsParis: UNESCO.

Ni, A.Y. (2013). Comparing the Effectiveness of Classroom and Online Learning: Teaching Research Methods, JPAE 19(2), 199-215.

Nooriafshar, M. (2008). The Role of Technology based Approaches in Globalizing Education. Hyderabad: Icfai University Press.

Noronha, F. (2003). Community Radio Singing: New Tunes in South Asia. Economic and Political Weekly, May 31, 2003.

Oboegbulem, A.I. and Ogbonnaya, N.O. (2008). Challenges in the application of information and communication technology (ICT) in the management of universities. In B.G. Nworgu (Ed.), Education in the information age: Global challenges and enhancement strategies. Proceedings of The First International Conference of the Faculty of Education, University of Nigeria, Nsukka.

Obota, N, Beldina, O. and Stanslous E. (2015). An assessment of the availability of ICT infrastructure for curriculum instruction in public secondary schools in Mumias. J. of research and methods in education, X(5), 52-57.

Olatokun, W.M. (2017). Availability, accessibility and use of ICTs by Nigerian women academics. *Malaysian Journal of Library and Information Science*, *12*(2), 13-33.

Oliver, R. (2000). Creating Meaningful Contexts for Learning in Web-based Settings. Proceedings of Open Learning, 5(8). Brisbane: Learning Network, Queensland.

Oliver, R. (2008). The Role of ICT in Higher Education for the 21st Century: ICT as a change agency for education. Hyderabad : Icfai University Press.

Olufunke, A. and Adegun, A. (2014). Utilization of open educational resources and quality assurance in universities in Nigeria. European scientific J., 10. Retrived from http//www.eujournal.org.

Olympiou, G. and Zacharia, Z.C. (2012). Blending physical and virtual manipulatives: An effort to improve students' conceptual understanding through science laboratory experimentation. Science education, 96(1), 21-47.

OPEPA (2013). OPEPA (Odisha Primary Education Program Authority). Retrieved from http://www.opepa.in/website/ICTProgramme.aspx.

Pal, J., Pawar, U.S., Brewer, Eric, A. and Toyama, Kentaro. (2006). **The case for multi-user design for Information and Communication Technology in developing regions.** Proceedings of the 15th international conference on World Wide Web (WWW 06), 781-789, NY, USA.

Parameswaran, M., and Whinston, A.B. (2007). Social computing: An overview. Communications of the Association for Information Systems, 19(1), 37.

Parliamentary Office of Science and Technology (2006). ICT in developing countries, *Postnote*, No. 261. Retrieved from http://www.parliament.uk/paliamentary_offices/post/pubs2006.cfm.

Patil, D.A. (2001). A Voice for the Voiceless: The Role of Community Radio in the Development of the Rural Poor. India International J. of Rural Studies (IJRS), 17(1), 3, 7-9. Retrieved from www.vrionline.org.uk/ijrs.

Paula, N. (1995). Helping your child with homework. Washington, DC: Office of Educational Research and Improvement, U.S. Department of Education.

Pavarala, V., Stalin, K. and Sajan, V. (2014). Community Radio Forum, India Working Paper CR Policy National Consultation on Community Radio Organised by Ministry of Information and Broadcasting (GIO) UNESCO, Community Radio Forum and Ford Foundation New Delhi, 13-15 December, 2010. Retrieved from http://www.communityradioindia.org/Working Paper on CR Policy.pdf.

Pelgrum, W.J. (2001). Obstacles to the integration of ICT in education: results from a worldwide educational assessment. Computers and Education, 37, 163-178.

Penn State (2005). Too Much Homework can be Counterproductive. Online posting. Physorg. com Home Page 31 May.

Pho, A. and Dinscore, A. (2015). *Game-based learning. Tips and Trends: Instructional Technologies Committee.* Retrieved from http://acrl.ala.org/IS/wp-content/uploads/2014/05/spring2015.pdf.

Piaget, J. (1950). The psychology of intelligence. London, UK: Routledge.

Pina, A. and Harris, B. (1993). Increasing teachers confidence in using computers for education. Arizona Educational Research Organization, Tucson, AZ.

Player-Koro, C. (2012). Factors influencing teachers' use of ICT in education. *Education Inquiry, 3*(1), 93-108.

Plowright, D. (2011). *Using mixed methods: Frameworks for an integrated methodology.* Sage Publications.

Prabhakar, V.P. (October, 2012). Community Radio Station – Success stories. Media –A Bilingual Monthly J. of the Kerala Press Academy, Retrieved from http://mediamagazine. in/content/community-radio-stations-%E2%80%93-success-stories.

Prasad, D.F. (2015). Impact of social network sites on perception of sociability and academic performance of college students in Bangalore City (PhD thesis, University of Christ). Retrieved from http://shodhganga.inflibnet.ac.in/handle/10603/77093

Radio Dunia (2008). Relevant Content and Talent Development. Radio Dunia, April, 2008, Retrieved from http://radioduniya.elesonline.come/?p=126

Rahim, B. and Shamsiah, M. (2008). Teaching Using Information Communication Technology: Do trainee teachers have the confidence? International J. of Education and Development using ICT, 4(1), 1-8.

Rajasekar and Vaiyapuri (2006). Construction and validation of computer phobia scale. J. of All India Association for Educational Research, 16(1), 56-58.

Rambhe, P. (2009). The impact of using social networking sites on academic relations and student learning in university settings (PhD thesis, University of Cape Town). Retrieved from https://open.uct.ac.za/bitstream/item/8434/thesis_hum_2009_rambe_p.pdf?sequence=1

Ramsey, G. (2000). Quality matters: Revitalising teaching: Critical times, critical choices. Report of the review of teacher education New South Wales. Sydney: NSW Department of Education and Training.

Rao, B. (2004). Methods of Teaching Educational Technology. New Delhi: Discovery Publishing House.

# Bibliography

Reed, L. (2000). Domerticating the personal computer: the mainstreaming of new technology and the culture management of a widespread technophobia. Retrieved from the ERIC database (ERIC.EJ 611089).

Reinoso, J. (2017). What are Real-Time Communication Tools? Blog entry. Available at https://www.nmc.org/nmc-research/real-time-communication-tools-2/?nmc_project_id=272743.

Ribeiro, D. (1978) A Universidade Necessária [The Necessary University]. 2. Ed. Rio de. Janeiro: Editora Paz e Terra, 312.

Rideout, V.J., Foehr, U.G. and Roberts, D.F. (2010). Generation M2: Media in the lives of 8-18 years old. Retrieved from: http:// www.kff.org/entmedia/upload/8010.pdf.

Ringstaff, C. and Kelley, L. (2002). The Learning Return on our Educational Technology Investment: A Review of Findings from Research. WestEd RTEC. [Online] http://www.wested.org/online_pubs/learning_return.pdf.

Robbins, C. (2016). *Foreword*. The Global Information Technology Report 2016: Innovating in the Digital Economy. Geneva: World Economic Forum.

Roh. K.H. (2003). Problem-based learning in mathematics. Eric Digest 482725. ERIC Clearing House for Science, Mathematics, and Environmental Education, 1-7.

Rolfe, V. (2012). Open educational resources: staff attitudes and awareness: Research in Learning Technology, 20. Retrieved from www.reserachinlearningtcechnology.net/.

Romeo, G.I. (2006). Engage, empower, enable: Developing a shared vision for technology in education. In M.S. Khine (ed) Engaged learning and Emerging Technologies, The Netherlands: Springer Science. doi:10.1007/1-4020-3669-8_8.

Rosenberg, M. (1965). Society and the adolescent self-image. Princeton, NJ: PrincetonUniversity Press.

Rouse, M. (2016). Social networking. Retrieved from http://whatis.techtarget.com/definition/social-networking

Rowell, L. (2015). Student Perceptions: Teaching and Learning with Open Educational Resources. Retrieved from www.dc.etsu.edu/cgi/viewcontent.cgi?article=3925andcontext=etd.

Royati, A.S., Ahmad, F., Mohd. A. and Rohani, A.T. (2010). The effects of GeoGebra on Mathematics achievement: Enlightening coordinate geometry learning. Procedia-Social and Behavioral Sciences, 8, 686-693.

Ruthven, K. and Hennessy, S. (2002). A practitioner model of the use of computer-based tools and resources to support mathematics teaching and learning. Educational studies in mathematics, 49(1), 47-88.

Sangra, A. and Gonzalez-Sanmamed, M. (2010). The role of information and communication technologies in improving teaching and learning processes in primary and secondary schools. ALT-J, Research in Learning Technology, 18(3), 207–220.

Santos, I.M., Hammond, M., Durli, Z. and Chou, SY. (2009). Is there a role of social networking sites in education? In A. Tatnall and A. Jones (Eds.), Education and technology for better world, pp. 321-330. Berlin: Springer. Retrieved from https://link.springer.com/content/pdf/10.1007%2F978-3-642-03115-1_34.pdf

Sargent, L.T. (1994). The three faces of utopianism revisited. Utopian Studies, 5(1), 1-37.

Sarkar, S. (2012). The Role of Information and Communication Technology (ICT) in Higher Education for the 21st Century, 1(1), 30-40.

Saxena, R. (2013). Innovative Teaching Methods. Jaipur: Rajasthan Hindi Granth Academy.

Schneider, J. (2014). From the Ivory Tower to the Schoolhouse: How Scholarship Becomes Common Knowledge in Education. Harvard Education Press.

Schwab, K. 2016. *The Fourth Industrial Revolution*. Geneva: World Economic Forum.

Scrimshaw, P. (1997). Computers and the Teachers Role, in N. E. Davis and B. Somekh (Eds) Using Information Technology Effectively in Teaching and Learning, pp. 100-113. London: Routledge.

Shadaan, P. and Eu, L.K. (2013). Effectiveness of Using Geogebra on Students Understanding in Learning Circles. The Malaysian Online J. of Educational Technology, 1(4).

Shah, B. and Agrawal, R. (1994). Teachers attitude towards computer-assisted instruction and Computers and Education in relation to sex, organization and experience. Indian Educational Abstracts, 37(l), 80.

Shah, D.B. (2003). Information technology and education: Vision and prospects. Allahabad: Kitab Mahal.

Shallsuku, Z. (2012). The Role of ICT in Education: Focus on University Undergraduates Taking Mathematics as a Course. International J. of Advanced Computer Sciences and Applications, 3(2), 136.

Shamatha, J.H., Peressini, D. and Meymaris, K. (2004). Technology-Supported mathematics activities situated within an effective learning environment theoretical framework. Contemporary Issues in Technology and Teacher Education, 3(4), 362-381.

Sharma, A., Gandhar, K., Sharma, S. and Seema (2011). Role of ICT in the Process of Teaching and Learning. J. of Education and Practice. Vol 2, No 5, 2011.

Sharma, R.A. (1983). Technology of teaching: (Teacher Behaviour). Meerut: Loyal Book Depot.

Sharples, M., *et al*. (2007). Mobile Learning: Small devices, Big issues (in Sharples, M. *et al*. (eds.). Technology-Enhanced Learning, 2009, Part IV).

Sharples, M., Roock, R., Ferguson, R., Gaved, M., Herodotou, C., Koh, E., Kukulska-Hulme, A., Looi, C.K., McAndrew, P., Rienties, B., Weller, M., Wong, L.H. (2016). *Innovating Pedagogy 2016*: Open University Innovation Report 5. Milton Keynes: The Open University.

Sharwood, S. (2017). Developing world hits 98.7 per cent mobile phone adoption. Internet News posted on 3 August 2017, available at https://www.theregister.co.uk/2017/08/03/itu_facts_and_figures_2017/.

Shaunessy, E. (2007). Attitudes toward Information Technology of Teachers of the Gifted Implications for Gifted Education. Gifted Child Quarterly, 2 (51), 119-135.

Shavinina, L.V. (2001). A new generation of educational multimedia: High intellectual and creative educational multimedia technologies. In L. R Vandervert, L. V. Shavinina and R. A. Cornell (Eds.), Cyber education: The future of Distance Learning. Larchmont (pp.63-82). New York, NY: Mary Ann Liebert, Inc.

Shraim, K. and Khlaif, Z. (2010). An e-learning approach to secondary education in Palestine: Opportunities and challenges. *Information Technology for Development, 16*(3), 159-173.

Shukla, C. (2008). Essentials of educational technology and management. New Delhi: Dhanpatrai Publications

Shukre, A. (2008). The Future of Online Education in India. Hyderabad : Icfai University Press.

Siemens, G. (2011). The race to platform education. eLearnspace, Retrieved from http://www.elearnspace.org.

Siemens, G. (2012). MOOCs are really a platform. eLearnspace, Retrieved from http://www.elearnspace.org.

Simin G. Wan, A. and Wan, R. (2015). Teaching and Learning with Technology: Effectiveness of ICT Integration in Schools, International J. of Research in Education and Science, 1(2), 174-190.

Simonson, M., Smaldino, S. and Zvacek, S.M. (Eds.) (2015). *Teaching and learning at a distance: Foundations of distance education.* North Carolina: IAP.

Singh, R. (2005). Role of ICT in developing teaching competency. Teacher education in dilemma. 139-143.

Siva, K.R. (2000). Computer awareness among Higher students. Unpublished M.Ed Dissertation submitted to University of Madras.

Smeets, E., Mooij, T., Bamps, H., Bartolome, A., Lowyck, J., Redmond, D. and Steffens, K. (1999). The impact of information and communication technology on the teacher. Nijmegen, The Netherlands: ITS.

Social (2017). Retrieved from https://en.wikipedia.org/wiki/Social

Sposito, M.P. and Corrochano, M.C. (2005). A face oculta da transferência de renda para jovens no Brasil [The hidden face of the income transference for youths in Brazil]. Tempo Social, 17(2), 141-172.

Stolley, K., Brizee, A. and Paiz, J.M. (2013). Is it plagiarism yet? Retrieved from https://owl.english.purdue.edu/owl/resource/589/2/

Suleman, M. (2016). Statistics in Psychology, Education and other Social Science. New Delhi: Motilal Banarsidas.

Sun, A. and Chen, X. (2016). Online education and its effective practice: A research review. J. of Infor-mation Technology Education: Research, 15, 157-190. Retrieved from http://www.informingscience.org/Publications/3502.

Sutherland, R., Armstrong, V., Barnes, S., Brawn, R., Breeze, N., Gall, M., *et al.* (2004). Transforming teaching and learning: Embedding ICT into everyday classroom practices. J. of Computer Assisted Learning, 20(6), 413–425.

Tanner, D. and Tanner, L.N. (1980). Curriculum development. New York: Macmillan. von Hofe, G. D., Jr. (1916). The development of a project. Teachers College Record, 17, 240–246.

Tanzanian Open University (2017). *Facts and figures 2016/2017.* Tanzanian Open University: The Directorate of Quality Assurance and Control.

Teaching with Technology (2006) Retrieved from http://cte.uwaterloo.ca/teaching_with_technology/

Technology (2017). In Oxford Dictionaries. Retrieved from https://en.oxforddictionaries.com/definition/information

Techpedia (2018). Information and communication technology (ICT). Retrieved from https://www.techopedia.com/definition/24152/information-and-communications-technology-ict

Teed, R. (2012). Game-based learning. Retrieved from http://www.newmedia.org/game-based-learning--what-it-is-why-it-works-and-where-its-going.html.

Tezci, E. (2011). Factors that influence preservice teachers ICT usage in education. European J. of Teacher Education, 34(4), 483-499.

The Science Probe, 1(1), May, 2012, 30-40.

The Scottish Government (2015). Consultation on the development of a Digital Learning and Teaching Strategy for Scotland supporting school years education. The Scottish Government.

Thioune, R. (2006). Information and communication technologies for development in Africa: Opportunities and challenges for community development. Vol. 1 Ottawa: IDRC. Available:http://www.idrc.ca.

Thomas, K.O. (2004). Practical Application of ICT to Enhance University Education in Ghanna, Feature Article, Ghana.

Thomas, R.M. (1987). Computer technology: An example of decision-making in technology transfer. In R. M. Thomas and V. N. Kobayashi (Eds.), Educational technology: Its creation, development and cross-cultural transfer (pp.25-34). Oxford: Pergamon Press.

Timothy B.J. (1981). Computer Phobia: What to do about it? Educational Technology, 21(1), 47-48.

Todman, J. and Dick, G. (1993). Primary children and teachers attitude to computers. Computers and Education, 20(2), 199-203.

Trentin, G. (1999). What does using the internet for education mean?. Educational Technology, 39(4), 15-23.

Tripathi, L.B. (2012). Psychological Research Method. Agra: HP Bhargava Book House.

Trybus, J. (2009). Game-based learning: What it is, why it works, and where it's going [Blogpost] World of Cheddar: Financial Literacy through Gamification. Retrieved from https://www.worldofcheddar.com/new-blog/2017/3/3/game-based-learning-what-it-is-why-it-works-and-where-its-going

Tsai, C., Lin, S. and Tsai, M. (2001). Developing an internet attitude scale for high school students. Computers and Education, 37, 41-51.

Turner, P. (2017). What are Internet of Things? Blog entry made on 5 October 2017. Available at https://www.nmc.org/nmc-research/internet-of-things-6/?nmc_project_id=272743.

Tutkun, O. (2011). Internet access, use and sharing levels among students during the teaching learning process. The Turkish Online J. of Educational Technology, 10(3)

Twenty First Century Learning Reference Group (2014). Future-focused learning in connected communities. Retrieved from http://www.education.govt.nz/assets/Documents/Ministry/Initiatives/FutureFocusedLearning30May2014.pdf

# Bibliography

UGC (2004). Annual Report 2002-03. New Delhi: University Grants Commission.

UGC (2017). University grants commission (Promotion of academic integrity and prevention of plagiarism in higher education institutions) regulations 2017 (Draft). New Delhi: UGC.

UNESCO (2000). Information and Communication Technology in Education, 23-27.

UNESCO (2001). Community Radio in India. Communication and Information Sector United Nations Educational Scientific and Culture Organization.

UNESCO (2002). Information and Communication Technologies in Teacher Education. A Planning Guide: UNESCO Publication. Retrieved from unesdoc.unesco.org/images/0012/001295/129533e.pdf

UNESCO (2003). Implemented project on training and professional development of teachers/facilitators in the effective use of ICT for improved teaching and learning supported by Japanese funds-in-trust programmes. Asia and Pacific regional bureau for education, UNESCO Bangkok, Beijing, China, September 27-29. Retrieved from http://unesdoc.unesco.org/ images/0013/001356/135607e.pdf.

UNESCO (2005). UNESCO Report: How ICT Can Create New, Open Learning Environments Information and Communication Technologies in Schools A Handbook For Teachers, Division of Higher Education, UNESCO.

UNESCO (2008a). ICT Competency Framework for Teachers: Implementation Guidelines Version 1. Retrieved from http://unesdoc.unesco.org/images/0015/001562/156209E.pdf

UNESCO (2008b). ICT Competency Standards for Teachers: Competency Standard Modules. Retrieved from http://unesdoc.unesco.org/images/0015/001562/156207e.pdf

UNESCO (2011). UNESCO ICT Competency Framework for Teachers Version 2.0. Retrieved from http://unesdoc.unesco.org/images/0021/002134/213475E.pdf

University of Cape Coast website (2017). College of Distance Education. Retrieved from https://ucc.edu.gh/node/126

VanTassel-Baska, J. (2013). Curriculum issues: Curriculum, instruction, and assessment for the gifted: A problem-based learning scenario. Gifted Child Today, 36, 71-75. doi:10.1177/1076217512465289

Varma, A. (2008). ICT in the Field of Education. Hyderabad : Icfai University Press.

Veen, W. (2004). Coping with Homo zappiens. http://bunet.karlsborg.se/sikt/veen gothenborg.ppt.

Venkaiah, V. (2015). OER in India: A study of attitude and Perception of Distance teachers retrieved from https://wikieducator.org/images/d/d7/PID_386.pdf.

Venkataiah, N. (1995).Educational technology. New Delhi: Atul Publishers.

Viji, S. (2000). Computer self-confidence and computer experience in relation to computer related attitudes and commitment to learning. Unpublished M.Ed. Dissertation submitted to University of Madras.

Virkus, S. and Bamigbola, A.A. (2011). Students' conceptions and experiences of Web 2.0 tools. New Library World, 112(11/12), 479–489. doi:10.1108/03074801111190473.

Visscher, A.J. and Wild, P. (1997). The potential of information technology in support of teachers and educational managers managing their work environment. Education and Information Technologies, 2 (4), 263–274.

Visscher, A.J., Wild, P. and Fung, A.C. (2001). Information Technology in Educational Management: Synthesis of Experience, Research and Future Perspectives on Computer-assisted School Information Systems. The Netherlands: Kluwer Academic Publishers.

Volman, M. and Eck, E.V. (2001). Gender Equity and Information Technology in Education: The Second Decade, Review of Educational Research, 71(4), 613-634.

Vygotsky, L.S. (1978). Mind in society: The development of higher psychological processes. Cambridge, MA: Harvard University Press.

Walker, M. (2011). The history of social networking: A brief look at the history and rise of social networks. Retrieved from http://www.webmasterview.com/2011/08/social-networking-history/

Wang, Q. and H.L. Woo (2007). Systematic Planning for ICT Integration in Topic Learning. Educational Technology and Society 10(1), 148-156.

Wang, V.C. and Cranton, P. (2017). Transformative learning and technology in adult and vocational education. In *Exploring the New Era of Technology-Infused Education* (pp. 34-48). IGI Global.

Webb, M.E. (2005). Affordance of ICT in science learning: Implications for integrated pedagogy. *International Journal of Science Education, 27*(6), 705-735.

Webdesigner (2016). The history of social networking: How it all began!. Retrieved from https://1stwebdesigner.com/history-of-social-networking/

Wikipedia (2018). Internet of Things. Available at https://en.wikipedia.org/wiki/Internet_of_things.

Williamson, K. (2004). A structured framwoerk for using games to teach mathematics and science in K-12 classrooms. The Technology Teacher.

Willis, J., Thompson, A. and Sadera, W. (1999). Research on Technology and Teacher Education: current status and future directions. Curriculum and Instruction, 47(4), 29-45.

Witt, N. (2017). What are Analytics Technologies? Blog entry made on 10 October 2017, available at https://www.nmc.org/nmc-research/analytics-technologies/?nmc_project_id=272743.

Wood, D. (1995). Theory, training, and technology: Part I. Education and Training, 37(1), 12–16.

World Bank Group Education Strategy 2020 (2011). Learning for All: Investing in Peoples Knowledge and Skills to Promote Development. Retrieved from http://siteresources.worldbank.org/EDUCATION/Resources/ESSU/Education_Strategy_4_12_2011.pdf DIGITAL STRATEGY FOR SCHOOLS – ENHANCING TEACHING, LEARNING and ASSESSMENT

XIMB (2008). Performance Assessment Survey on CAE. Study by Xavier Institute of Management, Bhubaneswar supported by OPEPA.

Yadav, N. (1957). A Handbook of Educational Technology, New Delhi: Amol Publications (P.) Ltd.

Yadav, N. (2003). A Hand book of Educational Technology. New Delhi: Anmol Publications Pvt.Ltd.

Yasothapriya. M. (2010). The Role of ICT in Improving Education. EDUTRACKS.

# Bibliography

Yelland, N. (2002). Teaching and learning with information and communication and communication technologies (ICT) for numeracy in the early childhood and primary years of schooling. Australia Department of Education, training and youth affairs.

Yerrick, R. and Moving T. (1999). Obstacles confronting technology initiatives as seen through the experience of science teachers: A comparative study of science teachers' beliefs, planning, and practice. J. of Science Education and Technology, 8, 291-307. Retrieved from http://www.sci.sdsu.edu/CRMSE/old_site/yerrick.html

Youssef, A.B. and Dahmani, M. (2008). The Impact of ICT on Student Performance in Higher Education: Direct Effects, Indirect Effects and Organisational Change. RUSC, 5(1).

Zacks, J. (2009). Reading creates simulations in minds. Science out of the Box [radio broadcast]. Washington DC: National Public Radio. Retrieved from http://www.en.wikipedia.org/wiki/Information_and_communication_technologies_in_education.

Zago, N. (2006). Do acesso a permanência no ensino superior: percurso de estudantes universitários de camadas populares [Access to permanence in higher education: the trajectories of university students of popular classes]. *Revista Brasileira de Educação*, May 15, 226-370.

Zaidieh, A.J.Y. (2012). The use of social networking in education: Challenges and opportunities. World of Computer Science and Information Technology J. (WCSIT), 2(1), 18-21.

Zakaria, M.H., Watson, J. and Edwards, S.L. (2010). Investigating the use of Web 2.0 technology by Malaysian students. Multicultural Education and Technology J., 4(1), 17–29. doi:10.1108/17504971011034700.

Zhao, Y. and Cziko, G.A. (2001). Teacher adoption of technology: a perceptual control theory perspective (Technology Information). J. of Technology and Teacher Education, 9(1), 5-30. Retrieved on 30 April, 2008 from EBSCOhost (Academic Search Elite) database.

Zhu, J. (2003). Application of computer technology in public school classrooms: usage dimensions and influencing factors, The Pennsylvania State University. Retrieved from http://portal.acm.org/citation.cfm?id=997354.

# KEYWORDS

5E Model

Achievement

Administration

Administrators

Attitude

Attitude towards Using New Technology

Benefits for Learning

Blogging

Bricks

Cartesian Plane

Challenges

Computer Games

Computer Phobia

Connection

Control Group

Digital Education Revolution

Digital Games

Edmodo

Education

Educational Administration

Educational Psychology

Educational Technology

Effectiveness

Environmental Education

Experiential Learning

Experimental Group

Future of ICT

Game Based Learning

Games for Math Education

Government School

Hatred towards Homework

Higher Education

Homework

ICT Enabled Learning after School

ICT Integration

ICT Related Problems

ICT Skills

ICT@School Scheme

Information and Communication Technology (ICT)

Information and Communication

Technology Programme
Innovative Homework Practices
Instruction
Integrating Technology
Interaction
Internet
Intervention
Learning
Learning Modules
Madhya Pradesh
MOOCs
Multimedia
Online
Online Courses
Pedagogical
Perception
Possibilities of ICT
Post-Assessment
Pre-Assessment
Private School
Project-based Learning
Psychosocial
Quality in Education
Radio Jamia

Repositories
School Education
School Functioning Education
School Learners
Science
Self-Esteem
Serious Games
SNSS
Social Media
Social Networking
Spatial Awareness
Student Teachers
Students
Sustainable Development
SWAYAM
Teacher Preparation
Teaching
Teaching-Learning
Technology
Traditional Pedagogy
Transacting
Visuals
Web 2.0 Technology
Wikis